EMPIRES
AND COLONIES

EMPIRES AND COLONIES

Jonathan Hart

polity

First published in 2008 by Polity Press

Polity Press
65 Bridge Street
Cambridge CB2 1UR, UK

Polity Press
350 Main Street
Malden, MA 02148, USA

ISBN-13: 978-07456-2613-0
ISBN-13: 978-07456-2614-7 (pb)

A catalogue record for this book is available from the British Library.

Typeset in 10 on 12 pt Sabon
by Servis Filmsetting Ltd, Manchester
Printed and bound in Great Britain by MPG Books Ltd, Bodmin, Cornwall

The publisher has used its best endeavours to ensure that the URLs for external websites referred to in this book are correct and active at the time of going to press. However, the publisher has no responsibility for the websites and can make no guarantee that a site will remain live or that the content is or will remain appropriate.

For further information on Polity, visit our website: www.polity.co.uk

Contents

It was the best of times, it was the worst of times.
Charles Dickens, *A Tale of Two Cities*

In memory of my mother, Jean Jackman Hart (1922–2005), and to my father, George Edward Hart

Preface and Acknowledgements

⟋⟍

This book is relatively brief for the vastness of the topic. It cannot discuss all it should. Its main focus is on the expansion of western Europe and thus examines mainly the seaborne empires and their successor, the United States. Whether the United States is an empire is an open question, but some of its citizens and presidents, such as Thomas Jefferson, have thought so. It has governed, and governs, territories that are not full states in its union, and has an informal power, as the British empire did, over territories beyond its direct political control. The words 'empire' and 'colony' are sometimes loosely used, or at least rhetorically, and change over time, but they are important terms that I have tried to define. There have been empires in many parts of the globe, but I have concentrated most on the West, mainly from the Portuguese expansion into Africa to the present. In the story of empire, I have touched on Russia and its successor the Soviet Union, China, Japan and other key empires and states. The point of view of the book is as it is because of the unfolding of empires in what has come to be known as the West, even though an equally interesting story could be told about Russia, India, China and Japan, or the Aztec and Inca empires, from their vantage. This is not the story of triumph or superiority, but of how things turned out. Although I focus on western European empires, I also try to decentre that narrative with alternative points of view, like those of Natives, slaves and others who were not in power in those empires.

Another aspect of the book is that it assumes that economic, political and military history are key to an understanding of the expansion of empires but it brings to bear on them a cultural turn, in which culture and individual voices qualify the drive to patterns, systems and statistics. The focus on alternative voices, religion and human rights is meant to juxtapose the personal and cultural with the impersonal and larger economic forces that underpin military and political power. I have wished to tell some of the story from those marginalized, traumatized and, at the time, almost left out. I have also wanted to stress the ambivalence and contradiction of empire within people as well as within their cultures and political institutions and practices. Tensions also occurred within and between empires and their colonies. A book can only tell so much, and so while too much will be left out by definition, it is my hope that what remains within this relatively short book opens up for the reader some vistas about empires and colonies. This is a subject not without controversy, which means it has a built-in tension.

In the writing of a book, many people and institutions deserve credit. Over the years, in my books, I have thanked many specifically and expressed gratitude to all those who have helped and supported my work in friendship and intellectually. There are too many names to list here. My particular thanks to my editors at Polity, Lynn Dunlop, Sally-Ann Spencer and Andrea Drugan, who invited the book, believed in it, and helped it to change shape over a period more extended than any of us would have anticipated. I am fortunate indeed to be blessed with such fine editors. We all thought of what the readers might most need in a book on empires and colonies as part of the new series, Themes in History, and this changed over time. In the last iteration, Andrea Drugan showed great understanding and wisdom in guiding the book into publication. The anonymous readers (assessors) deserve thanks for their perceptive comments and suggestions. My editors and the assessors greatly improved the final version. Thanks to the dedicated group at Polity who saw this book through production and into publication. At Polity, I also wish to thank Jonathan Skerrett, Helen Gray and Annette Abel for their work on editing and production.

For a long time, the University of Alberta has been generous and enlightened in supporting my leaves for fellowships and visiting appointments. Kirkland House and Harvard University kindly welcomed me when I was beginning my concerted work on empire. The President, Fellows and students of Clare Hall and the Faculty of History at the University of Cambridge have also been good to me over the years. Thanks also to the Director, Fellows, Staff and Board of the Camargo Foundation for a fellowship in France and the opportunity to consult the archives of the French overseas empire. At Princeton, Canadian Studies, History, Comparative Literature, and the Master, Fellows and students of Wilson College gave me a warm welcome and support. The librarians and staff at these universities and their libraries have been helpful and kind, as have those at the British Library, Bodleian, Bibliothèque Nationale, L'Archive d'Outre-Mer, the National Library of Canada, and other libraries and museums.

In the study of history and empires, I thank Anthony Pagden in particular. In this field, I am also grateful to Jeremy Adelman, Peter Burke, Nicholas Canny, Olive Dickason, Robert Duplessis, Anthony Grafton, Roland Le Huenen, Anthony Low, Kenneth Mills, François Moreau, Peter Sinclair and John Herd Thompson for their advice and example. Others have been supportive of my work generally in history and literature: Anne Barton, Sandra Bermann, Louise Clarke, Margaret Ferguson, Stephen Ferguson, Philip Ford, Marjorie Garber, Thomas Healy, Barbara Johnson, Michèle Lamont, Dale Miller, J. Hillis Miller, Don Skemer, Gordon Teskey, Godfrey Waller, Michael Worton and Jan Ziolkowski. Thanks, too, to my hosts for inviting me to speak about empire at conferences and universities in various locales. At Alberta, many have been encouraging of my research in recent years, including Kris Calhoun, Kerri Calvert, Patricia Demers, Julian Martin, Juliet McMaster, Douglas Owram and Irene Sywenky. I owe a debt to my students in courses on empires, colonialism and post-colonialism, especially those at Alberta and Princeton. For those who suggested, gave or lent me books that made a difference, my thanks: Alan Hart, George and Jean Hart, Shelagh Heffernan, John Hickie, Daniel Johnson, Mary Marshall, Stephen Mobbs, Peter Sinclair and Pauline Thomas. To many friends, thanks, including Alfred and Sally Alcorn, Judith Hanson, Allan and Laura Hoyano, Lenore Muskett, and Donald and Cathleen Pfister. In the past year or two, I have lost friends and colleagues, including Milan Dimić, G. Blakemore Evans and Elena Levin, whose kindness and wisdom were exemplary. Many thanks to my brothers and sisters, Charles, Gwendolyn, Deborah, Alan and Jennifer. To my wife, Mary Marshall, and our twins, Julia and James, my deepest gratitude. This book has grown up while our children have. Finally, this book, which was begun some time ago, is dedicated to my mother, Jean, who died on 26 August 2005, and to my father, George. While she painted, he wrote. They both instilled in me a fascination with history and literature.

Introduction: Empires and Colonies

The interest in empires and imperial history in the past decade or so has been keen. Why are authors and readers and people generally interested in the rise and fall of western empires from the Portuguese to the present? Various reasons have arisen in the period during which I have worked on this topic. For instance, the five-hundredth anniversary of Columbus's landfall in the western Atlantic, the First Gulf War, the attack on New York and Washington, and the invasions of Afghanistan (with the sanction of the United Nations) and Iraq (without the approval of the UN) are all events that have generated contemporary interest in the colonial and imperial past. Other defining moments in a changing world developed this interest. The signing of the Helsinki Accord in 1975 guaranteed respect for human rights and fundamental freedoms among member states in eastern and western Europe. The fall of the Berlin Wall in 1989 opened up eastern Europe and weaned it from Soviet dominance. Moreover, in 1991, the dissolution of the Soviet Union occurred; this took the world's second industrial power and third most populous state and largely broke it up into Russian and non-Russian states. President Ronald Reagan and some members of his administration in the United States during the last phase of the Cold War called it the Soviet empire, or even the 'evil empire'. Was the collapse of the Soviet Union (USSR) some kind of end of the last European empire? Alternatively, is the United States, which expanded into lands as a successor to the British, French and Spanish empires in northern America, an empire? Is this much-expanded Russia, which grew from Muscovy over the centuries into the lands of other peoples, yet an empire? Are these two great states in some form, even after the end of the Cold War and the loss of federated republics by the Russians, empires still? Given the Cold War from about 1945 to 1991, these two rival states, the United States mainly capitalist and the other mainly Communist or socialist, still generate a great deal of interest in the case of empires and colonies and what constitutes imperialism. In the chill of propaganda wars, there were those on both sides who spoke in derogatory terms of the other state as an agent of imperialism. This move is telling because it means that in some sense being an empire and embodying imperialism was not considered good in this period. From the early part of the twentieth century to its end, V. I. Lenin and Ronald Reagan both used 'imperialism' and 'empire' as negative terms. So there was and is a lot at stake over terms like 'empire', 'colony' and 'imperialism'. That makes the debate an exciting one and not something moot. In the conflicts, verbal, political and military, in whose midst we have been since the Second World War and where, unfortunately, we still find ourselves, these terms are still used as weapons. They do not have fixed definitions, so that makes it necessary to give some of the contours of the debate. In such a context, it is also important to provide a historical view of these persistent and vital themes. For instance, if the United States is not considered an empire, then, of the empires in Europe that began their expansion in the fourteenth and fifteenth centuries, the Russian (Soviet) empire was the last to dissolve. It is also possible to think of Russia as being, like the United States, a continental empire that involved expansion overland. One difference, however, is that the English had to sail to the New World to expand, whereas the Russians just spread out from Moscow in all directions.

However that might be, the United States became the dominant superpower with the decline of the Soviet Union, although the USA and Russia, as Alexis de Tocqueville noted, were great continental powers that were destined to become the great world powers. In the middle of the story at hand, during the 1820s de Toqueville looked beyond the past glory of Portugal, Spain and the Netherlands, the memory of the French Revolution and the recent rise and defeat of Napoleon, and declared the future to be American and Russian – something that came to be especially the case after 1945:

> There are now two great nations in the world, which starting from different points seem to be advancing toward the same goal: the Russians and the Anglo-Americans.
>
> Both have grown in obscurity, and while the world's attention was occupied elsewhere, they have suddenly taken their place among the leading nations, making the world take note of their birth and of their greatness at almost the same instant.
>
> All other peoples seem to have nearly reached their natural limits, and need nothing but to preserve them; but these two are growing. . . .
>
> To attain their aims, the former relies on personal interest and gives free scope to the unguided strength and common sense of individuals.
>
> The latter in a sense concentrates the whole power of society in one man.

One has freedom as the principal means of action; the other has servitude.

Their point of departure is different and their paths diverse; nevertheless, each seems called by some secret design of Providence one day to hold in its hands the destinies of half the world.[1]

This prophecy shows that amid the shape of the world as it was and is, the configurations of what will be fascinate people, whether in de Toqueville's time or now. A typology or double vision on power and expansion takes effect between the time not now and the present. While the British empire was the greatest state, de Toqueville was looking to future empires or powers.

Russia remains a power still, while Japan remains the world's second economic power. The rise of China and India, or their resurgence, is also causing great interest: these states are products of non-European imperial expansion, but they have also traded with Europe. Furthermore, for between one and two hundred years, China was subject to Europe informally and India formally. Both asserted their independent paths during the late 1940s in the wake of the cataclysm in Europe and Asia. These are ancient places with a plethora of languages and cultures and have taken on various political shapes over the past few thousand years. Alexander the Great made it to India and died there: Robert Clive helped the British stay there. Both China and India have long played central roles in the world economy and they appear poised to resume leadership in that sphere. When Britain gave back Hong Kong to China in 1997 and Portugal returned Macao to China in 1999, a circle had been closed or the tag ends of European expansion had been gathered. Both religious and secular books tell about the coming and going of empires and about the hubris of those who think they will never end.

The Irony of Empire: Limitation, Ambivalence and Contradiction

The story is more complicated than that because most administrators of empire and their peoples know that empires do not last. Guessing when states crest and when they ebb is something for prophets and soothsayers. In a world of models, projections and computers, people try to be precise about these matters. A typology or a double image of past and present haunts great powers in trying to guess their fate. The translation of empire is a myth of continuity between empires as a means of making an empire without end, but there is also a fear of chaos from the fall of an empire. The end of Rome provides such an image.

Empires can make people, even those at their centre, uncomfortable and ambivalent about them. If empires do not endure and are part of a fleeting earthly power, then why work for an empire or why suffer under the anxiety of trying to keep one going as long as possible? Are empires and colonies all about profit? Do those who live in the colonies suffer most to enlarge the imperial or metropolitan centre and its profits? For Christians, Rome was the empire that both helped crucify Jesus and persecute Christians and then became the empire that latterly made Christianity its official religion. The image of the Roman empire was ambivalent and contradictory. Ironically, empires are limited in time because they rise and fall or have a beginning, middle and end, even if they project power and endurance. Some of those who administer or write about empire are keenly aware of this contradiction. In the typology of time among past, present and future, in the theme of history concerning empires and colonies, historian and reader are also aware that change will make Rome, or any empire claiming that the sun will never set on it, less than eternal.

Power is also powerless in time. The very Christian religion which was at the heart of the expansion of Europe from the fifteenth century, despite the echoes of the classical and pagan world of Greece, Rome and the Europe beyond the pale of those empires, showed in its scriptures, especially in the New Testament, the chastening of power. The city of God and the earthly city coexisted symbolically and in the daily view, but earthly power would give way, like the empires, before the truth of religion, on the way to the end of things, as predicted in Revelations at the end of the Bible. While the powerful often prevail on earth, the meek shall inherit the earth. Secular and religious worlds came to collide in individuals, societies and states. The missionary urge was often enough in tension or in tandem with the quest for economic and political power.

The Argument and Emphasis

Nor is power the only matter at hand, whether it is trying to speak about the expansion of western Europe or the United States or setting out world history in terms of the power and might of China or India in historic and future terms. *Empires and Colonies* will provide an exploration of the expansion of the seaborne empires of western Europe from the fifteenth century and how that process of expansion affected the world, including their successor, the United States. While paying particular attention to Europe, this study will be careful to highlight the ambivalence and contradiction of that expansion. The book will also illuminate connections between empires and colonies as a theme in history, concentrating on culture while also discussing the significant social, economic and political dimensions of the story.

Empires and Colonies will recognize that while a study of the expansion of Europe is an important part of world history, it is not a history of the world *per se*. Its focus on culture will be a means of asserting that areas and peoples that lack great economic power at any given time also deserve attention. The alternative voices of slaves, indigenous peoples and critics of empire and colonization will be a vital aspect of the book, which is meant to appeal not only to students of imperial history, but also to anyone interested in the makings of the modern world.

Terms and Background: Empires, Colonies and Imperialism

Before we look in detail at the period and themes in question, it is worth taking some time to understand what we mean when we talk of empires and colonies. The background to the beginning of western European expansion in the fifteenth century shows that the story of empires and colonies is not new. This tale of empire and colony is an important one that still lives with us, however repugnant empire is to many in what has been called, in hope, the postcolonial world. In classical antiquity the Greeks and Romans discussed the nature of politics and history, which included discussions of empire and colonies. For instance, the Greeks explored other cultures. Herodotus wrote about the Persian empire and its clash with the Greeks. Thucydides represented internal strife in Greece and the fall of the Athenian empire and its democracy. Plato, through his teacher and the protagonist of his dialogues, Socrates, set out a cycle that included aristocracy and democracy and the nature of tyranny. Aristotle, who was Plato's student, studied politics systematically and was, for a brief time, the tutor of Alexander the Great, the Macedonian, who extended the imperial sway of greater Greece from northern India to Egypt and beyond. Alexander became a model for future emperors in Europe: he was observed even as his successors in the mythology or translation of empire departed from his example.

The Romans had the Greek imperial past to reckon with, and as they emulated Greece, they also displaced it as the *imperium*. Rome swept away rivals such as the Etruscans and Carthaginians (descendants of the Phoenicians) as well as the Greeks, but in doing so they absorbed what each of these cultures had to offer, for instance Carthaginian ship-design and Greek philosophy. Livy and Tacitus recorded the changes in the Roman polity from republic to empire, and Cicero was sceptical of the withering of the republic. These writers came to influence writers, advisers and rulers of the Middles Ages and Renaissance in western Europe, where the focus of this study begins.

'Empires' and 'colonies' are terms that we understand in a general sense, but the closer we examine them, the more fractured and intricate they become. Part of the reason for this is that an empire in the ancient world of the Mediterranean served as a model to those modern empires that will be discussed here, but that the ancient empires differed from those latter-day empires. Even if each of the western European empires from the fifteenth century onwards were distinct, it shared certain key characteristics with the others. In the confines of this book, I can mention but cannot explore other empires that inhabited the reaches of the globe, continent to continent, period to period, but these different polities strain the word 'empire' even more. Various European languages, not to mention others with related terms, have distinct but connected uses of this key word for this study. Still, as with the term 'colony', with 'empire' there is a practical field of use. Etymology, although it has its limits, is a good place to begin.

'Empire' and its cognates have a certain grounding. The English word 'empire', which has different uses, derives from the Latin 'imperium', which is related to 'imperare' – to command – from which comes the term 'imperator', the origin of our word, 'emperor'. This sense of 'Supreme and extensive political dominion', particularly 'that exercised by an "emperor" . . . or by a sovereign state over its dependencies', entered the English language about the first quarter of the fourteenth century, although related meanings seem to have occurred at the end of the thirteenth century.[2]

'Colony' also has a suggestive history as a term. The Latin 'colonia' came from 'colonus', a 'tiller, farmer, cultivator, planter, settler in a new country', and ancient Roman writers used it to translate the Greek word for 'a settling away from home'.[3] The word first appeared in modern languages, particularly in relation to the Roman 'coloniæ', in French and then in English. In the sixteenth century Latin and Italian writers, such as Peter Martyr, used the term 'colonia' from ancient Greek and Roman precedents to apply to settlements newly 'discovered' and planted in places outside Europe such as the New World, and Richard Eden translated some of these works into English, for example Martyr's *Decades* (1516, translated by Eden, 1555), and so gave this new context for the word a proper place in the vernacular of England. Other writers in English took up this meaning over the following centuries: for instance, in his continuation of the work of Richard Hakluyt the Younger, Samuel Purchas in the edition of 1613 declared 'O name Colon . . . which to the world's end hast conducted Colonies'. In *Leviathan* (1651) Thomas Hobbes spoke about colonies from England planted in Virginia. In 1775 Edmund Burke mentioned how the colonies in America complained that a Parliament in Britain taxed them without including their representatives. In 1883 Seeley, in *The Expansion of England*, provided the following definition, which builds on the classical and modern vernacular inheritance: 'By a colony we understand a community which is not merely derivative, but which remains politically connected in relation of dependence with the parent community.' In the year of the Declaration of Independence of the United States of America, Adam Smith's *The Wealth of Nations* appeared, a reminder of the political economy of empires and colonies. Smith proclaimed: 'The colony trade has been continually increasing.'[4] Recently, Robert Aldrich and John Connell admitted that while colonies are generally accepted to be distant, established by settlers and politically connected to an independent state, formal definitions of 'colony' do not reflect the complexity of the term: 'Since political shifts are crucial to colonialism and decolonization, any definition of a colony is condemned to flexibility and variable interpretations.'[5] Although my study is comparative, it is written in English, so that the very language I use involves the translation of empire as a theme but literally in the language.

'Empire' and 'colony' and their cognates are translations and came to have a practice in the language and lives of the English-speaking nations.[6] There were empires and colonies long before the English tongue was born, and the imperial centres and the overseas settlements of these seaborne empires between 1415 and 2000 were Portuguese, Spanish, French and Dutch as well, to name a few. German, Swedish, Danish, Russian and other colonies were also part of the concurrent European expansion.

The story of empire – although in English it is often, owing to language and culture, a story of Anglo-American expansion – is not of one language and nation. Even these key terms in English are related to earlier uses in Greek, Latin, French and Italian. To speak English is to speak the language of the colonized and colonizer even in the heart of London, once a colony of ancient Rome. England itself was invaded or colonized so often: in the past two thousand years alone, the Romans, Angles, Jutes, Saxons and Normans, to name a few, came into conflict with the Celts and the already hybrid ancient cultures of the British Isles. The great empire ruled from London, like that governed from Washington, was born of a colony turned empire. Whereas I include the United States in this study, as an extension and a development of the English/British empire from which it broke, it is not a traditional seaborne empire. The technologies that brought the United States to the fore may have helped it to build on the empire that gave birth to it, but radical technological changes in industry, agriculture and the military also gave it distinction. It developed the very sea and air power that Britain built up for the last great conflicts – those

two great civil wars in Europe that drew in the whole world which we call
the world wars – only to decline precipitously. Germany had aspirations
to empire and, having been denied those by Britain and France, with the
help of their empires or former colonies and the United States and Russia,
the German state took Europe with it into an earthly apocalypse.
Germany's ally, Japan, had similar ambitions in Asia and was defeated by
all those who fought Germany as well as by China. Perhaps politically the
greatest casualty of these wars was the British empire, which in 1914 was
the world power. The United States, already gathering strength economically from 1870 (as was Germany), rose from those ashes – having helped
the mother country – and developed over the course of the century, and
certainly by the end of the Second World War in 1945 it was the foremost
world power.

From the early or mid-eighteenth century and certainly from the defeat
of Napoleon in 1815, Britain was the dominant country in the world, so
that for about two hundred years or more, the English-speaking power of
either Britain or the United States was first among nations, even if these
were contending nations. Being first does not mean having its own way
or that other states within Europe or in other parts of the world did
not have their own influence. It would have been difficult for Britain to
survive these terrible wars, which also had horrific effects on Germany,
Japan, Russia and other countries, without its colonies such as India and
its former dominions (but still dependent for foreign policy on the empire
and then the Commonwealth) such as Australia, Canada, New Zealand
and South Africa. Its first great former colony – the United States – was
also a key support that helped Britain to victory in both world wars, even
if Britain became weaker and weaker and would in time become, even
with lessening power, a help to the United States in the Cold War and later
conflicts. In other words, to leave the United States out of this narrative
of empires and colonies, especially as this relation between the centre and
its settlements is an aspect of this imperial theme, would be to tell only
part of the story.

Empires have come and gone in different ways and shapes, making
colonies or other dependencies, whether these were envisioned as part of
expansion or not. As this is a study of empire in a specific sense and not
a meditation on empire in the sense of a history of the world from antiquity to our time, it will not cover the imperial yearnings of Alexander the
Great or Augustus Caesar or chronicle the diverse empires of the Chinese,
Mongols or Mughals. The body of this book will take as its beginning the
rough date of 1415, when Portugal began its expansion into Africa and
not long before the Portuguese rounding of the Cape of Good Hope to
India and the Spanish landfall in the western Atlantic. This date will be
observed as much in the breach as in the rule, but most of what follows

will derive from the fifteenth century onwards and will concentrate on the seaborne empires of western Europe – Portugal, Spain, England (Britain), France and the Netherlands – and their chief successor the United States.[7]

This last 'empire' breaks the rule of this book, and while the United States, like the Russian (later Soviet) empire, was and is largely continental, its presence here is in large part as a translation of western European empires, especially that of the British empire, whose principal 'colony' it was and whose tongue and institutions it has propagated, modified and repudiated. As these western empires, built on sea power, from which the United States developed late but in earnest, came into contact with other empires and peoples, they will be discussed, but within the scope of a book it would be difficult to examine all these matters and even begin to do them justice. Many of these powers came to see themselves – as the Byzantine emperors, the popes, Charlemagne and his successors had done – as those chosen to inherit from, or embody, the Roman emperors and empire in a kind of *translatio imperii* or translation of empire. The architecture of Washington shows that this translation was and is alive long after the fact.

This study will avoid conflating different kinds of phenomena under the rubric of 'imperialism'. Norman Etherington warned against a loose application of classic theories of imperialism in the historical study of the European colonial empires. Like Eric Stokes, Etherington thought that these theorists had not intended their theories to account for the growth of those empires. Etherington saw in H. Gaylord Wilshire, J. A. Hobson, V. I. Lenin and other important figures a study of capitalist sources for their theories of imperialism – how the imperial urge functioned as an outlet for surplus capital. Moreover, Etherington argued that imperialism, colonialism and the expansion of capitalism were not the same.[8] The colonial fits and starts from the fourteenth century to the eighteenth, especially among the French and British, for instance in the Americas, were nothing like the so-called high imperialism of the scramble for Africa in the nineteenth century and before the First World War began in 1914. Even then Etherington observed that there was a confusion of terms. He argued that the first capitalist proponents of imperialism saw it as justification for action, a policy that would allow an outlet to surplus capital, a civilizing mission or a struggle for survival among states. By imperialism, Marxists meant applying beliefs about causation in history to an analysis of international aggression, that is, they connected and confused (in Etherington's view) aggressive capitalist states and their financial press that justified imperialism. Later, historians who were not Marxists used the term 'imperialism' to include explanations of the expansion of colonial empires and split the term into specialities such as economic imperialism and capitalist imperialism. Etherington provided a reminder that capital exports alone cannot explain colonialism. The theory of imperialism, then, should not confuse these three factors: imperialism, colonialism and the expansion of capitalism. Etherington also called attention to Charles A. Conant's theory of capitalism which justified a policy, V. I. Lenin's application of a theory of history to a given phenomenon, and D. K. Fieldhouse's explanation of the scramble for Africa according to national rivalries. For Etherington, it is important to place these theories in their own historical contexts before testing them, and he noted that theories of imperialism are still useful. More specifically, it is vital to distinguish what these theories say about the different phenomena of the building of empires, the expansion of capitalism and the military rivalries that emerged at the end of the nineteenth century.[9]

By choosing the terms 'empires' and 'colonies', I am emphasizing the different kinds of empires and colonies even over time in the expansion of western Europe. As this region expanded overseas and its economic power increased, imperialism was part of the story but not all of it. Part of the expansion from about 1415 to 1750 was based on an agrarian, commercial and pre-industrial society that involved capital but was founded primarily on crafts and manufactures supplied by energy from the biological world of wild and cultivated plants and trees. The expansion from 1750 was derived from coal and other sources, such as oil, that drove an industrial revolution begun in England. In the twentieth century a technological revolution built on the agrarian and industrial bases of the economy.

Expansion involved the use of capital from the beginning of this period, but banking and investment intensified over time and, through the industrial and technological revolutions, displaced land more and more as a source of wealth and power for individuals and states. The European economy began to expand before intense colonization and capitalism were developed. Colonization and industrialization occurred in England before the high and centralized imperialism of late Victorian times. Capitalism and technological invocation continue in Britain despite the formal decolonization of its empire in the decades after the Second World War.

Decolonization occurred to some degree with the loss of the American colonies by Britain, but the British empire subsequently amassed more colonies. This empire was also a patchwork of various kinds of polities. Beginning with Canada in 1867, at about the peak of power but not of size of the empire, the settler dominions began to gain self-governance in domestic matters and gained that right over foreign affairs between the two world wars. Even between the imperial centre and settler colonies, where there was much in common, frictions occurred. The tension between empire and colony in this expansion is a reminder against the urge to flatten out everything in a flattened-out 'imperialism', which has its own confusions, fissures and intricacies. There were many empires among the western Europeans and they sought origins in their classical past.

Focus, Context and Method

By necessity, this book has Europe as its primary focus, because it explores the expansion of western Europe, its influence and its overseas colonies from the late fifteenth century to the beginning of the twenty-first century, but that does not mean that the argument need be celebratory, teleological or triumphant. In other words, a volume about the development of Europe in the modern world need not be 'Eurocentric' in what has come to be a derogatory sense. Instead, the story that this book will tell is of ambivalence and contradiction in terms of the themes of history as they apply to imperialism, colonialism and decolonization, or what might be considered by some as neo-colonialism or neo-imperialism.

There are many different ways in which one could approach the writing of a book on such a broad subject matter as empires and colonies. Choosing to emphasize different themes or criteria would delimit the chronological and geographical scope of such a book in varied ways. For instance, if economics were the sole criterion for writing about the expansion of western Europe and its power, then the book might constrain itself to the period of about 1800 to 1945. Another way of shaping a history of western expansion would begin in the classical or medieval periods. The westering of empire is an old theme that scholars have traced, and one theme is that this movement from the east would lead to doom in the west, where learning and knowledge (science) would have its end. This idea occurred in Christian writings, from Severian of Gabala (in the fourth century CE) to Hugh of Saint Victor and Otto of Freising (twelfth century CE).[10] The expansion of Europe could also begin much earlier, for instance with the Norse expansion to Iceland and Greenland, which ended in the fifteenth century. That way there would be a continuity between the Vikings and the Portuguese and Spanish voyages to Africa, India and the New World.[11] It would also be possible to view the expansion of Europe in terms of ecological and epidemiological damage or imperialism, beginning with the plagues. Some of them, like the Black Death, originated from China when Mongols, who controlled a vast empire in Eurasia (which fell about 1350), spread the bubonic plague (carried by the fleas on rats) from China into Europe, devastating populations from the east to the west, from 1331 to 1350 and beyond. By the end of the fourteenth century, the population of China and Europe, both connected through the Mongol empire, fell by about a third. The effects of weather and disease on food production, labour and the economy altered political, social and cultural practices in Eurasia and elsewhere. It is possible to see that this death count created a labour shortage in places like Europe that drove up wages and made these states look for gold and silver and for slaves to replace the dead. That seems to have caused an exploration of the New World, where Native populations died in vast numbers from diseases to which Asians and Europeans had been exposed over a long time, and this shortage of labour for exploitation led to the seeking of African slaves.[12] Such a narrative would see that a division between Asia and Europe is really artificial and would suggest that a global society and economy included Africa, America and elsewhere in a biological and cultural regime.

Whatever the focus chosen may be, in a comparative study of cultures and empires and colonies such as this one, it is vital to provide other contexts that serve as a reminder of the obvious, that other peoples besides Europeans had strong texts, images and actions that related to expansion, empire and relations with other cultures, some colonized or tributary. The tensions among Europeans and those they encountered during their expansion were multifold and had a context: that is, past as precedent as a future that soon becomes the past. The narrative or thesis this book sets out is one among many possible worlds, as Leibnitz might have framed it.[13] Even if from one point of view, nothing was or is inevitable, what has happened has happened. Thus, if the inexorability of the expansion of the western European empires is possibly a tool of triumphalism or mythology as much as something related to historiography, to get too deeply into the what-ifs of history might well, if taken too far, serve to deflect attention from what occurred during the expansion of these empires into the world beyond Europe. Alternative histories are a form of speculation, a philosophical view of human time not too different from fiction, more particularly historical fictions in the novel, drama and poetry. Aristotle had considered history to be that which represents what happened and poetry what might have happened, so that while the historian could not rearrange events for effect, the poet could.[14]

Although I have chosen the title *Empires and Colonies*, which emphasizes the relation, and sometimes tension, between the centres of the colonizing powers and their colonies, it could have been called *The Expansion of Western Europe*. This title, while perhaps more descriptive, might have suggested more of a focus on western Europe than the expanding role of Europe in the world in the period under discussion. Expansion includes empires, colonies, imperialism and related matters, but it allows for a distinction among them as well as within terms. For instance, these key terms are contested, and to assume that all empires are alike or that all their constituent parts are the same is something that this book argues against. One of the ways that empires are different, even from themselves, is over time. It is appropriate, especially in a volume that is part of a series on the themes of history, for this book to be structured in a way that explores the theme of empires and colonies chronologically. England grows into the English and then the British empire, and even the British empire is different in 1707, 1807 and 1907, and, by 2007, has long since ceased to exist except as a memory, trace and remnant. The same could be said for the Portuguese, Spanish, French and Dutch empires. As this history has many points of view within Europe, it needs focus, for the sake of coherence and detail, given the scope of the topic at hand. While China, India, Africa and other parts of the world were and are of great import-ance, it would be unwieldy to concentrate on the place of Europe in the modern world mainly from the point of view of the many colonies and states that came under pressure from Europe, especially from the middle of the eighteenth century or beginning of the nineteenth. Instead, while focusing on western Europe and showing the tension between these seaborne states and their colonies and with other parts of the world, this study cannot, within this scope, do justice to many of the aspects of the world beyond Europe or these empires.

The title of the book shows the tensions between imperial centre and colonies, but the volume tries to complicate and qualify notions of European superiority and to avoid reading history backwards by arguing for the inevitability of European power, and for that of the United States and Russia (later the Soviet Union) as societies that grew out of Europe. Despite this attempt at balance, this study is not, however, a completely decentred world history. In other words, while this book gives one way into the modern world and into globalization, it does so from the point of view of an expanding Europe and the world, no matter how ambiva-lent that expansion might be in the eyes of Europe, the world and pos-terity. It is important not to read history backwards in another sense, that is, to renovate the past or to reconstruct it for present purposes. All his-tories are written in the present, so there is always a dialogue between past and present, but to provide a revisionary history for the purpose of present political and scholarly trends is another form of teleology. Whereas that teleological urge might be difficult to avoid, it is worth resisting. It is possible for a historian to be too much of his or her times. While this book should contribute to the field of world history, it is doing so from a European point of view, with all the blindness and insight a vantage can provide. The same would be said about viewing world history from a Chinese or Indian view, especially up to 1750 or 1800, when both were world powers. Both states might well again be great powers in the world, but that would not detract from the story of about 1415 to the present, in which Europe expanded for much of that time. That expansion might not have meant, for about the first half of this period, that Europe was anything like as economically or technologically dynamic as Asia, but this growth in the western part of Eurasia affected the world, even when Europe was a lesser force in the world.

Culture

Economics and technology are not the whole story. It would be one-sided if we discussed Europe, India or China because they were economic powers and assumed that that was the central criterion in the study of history. One of the central concerns of this book, despite its attempt to examine social, economic and political factors, is 'culture'. That word is another notoriously fraught term, like 'imperialism', but it is one that Clifford Geertz said was 'Almost as bad as matter'.[15] As people cannot enact the lives of others, as Geertz notes, they can try, instead, to understand other frames of meaning. The meeting of cultures – different peoples in different places and time – is a key to the expansion of Europe and its encounter with the world and lies at the heart of this book. Moreover, the voices of people and their cultural practices, as they occur in texts and images, represent important parts of this study.

One of the assumptions of this book is that the meeting of cultures – even under stress from invasion, disease and ecological trauma – is the exchange of intricate cultures full of ambivalence and contradiction. The irony of a sense of superiority is that empires pass and cannot be sustained and that, by definition, no culture can sustain an argument for superiority. What is most productive is to bring out some of the intricacies of some of the relations between and among cultures at the time that Europe slowly then steadily went out into the world for better and worse.

It is important to remember that in the fifteenth century Europe was a creative, violent, multilingual and multicultural peninsula, which may have declined from the power and influence of Greece and Rome. However, even in the centuries afterwards, no matter how much power and influence Europe gained, it remained fractious and bent. If taken as a whole, Europe – which is supposition, as it was and is an idea perhaps more than an actuality – was given to civil war.[16] Rivalry, self-destruction, violence and social, economic and political friction characterized Europe on the verge of expansion as much as it has since. The world wars of the twentieth century (CE) show the sheer destructiveness that Europe brought on itself and on the world. So Europe was and is no Edenic or utopian world bringing civilization to the world, whatever was said, but it did and does make a contribution to the global community and changed it utterly.

The story of western European expansion, as this book will show, is ambivalent and contradictory. The western European seaborne empires and their successor, the United States, provided in economics, politics and social structures the good and bad, mixed sometimes inextricably. Those who would make this expansion into a triumph have one eye closed, and those who would make it into a disaster have the other eye closed. This book is neither an apology for European expansion nor a denunciation of it. The expansion occurred, and the task at hand is to see some contours of what that meant. This story of expansion is the focus of the book and gives it its shape.

Violence and Ecology: the Imperial, the Colonial and Expanding Capital

Imperialism, colonialism and the expansion of capitalism are key factors in the central concerns of violence and ecological change and degradation. During the period in question, violence against aboriginal peoples and others around the globe was widespread and the effects of disease and industrialization had complex interactions. The diseases the Spaniards brought to the New World and the mining for minerals such as gold and silver with slave labour were a form of violence against the land and peoples. The transportation of plants and peoples from different parts of the Atlantic basin, for instance, meant that, long before the Industrial Revolution and capitalism, trade and exploitation were present on a large scale. This occurred particularly through the institution of slavery, and through violence – physical, psychological and ecological. Colonies sometimes preceded formal empires. Feudalism characterized the Portuguese and Spanish empires, while the English (British) and the Dutch transformed their own colonies through capitalism, especially from the seventeenth century. The Industrial Revolution and the increase in capital certainly added to the strain, through technologies of warfare and ecological devastation, which we have been seeing on an ever-greater scale from about 1970.

The gap between the biological world and the industrial/technological world has been growing. Capitalism without classical imperialism seems to be doing an even greater job of ecological destruction. With the fall of the Berlin Wall in 1989, it became apparent that, if anything, the command or planned economies of eastern Europe had done even greater damage to the environment. The dictatorships of Stalin, Hitler and Mao showed that violence against people and the environment was more intense than in capitalist democracies and those with mixed economies. So from the colonization of Columbus, Cortés and the Pizarros through the division of China and the imposition of the Opium Wars and the scramble for Africa at the height of imperialism to the totalitarian horrors of the twentieth century, violence and wars against people and the land, air and seas are a central part of the story. Capitalism and socialism have at their extremes as much to answer for as the ideological wars of religion, society and politics. These are concrete examples that should serve as a reminder that to make one theme all themes, while tempting, is not possible. A mixture of ideological, physical, economic, technological and ecological violence has created a difficult situation in the time in which we live. This violence has historical roots and is a central part of this story.

Slavery, human rights abuses and the collision of cultures are key to the study of the expansion of Europe. As I have briefly discussed above, I will give due treatment to slavery, racism, the treatment of women and other related sub-themes so as to counter an economic history that might discuss production and power in the greatest states and neglect the violence, the ecological crisis and the legacy for aboriginal peoples and the descendants of slaves. There is a moral dimension to this history of empires and colonies. No one person or one people has the moral high ground, including the historian, and certainly not this historian. We are implicated and complicit. It is easy under the sway of models, graphs, statistics and other quantitative techniques, however useful they are, to forget about human voices and individuals and the culture of which each person is a part. Each culture has value, so that while empire, colony and imperialism can call up images of dominance and superiority, these are spectres and can lead to self-delusion on a personal, religious, social and political scale.

To these ends, in discussing the myths, theories and practices of colonization, or colonialisms, it is important to take a comparative approach to history. That way, one national tradition, or one imperial theme, does not seem so original or seminal. The appeal to wider contexts prevents the provincialism of each empire prevailing. Through a use of evidence from earlier periods and different cultures, it is possible to complicate and revise the notions of modern European imperial expansion and the apparently 'postcolonial' period we are said to inhabit.

Coming to Terms Once More

In what follows, taking into account the additional contexts set out since the discussion of the key terms of the study, I seek to make further suggestions concerning the intricacies of changing words, like 'empire' and 'colony', and to question the ready division between imperial centre and colonies as well as the claims that empires make for themselves. As Hans Kohn has suggested, not every imperial relation is colonial, and, in its baldest terms, colonialism, which has many intricacies, might be said to be 'foreign rule imposed upon a people'.[17] For Kohn, empire and imperialism imply power and domination, but however corrupt and greedy these systems can be, it is really a question of the abuse of power that is the root of the political problem. Domestic and foreign governments can abuse power. The words 'colonialism', 'empire' and 'imperialism' developed pejorative connotations in the twentieth century, but they had been laudatory terms until the end of the nineteenth: 'The Roman empire had been a model for Western political thought for over a thousand years. Americans at the end of the eighteenth century spoke proudly and hopefully of their "empire." The French revolutionaries proclaimed the "imperial" expansion of their leadership.'[18] A view that corroborates this one is that, as Jean-Marie André asserts, 'Roman imperialism has modelled our daily life and our culture'.[19] Michael Twaddle's definition is a variation on Kohn's: 'Imperialism, interpreted as the rule of foreigners by strangers, is as old as human history.'[20] This study discusses colonies in British, Spanish and Portuguese America, for instance, that were both colonial in the sense that they colonized many settlers in new lands that were invaded or conquered and imperial in that they came to rule over subject peoples. 'Empire' and 'colony', then, are caught between colonialism and imperialism because, depending on a greater or lesser degree of European settlement, they are imperial and colonial at once, so much so that in certain cases the two aspects become blurred. Lenin saw a sea-change in 1890, from a different point of view from Kohn, when the most advanced capitalist countries became monopolist and competed one with the other for direct control for the world's unconquered lands.[21]

Even if 'empire' and 'colony' are vexed terms and imperialism and colonialism have begun to be questioned in a widespread fashion over the past century or so, it would be an over-simplification, despite their drawbacks and abuses, to blame all the woes of the world or of a given people entirely on the colonial expansion of western Europe. Violence, disease and death did come with the Europeans, especially in the Americas. Moreover, they did exacerbate the already existing networks of slavery, especially in Africa, but war, violence, illness and domination were already in most cultures across the world. Empire and colony, then, have been subject to a shift in views in recent times and for good reason when considering the abuses of colonialism and imperialism, but there is also an ambivalence because many of the institutions, ideas and cultural practices that questioned or vilified empire derived from the critical nature of European culture. These empires were not above self-criticism.

Structure

The structure of the book is set out chronologically in order to provide context. Each chapter is based on major events for western European empires and their colonies, which constitute the focus of the study. The first chapter (1415–1517) focuses on the first years of Portuguese expansion into Africa until Luther began the Reformation; the second (1517–1608) goes from then to the founding of the permanent settlements of Jamestown in 1607 and Quebec in 1608; the third proceeds from then to the peace at the end of the War of Spanish Succession; the fourth (1713–1830) moves from then to the time when most of the European colonies in the Americas became independent; the fifth (1830–1914) is the era of high imperialism in which European powers expanded elsewhere, especially in Africa until the cataclysm of the First World War; the sixth (1914–1945) moves from the Great War to the end of the Second World War, which were shocks to Europe and the world, and which began stresses in and between European empires; the seventh (1945 to the present) deals with the postwar period of decolonization, which might also be viewed as an age of neo-imperialism.

Within these chronologically ordered chapters, key sub-themes of the main theme of imperialism will be explored. A significant emphasis will be on the legal, economic and technological aspects of the political culture of empire. Culture, and in particular the meeting of cultures, is a key part of the story. Culture is also one of the main lenses through which we gain insight into the friction between the religious, social, legal, political and economic histories of empires and colonies on the one hand, and alternative histories through the voices of individuals on the other. The human voice and statistics will qualify each other in a story-argument in which the private and public, the micro and macro, work together to give as broad a perspective as possible within the constraints of this book. Even in periods of economic expansion and changes in warfare, issues such as slavery and women's rights were on the minds of those alive at the time.

Ambivalence and contradiction abide in the theme of empire and colony. The tension between the imperial centres and the colonies themselves is sometimes stressed to suggest that there is no one point of view even within an empire at any given time, let alone from without or in subsequent eras. While taking a sceptical view of the self-promotion of empires, the study will also point out how new cultures and practices are born of colonization. While the ill-effects of empire are abhorrent, the imperial theme is not a simple moral tale.

1

First Expansion: 1415–1517

❦

In the early fifteenth century it was not certain that the Iberian or any other western European countries would expand in any significant way or that they would become important contributors to global culture, economics and politics. The first expansion was tentative, halting and unexpected. Matters of expansion moved in different and sometimes opposing directions, so that this spreading out was full of problems, questions and failures. Empires and colonies were not certain, and there was no march to triumph. Within and between the Iberian states, Portugal and Spain, there were tensions, and Europe itself was so often in conflict that to speak of Iberia or Europe as a whole with a single purpose towards imperialism and colonization would deny the ambivalence and contradiction of these states and this continent. There were times when a nation seemed to work together or when Europeans cooperated, but there were more often moments when rivalries meant that Europeans were busy conducting violent campaigns against their own people and against other European states. By the Reformation in 1517, religious tensions and conflicts meant that Europe acted even less in concert.

In 1415, these Europeans began coming into contact with peoples who had less or more technical knowledge. Some peoples considered the Europeans to be barbaric, poor, weak and few. It is also important to remember that while this study is about the expansion of Europe, the continent was also contracting in places. Elsewhere, changes affected religious, political and economic patterns that in turn affected the Europeans. The powerful Tartar dynasty, which had welcomed Europeans and their missionaries and had governed the Chinese empire, also included Mongolia, part of Russia, as well as Turkestan. By the middle of the fourteenth century, the Ming dynasty had defeated the

Tartar khans. The states in central Asia, either Muslim or Buddhist, did not allow European Christians and the Chinese to continue their trade as they had under the Tartars. In the fifteenth century the Hindu kingdoms in Indo-China and the islands of east Asia were becoming Muslim. In India itself, Muslim states were pressuring Hindu polities. The Ottoman Turks came to dominate other Muslim states in the Near East and took Constantinople, the last remnant of the Roman empire and the capital of the Byzantine empire, in 1453. During the sixteenth century, the Ottomans would take Egypt, Syria, the Balkans and lands along the Danube in the heart of central Europe. Islam was expanding while Christianity was contracting.[1] The expansion of the Iberian powers was a modest counterbalance to this growth of Islamic powers. This is a framework that is worth remembering for the ensuing discussion of European expansion.[2]

This chapter will begin with Portuguese expansion and move through Columbus and Spain to the Reformation, when religious divisions complicated political and economic rivalries between European states. The power of Portugal and Spain will be the main concerns here, but the role of Italians, who were leaders in Europe until the rise of the Iberian states, and the growth of their northern rivals, England and France, will also be important topics. The rise of Europe and its expansion will be preoccupations in the context of some adjacent empires. Moreover, the role of Europe will be discussed, not with one answer in mind, but as a way of opening up the question for readers as they move through the book. In this period the role of the Catholic Church, even beyond the Reformation (from 1517), is significant and haunts the period and beyond. The Italian states, Portugal and Spain, which dominated the expansion of empire and the establishment of colonies in this period, were all Catholic powers after the Reformation.

Backgrounds: Cultures, Trade and Commerce

The strands of Portuguese expansion in this period were manifold and, as we shall see, their effects long-lasting. Portugal led the way in the expansion into Africa, India and the East Indies. The technology of ships and naval guns was something the Portuguese developed over the course of the fifteenth century. The capture of Ceuta opened up knowledge of Africa to Portugal. Prince Henry established a court at Sagres on Cape St Vincent in the Algarve in southwest Portugal that concentrated on nautical knowledge. The desire to find the Christian empire of Prester John in Abyssinia (Ethiopia) and to contain Muslim power was a motivation of

Portugal. Henry derived from his brother, the king, a monopoly on the trade on the Guinea coast and also received papal support for it as a means of converting the Africans. Prince Henry, who died in 1460, also financed expeditions by those who were not Portuguese, for instance Alvise da Cadamosto, a Venetian.

The Portuguese accomplishments were gradual. In 1483, Diogo Cao got to the mouth of the Congo and in 1487 Bartolomeu Dias sailed on a route around the southern tip of Africa. Columbus's voyage to the New World helped delay the Portuguese fleet in going to India until 1497 as the court assessed the impact of Columbus's claims. When Vasco da Gama arrived at Malindi, he found Ibn Malid, a Muslim pilot of great talent, who helped him to navigate across the Indian Ocean to Calicut. There, the Hindu leader did not welcome this change from dealing with the Arabs, and the Portuguese had trouble trading for spices given the inferiority of their goods to those in India.

There is much talk about globalization today, but a global economy did exist at this time, although not with the intensity, variety and scale that have developed in the past few decades. Still, in the Middle Ages, Europeans had shortages of feed for their animals and had to slaughter a good portion, and so needed preservatives, such as salt. Spices could also be used to preserve food. Pepper, cloves, ginger and cinnamon, all from Africa, India and China, became valued in Europe. As Muslim states expanded at the expense of Christian and Hindu countries, they came to control the spice trade by about 1500. The Arabs traded with the Venetians for spices and other precious goods from the East, such as Chinese silk and Indian cotton. The Portuguese feats in sailing around Africa would challenge this trade, affecting the dominance of Venice and the Arab and Muslim control of the exchange of spices and precious goods. In 1502, Da Gama was able to destroy a larger Arab fleet in the Indian Ocean because of military tactics and the use of guns. Under Affonso Albuquerque, the Portuguese established forts off the Arabian coast and took Goa on the Malabar coast of India in 1510. They also took Hormuz, a strategic market at the mouth of the Persian Gulf, and also Ceylon (Sri Lanka) and Malacca, the key place for trade with east Asia, in 1511. The Portuguese were in Canton by 1513 and set up soon after in Macao. By controlling the Straits of Gibraltar in Ceuta and the straits to the Far East in Ceuta, the Portuguese were in a strategic position to dominate trade. War was the way Portugal sought to control the trade in the Indian Ocean and well beyond.[3] All this was in about a hundred years, the period that this chapter discusses. In other words, in a relatively brief time and in an unexpected fashion, Portugal, a small nation on the edge of western Eurasia, altered through force a trade network that stretched from Europe to China. It would be a long time before Portugal, or any European nation, could rival the Indian states and China in wealth and strength, but in these early years the groundwork was set.

Some background will suggest that there were other factors in the context leading to Portuguese expansion into Africa and Asia. Cultural encounters complemented and supplemented the legal texts of the expansion of Portugal and other European powers later on. Columbus would show this ambivalence towards the Natives of the New World. Cultural, financial, religious and other values were intertwined with the legal framework of expansion. A proleptic aspect of these texts of early European expansion into Africa for those accounts of a similar exploration of the western Atlantic is that of the bad tribes or peoples. For instance, in Alvise Cadamosto's account of the Portuguese in Africa in the fifteenth century, the Barbazini (Barbacenes) and Sereri (Serer) partly play this role: 'They will not recognize any lord among them, lest he should carry off their wives and children and sell them into slavery, as is done by the kings and lords of all the other lands of the negroes. They are exceedingly idolatrous, have no laws, and are the cruellest of men.'[4] They seemed to be without class, religion, law, restraint and civility. Even though the king of Senega tried to subdue these peoples, he suffered at their hands, their poison arrows having presumably been too much to overcome. A certain unruliness and danger, a group escaping but needing control, created a tension that would welcome later European intervention.

Countries and continents were closely linked long before Columbus set sail. Europe in the late Middle Ages was short of gold, which was available through African trade routes. The expansion of Europe in the fifteenth century involved intertwined motives of God and gold. The fate of merchants depended then, as they had before, on war, investment and resources. In the late fourteenth century the climate for business was not good. The Black Death devastated the population and contracted the economy. The Persians and the Chinese had little time for the Europeans, but the technology that drove them to expand by land and sea helped to create a more global world than ever before and to bring about modernity. The Russians spread by land while the Portuguese, Spaniards, English, French and Dutch moved by ship. People, crops, diseases and goods crossed boundaries and changed and devastated the New World or Americas. Italians were crucial in banking and navigation in the late Middle Ages and early Renaissance and they would continue to play crucial roles in the economic expansion of Europe, sometimes within the Italian city states and other times in the service of the monarchs of Portugal, Spain, England and France.[5]

Portugal and Spain: Their Expansion and the Role of the Church

Papal donations and bulls played a key role in the expansion of European powers. What authority did the pope have in dividing the world unknown to Europe between Portugal and Spain? The monarchs and writers of England and France asked this question repeatedly for centuries.[6] In the expansion of Portugal and Spain the Church played a role that supplemented conquest, reconquest and trade. This expansion often involved religious, political, economic and cultural motives. Documents of various kinds, whether ecclesiastical or civil, were not only promulgated but also engendered interpretations by those who seemed to benefit from them and those who complained they did not. Even before the Reformation in central and western Europe in 1517, Christian countries in those regions were engaged in disputes over the influence of the pope and the Roman church in areas that we would now call international law and trade.

In the fourteenth and fifteenth centuries Portugal and Spain were rivals in exploration. The rediscovery of the Canary Islands created a conflict between Portugal and Castile in the late thirteenth century. In 1344, Don Luis de la Cerda, admiral of France and great-grandson of Alfonso the Wise, obtained a bull from Clement VI to Christianize these islands, believed to be the *Fortunatae Insulae* of the ancients, and was crowned prince of this domain in Avignon. Castile and Portugal put aside their differences and supported Luis, but, after he did not take possession, they continued their struggle. Subsequent papal bulls favoured one side then the other, and the question of ownership was not settled until 1479 when, by the treaty of Alcaçovas, Portugal ceded the Canaries to Castile.[7] The second controversy between Portugal and Castile was over Africa. After the conquest of Ceuta in 1415 with military expeditions in Morocco and with voyages to Guinea, Portugal made its claim in Africa. In the 1440s and 1450s slaves and gold made for a lucrative trade there. As they had in the case of the Canaries, the kings of Castile based their claim to conquest in Africa on its possession by their ancestors, the Visigoths. By 1454, the two countries were embroiled in this African controversy. On 8 January 1455, Nicholas V issued the bull *Romanus pontifex* that gave exclusive rights to King Alfonso of Portugal in this African exploration and trade. This ruling extended the bull *Dum diversas* (18 June 1452), in which Nicholas had given Alfonso the right to conquer pagans, enslave them and take their lands and goods. Nicholas's predecessor, Eugenius IV, had, in the bull *Rex regum* (5 January 1443), taken a neutral stance between Castile and Portugal regarding Africa. The Castilians would not accept the authority of the papal letters and continued to claim Guinea until 1479. That year, after the War of Succession (in which Alfonso invaded Castile in an attempt to annex it), Portugal ceded the Canaries, and Castile acknowledged Portugal's claim to Guinea, the Azores, Madeira and the Cape Verde Islands.[8] Conflict and rivalry, as well as the dynastic intertwining of the royal houses, complicated the relations between Portugal and Spain as well as their expansion beyond their peninsular boundaries.

The legal authority of the See of Rome was also a complex matter, and papal authority, even in places as apparently devout as Portugal and Spain, was not always secure. As these tensions and conflicts between Spain and Portugal suggest, papal bulls were not permanent laws and were not always accepted as remedies by the parties involved in the disputes. From the late fifteenth century onwards, Portugal and Spain would, however, insist that other nations, such as France and England, abide by the papal bulls dividing the 'undiscovered' world between the Iberian powers. After 1492, Spain dominated the discourse about the New World. The temporal power of Spain used the spiritual authority of Rome to underpin the Spanish empire.

Lost opportunities were a theme of France and England in this period. The French and the English, who had not taken up Columbus's Enterprise of the Indies as Spain had, now had to try to catch up to the Spanish. Columbus had given Portugal the right of first refusal. In this they had to contravene the wishes and the gift of the pope, set out in the bull of 4 May 1493, which, in response to Columbus's first voyage to the New World, divided the parts of the world yet unknown to Christians into two spheres, one for Spain and the other for Portugal. The pope, who had Iberian connections, issued a direct threat to those who might not accept his donation 'under the penalty of excommunication' if they contravened the gift of these new lands to the Iberian monarchs.[9] Church and state were intricately integrated in Europe in the early phases of the age of exploration.

Papal warnings were not new. This kind of threat against other Christian princes breaking the exclusive rights of the parties named in the donations occurred in earlier bulls, such as *Romanus pontifex*. The Spanish and the Portuguese accepted the terms of this bull, except that they shifted the line of demarcation from 100 leagues to 370 leagues west of the Cape Verde Islands in the Treaty of Tordesillas in 1494. Although claiming the spheres of ownership that the pope had set out, these Iberian states gave each other rights of passage across each other's territory. Spain and Portugal confirmed these terms, including the changes to the bull *Inter caetera*, in the Treaty of Madrid in 1495. The bull *Ea quae* of 1506, issued after Vasco da Gama had rounded the Cape of Good Hope, also made this confirmation. The Reformation changed the attitude of other countries, such as England and the Netherlands, to the authority of the papal disposition. Catholic France also resisted this donation. Monarchs, when issuing commissions to their own explorers, instructed them not to seize land already claimed by another Christian prince. To claim title, the explorers supplemented the bulls by planting crosses with the royal coats of arms on the 'new-found' lands.[10]

If there was disagreement within European nations over expansion to the New World, Europe itself was divided. This division possessed its own form of opposition. The English and French opposed the papal donation to Spain and Portugal even while they imitated these leading colonial powers. That the English and French monarchs sent out their own expeditions to the New World showed a practical disregard for the papal bulls. A gap between theory and practice, church and state, widened as the rivalry among the European powers intensified. After the Reformation took hold, at various times in different countries from 1517 onwards, the primarily Protestant powers of England and the Netherlands came to oppose Portugal and Spain, with France, a Catholic country with a large Protestant population, poised between. In Germany and the Netherlands, where many Habsburg interests lay, the situation was even more complicated in relation to that great Habsburg power – Spain.

Early on, the two powers the pope favoured could not always get along. 'Spain' was a rival of Portugal in expansion and colonization. Whereas in 1488 Dias rounded the Cape of Good Hope, in 1492 Columbus set sail to the western Atlantic. The Portuguese, as we have seen, entered with Spain into the Treaty of Tordesillas in 1494: Vasca da Gama reached India in 1498 and Cabral, Brazil in 1500. In 1514, Pope Leo X granted, in the bull *Præcelsæ Devotionis*, to Portugal all places they encountered by sailing east that could be seized from heathens. This, as we will see, was a challenge to Spain when Magellan, a Portuguese, sailed for Spain in search of a western route to Asia in 1519, the year Hernán Cortés invaded Mexico. Even in the papal division of the world between the Iberian powers, there was friction between them. The Portuguese, who could not tell the longitude of the Moluccas, which was lucrative for them, did not want to take the chance of the islands falling into the sphere of Spain. This is why Leo's ruling was so crucial to Portugal and anathema to Spain, which had understood the papal line of demarcation as dividing the whole world between the Iberian states and not just in the Atlantic. Most of the time, the Portuguese did well in its relations with the papacy regarding these donations.

Donations and other quasi-legal documents could cause discontent as much as order. A religious and legal framework was developed as the Iberian powers expanded. Until the fifteenth century relations with Islam had been a significant political and juridical consideration. In Iberia or Hispania, the Moors were thought to inhabit *terra irredenta*, lands that needed to be restored to legitimate Christian rulers, whereas pagans' lands in Africa were *terra nullius*, uninhabited lands in the sense that these people lived without civility or a polis. Earlier writings, such as those of Hortensius (Cardinal Henry of Susa, d. 1271), were used to justify Portuguese claims in Africa: Christ embodied temporal and spiritual lordship over the world, and this dominion was passed on to His representatives, the pontiffs or bishops of Rome, who could also delegate lordship over non-Christian lands. This doctrine imbued a papal bull in 1452, which donated to the Crown of Portugal sovereignty over subjects in the lands that the Portuguese had discovered, and another in 1454 over peoples in lands that the Portuguese might discover in Africa as they proceeded south. The Crown was obliged to convert these peoples, who could be conquered if they resisted trade with, the dominion of and evangelization by Christians. In these bulls the pope gave Portugal a monopoly in the expansion south of Morocco on the Atlantic coast of Africa.[11] Conversion and monopoly were just two aspects of these papal bulls.

Law, religion and culture could not be separated. Cultural encounters include stereotyping or depreciating groups as in Cadamosto's account of the Barbazini and Sereri.[12] They lack important traits like civility. This old trope that if people could not govern themselves, then they needed to be governed was something as old as Tacitus.

The Treaty of Alcáçovas in 1479, Pope Alexander VI's bulls in 1493, and the treaty between Portugal and Spain at Tordesillas in 1494 are, as mentioned, important landmarks.[13] The printing of the '*Inter Cætera*' bull (1493) in northern Spain in 1511 showed how important the church and its documents were to the history of expansion.[14] The world within and beyond Europe would change radically in the years to come.

The Rise of 'Spain'

It is important to see states and cultures in various contexts and not to see one in isolation as a dominant empire that could be self-sufficient. There are always trading partners and different cultures at work in European states and their empires. To speak of 'Spain' is not to describe a unity, but, as Henry Kamen has noted, the empire made Spain, which did not exist as such and which grew out of a joining of different peoples in the peninsula. During the fifteenth century, after long civil wars, Castile and Aragon were united ten years after the marriage of Isabella of Castile and Ferdinand of Aragon. Castile made up two-thirds of the country and four-fifths of its roughly five and a half million inhabitants. Spain was poor and exported wool to northern Europe in exchange for manufactures, grain, textiles, paper and other commodities. France, Portugal and the Muslims in southern Spain (al-Andalus) were a challenge to the Spanish monarchy.[15]

Portugal and Spain clashed over expanding their influence, trade and territory. As Portugal expanded, it was wary of the larger nation with which it shared the Iberian peninsula and Spain's claim to the Canary Islands, which made them vulnerable in their expansion into Africa. The Spaniards had conquered the Guanches there, and in 1479 Portugal recognized the Spanish claim to the Canaries. Portugal had explored the Azores in the 1430s. Columbus's westward journey in 1492 meant that the Portuguese now had serious rivals in expansion.

Columbus's landfall in the western Atlantic helped to shift the balance of power in Europe from the Mediterranean to the Atlantic. He brought the New World, which had been mainly isolated from other parts of the world, into a global economy and many of its peoples into the shock of disease, misery and death as a result of European expansion. After serving the Portuguese and after the death of his wife, a member of the Portuguese nobility, in 1485, this Genoese settled in Spain and, after much difficulty, convinced the monarchs, Isabella of Castile and Ferdinand of Aragon, to back a sea voyage westward in search of the gold and spices of Asia. Columbus, it may be said, ushered in an era in which the Americas played a key role in the world and what may, therefore, be truly called a global epoch.

After his arrival in the West Indies, Columbus claimed these lands for the Catholic monarchs. The possession of gold and the notion of force reassert themselves when Columbus, who was to share profits with the monarchs, promised Ferdinand and Isabella goldmines and great riches, and when he spoke about his fortification of the town, which he named La Navidad. Lordship over, and Christianization of, the Natives were also part of this claiming of new lands. Portuguese and Spanish Christians had reclaimed the Iberian peninsula and now took that zeal into the furthest reaches of the world. Columbus's view of the new land is ambivalent: it is a place of innocence and profit.[16] The peoples of the New World, like their lands, become subject to, and in many ways a possession of, the king and queen. The letter of Columbus (also called the Spanish letter) was addressed to Luis de Santangel, the Keeper of Accounts of Aragon, and recorded his great expectations. Columbus, as we have him here, clearly wanted to find evidence of a great civilization to convince his sovereigns of the importance of his voyage and the wisdom of their investment. Columbus said that he soon prevented his men from trading worthless things for gold.[17] God and gold go hand in hand once more. The legal and the political join the religious and economic.

Columbus found gold and caught the imagination of Spain and, through editions in different languages, Europe. During the second voyage in 1494, in the year Charles VIII of France invaded Italy, the local Natives rebelled because the Spanish mistreated them. The Spaniards called these indigenes Indians ('Indios'), so called because they referred to these as the Indies in hope of their being part of Asia. Columbus took slaves in Hispaniola. Like the Portuguese, the Spanish soon kidnapped slaves and used violence in their expansion. Columbus and members of his family, after the third of his four voyages when he explored Trinidad and the northern coast of South America in 1498 to 1500, were sent home in leg irons. There was conflict among the Spanish colonists. So violence towards others and internal dissention were part of the first few decades of the Spanish colonization of the Caribbean. Food shortages, a new climate and friction with the Natives made colonization difficult. Columbus helped 300 settlers, including Bartolomé de Las Casas's father, return to Spain. Those who stayed survived because the Natives fed them.

Once the wealth of the New World was proven and the population of settlers grew there, the Crown asserted its control over these dependent territories. Ferdinand and Isabella had exerted their authority in Castile through law. Courts and the Roman law they dispensed were instruments of that strategy. In Castile, the royal administration made much use of judicial bodies, which, in the form of *audiencias*, became crucial in major colonial cities and whose powers extended beyond those at home. The first *audiencia* or tribunal in the Americas appeared in Santo Domingo in 1511. As part of an extension of authority in the colonies, the Crown retracted the privileges granted to Columbus, and Charles I kept his eye on *encomenderos*. If, as J. M. Ots y Capdequí has maintained, the problem for the Crown was to conquer the conquerors (*conquistadores*), then, as Mark A. Burkholder and D. S. Chandler have suggested, the solution for the Crown was to extend the Castilian administration to the New World.[18] Politics and law as well as economics – especially the issue of slavery – were hard fought early in the history of Iberian overseas history.

With expansion, Spain became part of a vast web of lands in the Habsburg empire. The very existence of this economic and political power concentrated in the hands of one family caused alarm in many states, and particularly in France, whose lands were surrounded by various territories the Habsburgs controlled. The one person who seemed to be able to rule this 'empire' was Charles, grandson of Maximilian I of Austria (1493–1519; Holy Roman emperor, 1508–19) and of the same monarchs, Isabella and Ferdinand, who sent Columbus on his voyage to the New World.

Although Spain and Portugal were rivals, they were also closely connected. Portugal was making breakthroughs, but its exploration was in relation to that of Spain and subject to the authority of the pope. The Iberian states, then, experienced a double movement of rivalry and shared advantage owing to the papal support for their expansion and colonization.

The Spanish Crown came to play a large role in Italy for 300 years and in the wars against Muslims in Iberia and beyond. The monarchy forced conversions of Muslims in the peninsula partly because the conditions for emigration were so harsh when they were given the choice. The extension of the war against the Muslims extended to a dream of empire in Africa. So Italy, the reconquest, expansion into Africa and to the New World and Asia were all happening simultaneously over these key decades. Isabella died in 1504 and Ferdinand in 1516, when the thrones of Castile and Aragon passed to his grandson, Charles of Habsburg, the son of Ferdinand's daughter, Juanita, who was queen and joint ruler of Castile until her death. Charles was born in Ghent in 1500, grew up in the Netherlands and barely spoke Castilian, and had advisers mainly from the Netherlands. Spain and Charles's other possessions were polyglot, so his empire was neither simply German nor Spanish. At the end of the period, on the verge of the Reformation, 'Spain' faced its own challenges internally.[19]

Slavery

Portugal and Spain benefited from slaves early on in their expansion. Here is a fulcrum for looking backwards and forwards to a key underpinning of this imperial and colonial regime: slavery. Aristotle's theory of natural slavery was set out in his *Politics* and divided the world into masters and slaves. It was in circulation about 1,800 years before the court chronicler, Gomes Eannes de Zuzara, attached to Prince Henry of Portugal, described how in August 1444 the Portuguese landed 235 African slaves near Lagos in southern Portugal, sobbing, lamenting, throwing themselves prostrate as they were divided from family members, one from the other. This was the beginning of the transformation of an ancient and lamentable practice, an inhumane institution so long engrained in so many human societies: slavery.

Africa, which had seen Islamic powers involved in slavery, now had to face European involvement. The Iberian powers did intervene. The Portuguese and Spanish, in pursuit of their delegated monopolies, enslaved Africans, who were considered pagans and savages, and sold them in Portugal, Spain and the Atlantic islands. In the fifteenth century, as we have observed, black slaves were sometimes considered to be ill-formed and inferior.[20]

Thus, the issue of slavery arose early in the expansion of Spain and Portugal. The bull *Romanus Pontifex* had given the Portuguese the right to reduce the infidels to slavery, so that the inhabitants of these new lands – 'so unknown to us westerners that we had no certain knowledge of the peoples of those parts' – had no rights because they were not Christian.[21] This pattern was similar to the one the popes made in their donations concerning the New World, except that the Natives were deemed barbarous and not infidels, so that their potential for conversion saved them, at least theoretically, from slavery. The papacy continued to play a role in legitimizing exploration after Columbus's landfall in the New World. Church authority allowed for expansion and slavery to underwrite the political and economic power of Catholic Europe.

The change was that Europe would now use African slaves to feed its production of sugar, first in Europe and in the islands that Portugal and Spain possessed in the eastern Atlantic and then in the West Indies and the mainland of the Americas. Cotton would follow as a crop that slave labour maintained. Mining and domestic service were other work that drew heavily on African slaves. The seizure of slaves, or *razzias*, rather than their purchase, was practised by Muslim merchants in Spain and Africa during the Middle Ages, and Christian merchants had similar practices. The Portuguese, who themselves used slaves on the sugar plantations that the Genoese had established in the Algarve, also sold slaves into Spain. By 1475, Spain appointed a magistrate, Juan de Valladolid, who was black, for the growing population within the country itself of *loros* (mulattos) and blacks. Bartolomeo Marchionni, a Florentine banker who was one of the wealthiest people in Lisbon and had agents in Seville, became involved in the African trade and also had connections with Christopher Columbus (Colón). His son, Diego Colón, became governor of the Spanish possessions in the Caribbean in 1509 and wrote to King Ferdinand, saying that the Natives were not able to bear the work and asking for African slaves. Despite Ferdinand's irritation – he had authorized the kidnapping of Native slaves from adjacent islands – he did in January 1510 authorize the sending of fifty African slaves to work in the goldmines of Hispaniola. Very soon after Columbus's landfall in the western Atlantic, sugar cane was being cultivated in the Caribbean. This was the same king who had deported Jews and Moors from Spain and had enslaved many of his Moorish and some of his Jewish subjects.

Columbus's landfall also, along with the Portuguese exploration of Africa, changed the face of slavery. In the fifteenth century and sixteenth centuries, a shift occurred. Whereas Slavs, Turks and western Europeans had also been part of a slave economy based on war and piracy, Africa now became the predominant source of slaves. When the sugar economy spread from the estates of southern Portugal and the Portuguese Atlantic islands to the large plantations of Brazil and the West Indies, the demand for slaves increased sharply. The Muslim rulers of West Africa had increased the trade in slaves, but the European demand for slaves after the coming of the Portuguese in the sixteenth century intensified the trade and made it all the more devastating. American sugar plantations would be the machine into which so many people were fed and which helped to ruin families, tribes and states in Africa. Columbus, as Hugh Thomas has pointed out, was a product of a new Atlantic economy in which sugar, and the slavery that underpinned it, played a large part. To his Florentine friend in Seville, Juanotto Berardi, an associate of the great merchants the Marchionni, Columbus himself sent from Santo Domingo the first known shipment of slaves – Taino Indians. Soon the Crown was annulling such sale of Native slaves because of the uncertainty over the legality of this scheme. The queen was reported to be cross with Columbus over his repeated attempts to sell or give her vassals away as slaves.[22] Columbus and his king were content with Native slaves, but by 1510, owing to the decimation of the indigenous labour force, King Ferdinand ordered that 200 African slaves be sent to the New World. In the Spanish colonies – from the Philippines to Peru – the three chief institutions were the *audiencia* (judicial tribunal), the office of the viceroy (captain-general) and the church, the first two representing the royal interests and the third attending to 'the conversion of the infidels and the subsequent care of their souls'.[23] Material benefit and the spiritual conscience collided in the slave trade and the institution of slavery.

The Challenge from England

Columbus's landfall in the New World seems to have prompted the English court to seek out the possibilities of exploration. In the first letters patent granted to John Cabot, citizen of Venice, and his sons, on 5 March 1496, Henry VII granted to them and their heirs and deputies the right to sail to any foreign parts in the eastern, western and northern sea, at their own expense, and would allow Cabot and his sons and heirs to have all the profits and goods, free of customs, except for the fifth that must be paid to the Crown.[24] The 'discovery' of the Grand Banks and the search for a northwest passage to Asia would change the course of English, European and world history. The race for the passage and for Newfoundland was on from the 1490s onwards. Although this race is under this section about England, it is there because the English were the first to draw attention to the fisheries there through Cabot's voyage and because it later became an English colony.

The legal and political questions started early in the history of European expansion to the western Atlantic and depended on matters of the discovery and possession of territory. England followed Spain most closely in exploring the New World. Henry VII seems to have ignored the papal bulls and treaties between the Iberian powers during the 1490s dividing the world-to-be-discovered.[25] On 5 March 1496, at Westminster, the Lord Chancellor of England considered a bill of John Cabot and his sons.[26] Henry VII provided a grant but not the finances.[27] During the last half of the sixteenth century, the English anxiety over Spanish claims to the New World and their own desire for legitimization there would make Cabot part of a search for a claim to the Americas prior or nearly contemporary to Spain's.

Intelligence was one way to attempt to bolster the legal claim to the New World. Spain itself opposed the expansion of England and France to the New World. Spanish intelligence must have been sensitive to English and French rivalry, for in Tortosa on 28 March of that same year, the Spanish sovereigns wrote to Gonzales de Puebla:

> In regard to what you say of the arrival there of one like Columbus for the purpose of inducing the King of England to enter upon another undertaking like that of the Indies, without prejudice to Spain or to Portugal, if he [the king] aids him as he has us, the Indies will be well rid of the man. We are of opinion that this is a scheme of the French king's to persuade the king of England to undertake this so that he will give up other affairs.[28]

The Spanish king and queen, showing some anxiety and self-interest of their own, obviously took seriously the English threat to the monopoly that Spain had with Portugal in the New World, which the pope and the two countries had worked out in the previous three years. This anxiety extended to a rivalry with the French in Europe generally and in Italy specifically, which could not be suppressed even in the Spanish monarchs' interpretation of English preparations to stake a claim in the New World. This empire had its own anxieties about its power: its rivals and opponents did not have a monopoly on these worries.

Diplomacy is a good way to observe the official expression of these tensions and concerns. The ambassador of Spain to England said that the success of Cabot's first voyage had made Henry outfit five vessels with a year's provisions for the second voyage.[29] Cabot was expected back in September and Pedro Ayala would inform the king and queen what had happened. If the ambassador acknowledged the discovery, then he would not allow for its legitimacy. In this account Henry VII would have none of this.[30] The dispute was twofold. The first issue was whether England accepted the papal bull dividing the 'undiscovered' lands in the Atlantic between Portugal and Spain. The second matter was whether England had 'discovered' lands that Spain had already claimed. England and Spain were engaged in a kind of political, economic and diplomatic hide-and-seek game.

The Portuguese thought that the land Cabot encountered was quite possibly in their sphere as set out in the Treaty of Tordesillas (370 leagues west of the Cape Verde Islands). It was possible that after Vasco da Gama lost two-thirds of his crew on his eastern voyage (he returned in September 1499), the Portuguese considered a westward route to be shorter, cheaper, and less punishing. Having watched Columbus's success and heard about Cabot's news of fish, timber and a possible northwest route to Asia, the first great exploring nation of the fifteenth century now followed the English lead. On 28 October 1499, King Manuel of Portugal issued letters patent to João Fernandez to make a voyage to discover new islands in the North Atlantic.[31] The Portuguese king issued similar patents to Gaspar Corte Real on 12 May 1500, and for a second voyage in 1501; to Miguel Corte Real in January 1502; for a fourth voyage in 1503. When the Corte Real brothers were lost and the hope for a northwest passage grew dim, the Portuguese gave up on Newfoundland for some time to come, except for the fisheries. Fernandez took his ideas to Henry VII just as Sebastian Cabot would leave England for Spain in order to find backing for his expeditions. In 1501, from Bristol, merchants from the Azores and England joined together to petition for a patent to seek out the new lands in the northwest Atlantic.[32] The Company of Adventurers to the New Found Lands was to serve as a model for later companies that helped to extend English trade and settlement to new lands.

John Cabot's voyage had alerted other nations to the great stocks of fish in the banks off the northeast coast of North America, and the fishermen of western Europe soon sought this fishery, sometimes despite the official policies of their respective countries.[33] Cabot and his crew claimed that England would no longer need the Iceland fishery and described the role of Corte Real in the establishment of a Portuguese fishery in Newfoundland that flourished until the end of the sixteenth century. The Newfoundland fishery would be a place of conflict. In 1506 the Portuguese imposed a tax on Newfoundland cod brought to Portugal.[34]

Perhaps the most tenacious heirs to the elder Cabot were the French fishermen, later the men of the French shore in Newfoundland and of St Pierre and Miquelon. Two decades before official French voyages to North America, French fishermen were involved in the fisheries near Newfoundland. In some ways the fishermen kept up contact with and interest in North America for the French between Cartier and Champlain.[35] According to Ramusio, by 1504 Breton fishing vessels went as far as Newfoundland, and in 1508 the *Pensée* sailed from Dieppe to Cape Bonavista. The ship, which belonged to Jean Ango, later viscount of Dieppe, brought back seven Natives and their arms, canoes and belongings. This followed the Columbian tradition of kidnapping Natives in the New World, something Paulmier de Gonneville had done on his return from Brazil to Honfleur, when he took Essomericq back with him.[36]

The dispute endured a long time. Later, King Ferdinand of Spain continued his interest in the lands the Cabots had visited. In October 1511 he concluded a compact with Juan de Agramonte, a Catalan, for a voyage to Newfoundland, which Queen Joanna ratified, but no record exists to show whether Agramonte and his Breton pilots ever made the journey.[37] The documents mention that Agramonte was to set out to find 'the secret of Newfoundland' with a crew of Spaniards (except that two of the pilots might have been Bretons or from another nation with experience there). Nevertheless, owing to the agreement between Spain and Portugal (the Treaty of Tordesillas), Agramonte was not to venture on to the lands of Manuel, king of Portugal, who had married Ferdinand's daughters, Isabella and Maria.[38] Ferdinand faced a contradictory situation: he would not recognize any discovery of Newfoundland outside his Iberian family, whose bonds treaties and marriages had cemented, but he needed the help of Portuguese, French or English pilots. The Breton pilots seemed acceptable to the king of Spain, who gave Agramonte permission to buy provisions in Brittany. The king, who hoped that Agramonte would find gold and other useful things in Newfoundland, also obliged himself to free Agramonte from prison should anyone detain him at the instance of any Christian king, thereby admitting the existence of nations 'hostile' to Spain's claim to the New World.[39] The tension between ideals and practical concerns was and is a recurring theme of empire. The potential is that if the practice qualifies or contravenes the ideals too much, then the law might seem an ass and be undermined. Practices and details could call into question the ideology – the moral, religious and legal authority – of empires.

What England was doing in the western Atlantic was also of interest to Portugal. The oceans near and about Newfoundland were a great source of fish, but establishing dynamic permanent settlements by any of the European powers would prove difficult. The race for Newfoundland was intermittent but sometimes intense.

European laws, ecclesiastical and secular, affected the lives of the local peoples that the explorers and settlers from Europe met. The Natives whom the Spanish, Portuguese and other Europeans encountered were also subject to various legal explanations and categories. For instance, in French and English America, Natives came directly under the spiritual jurisdiction of the pope, whereas in Iberian America they were under royal patronage (the *patronato real* in the Spanish colonies by 1508 and the *padroado* in Portuguese colonies by 1514).[40] What might be legal justification for Europeans had hard consequences for indigenous peoples.

Sebastian Cabot had become useful to Ferdinand, who wrote to him on 13 September 1512, and whose chief chaplain and secretary, on behalf of their monarch, spoke with Cabot in Burgos about 'the navigation to the Indies and the island of the Codfish', that is, to the West Indies and Newfoundland.[41] By this time, the Breton, Portuguese, English and French fishermen seem to have been making annual trips to the fishing banks off the coast of Newfoundland. Records suggest that Newfoundland cod was having an economic impact on the western coast of France.[42] The records also show the English fishing fleet active in the Newfoundland fishery.[43]

The Challenge from France

France was involved in crusades and exploration. Rivalry between the French and the Castilians began early. The French, having played a central role in the crusades, tried to re-create their glory. In 1390, the Duke of Bourbon set out for Barbary in the quest for holiness and gold, and perhaps as a means of eradicating corsairs for the Genoese proponents. Two men who served with Bourbon were Jean de Béthencourt and Gadifer de la Salle, who, on 1 May 1402, set out to conquer the Canary Islands for France. Relying on Castilian supplies and facing the jealousy of Castile and the indifference of France, the two French explorers saw the islands become Castilian. Castile gained much as the Canaries, whose winds were connected to the New World, became strategic for supplying ships making the voyage. De Béthencourt and de la Salle were to honour God, increase the Christian faith and seek the River of Gold.[44]

At the end of the fifteenth century, the English were making important contributions to European exploration. After the accomplishment of John Cabot in 1497, however, the English began to lag behind the French, who were in Brazil as traders and pirates and who challenged the Portuguese there until they were driven out in 1603. Unlike Henry VIII, François I made a concerted effort to explore and claim new territories in the New World. Like Henry VII, he ignored the authority of the pope to donate these lands to Spain and Portugal. François built up a policy of discovery, conquest and settlement that challenged the bulls, and that was, as in Henry VII's case, a version of *terra nullius*. The French use of the principle of 'no settlement, no possession' goaded the Portuguese and the Spanish and was a position that Elizabeth I would take up. There were, then, some affinities between the English and the French in their strategies to circumvent the legal and practical obstacles that the Spanish and Portuguese empires threw up before them.

France made an impact of its own in the exploration of the southern part of the New World. Binot Paulmier de Gonneville, a Norman, sailed to Brazil on the aptly named ship, *L'Espoir* (1503–5). The opening of Gonneville's account explained how two Portuguese, 'Bastiam Moura' and 'Diègue Cohinto', helped the Normans know the route to the Indies, something illegal under Portuguese law at the time.[45] The French were beginning to challenge the Portuguese in Brazil and the Spanish in North America.[46]

In the first three decades of the sixteenth century, the governments of England and France were still committed to the Catholic Church. These links to Rome qualified attachment to one's country. Gonneville's act of possession was not straightforward. In spite of all the talk of an opposition between Rome and France over the bull of 1493, Gonneville described the inscription on the cross in a way that accounted for both parties.[47] He represented Pope Alexander VI, King Louis XII of France and the French admiral Mallet de Graville in apparently descending order as a sign that Christians had arrived in that country, hardly a defiant patriotic gesture against the author of the donation that was supposed to divide the undiscovered world between Spain and Portugal. Moreover, another part of the Latin inscription suggested how the regional or provincial aspect of this voyage and ceremony also complicated national sentiment: 'Here Paulmier de Gonneville raised this sacred monument while associating intimately the tribe and the Norman lineage [descendants].'[48] Like the aboriginals Bernal Díaz described in his account of Cortés's conquest, those Gonneville met were much taken by the power of writing.[49] Gonneville saw bringing Christianity to the Natives as the custom of all those who came to the Indies and said that the Native chief, Arosca, wanted his son, Essomericq, to return to France to live in Christendom. The French promised the father and the son that Essomericq would be returned home after twenty moons at the latest.[50] Like Christopher Columbus, Gonneville read the signs, but their meaning was not always as simple and clear as these European captains thought.[51] On the way home, the French were stricken with sickness. Monsieur Nicole administered the sacrament to Essomericq, who was sick, and baptized him Binot, after one of his godfathers, Gonneville. The baptism seemed to serve as medicine to body and soul because 'the said Indian' recovered and was now in France.[52] After two years, he arrived in Harfleur with twenty-eight of fifty-eight men.[53] Gonneville, Andrieu de La Mare and Anthoyne Thiéry lost their journal with the ship, which Gonneville preferred to lose rather than yield to the Breton pirates (7 May 1505), and so presented their report in the form as set out by law.[54] Differences within 'nation states' also complicated the national identities and made difficult the expansion of these European 'empires'. Overseas territories and cultures were beginning to affect the culture and law in Europe.[55]

Legal matters were part of a wider cultural, political and economic dimension of expansion. France was long a key place in Europe and would have, in varying degrees, great influence on the continent and beyond. The governments of the Iberian powers would have been well aware of the geopolitical importance of France. Well before Columbus's landfall, as we have seen, France was interested in, and participated in, expansion overseas so it challenged the monopoly that the pope had granted them in exploration and dominion of unexplored lands.[56] The French had been in the Grand Banks since the first decade of the sixteenth century. Their efforts at colonization would increase after the beginnings of the Reformation.

An Expanding Europe

Europe was not as economically strong as India and China in this period. These European states would have seemed unlikely at the time to become central in the future. This question of why Europe expanded into great empires east and west, by land and sea, is an old one among scholars. Behind this question lies another: Why did the European economy begin to be innovative and to take off above others for about 500 years, the years, coincidentally, that make up most of the period of this book? E. L. Jones, for instance, based his study on the idea of a 'European miracle'.[57] Paul Kennedy has offered a good summary of this scholarship on the economic history of European expansion in the context of other powers in the world and I will condense and supplement his findings further.[58] China, the Muslim powers, Russia and Japan were all worthy rivals of the western European seaborne empires. They had resources, technology and economic clout and, despite their great successes, they came under the influence of the western countries in the centuries to come. Why was that?

China had all the knowledge, technology and economic power to expand, but stopped short of doing so, partly because of threats from the north and desires to expand southwards. There were, however, other apparent factors. Zhang Ting-yu (Chang T'ing-yü) (1672–1755), a key historian of the late Ming dynasty who led a group of scholars who produced the *History of the Ming*, wrote about the sea voyages of Cheng Ho (Zheng He: c.1371–c.1433). The early Ming emperors, particularly the third, Zhu Di (Chu Ti: 1360–1424, ruled 1403–24 under the title Yongle or Yung-lo), expanded China's tributary network and promoted knowledge of the religions, social practices and culture of places outside China; their policies had the effect of promoting trade and emigration in southeast Asia. Yongle's successor Hsüan-te (ruled 1425–35 under the title Xuande) continued to send emissaries and expeditions; after saying that 'Chengo-Ho served three emperors with distinction and conducted seven voyages altogether', visiting thirty kingdoms from Champa to Battak, Zhang Ting-yu concludes: 'The amount of treasure he brought to China from these kingdoms was of course enormous, but the expense to China herself was even more staggering.' More specifically, starting 'in the Hsüan period [1426–35] these kingdoms, occasionally, still sent tribute missions to China, but they could not be compared with the tribute missions of the Yung-lo period [1403–24] that were not only more sumptuous but also more frequent'. By that time, although Cheng Ho, the leader of the voyages, was too old to continue, his reputation persisted: 'Long after his death, however, his achievement was still so highly regarded that Chinese generals and admirals, whenever serving abroad, kept mentioning it as a way to impress foreigners. Even laymen spoke of the Seven Voyages of the Grand Eunuch as a most outstanding event of the Ming dynasty.'[59] Huge costs over and above large revenues could not pay for the voyages, particularly as the network of tribute weakened. The voyage leader could no longer sail. These ideas differ from those proposed by western historians in answer to this key question: Why would the Chinese mothball their great imperial navy and not revive it when Japanese pirates threatened its coast a century or so later? Nor did the appearance of Portuguese ships cause the Chinese Confucian bureaucracy to reconsider. This is a general outline of Kennedy's bringing together the attempts of western historians to understand the Chinese retreat from seaborne expansion and the maintenance of an imperial navy and his presentation of an alternative interpretation to Zhang Ting-yu's.

Islam, for centuries before 1500, had been technologically and culturally more innovative and open than European culture; its universities and libraries, its medicine, mathematics and cartography, its mills, military and civil service were advanced and inclusive. The Ottoman Turks, however, could not maintain their long frontiers without great losses in soldiers and money and, unlike the Spanish, English and Dutch later, they did not bring back much that was profitable. The Ottomans had to maintain expensive defences against the Russians, the Shi'ites in Iraq then Persia (who were willing to oppose the prevailing Sunnis) and the western Europeans.

The Mogul empire – despite its brilliance in war, crafts and banking – depended on a conquering Muslim elite who ruled a vast number of indigent, largely Hindu peasants. Although there were a good number of innovative Hindu business families in the towns, the caste system and religious taboos that did not allow for the killing of insects and rodents, and social mores that discouraged the control of excreta and refuse, kept food production from growing and plagues from being brought under control, respectively. The sheer opulence and consumption of the Mogul courts required heavy taxes and consumed funds that might have been used to provide a few services to the population. By the time the Afghanis, the Marathas and the East India Company threatened this empire, it had suffered a good deal of internal damage.[60] As in China, there were various possible reasons why the Muslim states, though sophisticated and accomplished, did not continue to grow in power and influence vis-à-vis Europe. From the beginning, the Portuguese had been careful not to stray too far from the coast. In the Indian Ocean, they had destroyed Muslim sea power, but in China and Japan they, and later Europeans for some time to come, had to trade and have cultural contacts according to the desires and edicts of the Chinese and Japanese.[61] Although there was no manifest destiny why the European empires should grow in strength, they did continue to expand to a greater degree than other great states.

Europe had generally been fragmented politically, despite the attempts at various unified empires. This fragmentation was due largely, as Paul Kennedy has suggested, to its diverse geography. No immense plains cover central or western Europe, like those adjacent to the Yangtze, Yellow, Ganges, Euphrates, Tigris and Nile rivers, so that horsemen could not impose their rule over them.[62] Thus, a unified and enduring empire was difficult, if not impossible, to impose on these European lands, whose various climates produced a vast array of produce and products – wine, grain, timber, fish and wool – transported for trade at a relatively low cost along rivers and by way of the surrounding seas. Paradoxically, the difficulty of having a unified empire in Europe allowed for the innovative conditions that would permit these various and competing states to create empires that pushed each other through competition. The Black Sea, Mediterranean, Atlantic, North Sea and Baltic were all connected and supplemented by rivers, and were themselves harvested for food. This trade led to a credit and banking system as well as bills of exchange and insurance, so that trade – despite the disruption of war, natural disaster and disease – became more predictable. Shipping developed for rough waters in the North Sea and the Atlantic led to innovations that helped to shift economic power from the Mediterranean to the Atlantic. No uniform central authority in Europe could stop a particular commercial development, cause the growth or demise of a given industry or kill innovation and enterprise. Even before the Reformation, the Catholic kings, Henry VII of England and François I of France, would not accept the pope's division of overseas territories between Portugal and Spain. In such a world in which one ruler was willing to take advantage of the intolerance of another, Jews, Huguenots and the Flemish took their expertise to new lands. Peace, fair taxes, good laws and government produced prosperity, so that the occasional stubborn ruler would see his country's wealth and military power contract.

The flow of goods in Europe and worldwide trade intensified a trend that has grown ever more intense with new technology – globalization. To speak of Europeans as a whole, as if they were unified, would also be to forget their rivalries. Even the Iberian nations experienced conflicts with each other overseas. After the Revolt of the Netherlands and the

decline in the English cloth trade, the French, Dutch and English intensified their challenge to the Portuguese and Spanish in the Atlantic.
Religious division between Catholics and Protestants complicated this
rivalry. A revolution in knowledge and its dissemination occurred that,
along with the development of market economies, led to placing more
value on variety, openness and competition. Moreover, inquiry, experimentation, disputation and improvement were tolerated, allowed or
encouraged. All this meant that Europe, for some reason and perhaps
beyond a full and convincing proof, expanded and brought its imperial
reach to the four corners of a round world. Whether or not we agree with
Kennedy and other western historians in this hypothesis, it is worth considering, and they are right to stress the importance of trade, resources
and technology in this history of western European empires and colonies
from 1415. In the next chapter the question of why Europe expanded
when it did will continue, as we will examine the rise of this continent in
a wider context. Part of that background presents another point of view
through some voices of individuals among the people they encountered.

Native Voices and European Sceptical, Satirical and Oppositional Voices

In the meeting between European and other cultures, the local or Native
peoples had their own points of view, no matter how obscured and under-
represented in some cases, especially in cultures without writing in the
European sense. The contact between Natives and Europeans in the New
World was many-sided. For instance, the mixing of cultures or mediation
through kidnapping, interpretation, translation, trade and marriage constituted a complex and changing set of cultural practices. Go-betweens or
mediators, who mediated theses cultures, were sometimes made into scapegoats and could become 'excluded others' in any cultural negotiation.[63]

Go-betweens were a feature of encounters between European and local
populations over the course of the expansion of these empires overseas.
The Crown of Portugal must have realized that interpreters were necessary
to their success in trading in Africa. This can be seen through a narrative
of the fifteenth century. Alvise Cadamosto gave some further background
concerning these interpreters: 'These slaves had been made Christians in
Portugal, and knew Spanish well: we had had them from their owners on
the understanding that for the hire and pay of each we would give one
slave to be chosen from all our captives. Each interpreter, also, who
secured four slaves for his master was to be given his freedom.'[64] Language
and religion were part of the black African's training, and only enslaving

others would free him. Spanish, rather than Portuguese, was the language taught to the slaves. The king of Senega, it seems, had unleashed a new force in Africa as part of his trade in slaves. Through an interpreter, Cadamosto traded with Lord Batimaussa, exchanging many articles for gold and slaves. Differences in values and valuation occurred in this relation between Portuguese and the blacks of Gambra: 'Gold is much prized among them, in my opinion, more than by us, for they regard it as very precious: nevertheless they traded it cheaply, taking in exchange articles of little value in our eyes.'[65] These Africans spoke many tongues and traded varieties of colourful cloth, apes, baboons, civet and wild dates and did not venture from their own country because they were 'not safe from one district to the next from being taken by the Blacks and sold into slavery'.[66] Besides gold and slavery, Cadamosto also described the hunting of wild elephants and other matters of interest and wonder. Descriptions of cultural contact and economic exchange go back much further.

Ventriloquy could happen in European representations of Native voices in their texts. The case of Columbus provides an illustration. Even before Columbus left Europe to explore the western Atlantic, there were European voices raised against him. A royal council in Spain rejected Columbus's petition, so he sought an audience with Ferdinand and Isabella, to whom he was connected through his Portuguese wife. During meetings in December 1486 and January 1487, the Columbus commission rejected Columbus's arguments and passed their findings along to the Spanish sovereigns.[67] Even though this kind of opposition was not enough to stop Columbus's project, it modifies any idea of Spain, or Europe, as embracing expansion and empire without reserve and caution. But Columbus did sail. And he came upon peoples native to the western Atlantic and represented them in texts that themselves are complex. In other words, the moment of contact is fraught with difficulty for those who would interpret them as part of the history of European expansion.

These works are part of a great network of mythology, ideology, culture and history. As Columbus's texts were and are mediated, his views of the Natives come to us through collective eyes. A recognition of ambivalent and resistant voices in the documents surrounding Columbus's four voyages to America serves as a reminder that these doubts and oppositions in the text involve all kinds of mediation. The image of the Native has been translated, ventriloquized and involved in a high degree of mediation and textual uncertainty. As the voices of Natives were reported in European texts, it is vital to consider the problem of mediation in the writing and reading of the accounts of the contact between indigenous Americans and the European invaders.

Another kind of opposition from within occurs in the ambivalence in European representations of the lands and peoples of the New World, who are both fierce and paradisal. For example, Columbus and Verrazzano (at least as we have his account in Italian) can display that ambivalent attitude in the same sentence. The idealization of the land and its peoples as comprising paradise is a promotional strategy that might appeal to religious dreams of the Ten Lost Tribes of Israel and conjure the riches of Asia. This trope of God and gold can be implicit and explicit. Another possibility is for the ideal aspect of the representation of the Natives and the new lands, which provided a standard against which to judge the corruption of Europeans. As much as these early representations in Columbus and Verrazzano might owe to classical myths and to Marco Polo, they prepared the way for Las Casas, Montaigne and others, who would turn the Natives into critics of Europe.

This second kind of opposition often combines with a third, the Christian critique of riches and power. European expansion was not as univocal and as triumphal as it might appear five centuries later. Humanism was not simply the standard of the imperial theme. Humanists were trained in the classics and dwelt on the classical past, sometimes critically, sometimes not. This interpretation of the classical past affected their framing of scholarly and social problems in the present.[68] Las Casas and Michel de Montaigne considered the follies of expansion, colonization or the mistreatment of others, including Natives, although they did not come down entirely on one side of the question or the other.

The religious could criticize the excesses of colonization. Las Casas, who was not the first religious to attack Spanish excesses in their treatment of the Natives in the Caribbean, edited Columbus. The Dominicans or Black Friars opposed abuses of the Natives. From an order founded during the thirteenth century in Spain, these friars arrived in 1510 in Hispaniola, where they protested in private over the decline in the Native population of the island. They concentrated on the abuses of the Spanish domination of the indigenous peoples rather than their right to dominate. The Dominicans were founded to travel the roads and preach against heresy, and directed the Papal Inquisition in the Middle Ages and the Royal Inquisition in Spain later on (and were also involved with the expansion of Portugal, Spain and France; they came to defend the Natives against abuses by Spanish colonists).[69] One instance will illustrate the Dominican opposition. In December 1511, one of the members of this order, Antón Montesino, preached two sermons that were critical of these abuses. In writing a history of the Indies, where Las Casas described the work of the Dominicans and told of these Advent sermons, he observed two types of Spaniard, 'one very cruel and pitiless, whose goal was to squeeze the last drop of Indian blood in order to get rich, and one less cruel, who must have felt sorry for the Indians', although Las Casas said that they both 'placed their own interests above the health and salvation of those poor people'.[70] According to Las Casas, all the Dominicans signed the sermon to present a common front, and, as their representative, Montesino delivered it before Diego Columbus, the admiral, and other important people they had invited. The sermon was on the theme: *Ego vox clamantis in deserto*, this voice in the wilderness that declared 'that you are living in deadly sin for the atrocities you tyrannically impose on these innocent people. Tell me, what right have you to enslave them?' Montesino asked: 'What authority did you use to make war against them who lived at peace on their territories, killing them cruelly with methods never before heard of?' He wondered why the colonizers oppressed the Natives and failed to 'look after their spiritual health' and to treat them as human beings that are like the Spaniards.[71] The sermon attacked the governor and the established settlers of the colony as infidels. This sermon brought about different reactions among the colonists. Las Casas said that the powerful in the congregation gathered at Diego Columbus's house, where they decided to frighten and punish Montesino for questioning the king's authority in them. Pedro de Córdoba, Montesino's superior, would not permit the admiral and his royal officials to see Montesino in person. The intimidation included a demand for an apology and a threat to send the friars back to Spain: it did not work. The following Sunday Montesino amplified his condemnation of illegal Spanish tyranny and asked them to mend their ways, so the enraged Diego Columbus appealed to the king directly, who ordered the Castilian provincial of the Dominican order to correct the situation. From this incident, Las Casas drew a moral that stressed the free speech and the courage of the religious.[72] A landowner, Las Casas became a Franciscan and would become part of this crusade for the conversion and care of the Natives. A kind of awakening or conversion could happen among these Spanish Christians.

A few problems in transmission and representation occurred and remain with us in examining the relation between invader/settler and the Natives in the New World, the place that was a key to European expansion, especially from the 1490s to the later years of the eighteenth century. Early on, point of view and 'translation' became key issues in this tension between empires and colonies. Europeans and their settlers in the Americas often wrote about the Natives from the vantage of conquest and triumph.[73] The European colonizers developed a myth that the American 'Indians' had no writing because these records threatened the Scripture and European authority and tradition.[74] The Natives did not have the opportunity or forum to represent themselves. From 1492 to 1519, there was no American Native chronicler of the exchange.

Within Europe and the European community in the New World there were some oppositional voices. Bartolomé de Las Casas wrote a defence of the Native population.[75] In a debate with Juan Ginés de Sepúlveda, Las

Casas defended the Natives at Valladolid in Spain. There, the debate focused on whether the Indians were human beings with culture or brutes, as Aristotle defined them, who could become servants to the civilized nations. Since 1492, the Europeans had viewed the Natives from a theological perspective that identified them with the lost peoples of the New Testament or as brutes who originated in the 'Americas'.[76]

Ecological Imperialism

The Natives and the Europeans soon found themselves amidst epidemics and the degradation of the land, largely from European efforts to get rich and exploit the environment. There is an intermediate stage before the Columbian landfall that showed the reckless European attitude towards ecology. During the 1420s, the Portuguese settled a place apparently empty of people – Madeira. They burned and cut the great forest and soon found an eroded island. The settlers found that sugar could make them rich, owing to the demand throughout Europe. Vast irrigation projects and slaves helped drive this industry. It may be that many of these were Guanches, who seem to have been related to the Berbers, but black African slaves would not have been available until the 1440s when Portugal entered the slave trade in Africa. Europeans had gone to the Canaries in the 1290s or in the first decades of the fourteenth century. Alfred Crosby takes 1492 to be the birth of modern European imperialism, when the French, under the auspices of Castile, defeated the Guanches. The Portuguese took these Natives of the Canaries as captives to Madeira. By 1475, the Spaniards had taken all but three of the Canary Islands from the Guanches. From 1478 to 1483, Spain, under the instructions of Ferdinand and Isabella, sent soldiers with artillery, cannon and horses to conquer Gran Canaria. The Portuguese allied themselves with the Guanches in their guerrilla war until Portugal and Spain made peace. In 1583, only La Palma and Tenerife remained unconquered. Against resistance, the Spaniards took La Palma in 1492 and Tenerife in 1496. This was a bloody and long-lasting invasion. The Guanches fought bravely and effectively, but were not united as they lived on seven islands and different regions of each island and spoke different dialects and perhaps languages. Nor were they used to facing soldiers on horseback. The Guanches had to yield the lowlands where they grew grain for the hills where they could fight a guerrilla war. The pathogens the Europeans introduced to the islands killed perhaps two-thirds to three-quarters of the Guanches and so weakened them in their fight against the Spanish invaders. The Spanish deforested the island and introduced livestock, other animals and plants. The Guanches suffered into the sixteenth century, had their land taken, were sold into slavery and were infected with all kinds of diseases. Had they kept up their original knowledge of sailing, they would have been in contact with the Berbers and not isolated, a vulnerable situation before the coming disease. In 1492, on his way to Asia (he thought), Columbus stopped in the Canaries amidst the long campaign to subdue them.[77]

What sort of Spain did Columbus leave behind on this voyage? David Stannard has characterized it as a place of squalor, violence, treachery and intolerance, no different from the rest of Europe, a continent given to epidemic outbreaks of smallpox and plague with habitual attacks of influenza, measles, typhus, diphtheria, typhoid fever and other diseases that would kill 10 or 20 per cent of the residents of its cities at once. And famine was also common, partly because of great disparities in wealth and great fluctuations in prices. There was a thin margin and any change could cause starvation among a considerable portion of the population. The poor froze to death in winter in colder climes, and half the children born did not live to see their tenth birthday. Witch-hunts, civil wars and other kinds of violence were prevalent if not officially sanctioned. These cities needed in-migration from the country to keep the population from declining precipitously. Here was a world in which most went hungry and the wealthy hungered after silver and gold.

And Columbus, who had once traded in African slaves, looked for Asia and found a paradise with rumours of gold. More than seventeen editions of translations of Columbus appeared within five years of his first voyage, thus spreading his view of this encounter between Natives and Europeans. Columbus and his successors perpetrated great violence against the Natives. The *Requerimiento*, a document the Spaniards read to the indigenous peoples as they were manacled, proclaimed the truth of Christianity and demanded that the Natives swear alliance to the pope and the Crown of Spain. Columbus began this scheme of kidnapping and enslavement, something we have seen and will see throughout the expansion of Spain and of Europe. The systematic destruction of the Natives and their lands began with Columbus's second voyage, which ended in January 1494 on the northern coast of Hispaniola. A third of the crew and many of the Natives fell ill. Meanwhile Columbus sent some of the healthy crew to explore for gold. This epidemic may have been as devastating as the swine flu of 1918. The Natives had few domesticated animals and the livestock among the Spaniards may have helped spread this epidemic. And Spanish violence led to death and the flight of the Natives led to starvation. Columbus and his men massacred or enslaved the indigenous peoples. Violence and cruelty were widespread.

The population of Hispaniola and adjacent islands in the Caribbean declined precipitously in the first twenty-five years after Columbus's landfall. The land and the people groaned under the weight of this Spanish invasion, what the Spaniards themselves called pacification. The *repartimiento*, or Indian grants, and the later *encomiendas*, which divided up communities and peoples among Spanish masters, increased the devastation and cruelty. This is the beginning of what Stannard has called the American holocaust. By 1496, the population of Hispaniola, which may have been eight million, fell to about four to five million, to less than one hundred thousand in 1508, to less than twenty thousand in 1518 and to virtual extinction in 1535. However much one disputes these numbers, the percentage of dead among the Natives and their ill-treatment, starvation and violent deaths at the hands of the Spaniards mean that this meeting of cultures was devastating and full of terror. This pillage of the land for riches and gold fed the Natives into an unseen web of disease and an all too visible machinery of greed. And the Caribbean islands and mainland would soon suffer what Hispaniola had.[78] Eric Wolf has framed the encounter between the Natives and the Spanish in the Americas ironically in terms of Europe and the people without history. He has examined how the pathogens from Europe contributed to the great dying. Wolf has said that this was not the whole story in the islands and the borderlands of the Caribbean, but it occurred in conjunction with a profligate abuse of Natives and their labour in search of gold, and an intensification after 1494 of slave raiding and slavery.[79] The expansion of Spain meant that their technology of empire, mixing writing, military power and economic greed, meant that human and environmental ecology was assaulted. The Norse could not or would not achieve the same full and awful effect in Iceland, Vinland and Greenland. The Columbian legacy combined military, legal, bureaucratic and economic power with terrible effects on the Native peoples.

Transitions

The expansion of Europe, for better and worse, meant that European economic, political and cultural power in the world grew steadily and rapidly. Europe, being made up of strong and rivalrous states, would not know peace. Wars, at home and abroad, punctuated the rise of Europe. One of those battles was a split in the Roman Catholic Church. With the birth of Protestant branches of Christianity, the violent division in Europe and in its empires became more intense. After 1517, a revolution came that would create Protestant powers, such as England and the Netherlands, that would in time, but not for some time yet, become the greatest trading and commercial powers in Europe and the world. India and China were still the economic powers, and it is important to remember the ecological damage and suffering and violence the European expansion brought to various parts of the globe, some of which had their own divisions, tribulations and war. This was a period in which the states of Islam and Christianity grew rapidly while shrinking one before the other. These states and empires were mixed, and involved the holy wars of converting or subjecting other cultures. The results of expansion could bring dire results. The papacy and Iberian states created a legal and theological framework for the expansion of western Europe that had demographic, epidemiological, ecological, economic, ideological, political and theological consequences for Europe, the Mediterranean and Atlantic worlds and, very soon, for the globe.

2

From the Reformation to English and French Settlements in the New World: 1517–1608

෬෬

The framework of Portuguese and Spanish expansion had to do with gradual exploration by sea and was defined by a series of papal donations in which, as we have seen, the Portuguese largely outmanoeuvred the Spanish, who, perhaps unwittingly, owing to the limited knowledge of geography and longitude of the time, allowed Brazil to slip away from their colonial sphere and were unable to establish themselves in the Moluccas, a key place in the spice trade. This religious and quasi-legal framework set out by the church (the pope had moral authority but not the legal authority he tried to project) is key to how the Iberian states viewed expansion until the Reformation. The frame of wars against Islam, the hope that Christianity could expand and connect with ancient Christian communities in Africa and Asia, the desire for expanded trade with the East, the demand for gold, spices and other precious commodities, all drove western European states to reach out beyond themselves. In some ways, as I have argued, the paradox or weakness and scarcity in the face of an expanding Islam and a more economically powerful south and east Asia led the kingdoms on the western edge of Eurasia to go beyond themselves. These religious, cultural and economic motivations drove the political course of empire, which could not have been foreseen at the time. The New World was, except to the Scandinavians, too unknown to be factored into the vision of empire.

It was not surprising that Europeans would see the world from their own point of view, which has been called 'Eurocentric' in debates over the past few decades.[1] The Portuguese set the scene for the Dutch and the English in Asia, but how much that example was followed in the breach is similar to the question I have asked elsewhere about French and English uses of the example of Spain in the New World.[2] Texts from other cultures sometimes distinguish Europeans by nationality and show their own shades of distinction, something that Sanjay Subrahmanyam reminds us of in his analysis of an untitled Malay text from the late seventeenth or early eighteenth century describing the Portuguese arrival at Melaka and the later Dutch and Malay collaboration in defeating them. This text mixes myth and history, as so many texts do. It also distinguishes between the Portuguese, who earn grudging admiration for their steadfastness in fighting, and the Dutch, who work and share with the Malays, unlike the Portuguese who insinuated themselves with lies and other deceptions. The text also shows Portugal as an Asian power centred in Goa and represents the Malays as holding the balance of power and, through craft, helping the Dutch win.[3] Like Subrahmanyam, I have, over the years, used Native and local voices and sources, as I do in this book, because they bring something to the discussion, complicate the history, and mix fiction and fact as European texts do. There are liminal spaces, and this inbetweenness calls for two sides and parties, if not more. So while the expansion of European empires often takes on points of view from Europe, it is important to recall that other vantages occur even if only a few can be mentioned here. Native texts or the representation of Native or local voices is part of the mix, which on the ground is about culture, trade, conflict, justice and other themes and not exclusively about empires and colonies.

All the ecological, moral and economic implications of this expansion cannot be summed up entirely by discussing empires and colonies because the depredations and excesses applied to feudalism, capitalism and, later, totalitarianism. In all this, the Christian churches, and their desire for missions and conversions, played an ideological role, so that heathen and pagan were subjected to pressure and exploitation or pushed aside, whether intentionally or not. Sometimes the churches and their clergy and lay members championed the victims of European invasions and expansion, sometimes not. Often Europeans viewed others ambivalently and were viewed in a similar fashion. Mixed motives, emotions, intentions and results were part of this slow, halting but growing expansion of Europe. Divisions within each state and within Europe always serve as reminders that just as the peoples the Europeans encountered were multifold and involved in internal and contiguous conflicts, so too were the Europeans. Individuals as well as groups experienced this strife, and one such key person was Martin Luther.

Luther's defiance of the Catholic Church had political and economic implications as well as religious ones. Northern Europe was part of a shift away from the traditional cultural sway of Rome, southern Europe and the Mediterranean. After all, Israel, Greece and Rome were the foundations of the religion and culture of much of Europe. While in 1517 it was unimaginable that anything but Catholic power would dominate Europe, the years would bring French, Dutch and English Protestant influence in Europe and the overseas empires. A challenge to the Catholic powers of Portugal and Spain occurred. England would no longer be a monolithic Catholic state and shifted more and more to Protestantism from the 1530s onwards. Even if Philip of Spain and Mary Tudor of England were married in the 1550s, this would not keep England Catholic. The pope excommunicated Elizabeth I in 1570. France was riven with civil wars between Protestants and Catholics (about 1559–98).[4] The Revolt of the Netherlands (1555–1609) helped to weaken the power of Spain, so much so that this new, largely Protestant power left a Spain driven into bankruptcy in the wake of the founding of Jamestown in 1607 and Quebec in 1608, the former the first permanent English colony in North America and the latter the first French one there.[5]

Portugal and Spain

'Spain' was not a unity when the Iberian states began to expand, and Portugal was also varied in its views and interests. Lisbon and the rest of the country, north and south, littoral and interior, were some of the divisions in the country. The court nobility, who were made up of bourgeois and migrants from Galacia, France and Castile, thought of expansion in terms of military prowess, but were not interested in royal centralization. The bourgeois in the city had supported expansion in the fifteenth century, but were less keen when the Crown began to keep the profits. So the king turned to the service nobility, urban labourers, and the Florentine and Genoese bankers and financiers in Lisbon to serve the interests of expansion. In the sixteenth century, the north of Portugal was much more densely populated than the south and provided more of those who went overseas. The internal expansion of Portugal was halting. At various times, Arabs ruled all parts of Portugal, beginning in 712, and these Muslims became the defining feature in the Christians' struggle. The name Portugal derived from the city of Portucale near Oporto, seat of the count in the mid-ninth century. It was only by 1147, with conquests including that of Lisbon, that Affonso Henriques called himself *rex* rather than *dux*. By 1250, the Portuguese Christians expelled the *mouros* or Moors and defined the *reino* or homeland of Portugal. North of the river Douro a traditional nobility was strong. Between Douro and Tejo, in a region once contested between Christians and Muslims, a comfortable peasantry held influence. In the south, where in the *reconquista* the military orders and nobility held sway, these forces were still dominant. Between 1300 and 1500, a tension occurred between a centralizing monarchy and resisting groups, such as the church, military orders and the nobility. In the fifteenth century Philippa (Filipa), from the House of Lancaster in England, seems to have helped introduce a hierarchy of titles in fifteenth-century Portugal that was similar to those in her native country. During the schism, Portugal followed Rome, and Castile supported Avignon, which meant more independence for the Portuguese military orders, which most often had been connected with those of Castile. In 1347, Portugal had a population of about 1,500,000 and two hundred years later it was slightly smaller owing to the Black Death. By the turn of the sixteenth century, Lisbon had Italian, English, French and Flemish merchants. It had a Moorish quarter (*mouraria*), and the privileges of the Muslims, who were mostly artisans, were eroded until the end of the fourteenth century. The Portuguese had been more tolerant of Jews than the Spanish, who had persecuted them in 1391. In 1496, Dom Manuel, an admirer of the skills of his Jewish subjects, accepted the pressure from Ferdinand and Isabella, whose daughter he was to marry, to expel the Jews. Dom Manuel did not want to lose the skills and he forced their conversion as New Christians (*cristãos novos*) in 1496–7. And so as Vasco da Gama set sail for Asia, the tense, heterodox and contradictory world of Portugal showed anything but stability.

Change was rapid in Asia as well as in Europe. All of Eurasia was recovering demographically from the effects of the Black Death in the fourteenth century. In 1500, Asia probably had a population of about 200 million, which doubled by about 1700. China itself grew from about 60 million in 1400 to about 180 million in 1750 (this second figure is similar to the population of the United States in the 1950s). In the seventeenth century, China and India may well have produced over half the textiles in the world. Wide-ranging changes occurred in Asia from 1300 to 1700, including a shift from east–west dominant trading patterns to those of north–south. In addition to Arab traders in the Indian Ocean, who were certainly important, Tamils, Chinese, Iranians and others made contributions to the trade. The Portuguese came to Asia in 1498, whose legacy, particularly in regard to Vasco da Gama and Pedro Álvares Cabral, was described in the late 1570s in Zain al-Din Ma'bari's chronicle, *The Gift of the Holy Warrior* (*Tufat al-Mujahidin*). Here, on the Malabar coast of the southwest tip of India, in the rhetoric of this text but not actually, two holy wars met: the *guerra santa* of the Portuguese and the *mujahidin* of the Muslims. In something eerily similar to distinctions made in recent years, the Portuguese distinguished between Moors native to the land and those from the Middle East (*mouros da tera* and *mouros de Meca*). Piracy, sanctioned by the Crown or not, required that the king receive a *quinto* or fifth of the share, something that ironically the Portuguese seem to have borrowed from the *khums*, an

Islamic tradition of a fifth of the plunder made to the Caliphate or over-lord. So Portuguese plundering before and after their entry into the Indian Ocean borrowed from an Islamic practice and was often used against Muslims. The cargoes of the Portuguese trade in Asia included pepper mainly from Malabar in India, cinnamon from Sri Lanka, and nutmeg, cloves and spices from the Moluccas. The Portuguese route around the Cape provided competition and threatened the prosperity of the spice trade that had been carried on by the Venetians, the Mamluk sultans of Egypt and other polities like Calicut and Kilwa. Until 1509, a major accomplish-ment of Francisco de Almeida's viceroyalty was to defeat the Mamluk fleet, hastening the collapse of the Mamluk Sultanate in 1516–17.[6] Over the cen-turies, European Christians would ally themselves with other peoples against other Europeans. From 1511, with the capture of Melaka, to 1516, when Albuquerque, the Portuguese governor, died, the Portuguese Crown cooperated with Keling merchants in a number of maritime enterprises.

The Portuguese monarchy was crucial in shaping the trade with Asia, which differed from the English and Dutch private companies that were set up for the Asian trade in the end of the sixteenth and beginning of the seventeenth century respectively. The Portuguese defined themselves against the two groups with which they had the most in common cultur-ally – the Castilians and Moors.[7] The ambivalent and contradictory motives of king, court and country meant that Portugal was a changing place as it brought change to other places. It was both vulnerable and assertive: the monarchy tried, through ideological centralization, to shape a nation tied to Islam and to Castile but attempting to define itself against them even as its people moved amongst the Castilians and Moors. This religious orthodoxy occurred before the coming of the movement to reform within the Roman Catholic Church.

Still, the activities in the Indian Ocean complicated any dichotomy between Portuguese and others. The development of the interior of Brazil as a colony in the 1530s, the expansion of the Ottomans in the 1530s and 1540s, and the growth of a new and powerful sultanate in Bengal all made matters intricate. Portuguese energies in Asia seemed to be critically chal-lenged. The influence of Spain was felt in the Inquisition (conducted mainly by the Dominicans) and in the Society of Jesus (Jesuit order), both weapons in the Counter-Reformation against heretics or Protestants, and in spreading a pure Catholic faith overseas. It is easy to overstate this crisis. After the success of the Ottoman fleet against the Portuguese in the early 1550s, the Portuguese routed it.[8] In China, the Portuguese attracted some negative official attention, so that Ho Ao, a censor, called them 'cruel and crafty' and concluded that 'if we allow them to come freely and to carry on their trade, it will inevitably lead to fighting and bloodshed, and the misfortune of South China may be boundless'.

During the 1540s and 1550s, pirates or *wo-k'ou* (*wako*) allowed the Portuguese to be involved in a clandestine trade in the South China Sea and, in 1543, may have helped the Portuguese get to Japan. Soon the trade with Japan was centred on Kyushu, under the control of the Otomo clan. Jorge Álvares' fleet of 1546 was key, partly because when he returned to Malaka in 1547 he met Francis Xavier, a Jesuit, whose order was founded by a Spanish Basque, Ignatius Loyola. Álvares introduced Xavier to Yajiro, a Japanese, brought back to Goa, where he converted to Christianity in 1548 and provided economic, social, political and religious information about Japan that Xavier translated into European terms. In 1549, on a Chinese junk, Xavier and two Spanish Jesuits went to Japan, where he stayed for two years. By 1552–3, the Portuguese were trading regularly in Kyoto. Trade and mission work went together. With China, this was one of the lands Columbus hoped to find but did not. The occasional violent clash with the Japanese occurred as part of this trade. After 1570, when the trade between Macau and Japan settled on Nagasaki, the violence quieted and missionary work increased. Japan supplied silver. For about fifty years to come, the Portuguese benefited from the Chinese government restricting trade directly with Japan for its subjects. By 1570, Portugal was involved in trade in territories from east Africa to east Asia that they would develop further in the next two centuries. From that point on, however, Portugal began to look inland, away from the coasts to which their maritime power had given them access.[9]

The Reformation, which began in 1517, did not at first seem to be a threat to the great Catholic powers of the Iberian peninsula. By 1519 Charles was Duke of Burgundy, Charles I of Spain and Charles V, Holy Roman emperor, and he and his successors threatened to throw off the balance of power in Europe and became defenders of the Catholic faith against Protestantism, so that religion had an additional political angle. Charles, who was often absent from Spain, unlike Isabella and Ferdinand, and whose advisers were often from the Netherlands, heard often from the Cortes that he should spend more time in Spain. He faced a revolt there in 1520.[10] For the most part, however, the power of the Habsburgs in Spain and elsewhere did not seem under serious threat. That was to change over the course of the sixteenth and seventeenth centuries.

Portugal was making breakthroughs, but its exploration was in relation to that of Spain and subject to the authority of the pope. In 1529, after the question of the Moluccas was settled, Portugal and Spain agreed to set out another line of demarcation in the Pacific. For the Iberian powers, the sea was closed and the world was effectively divided between them. For the first time since independence, Portugal now saw its national interest as coinciding with Castile. Owing to Portugal's imperial interests and to the Reformation, it loosened its ties with England. Whereas João

II (John II) had admitted Spanish Jews, Manuel expelled them and thus kept in line with the policy of Isabella and Ferdinand. Dynastic marriages yoked the two nations: João III and Sebastião (John III and Sebastian) were half Spanish and Philip II was half Portuguese. Other institutions drew them together: for instance, the Jesuits, who began in Spain, gathered great power in Portugal and were key in education there. Castilian became one of the languages of the Portuguese court, and writers, such as Luis de Camões, also wrote copiously in that language. John III, married to the sister of Emperor Charles V, had as his heir a grandson, Sebastian, who ascended to the throne at three years old and who, unmarried and without a clear heir, died in 1578 when his army was soundly defeated at Alcazar-Kebir in Africa. After his aged great-uncle King Henry, a cardinal, died, having ruled from 1578 to 1580, his kinsman, Philip II of Spain, ascended the throne. This Iberian union, a kind of greater modern version of pagan, Visigoth and Christian Hispania in which the Portuguese and Spanish empires complemented each other in trade, is something that was attractive to more than a few in Portugal, so that in the last half of the sixteenth century Seville, and not Antwerp, was the main connection for Portuguese trade.[11]

From about 1570 to 1610, the Portuguese continued their maritime enterprises overseas, but they also became interested in territorial expansion. How much of this was owed to the union of the Spanish and Portuguese Crowns in 1580 is a central question. Whereas the Portuguese tended to seek out trade, the Spanish, even in Asia, followed the practice of conquistadores like Hernán Cortés, who conquered the Aztec in 1519, and Francisco Pizarro, who entered the Inca capital of Cuzco in 1534 – they profited from controlling labour. The use of the *encomienda* gave the *encomendaro* the right to collect a tribute or *tributo*, in labour, goods and money, from the Natives (Amerindians). Although the monarchy was not successful in abolishing this system in 1542, it was more so at the end of the sixteenth century. Even so, the Spaniards, who had agreed in the Treaty of Saragossa in 1529 to leave Asia to the Portuguese, began in the mid-1560s to introduce the system of the *encomienda* to the Philippines, which grew, and by the 1590s ended up claiming control over nearly 700,000 inhabitants. The Portuguese monarchs owned ships and were traders; the Spanish monarchs taxed private ship-owners. In the decades before Philip of Spain (Dom Felipe) also became king of Portugal, the influence of the Habsburgs grew, and the Portuguese monarchy began to resemble that of its Spanish neighbour. Philip's policies were often continuations of those of his nephew, Dom Sebastião, and the Cardinal Dom Henrique. The Crown cut back on its ships and began leasing out voyages to private interests, the so-called concession-voyages (*viagens de lugares*). The Portuguese also started to shift more of their attention from Asia and North Africa to Brazil, where they rapidly increased the settler and African slave population as sugar production tripled from about 1570 to 1600. The New Christians or former Jewish converts in Portugal had vast trade networks and benefited from the union, which connected two empires. They became involved in the Acapulco–Peru–Philippines trade. From about 1560 to 1580, the Inquisition was especially active in Goa and particularly concerned with Jewishness. By the 1630s and 1640s, in a second wave, the Inquisition was persecuting and executing New Christians in Peru and Mexico. The Spanish commitment to religious purity, something that Loyola had flirted with but renounced, came once more to haunt the Portuguese and especially those of Jewish descent. Another aspect of this period was the reform of government that began before Philip, which divided the Estado da Índia in three parts: east Africa, Hurmuz to the Bay of Bengal, and eastern Bengal to Macau. These were supposed to perform *conquista*, often dissimilar to those undertaken in Angola and Brazil, which, like the Spanish conquests, set out to plunder, and to control produce and people and their labour. Religious and legal reasons or pretexts were marshalled to justify expansion in east Africa and east Asia. In sixteenth-century Sri Lanka the Portuguese got involved in the cinnamon trade and in dynastic politics among the three states that made up the island, with all their shifting balances in power. In the 1540s, Portugal guaranteed the sovereignty of Kotte as opposed to Sitavaka, which collapsed in the 1590s. Each colony was different, but during the sixteenth century Portugal came to be interested more in territorial expansion. Even still, maritime interests persisted. The Sultanate of Aceh in the north of Sumatra came to challenge the Portuguese during the 1560s and 1570s. It had ties to the Ottoman empire, had a maritime network in the Bay of Bengal, and had grown in influence in the Moluccas and the north coast of Java. The Ottomans themselves had a navy in the western Indian Ocean, so this alliance threatened Portuguese naval dominance. But Aceh was able to maintain trade with the Ottomans and in the Bay of Bengal and Indonesia and so challenge Melaka. Moreover, the Mappila Muslims of the Malabar coast challenged the Portuguese at sea. The Portuguese were still strong, and merchant capitalists like the Welsers and Fuggers played a growing role while the Crown backed off financing the voyages. Portugal gained territory at this time. While in 1610 Philip III could dream of a land empire in India, in 1615 the Portuguese were on the defensive against the Dutch.[12] This Iberian union (1580–1640), as we have seen, was attractive to some key people in Portugal.[13] Ultimately Catalonia and Portugal rebelled successfully in 1640.[14]

Spain also developed its own expanded domain, the so-called silver empire. Between 1520 and 1550, the *conquistadores* or conquerors, many with experience in the wars in Italy or against the Moors, subdued much of central and southern America. Before that, the Spaniards had explored and settled much of the West Indies, but concentrating their efforts most on Hispaniola and Cuba. The settlers or ranchers used African slaves to replace the Native labour (mainly Arawaks) and imported horses and cattle. These adventurers sought gold, and after Balboa's view of the Pacific in 1513, a number set out to find a passage to it, and to explore for precious metals. The Spaniards heard of vast and rich kingdoms or empires on the mainland. Native allies, firearms, horses, discipline, timing, circumstances, myths, religious zeal and other factors allowed the Spaniards to conquer the Aztecs and Incas against the odds. In 1519, Hernán Cortés made himself independent from the governor of Cuba, who had backed his conquest of Mexico. The Native allies and Cortés' diplomatic ability to negotiate with Montezuma's envoys allowed the Spanish leader to enter the Aztec capital, Tenochititlán. Despite a brief peace, the Spanish zeal in destroying temples there caused a conflict in which the Aztec leader was killed, and Cortés and his men, under the cover of darkness, escaped. They suffered many casualties, and only after the Native allies remained at their side, and with reinforcements from Cuba, did Cortés subdue the city in 1521. The Spaniards took over the tribute system of the Aztecs.

Other conquests were more violent still, and less successful. Cortés' own lieutenants used terror to subdue the Mayan territories. Cuzco, the capital of the Inca empire, was 'discovered' in 1530. Francisco Pizarro led the expedition and found Atahualpa, a usurper, on the Incan throne, and, following the model of Cortés, seized and executed the Incan leader. Like Cortés, Pizarro founded municipalities and sent out expeditions, but he lacked Cortés' political sense. Civil wars soon broke out. Francisco and Gonzalo Pizarro and their rival Alamagro were killed and their factions fought on and off for almost twenty years. The government of Spain inter- vened to restore order. The Natives battled against the Spaniards, but only in southern Chile did they defeat the Spanish forces. By 1550, much of central and south America was under the control of the Spanish Crown. In the 1560s, the Spaniards took the Philippines in a less bloody way to the conquest of America.

The Spaniards debated the nature of empire and of the relation with local peoples. The Spanish Crown had curtailed the power of feudal lords, knightly orders, and corporations. This centralizing monarchy could not tolerate the *conquistadores* wanting to be feudal lords in the New World. The church and lawyers were able to help in the consideration of the expansion to the New World in terms of authority, conscience and justice. Whereas many of the Spanish colonists wanted to be lords over the 'Indians', a large number of the missionaries saw them as spiritual beings who would benefit from the liberty and justice that came from obedience to the Spanish Crown. The principal debate in this controversy over the Natives was between Bartolomé de Las Casas and Juan Ginés de Sepúlveda. The importance of debate and law to Spanish government and ideas of empire contrasts with the quick violence of the conquests. Even so, Cortés made sure that he set up a legal framework for his conquest. How did the New World become constituted? The Indies were kingdoms of the Crown of Castile that were separate from the kingdoms of Spain. A separate royal council administered them. The Natives were subjects of the Crown. As such they were free and could not be enslaved unless taken in rebellion. They were not subject to any Spaniard or to the Spanish state. The Natives had their own land and property which could not be taken from them. Their own laws were in force unless they contradicted the Spanish laws of the Indies. The Natives were to be converted freely and not by force and their lapses were to come under the jurisdiction of bishops and not the Inquisition. The protection of the Natives was not always as good in practice as in theory. A conflict often occurred between these soldier-conquerors and their descendants on the one hand and the churchmen on the other, because the latter sought to learn Native languages, create mission churches and were not in favour of the settlers establishing a lord and vassal relation with the Natives. The Crown was caught in this tension, but it did retain salaried advocates to hear the pleas from Native people. The courts of appeal (*audiencias*) were a central institution, and the *audiencia* judges were from Spain and represented the monarch. The Council of the Indies was also a legal body and listened to these judges, who also acted as a kind of advisory body or cabinet to the governors, whose power the Crown circumscribed even if those of Mexico and Peru had many of the powers of viceroys. The Crown really centralized authority and decisions in Castile itself. Ranching, sugar and tobacco became the sources of agricultural wealth in Spanish America. Slaves were used for the production of sugar and tobacco, and because these slaves came from non-Christian Africa and were not subjects of the king of Spain, they did not receive any legal or spiritual protection as the Natives did. In the middle of the sixteenth century, great silver-mines were founded in Mexico and what is now Bolivia. The Crown claimed a one-fifth share of the profits. From 1564, one fleet went to Mexico and another to Panama each year to escort the silver back to Spain, and only three times, once by the English and twice by the Dutch, was the whole fleet seized. These two fleets sailed regularly for about 150 years. Unlike Portugal, where the Crown had the monopoly on colonial trade, Spain created a monopoly for the merchant guild of Seville (the *consulado*) which, through fictions, acted as proxies for, and collected commissions from, merchants from other parts of Spain and from Germany, England and Flanders. Owing to a shortfall or a reluctance to export in Spain, the trade with the New World became open to illicit traders from various states, whether pirates, slavers or smugglers. Within and between empires and colonies a multilateral and liminal aspect developed that complicated the nature of the polity and its social, cultural and economic relations.[15]

Two important factors in the globalization of trade in the sixteenth century were the importation of American silver into Spain and the discovery of the route round the Cape to the East Indies.[16] But Spain was to lose the Netherlands to revolt, so that with each decade of the seventeenth century the Dutch became more a force for and in and of themselves.

Despite Philip II's attempts to separate the administration of the two kingdoms, warfare brought them closer together. The great armada of 1588 was formed in Lisbon; Portugal lost its English and Flemish trade; and the Dutch, excluded from the emporium, sought the products at source. Philip III and Philip IV were less concerned about Portuguese interests than Philip II. Soon the Dutch had a presence in the Portuguese sphere in Asia, Africa and America. Taxation and wartime levies of troops, imposed by the Spanish, were two aggravations for the Portuguese. The French tried to foment rebellion among them and when Catalonia rebelled in 1640 so too did Portugal – and successfully.[17] Laws, then, attempted to keep the course of empire smooth, but the empires of Portugal and Spain sometimes experienced disruption and friction.

In fact, the Habsburgs failed to achieve some of their key military aims – Charles V's destruction of the Protestant princes in Germany in the 1540s; his son Philip II of Spain's suppression of the revolt in the Netherlands in 1566 and his invasion of England in 1588. Instead, the Habsburgs of Madrid and Vienna had a great deal to do to maintain their power in Europe let alone see it expand, and they had to finance their almost constant warfare, which became more expensive owing to innovation. Charles V had to fight the French, Turks, Barbary corsairs and papal forces: he abdicated in 1555 as Holy Roman emperor and as king of Spain in 1556. The Spanish branch of the Habsburgs in the next few decades was involved in more wars than the Austrian branch. Philip II faced wars with the corsairs, with the Ottoman empire, and with the Netherlands, owing to religious and taxation policies. It is possible that the very imperial expansion of the Habsburgs made other powers nervous to check their hegemony.

The five principal sources of Habsburg finance were Castile; the Italian states; the Netherlands; the American empire (including the royal fifth of the gold and silver mined there); and the leading mercantile and financial houses in Europe (all of them in Habsburg lands in Antwerp, southern Germany and Italy). The most important of these sources was Castile, which the Cortes and the church had conceded to the Crown and which yielded regular taxes such as the sales tax and a tax on religious property.

The Low Countries and the Italian states, being so wealthy, also yielded funds from their capital and the wealth of their merchants. The wealth from America, whether taxes on individuals who benefited from that trade or from the royal proceeds of 20 per cent from the gold and silver mined there, provided revenue and credit for Spain. The Spanish-trained infantry gave the Habsburgs perhaps the greatest military weapon in Europe. Although the dynastic alliance between Spain and Austria was powerful, it never had financial and military resources to meet what its interests required. Through technological change from about 1520 to 1670, the cost of running a military was much larger. The use of arquebuses, swords, crossbows and pikes meant that there was a shift from cavalry to infantry. The Italian development of fortifications also meant that large numbers of troops were necessary to man and besiege them. During the 1540s and 1550s, Charles V fought the German Protestants, the French and the Algerians, and these and subsequent wars drove the Habsburgs into seeking out loans to stave off insolvency. When Charles abdicated, Philip II of Spain inherited a debt of 20 million ducats and a war with France, so that in 1557 the Spanish Crown declared itself bankrupt, as France also did in that year. Peace with France was followed by twenty years of war in the Mediterranean, the battle of Lepanto having cost the Spanish, the papacy and the Venetians enormous amounts. Philip was chronically late in paying his troops, who were trying to put down the revolt in the Netherlands, so that in 1575, after Philip suspended paying interest to his Genoese bankers, the soldiers themselves revolted. The revenue from the American mines, which had grown from about 200,000 ducats annually in the 1540s to 2 million in the 1580s, helped to bail out the Crown.

The cost of the Spanish armada of 1588, however, was 10 million ducats. The armada meant something else for the English and was, according to Felipe Fernández-Armesto, a self-defining moment for English identity in making the underdog and sangfroid part of the national self-image. Moreover, the armada was not in fact but only in English mythology a translation of empire: England did not gain an empire nor Spain lose one because of this battle in 1588. The English victory was, however, a step along the way to empire and to being the dominant sea power, an actuality that remained some generations away. The armada was a dream and myth that was a beacon, especially for those who looked back from the greatness of the British empire.[18] That boost to English morale, based on myth as it might have been, was palpable and its sum was much more than its analysed parts. For Spain, the defeat of the armada was another costly action that drained the treasury. By 1596, Philip once more defaulted. In 1598, when he died, Philip left a debt of 100 million ducats, whose interest payments equalled about two-thirds of all Crown revenues. The problems continued. By 1607, the Spanish crown declared bankruptcy once more and the Spanish army mutinied, prompting a truce with the Dutch in 1609.

Slavery

Spain learned from Portugal about how lucrative the slave trade could be. Until about 1550, more slaves were shipped to Europe than to America, and in that year one in ten people in Lisbon were slaves. A black slave was the jester of João III, who extended his empire to and in Brazil. The Portuguese sent back slaves from Malacca and China, so not all slaves were African. In Seville by 1565 slaves made up about 7 per cent of the population, and among the African slaves the blacks outnumbered the Berbers or 'white slaves'. In mining, textiles and agriculture, the Africans worked in the New World.

In the sixteenth century, Bartolome de Las Casas and Pope Leo X could argue, contra Aristotle and his followers, like Ginés de Sepúlveda, that slavery was unnatural and inhumane in the case of the Indians in the New World, but they did not make the same argument for Africans. There were others, however, such as Domingo de Soto, Alonso de Montúfar and Martín de Ledesma – Spanish Dominicans – who spoke out against slavery, including that of Africans. Fernão de Oliveira – a military writer and captain – also criticized the slave trade in Portugal and Africa for its illegitimacy and immorality. Diseases had destroyed the indigenous slaves, smallpox in 1520 in the Caribbean and Mexico and dysentery and influenza in Brazil in the 1560s. The destruction of the Native population in Pernambuco and Bahia led to the importation of blacks from Angola and the Congo to work the sugar plantations.

These Africans, whether bought, kidnapped or taken in war, were severed from their families and worked in the most brutal fashion in an international web. Brazil supplanted São Tomé, which had succeeded the Canaries, Madeira and the Mediterranean islands, as the greatest supplier of sugar for Europe. The Italians produced sugar equipment, Madeira and the Canary Islands artisans, and Lisbon the marketing representatives of the Fugger commercial interests in Augsburg, while the Dutch provided much of the capital and many of the ships for transporting the sugar to Europe. Multinational interests and trade developed in an increasingly globalized world that had long had basic global trade networks. The paintings of the Dutch masters came to show the effect on the teeth of the subjects of the increasing consumption of sugar in western Europe, and the teeth of Elizabeth I and more and more people in England showed the effect of a taste for sweets. As the mouths of Europeans rotted, the lives of those subject to slavery grew rotten.

The slaves in the colonies did the backbreaking work while the peoples of Europe did the manufacturing in a kind of mercantilism in which resources from overseas fed European manufactures. Black African slaves were sold for almost three times what Native slaves sold for in Brazil in 1572.

The Challenge from England Continues

The 'race' for Newfoundland continued during the 1520s: the Portuguese, Spaniards, French and English all sent out voyages. During the spring of 1521, Cardinal Wolsey wanted to send five ships to Newfoundland, but the companies in the City would not provide adequate support.[19] The English had to wait until 1527 to send out a voyage. On 13 March and 22 May 1521, Alvares Fagundes, from Vianna, a fishing town with links to Newfoundland, received a grant of land from King Manuel of Portugal should he discover it in the Portuguese sphere. He explored the coast from Newfoundland to Nova Scotia.[20] On 27 March 1523, Charles V issued an agreement with Stephen Gomez, a Portuguese, to command a voyage in search of a northwest passage on behalf of Spain. Charles stipulated that Gomez not approach any of the possessions of his cousin and brother, the king of Portugal (John III was the son of Charles V's aunt Maria and married his sister Catalina).[21] During the winter of 1524–5, Gomez made the voyage. Newfoundland, as we shall see, continued to be a place of rivalries beyond the rich fishery there.

During the 1530s and 1540s, the English did little to maintain their claim to North America, which seemed to be becoming a French sphere of influence. The English also left fewer textual traces of their early exploration than did the French. Even though under Henry VII the Bristol merchants had explored America, no exploration literature appeared during his reign. Henry VIII took an interest in trade and navigation, but he did not, as François I did, make a concerted effort to explore or settle the New World. London participated in the Iberian trade through Antwerp, and Henry became preoccupied with the Reformation and his conflicts with the pope and Continental monarchs. In 1533 the only book published about European discoveries in the last two decades of Henry VIII's reign appeared. William Rastell, son of John, the author of *Interlude of the Four Elements*, printed *The Legacy or Embassate of Prester John unto Emanuell, Kynge of Portyngale*, the only translation from Portuguese travel narratives to the middle of the century.[22] John More, the son of

Thomas, was the translator, and the book may have had something to do with the interest in the 'Prester John' embassies from Ethiopia to Portugal in 1513 and 1531.[23] In surveying the search for him, Elaine Sanceau concluded when she looked back over the centuries: 'The quest for Prester John is one of the blind alleys of history, for it does not seem to have led anywhere.'[24] But that is hindsight and not the luring telos that Prester John appears to have been early in Portuguese exploration. The More–Rastell circle seems to have oscillated between utopian ideals and practical exploration.

During the 1540s, the English voyages to Brazil, which William Hawkins probably began in the 1520s through his contacts in La Rochelle and Rouen, appear to have been discontinued because large vessels were needed in the war with France.[25] Roger Barlow, a Bristol merchant who had been a resident in Seville and had known Robert Thorne there, had gone on a voyage on a Spanish ship en route to the East Indies in 1526 but had reached South America only.[26] With Thorne, he had hoped to present a plan to Henry VIII to send an expedition through a northeast passage to the East Indies, but Thorne died in 1532.[27] Failure was long part of early English colonization in the New World, as it was for the French. The Europeans relied on Natives and were not able to assert assimilationist policies in the early years.[28] This presentation was delayed until 1540, when Barlow accompanied his proposal with a manuscript translation of Martín Fernández de Enciso's *Suma de geographia*, in which Barlow interpolated his own experience, especially his voyage to South America. Henry, however, did not answer Barlow's wish to give authority so the manuscript could be printed.[29] Although the Spanish ambassador wrote from England in May 1541 saying that an expedition for a northwest passage was about to set off, no record for such a voyage is extant. From 1535 to 1547, no travel literature appeared in England.[30] Concerning the exploration of the New World, France had left England behind for the time being.[31]

In the middle of the sixteenth century, according to Theodore K. Rabb, England was, by the economic standards of the era, an underdeveloped country that had not kept up with the commercial expertise and financial techniques developed on the Continent during the previous centuries, so that foreigners controlled much of English trade. Italians had just finished their domination of Southampton and the Hanseatic and Italian communities were the main reason London was a thriving entrepôt.[32]

Illicit trade was also part of the story. Piracy was a recurring theme of the economics of expansion. Another example of the English imitation of France was in trade and piracy. The two states sometimes clashed over this issue. For instance, in a letter to Henry VIII of 13 March 1542, Paget, the English ambassador, reported François's reaction to the English request about stopping French pirates from piracy against the English. The French king promised to apprehend Sieur de Roberval.[33] When asked about restitution, the French king replied that he had merchants in England with like causes, so that if Henry VIII would consider their wrongs, he would do the same for these English merchants. Apparently much of the English and French concern surrounding the third expedition of Jacques Cartier was over piracy. François's talk of conquering echoed the language of Spanish expansion in the New World. How theatrical or sincere the French king was in this instance is an open question, but he wanted to impress Henry VIII, who was about to the join him in a war against Charles V, although François never punished Roberval.[34]

The example of Spain and Portugal as colonizers also included an aspect in which the Portuguese and Spanish were protective of their gains and anxious to keep away rivals or to get the better of them while other states struggled to keep up with them. The English struggled against Spanish domination. Like the French, they found that Spain was not easy to displace or overtake. The English thought that one way they could challenge Spain was by discovering a sea route to Asia. Seeking a northwest passage motivated the English despite the display of Spanish sea power. Many European cartographers and scholars saw promise in a northwest passage. So did John Dee, the leading geographer in England at the time. Humphrey Gilbert rekindled John Cabot's interest in discovering that route to Asia. In 1566, Anthony Jenkinson and Gilbert petitioned the queen for the right to discover it and for a monopoly in the passage. Gilbert, Martin Frobisher and Henry Sidney, supporters of this northwest venture, were in Elizabeth's service in Ireland, which was a type of 'Terra Florida'.[35] Thus typology between Ireland and Florida was sometimes an embarrassment: Sir Thomas Smith distanced himself from Stukely's [Stukeley's] fraud in raising money for the Anglo-Huguenot attempt at a colony in Florida.[36] The Canary Islands were for Spain what Ireland was to become for England – a testing ground for expansion.

Humphrey Gilbert's *Discourse of a Discoverie for a New Passage to Cataia* was an attempt to have the queen give him permission to sail in search of this passage and for a monopoly there, but Gilbert's efforts to that end were unsuccessful.[37] Not until about the 1580s, when Drake, Walsingham, Ralegh, Hakluyt and others made a concerted intellectual and material effort, did the English become serious contenders with the French for the lands north of the Spanish colonies. Even though the English and the French continued to seek the riches of the New World and rivalled Spain and Portugal in searching for a northwest passage, they began, from the death of these two dominant kings to the Spanish armada, to intensify their attacks on Spain. The rise of Protestantism and the jealousy over the riches and political power of Catholic Spain were largely responsible for this onslaught from Germany, the Netherlands, France and England. If the beginnings of the Black Legend (allegations of the cruelty of Spaniards in the expansion of their power) were in the anti-Spanish feeling in Italy of the 1490s to 1530s and in Reformation Germany from 1517 onwards, the climax primarily occurred as the result of the following factors: the rapid increase in Spain's economic and political power, Spanish insistence on its 'shared monopoly' with Portugal in colonizing lands unknown to Europeans, the Inquisition, the massacre of the Huguenots in Florida, the war in the Netherlands and the Spanish armada. The conquest of Ireland was the biggest military undertaking of Elizabeth I's reign, costing over £1,000,000, which, according to T. O. Lloyd, was the equivalent of the total royal revenue for three years: the search for land was key because the English had lost France and were hungry for land in Ireland and later America.[38]

At Elizabeth's court, a group favoured expansion, which took three major forms: the American enterprise and a search for a northwest passage, Ireland, and the trade with Muscovy and the push for a northeast passage. In England at this time there was no great public doubting voice like Montaigne's to question the right of the country to embark on empire, but there were many doubters, whose concerns and opposition the promotional literature often addressed. As Nicholas Canny points out, individual cases, like Thomas Stukely's fraud for an Anglo-French settlement in Florida in 1563, could put off potential backers and colonists for Ireland and America, but other more practical objections occurred amongst the English, for instance that, in Ireland, only financing from the Crown could lead to successful colonies and that private profit had been placed before social and religious reform.[39] Canny makes an interesting connection between Richard Eden and Sir Thomas Smith, once Eden's tutor at Cambridge and a champion of Henry Sidney's promotion of colonies in Ireland. The Elizabethans often compared their colonization of Ireland with that of the *conquistadores*. Whereas Smith worried about Stukely's voyage to Florida as a negative example, he did not mind a comparison of this Irish venture with English colonies in the New World. Canny cites Essex, Leicester and Davies as those who would probably know Eden's translation of Peter Martyr and who came to see the English in Ireland as following the harsh example of Spain in the New World.[40]

On 11 June 1578, Elizabeth I of England granted Gilbert letters patent of such scope that, in Samuel Eliot Morison's words, they 'deserve the title of the first English colonial charter'.[41] The letters patent of June 1578 allowed Gilbert 'to discover, finde, searche out, and view such remote, heathen and barbarous lands, countreys and territories not actually possessed of any Christian prince or people'.[42] The patent also reflected the care to tread softly amongst the Continental powers.[43] Moreover, this legal ground was consistent with the attitudes of England in Henry VII's time and of France at least since François I: do and do not recognize the papal donation to Spain and Portugal. Gilbert was given vice-regal powers like those delegated to Columbus. Roberval later held similar powers in Canada. Gilbert was instructed to give his colonists the rights and privileges of Englishmen as if they were born or living in England. This was to be the main way of English America up to the American Revolution.

In October 1576, Martin Frobisher returned to England from his first voyage thinking that he had found the northwest passage, having brought with him an Inuit and having discovered what he thought was gold. The first voyage had trouble attracting capital and subscribers (Lok was the key supporter), whereas the second voyage, under the aegis of the newly formed Company of Cathay, included a £1,000 subscription of Elizabeth I and the use of her ship. The goal of the voyage was gold. If Frobisher did not find gold, then he was to proceed to Cathay, but without the queen's ship.[44] The second voyage set out on 26 May 1577. Frobisher returned, as his orders specified, with three ships full of ore from Baffin Island, reaching England in September. The journey did have a chronicler in one of the participants, Dionyse Settle, whose epistle to the reader called the English to the conversion of the Natives.[45] He was also doubtful about the possibility of gold and silver and became perhaps the first of many Englishmen to speak of the Native goods or desired goods as 'trifles'.[46] Nor did he see evidence of the passage. George Beste addressed *A True Discourse* (1578), an account of the three voyages Frobisher made, to Sir Christopher Hatton, a member of the Privy Council.[47] This was part of promotional literature or what might be called the literature of justification. The more the English wanted a permanent settlement full of riches, the more they feared another failure. That led them to devalue the example of Spain and Portugal. An analogous operation occurred in many French promotional and justificatory narratives of the New World.

In 1580, when Francis Drake returned from his circumnavigation, it was apparent that England had a new route to the East. Drake's ship, full of Spanish gold, returned home to a nation split for and against Spain. Thomas Nicholas's translation of Augustín de Zárate's *Discovery and Conquest of the Provinces of Peru* in 1581 was the only book to praise Drake immediately following the voyage. Nicholas saw Drake as an example for the English to rival Spain, but also showed the example of Pizarro as a dutiful servant of the Crown. Nicholas also described his reward, the mines at Potosí, at length. The spectre of Spanish gold continued to haunt the English.[48] In 1585, in Newfoundland, Bernard Drake captured 600 Spanish prisoners.[49] Newfoundland itself became a figure for the rivalry between and cooperation of the European powers.

During the 1550s, the English woollen trade had been declining in Antwerp and during the 1560s, political and religious conflict made that trade even more difficult. As a result of the Revolt of the Netherlands, Spain moved its financial centre from Antwerp to Genoa. Following the example of France, the English began to exchange cloth for goods directly with the eastern Mediterranean. By 1580, the English gained entry into a direct trade with Turkey. In that year, Richard Hakluyt the Younger, who had been influenced in the study of geography by his elder cousin, Richard Hakluyt the Elder, a lawyer, encouraged John Florio, the son of an Italian Protestant refugee who, like the younger Hakluyt, taught at Oxford, to publish a translation of Ramusio's 1556 Italian version of the first and second voyages of Jacques Cartier, probably in aid of the Gilbert expedition to the northwest.[50] In his 'Preface' Florio claimed that Spanish success in its colonies was not based on wealth easily gained but on planting.[51] Piracy was another tactic for England as it had been for France. Between 1577 and 1580, England was officially at peace with Spain: Elizabeth I expressed regret at Drake's actions, but she knighted him and she and others who invested in his ventures received 4,700 per cent on their investment.

It was not as if it was apparent to all in the early seventeenth, let alone the fifteenth, century that England would develop into the world's greatest empire and power. There was no necessary march of economic and political progress for England from the Middle Ages. After the War of the Roses and the peace with France in 1492, Henry VII brought political and financial stability to England by paring his own expenses and paying off his debts, encouraging fishing, commerce and the wool trade, but Henry VIII spent much of what his father had saved in financing military campaigns in Scotland and Europe. The disastrous wars during the 1540s cost about ten times the crown's normal income: England was militarily backward and its finances could not fund a major war. Elizabeth could not go head-to-head with a great power like Spain and so used diplomacy and harassment at sea, thereby building a large surplus in the first quarter-century of her reign, which became useful when in 1585 she sent an expedition under Leicester to the Netherlands as part of a united Protestant front against the Counter-Reformation. Elizabeth understood that when Spain was finished with France and had subdued the Netherlands, it would then turn on England. This twin strategy of checking Philip II in Europe and disrupting his empire on the high seas placed great strains on the finances of England, but it never fell into bankruptcy.

During this period, Gilbert and Hakluyt the Younger thought that North America would provide bases against Spain, a policy Gaspar de Coligny had tried for France during the 1560s. France and England turned to each other for instances of how to circumvent or oppose the power of Spain. The implications of Drake's circumnavigation were not fully integrated into the English policy on exploration and expansion. On 11 June 1583, Gilbert sailed from Plymouth. On 5 August, he took possession of Newfoundland for England, which Cabot had done in 1497. Edward Haie's account of the voyage was found in every edition of Hakluyt's *Voyages*.[52] Origins haunted the textual history of the English and then British empire. Haie also focused on Columbus and Cabot, on the English right to Florida, which the French had tried to usurp, and attempted to set out two spheres of influence in the New World, the Spanish south and the English north (Florida being the divide).[53] The papal donation was being revised in practice.

During the generation before this peace between England and Spain, French and English Protestants sometimes cooperated in opposing Spanish power. Spain was a primary concern for Elizabeth and her court. In 1584, the Reverend Mr Richard Hakluyt was chaplain and secretary to Sir Edward Stafford at the English embassy in Paris, 'a focus of anti-Spanish sentiment' and a substitute for a listening post at Madrid, where the English had no envoy. There, Hakluyt the Younger wrote his 'Discourse on Western Planting', as it is now known. France could teach England a good deal because it was the first state to challenge Spain in its American empire, and Spanish ships sometimes called into French ports.[54] The 'Discourse' was presented to Elizabeth I in October 1584. Sir Francis Walsingham, secretary of state, seemed to have employed Hakluyt as a support to Ralegh both in giving advice and as a means of persuading the queen to back the venture. In the spring of 1584 Ralegh had sent Philip Amadas and Richard Barlowe to North America to look for a suitable site for a colony.[55] As Walsingham was a central force in English expansion, it comes as no surprise that Hakluyt, like Thomas Nicholas, worked within the secretary of state's network of patronage. Hakluyt, who was busy gathering information on rivals in North American colonization, especially on Spain, knew the work of Peter Martyr, Gómara, Oviedo, Benzoni, and others who wrote about Spanish colonization. This collector of travel narratives also knew the writing of La Popelinière (Lancelot Voisin) who described French colonies. As part of his project, Hakluyt often seemed to have sought out pro-Dutch and anti-Spanish work.[56] This world of English and French expansion, which had some interlocking parts among the Protestants, suggests that alliances and cultural factors like religion can be as important as a single nation or empire.

Nor can religion, economics and technology be readily separated. The issue of God also affected trade. In the king of Spain's dominions the English were driven to renounce their religion and obedience to their queen. The Spaniards confiscated English goods in the Barbary trade. If the English were blown on to the Spanish coast, the Spanish subjected the crew to the Inquisition. The king of Spain, for Hakluyt, was 'our mortall enemye'.[57] Hakluyt's text suggests that part of the rhetorical belligerence among the English was owing to England's economic reliance on Spain. Uncertainty over the increase of Spanish power and of religious tension only exacerbated the gap between the two in word and deed. Hakluyt catalogued the dangers and woes of English trade in Turkey, France, Flanders, Denmark, Russia, and other places. Another key problem was that Flanders had floundered on eighteen years of civil war that had ruined English trade there. Frustration and anger in these texts may have arisen from feelings of exclusion and persecution, but such rhetoric might well have been a pretext or justification for acting against Spain.

But that might be too simple. Hakluyt could level criticism against his own country. In his view, France might have been piratical, but England was engendering pirates, loiterers and vagabonds. This self-criticism in favour of the Iberian model (Spain had absorbed Portugal in 1580 and would govern it until 1640) had more than economic motives. Hakluyt's marginal notes presented starkly the political reasoning behind colonization: 'Idle persons mutynous and desire alteration in the state' and 'A remedy to all these inconveniences'.[58] Trade with the new lands would lead to manufacturing in England and this production of goods would be salutory for the soul. The idle should be employed in England in making trifles.[59] While this trifling with the Natives for the sake of full employment was hardly flattering, it is tempting to make too much of it. Hakluyt did not follow the example of the Iberian powers in some key areas. He did not propose enslaving or subjugating the Native populations as had occurred in the Portuguese and Spanish colonies of the New World. His proposals were much more humane than those in effect in England at the time.[60]

Wider comparisons also helped Hakluyt to illuminate what he thought England should do in the pursuit of prosperity and empire. The voyage Hakluyt proposed would allow England to arrest the Spanish in the Newfoundland fisheries.[61] The strengths and weaknesses of the Spanish empire were found in Hakluyt's argument. He supplemented the usual complaint with Spanish contempt for, and expulsion of, the Italians from their colonies. This action arose from the fear that they would reveal the weakness of the Spaniards there and reinforced Spanish exclusivity in the settlement of its colonies in the New World. In Hakluyt's version, depopulation from the wars in the Netherlands and tyranny plagued Philip's empire. This clergyman kept harping on the Spanish American treasury, without which, he said, France alone could drive Philip out of all his dominions.[62]

Philip II attempted to invade England in 1588 partly owing to friction over trading and raiding commerce in South America. Spain was preoccupied with the Netherlands and made peace with England in 1604, a pact whose unintended effects allowed the English to concentrate on expansion and to put pressure on the Spanish empire, especially in the New World. After the war with Spain ended, England entered forty years of relative peace, which allowed it to concentrate on permanent settlements in North America and the West Indies and trading posts in India.[63] This was the period in which Spain would reach its peak as an empire and begin its slow decline.

England looked east as well as west, even though westward expansion was Hakluyt's preference. On 31 December 1600 Elizabeth I issued a charter for the founding of the East India Company, which had 218 subscribers and a monopoly for English trade in Asia and the Pacific. The first four company ships left Woolwich on 13 February 1601, arrived in Bantam – now in Indonesia – on 16 December 1602 and returned safely to England by September 1603. Over five years before, the Dutch had reached Bantam. James Lancaster, who had raided Portuguese ships in early 1591 as far as Sumatra, commanded a ship that, along with a Dutch ship, fought and captured a Portuguese carrack in the Straits of Sumatra on 3 and 4 October 1602. The Portuguese and the Chinese traded in Bantam, which pepper had boosted. After landing that first time, the English rented accommodation in the Chinese quarter. Even though Portuguese was the language the English used at first to communicate in the area, they soon switched to Malay, which the Chinese had used as the lingua franca in southeast Asia before the arrival of the Europeans. Manuals describing how to trade in Malay, such as *A true and large discourse of the voyage . . . to the East Indies* (1603) and *Dialogues in the English and Malay* (1614), were the first publications from the East India Company. The expansion of France, like that of England, posed a test to the empires of Portugal and Spain.

The Persistence of the French Challenge

France also came to challenge overtly papal authority and the legal foundation of Rome's bulls. In a well-known instance, François I (1515–47) asked to be shown Adam's will as evidence of France giving up the right to territory in the New World.[64] The king shifted the ground of the debate and influenced English attitudes to Spanish and Portuguese claims to the New World. He would not accept this 'divine' law that underpinned the agreement between Portugal and Spain but, instead, adopted the principle of first possession by Europeans.[65] Law was a particularly contested matter in the decades surrounding Columbus's voyage to the western Atlantic.

The French took another major step in claiming new lands when in 1524 Lyon merchants had provided for Giovanni da Verrazzano, whose voyage brought him to North America and not the promised land of Asia. Furthermore, French corsairs, such as Jean Ango, raided the Spanish and Portuguese fleets in the waters off Europe, America, Africa and Asia. In 1536 François I made a treaty of friendship with Portugal and used its ports as bases to attack Spanish shipping. During the 1530s and 40s, amid these hostilities with Spain, the king of France sent Cartier and Roberval to North America, to regions that the papal bulls had designated as Spanish and Portuguese. In one of the wars, from 1542 to 1544, the French fared badly and signed a peace treaty at Crépy-en-Laonnois, which barred the French from colonization in the East and West Indies in exchange for the right to trade in these regions. This was a deal that the victorious Spaniards and the Portuguese were not happy with because it broke their traditional monopoly in the New World, so that this article of the treaty was never officially ratified. In 1545 François I banned his subjects from voyaging to the Spanish colonies.[66] Beyond the attempted circumvention of the papal bulls giving Portugal and Spain a monopoly on the unknown lands overseas, piracy, treaties and prohibitions became part of the debate in France over what was legal and illegal in expansion and empire.

These relations between powers were seldom bilateral and were also predicated on connections with the papacy. A double movement could also occur in France's relations with Rome pertaining to the monopoly it had given to Spain and Portugal in the exploration of the New World. The personal and political connections of the various popes may have made some difference to their positions concerning the Americas. During the 1490s, the pope had Iberian connections, whereas his successor in the early 1530s had a family member in a key post in France. In one instance, as much as François I seemed to ignore the papal donation dividing the 'unknown' world between the Iberian powers, he sought to avoid the condemnation of Rome. On his behalf, through his relations with Cardinal Hippolyte de Médicis, archbishop of Montréal and nephew to the pope, Jean Le Veneur, bishop of Lisieux, approached Clement VII. In 1533, Clement declared that the bulls of 1493 applied to lands known to the Spanish and Portuguese before that date. The success of that mission seems to have helped to make Le Veneur a cardinal. Clement's successor, Paul III (1534–49), did not intervene in the French colonization of America, something that concerned Charles V.[67] The papacy was not necessarily under the sway of Spain or the Holy Roman emperor, although this depended on personal connections and the balance of economic power and political influence at the time.

Jacques Cartier also took possession of land in the New World for France. He maintained that the Natives thought the French to be gods and, like Binot de Paulmier Gonneville, who travelled to Brazil in the first decade of the sixteenth century, he planted a cross as a sign of possession. Gonneville used the French pattern of taking possession, which involved Natives, symbolically or literally, as part of the audience during the ceremony of planting the cross. On 24 July 1534, Cartier planted a great cross in the Gaspé, which was a sign of taking possession of Canada for his king.[68] Apparently, René Laudonnière supposed that Verrazzano had planted a cross that had convinced the Spanish that the territory was French.[69] Even though François I had approached Rome with some care in order to legitimize Cartier's voyages and the French ambitions of exploration, he and his government were able to keep their plans quiet. The diplomatic correspondence and espionage in London, Lisbon and Valladolid on the eve of the third voyage imply that Cartier's discoveries were unknown to France's rivals.[70] The French king turned his attention to war with Spain until the truce at Nice on 18 June 1538. From 1538 to 1541, the king of France waited to see how the pope would respond to Charles V's wish. Charles expected a condemnation of those who would contravene the bull of Alexander VI. Conversion of the Natives – the official French goal of colonization – made it difficult for the pope to condemn the expansion of France. Gold, in Marcel Trudel's view, was the true motivation for French exploration.[71] Laws and economic motives could be at cross-purposes. The popes set out documents that represented the importance of conversion and the spreading of Christianity as part of the donation to Portugal and Spain and not simply the riches that the Crowns and subjects of western European powers seemed to value so much. At this time, however, it was difficult to separate God from gold.

François I elaborated a legal and political approach to empire and expansion that was to be influential. He attempted to reverse the principles used against France in its favour. In the course of discussions with the ambassadors of Charles V and John III of Portugal, François elaborated a new policy toward colonization. The doctrine was as elegant as it was simple: permanent occupation rather than discovery created possession.[72] He turned the Portuguese doctrine of *terra nullius*, begun in their exploration of Africa in the fifteenth century, against Portugal and Spain. In the fifteenth century, the Portuguese had posts, instead of colonies, in Africa, so that the exact nature of this claim to possession there is not entirely clear. One argument for the Portuguese precedence for possession of colonies was the use of *terra nullius* in Africa.[73] This legal doctrine of *terra nullius* came to affect the English colonies as much as those of the French.[74]

The French king issued formal orders to French seamen not to go to places in the New World occupied by the Portuguese and Spanish. On 27 December 1540, the Spanish ambassador in France wrote to the emperor

Charles V and outlined the nub of the issue between Spain and France regarding the New World: the popes, who had not consulted properly, had spiritual authority only.[75] France would stay away from areas that Spain possessed but not those in its sphere that were yet to be possessed. On this question of the Spanish and Portuguese appeal to the papal bulls for the authority of their overseas empires François seems to have wavered or been split. Perhaps some of this was tactical, a kind of diversion that involved diplomacy and discourse while his appointed subjects went about their business in extending French interests and curbing those of the Iberian powers.

In practice, the French did not appear to desist from encroaching on lands that Portugal and Spain considered to be in the sphere that Rome had granted them. The emperor and his government kept trying to determine where the French might land. In a letter of the emperor to the cardinal of Toledo on 7 May 1541, Charles V approved of the idea of sending arms to the Spanish colonies and hiding their gold and silver in a safe place.[76] The emperor did take the pope's role seriously. Thus, he tried to develop a policy that would counter or balance the position that François I was developing in regard to the New World. In the meantime, inside and outside the framework of the law, the French and Spanish were at odds.

Each side attacked the other. France and Spain had been at war in 1552. Spanish privateers raided the French fisheries in Newfoundland. Moreover, the French corsairs attacked Spanish fleets and colonies in the Caribbean and, under the command of Jacques de Sores, took Havana in 1555. A truce that gave up the right of the French to trade in the West Indies occurred in 1556, but this did not endure a year. Whereas the Spanish insisted on the monopoly powers in the papal donations and its treaties with Portugal, the French wanted an open seas policy. Instead, there was a compromise. The Indies were not mentioned in the Treaty of Cateau-Cambrésis (3 April 1559). This meant that the French might operate there freely, except in areas that Spain controlled and where it meted out its own punishment. The treaty also seemed to imply that there were two spheres for laws and conventions in Europe and the New World.[77] This framework allowed a challenge to the Iberian monopoly. Although the effort by Jean Ribault (Ribaud, Ribaut) and René Laudonnière to found a colony in Florida in 1562 failed in the face of Spanish force in 1565 and although civil wars had weakened France, the French made progress in the last decades of the sixteenth century. Samuel de Champlain founded Acadia and Quebec in the first decade of the seventeenth century. The political actualities on the ground or on the high seas affected how much the laws and the papal bulls could be enforced.

For a long time, slavery constituted part of the Iberian trade. The French and English disrupted this network. The Portuguese were involved in the black African slave trade in the fifteenth and sixteenth centuries and beyond. The Portuguese, according to André Thevet, altered their tactics when French corsairs and English privateers attacked a caravel, which had slaves as a crew.[78] This is the context for Nicolas Durand de Villegagnon's voyage to Brazil in 1555, and Léry comments on the monopoly that Portugal and Spain held so dear. The Spanish and Portuguese claimed to be the lords of the countries while the French bravely maintained and defended themselves.[79] In this prefatorial aside Léry encapsulated a French view of the conflict between the French on the one side and the Spanish and Portuguese on the other. While he chid the Spaniards – this strategy was part of the Black Legend of Spain – he represented the Portuguese as insisting more on their priority and precedence and as being more pusillanimous than even the Spaniards. In the sixteenth century, then, the French challenged the Spanish and the Portuguese in the New World. Pirates, Protestant clergy and settlers, and the Crown itself created problems for the Iberian empires, but the French civil wars would weaken France and make it less of a threat in the last three decades of the 1500s. At this point, England, which had experienced its own internal dissension between Catholics and Protestants, began to show a renewed interest in overseas colonies.

From the 1530s to the 1570s, the French had the upper hand over the English in the exploration of North America. French pirates terrorized Spanish America and disrupted the trade between the colonies and Spain well before Drake and the other Elizabethan seadogs harassed the great power. During the sixteenth century everyone but the French fishermen avoided sailing the North Atlantic in winter.[80] Through hunting, the Basque fishermen from northern Spain and south-western France developed an interest in the fur trade. They blurred the boundaries between the rival states of Spain and France. The Basques qualify my generalization about French dominance of the western North Atlantic in the sixteenth century.[81] The Bretons and Normans primarily were developing a fur trade along the St Lawrence river and had established a post at Tadoussac.

Between 1555 and 1565 the French colony in Brazil under Villegagnon and then the one in Florida under Jean Ribault and René de Laudonnière during the 1560s failed. However, according to Frank Lestringant, these colonial enterprises fascinated the French more than did Cartier's voyages because the tropics caught the imagination of France whereas the cold winters of Canada did not.[82] Although the French would succeed the Spanish as the great military power in Europe and would aid its expansion overseas, its position was also difficult. Whereas after the Hundred Years War the French Crown consolidated its territories in opposition to England, Brittany and Burgundy, developed a system of direct taxation in the *taille* or poll tax, created a central army with strong artillery and had capable administrative leadership, it, too, like Spain, suffered bankruptcy in 1557 and, unlike England and Spain, was torn asunder by civil wars of religion. A central conflict occurred between the French and Spanish in Florida – Thomas Hacket's translation of Jean Ribault (the original was lost) and Nicolas Le Challeux's narrative.[83] The Ribault and Le Challeux texts are French Protestant works that helped to produce, in France and England, the Black Legend of Spain. These important texts suggest a shift in the representation of Spain in the 1560s, when the French and then the English, mainly because of the events in Florida and in the Netherlands, started to create a complex anti-Spanish rhetoric. This propaganda arose in the French and English languages from London through Amsterdam and Paris to Geneva. A textual web – an intertextuality – was part of the story of empire and colony.

The translation of empire relied heavily on the translation of study, narrative and technology. For instance, texts represented the attempt by the French to establish permanent settlements in Florida, a territory the Spanish claimed. The first French voyage under Ribault in 1562 failed partly because the French depended on the Natives, who came to resent them, rather than on farming. Moreover, the second voyage under Laudonnière in 1564 was a failure because the settlers dreamed of riches, became involved in the wars of the Natives, traded guns to them and practised piracy against the Spaniards in the Caribbean. The third voyage under Ribault reinforced the settlers with labourers, artisans and soldiers. This was, however, primarily a military expedition to attack Spanish commerce in the West Indies. It came to grief because a storm drove Ribault's fleet off course as he was attacking Pedro Menéndez de Avilés, who had been sent to fight the French. Menéndez later massacred 132 French at Fort Caroline and may have tricked Ribault into surrendering so he could kill him and his men.[84] This conflict, and the controversy surrounding it, went deep.

By preventing Ribault from joining forces with Jacques de Sores – the Huguenot pirate – Menéndez seemed to have thought that he had saved the West Indies for the Spanish empire. Philip II approved of the massacre. He also employed some of the prisoners from that incident on his galleys.[85] A Protestant noble, Dominique de Gourgues, perhaps moved by the Huguenot pamphlets against Spain, raised volunteers. In 1568, he took two Spanish forts in the New World and hanged his prisoners in a similar fashion to the way Menéndez had the Huguenots.[86] Natives were often enlisted in conflicts between Europeans, and Gourgues raised them against the Spanish. The indigenes appear to have wanted to free their leader and so had another kind of liberation in mind.

The fourth voyage, led by Jean Ribault, is a key episode. Nicolas Le Challeux, one of the survivors of the slaughter on that journey, acted as the chronicler.[87] At the opening of *The Whole and True Discovery of Terra Florida* (1562), Ribault said that the admiral (Coligny) had long wished for the day when France could make new discoveries and find regions full of riches and commodities, which other countries have done to the honour and merit of their princes and for the great profit of their state, provinces and domains. Ribault followed this anatomy of riches with the ideal of God. The massacre of the French in Florida in 1565 evoked a strong reaction in France. The Spanish failure to conquer Florida seems to have created a vacuum for the French.[88]

Between the Brazilian colony and Léry's narrative lay Nicolas Le Challeux's account of the Spanish massacre of the French Protestants in Florida in 1565 and the Massacre of St Bartholomew's Day in 1572, not to mention the siege and famine of Sancerre that Léry survived. Le Challeux's narrative of 1566 and Léry's account were disturbing and showed the conflicts and tensions in the French realm in the Old and New Worlds.

Various types of texts were involved in this representation of empire and colonies. Translations could also represent traumatic encounters with the power of Spain. One of the events that turned the rhetoric of Huguenots against Spain was the massacre of the French colonists in Florida in 1565. Besides Las Casas, there were other significant sources for the Black Legend. The title page of Urbain Chauveton's text of 1579, which included a translation of Benzoni, demonstrated that the Italians, as well as the Dutch, French and English, fed this legend. Fifteen years later, Theodore de Bry's illustrations in Frankfurt would indicate the participation of artists and printers in Germany in anti-Spanish tracts. Chauveton's title stressed 'the rude treatment' of the Spanish to these peoples in the New World and that his book was 'A little History of a Massacre committed by the Spaniards against the French in Florida'.[89] There was no hiding the ideological intent. Spain was a preoccupation for the French and other European rivals in empire.

The landfalls of Columbus seem to have intensified this rivalry. Even though from 1492 to 1547 the English and French were mindful of the claims of Spain and Portugal in the New World, their monarchs traditionally did not recognize the pope's supreme jurisdiction in ecclesiastical matters, let alone in temporal affairs. Consequently, beginning with Henry VII, England and France proceeded with their own exploration.[90] Besides challenging the Iberian powers in Europe and overseas, the French and English committed piracy against each other, and the French long plundered in the Caribbean. English piracy in the West Indies came into its own with Francis Drake's plundering expeditions of 1570–3. Although the French seem to have been a few years slower to sail to the New World than were the English, they made a more concerted effort to explore the western Atlantic in the first six decades of the sixteenth century than did the explorers in England. The French privateers pursued the Portuguese and Spanish and France attempted permanent settlements in Brazil and

Florida before the French and the English finally established permanent colonies in North America in the first decade of the seventeenth century.

Spain influenced France in its colonization of the New World. The French set out for gold as Columbus had, but later settled for farming, the fishery and the fur-trade. This quest was something the hidalgo would not consider.[91] The three main French colonial enterprises of the sixteenth century were Cartier and Roberval in Canada, Villegagnon in Brazil, and Ribault and Laudonnière in Florida. The motives behind them were to look back to the Spanish conquest rather than ahead to New France.[92] French writers, like those in England, advocated attacks on Spain and its displacement. A good instance of this genre was Philippe Du Plessis-Mornay's 'Discours . . . sur les moyens de diminuer l'Espagnol' (1584).[93] France continued to challenge Spain even as it tore itself apart in the Wars of Religion.

Although the French would succeed the Spanish as the great military power in Europe and would spur expansion overseas, its position was also difficult. Henry IV did something with his war against Spain and his religious compromise to begin the healing. This country of about sixteen million, with its great natural resources and food supply, might soon rival in commerce, finance and urbanization, southeast England, the Netherlands and northern Italy. England had a population of about four million and Spain of about eight million. France, however, could not develop its potential for a long while because of internal strife.[94]

The Americas were precarious for the French. Still, despite the tensions between French Protestants and Catholics in Brazil in the 1550s, the Spanish destruction of the French Protestant colony in Florida (South Carolina today) during the 1560s, and the continued tensions between Protestants and Catholics in the early years of Acadia in the first decade of the seventeenth century, France managed to established what turned out to be a permanent colony at Quebec, under the command of Samuel de Champlain. This became in the later seventeenth and well into the middle of the eighteenth century a central battleground between France and England (Britain). The French Protestant influence on French and English exploration and settlement would wane in the decade after the assassination of Henry IV (1589–1610), who traded his Protestant faith for Paris. At this time other states, like the Netherlands, rose in power and developed an overseas empire.

The Netherlands

Even before independence from Spain, the Netherlands had its conflicts with the Spanish government. Early in the reign of Charles V, the States

General insisted on recognition of its privileges as it was asked to give more in tax revenue. Later, this body was asked to raise money for wars in Germany and Italy. Soon these demands, along with commercial problems and religious discontent, helped to raise ill feelings against Spain. The Revolt of the Netherlands drained the Spanish empire, whose Army of Flanders consumed for decades 25 per cent of the outgoings of the government of Spain. For 140 years, Spain also concentrated on war, expelled first the Jews and then the Moriscos, closed contacts with foreign universities, failed to protect commerce and began to lose out to its rivals, including parts of its former realms, like the Netherlands. Spain had to re-export its American gold and silver because of its imbalance of trade: by 1640 Dutch ships delivered 75 per cent of the goods in the ports of Spain.[95]

The independence of the Netherlands was not clear-cut diplomatically and lingered much longer than the negotiations between the American colonies and Britain would. In 1609 the Netherlands concluded a twelve-year truce with Spain, which tacitly recognized its independence. Not until 1648, however, did the Spanish Crown abandon its claims to the Northern Netherlands. These United Provinces became a great sea power that challenged Iberian power from China to Peru from the turn of the seventeenth century. England concluded a peace with Spain in 1604, whereas the Dutch left in ruins a Portuguese fleet off Malacca in 1606 and a Spanish fleet off Gibraltar in 1607. The Netherlands gained some rights to trade in the East Indies but much less so in the West Indies in the truce of 1609. The Dutch East India Company had made incursions into the Iberian monopoly in colonial trade since 1602. This instance gave credence to those, like Willem Usselincx (1567–1647), who wanted to found a West India Company. His view was that natural resources, such as sugar, dyewoods, indigo and pearls, were more valuable to the Spaniards in the New World than gold and silver. Thus, Usselincx wished to found Dutch colonies in America based on natural production and agriculture. Brazil produced no gold and silver at that time but possessed abundant natural products and so, for Usselincx, was a case in point.[96] The Netherlands were helping to transform the business of empire: trade and commerce would be front and centre.

Brazil was a key place where the Netherlands challenged Portugal. Spain and Portugal succeeded in expelling France from Brazil, where they had been trading since the turn of the sixteenth century. Sometimes in the sixteenth century Brazil was kept as a secret in Portugal or was neglected there in favour of trade with the East. In 1576 Pedro de Magalhães Gandavo praised Brazil, which other countries were trying to colonize.[97] The Franciscan and Benedictine friars played a central role in the early religious history of Brazil. It was not, however, until the arrival of the

Jesuits in 1549 that a systematic attempt at evangelization of the Natives happened. In 1663, Simão de Vasconcellos published an account of the Society of Jesus in Brazil, from their appearance in 1549 to 1570, including the founding of the Colégio de São Paulo, an important moment in the Jesuit contribution to education in the colony.[98]

Besides the crucial Revolt of the Netherlands against Spain, the growth of Dutch sea power, commerce and colonial influence came as a surprise to its neighbours, England and France, as much as to Spain itself. Early on, business was a significant part of the expansion of England. Trade and privateering had been keys to the voyages. Different English companies developed for the expansion of overseas trade. In 1552 the Muscovy Company was formed, during the 1580s the Turkey Company and the Venice Company: in 1592 they combined to form the Levant Company. In 1600 the East India Company was established with £68,000. Two years later, the Dutch East India Company started with £500,000 in capital.[99] The East India Company soon learned that bartering Asian goods, especially Indian textiles, for other Asian goods was the most profitable trade. They sailed the first English ships to India in 1608. In 1598, an English pilot, William Adams, sailed with a Dutch fleet en route to Indonesia via the Straits of Magellan and his ship alone reached Japan in April 1600. Despite imprisonment and interviews with the shogun Ieyasu, through a hostile interpreter, a Portuguese Jesuit, João Rodrigues, Adams became a retainer of Ieyasu and replaced Rodrigues as official interpreter for Europeans in that region. In this capacity, Adams helped the Dutch East India Company to set up a factory at Hirado in 1609 and was friendly to the English four years later. He died in Japan in 1620.[100]

Rivalries between these western European empires were strong in Asia as well as in the Americas. The Netherlands was emerging as a dominant power in east Asia. The Dutch were stronger than the Portuguese and English: in 1601 in the Bay of Bantam, they defeated a Portuguese fleet and, as Anthony Farrington has noted, the English found at Bantam and elsewhere that the Dutch had more money, ships, men and purpose.[101]

How did such a small country become so powerful? It was a small part of the dynastic empire of the Habsburgs and, after breaking away from Spain, became a great power in Europe and throughout the world, dominating the seas for about a century and developing an empire. The innovations of the Netherlands were in finance, industry and trade. The aid from England and other Protestant states helped make the Revolt of the Netherlands a success after a protracted period. After the sacking of Antwerp by the Spanish in 1576, the Netherlanders themselves became increasingly entrepreneurial. By 1600, they held much of the carrying trade in Europe, and, by 1622, 56 per cent of Holland's population lived in towns. Overseas expansion and Amsterdam's new role as the centre of

international finance (owing to the importance of the Netherlands in shipping, exchanging and dealing commodities) underpinned Dutch military
power. At the very end of the sixteenth century and in the first decade of
the seventeenth century, Dutch ships sailed to west Africa, Brazil, the
Caribbean and the East Indies; Dutch colonies were being established;
and Dutch trading posts and factories were set up around the Indian
Ocean, at the mouth of the Amazon and in Japan. The Dutch made money
available for the government of the Netherlands, which repaid its loans
promptly and, owing to its good credit rating, was able to borrow more
cheaply than its rivals. War strained the United Provinces, but the scale of
their financial institutions and economy and their prudent management
of finances gave them an advantage over their enemies.[102] The Dutch were
important to France and England, two states that were great rivals from
the last decades of the seventeenth century into the second decade of the
nineteenth century. All these empires built up wealth, but they also often
affected adversely the lands and peoples they colonized.

Violence and Demographic and Ecological Consequences

One key example of violence and the destruction of peoples and their land
was, as we saw in the last chapter and will discuss here, the early Spanish
conquest of the New World.[103] After the great dying in the Caribbean
from about 1492 to 1518, the Spanish moved to the mainland and
invaded. It seems that the violence and terror of the Spaniards in the
Caribbean would have been less successful had not the Tlaxcaltecs seen
the Spanish, under Hernán Cortés, as potential allies against the Aztec,
their traditional enemies. Cortés used treachery and trickery to attack the
Aztec and to capture Montezuma. After Cortés and his men retreated, following the resistance and subsequent fight that led to Montezuma's death,
smallpox ravaged the great capital of the Aztec. The epidemic weakened
the Aztec, and the Spaniards laid siege and burnt and laid waste to
Tenochtitlán, a city they had said was so beautiful. They starved out and
destroyed city and people. Cortés sought to kill those who remained alive
and admitted as much in his own writings. In 1553, Pedro de Cieza de
León observed that the Spaniards criticized the Natives for human sacri-
fices partly to cover up their own ill-treatment of these peoples. The
Spaniards killed women and children, burned sacred books and fed the
Aztec priests to their dogs of war. And the pattern in the Caribbean, if not
of the Canaries, repeated itself: the Spaniards enslaved the local population and worked many of them to death in search of riches and wealth.
Cortés and his army killed hundreds of thousands in war and through

disease. Pedro de Alvarado and his men, all under Cortés' authority, were especially given to killing and exploiting the Natives throughout what is now central America. Others were also involved in the massacre of Natives. Small percentages of certain indigenous groups remained a hundred years later. Pacification and enslavement were familiar patterns of the Spanish conquerors. Wolfhounds and mastiffs were weapons in terrorizing the Natives as if they were quarry in a hunt. The cruelty and violence, which drove Las Casas to rhetorical excess, was something that Michel de Montaigne had said some of the Spaniards themselves revelled in in their writing. The Spaniards also abused and misused the Native women sexually. Whether the population of central Mexico fell by about 95 per cent in the first seventy-five years after the Spanish invasion, it dropped off precipitously. The wasting of people and the land was one consequence of the expansion of Spain in the New World. The same dire events happened in neighbouring lands.[104]

Violence was a key part of this expansion. One Native Mayan book calls the Spaniards, 'Marauders by day, offenders by night, murderers of the world'.[105] The biggest change in population, as Jared Diamond has noted, was the colonization of the New World by Europeans and the reduction or disappearance of whole groups of Native Americans.[106] Diamond says the most fateful day was that of 16 November 1532, when Incan emperor Atahualpa and Francisco Pizarro, a Spanish conquistador, met in Cajamarca, a town in the Peruvian highlands. The emperor encountered a man whose own king, Charles I of Spain, was also the Holy Roman emperor, Charles V. Through treachery and trickery, probably following the example of Cortés, Pizarro seized Atahualpa, asked for a ransom of a large room full of gold, went back on his word and killed the Incan emperor. The usual story is that a small band of Spanish adventurers, under 200 in number, cut off from the Spanish settlements a thousand miles north, captured the Incan leader, who was surrounded by tens of thousands of warriors. Six of Pizarro's companions, including his brothers Pedro and Hernando, wrote accounts that help to make a heroic story of holy war, bravery and victory against the odds. The pretext for the attack was that when a friar gave Atahualpa the Bible and tried to help him open it, the emperor became angry, opened the book himself and threw it to the ground. The friar then called the Spaniards to war and they were all ready for the ambush. After the violent capture of Atahualpa, Pizarro justified it to him by saying that no Native could now offend a Christian. The episode is framed in terms of a holy Christian war. Despite what we might question as the ethical or moral aspects of this encounter and trap, it is also important to consider what Diamond does, which are the technical reasons for the defeat. Whereas Pizarro had steel swords, armour and horses, the Incas did not. Only later Native groups who acquired guns and horses were able to resist European expansion, however briefly, in North America. Pizarro later won battles at Jauja, Vilcashuaman, Vilcaconga and Cuzco in which anywhere from 30 to 110 Spanish horsemen engaged thousands and thousands of Natives and won with few or no losses to themselves. Native allies and myths about returning gods helped the Spaniards, but Diamond argues that the horse, steel swords and the gun are primary reasons for the victory. He also says that the subsequent Incan attempts under Emperor Manco at Lima and Cuzco failed for the same reasons. Atahuallpa was at Cajmarca because he had just won a battle in an Incan civil war, which had arisen because Spanish settlers in Panama and Columbia had spread smallpox and this epidemic in 1526 had killed the Inca emperor, Huayna Capac and most of his court. The epidemic caused a contention between Atahualpa and Huascar, his half-brother. It weakened the Inca. Epidemics had weakened peoples in Europe and the Americas before they lost decisive battles. The Incas did not have as widespread writing as the Spanish and lacked knowledge of them and their extensive centralized political structures. They did not know the Spaniards' military tactics, thirst for riches and precious metals and commitment to holy war and profit.

The Incan state covered the coastal regions of modern-day Peru and Chile and contained millions of people. Even before Pizarro arrived, smallpox and other epidemics came down from Mexico. The soldiers followed the disease they had brought elsewhere. The Spanish hunger for treasure drove them in violence against the indigenous peoples, something Pedro de Cieza de Léon, himself a conquistador, chronicles in gruesome detail. Natives were subject to enslavement in Spanish silver-mines and plantations and died of starvation and diseases. The search for El Dorado meant that the golden age was the age of gold, that peace and plenty yielded to cruelty and greed. Diego de Almagro described how Hernando Pizarro decapitated chained Natives when they grew exhausted and strew the roads with their headless corpses.[107] Terror was a way of keeping the Natives labouring for the enrichment of the Spaniards, and even clergy got involved in exploitation in the search for God and gold. The Inquisition was the main clerical contribution to violence. Holy terror or torture for truth was another trial for the Natives. Native mineworkers were forced labourers who usually died in several months. Although in 1551 in response to the outcry of some settlers and religious the Crown tried to end forced labour, this measure did not endure. The silver-mines at Potosí, discovered in 1545 by a Native prospector in what is today Bolivia, were a graveyard and were a tragedy for all the indigenous peoples who died there.[108] The Natives were caught between disease as they fled the Spanish and being worked to death. The Native population in the Caribbean, Mexico and South America fell to a small fraction of what it was at first contact.

In Brazil, the Portuguese also devastated the land and people. Tomé de Sousa arrived in Bahia in 1549. Whereas the Spaniards had come to base their wealth on silver for export, the Portuguese developed sugar plantations to create an export crop. In the seventeenth century, the Dutch, French and English came to rival the Portuguese by setting up sugar plantations in the Caribbean. Even by 1570, when King Sebastião decreed that the Natives could not be enslaved except in just wars, the aboriginal population was declining. The Portuguese killed many and others fled into the interior. Weakened by violence and enslavement, the indigenous peoples succumbed to a wave of epidemics, including influenza, dysentery and haemorrhagic fevers. Plague was also killing many in Lisbon and beyond, and in 1563, the plague and smallpox accompanied a ship to Brazil. So many thousands died that few were left to care for those among the Natives who survived. They in turn often succumbed to shock, dehydration and starvation. The Native farming and crops were devastated, and their land was changed. The slaving raids and the epidemics weakened the Natives to the point that they were no longer masters in their own land. Many among the Caribs, Mayans, Manau and others in the Caribbean, Mexico and South America tried to resist the Spaniards, but the waste of their land and communities and the work of microbes made that a battle without a victory in sight. In the eighteenth century, Ajuricaba, chief of the Manau, fought to keep his people from kidnapping and slavery and leapt to his own death rather than be captured.[109]

Throughout the New World, as Diamond points out, 95 per cent of the pre-Columbian population died from disease. The Mississippian chiefdoms disappeared from 1492 to the late 1600s before Europeans settled on the Mississippi. Other continents experienced this pattern of depopulation through disease. In 1713, a smallpox epidemic weakened the San in South Africa before the Europeans destroyed them. Epidemics ravaged aborigines in Australia soon after the British settled Sydney in 1788.[110] In 1806, a few European sailors were shipwrecked and brought an epidemic to Fiji. Other epidemics affected Hawaii, Tonga and other Pacific Islands.[111] Here, and elsewhere in this book, we have witnessed the role of disease and ecological degradation in the expansion of empires and the death of those they invaded. Disease affected Europeans and all the peoples they encountered. It was a key factor in the history of empire and colony and affected the patterns of slavery and violence that have also played a significant part in this study. And the individual voices of these Natives, against the odds, even though often translated or interpreted through European texts and images, provide another perspective.

Native, Local or Colonial Voices

Native voices were often filtered through European texts. Unfortunately, even the most informative among pre-Conquest Native documents were mostly redone under Spanish influence during the 1540s and after.[112] Las Casas insisted on a place for the Amerindians as members of a human civil society.[113] The Spanish set the tone for debates among the French and English. The conflicted and contradictory voices of Columbus, Las Casas and Sepúlveda and Oviedo find their echoes in Cartier, Thevet, Montaigne, Ralegh, Hakluyt, Purchas and Shakespeare.

Go-betweens, mediators and translators were important voices and actors in the colonies. For example, La Malinche, a woman and a mediator, helped translate and interpret Native culture while being Cortés' mistress and on his campaign to conquer the Aztec.[114] In the *Conquest of Mexico* Bernal Díaz suggested that La Malinche may not have been a Nathua or Aztec. He also said that she may have been seeking revenge for their exploitation of her people. In 1959, Miguel Leon-Portilla published his collection of various of Angel Maria Garibay K.'s translations into Spanish of Nahuatl oral accounts of this conquest. *Broken Spears*, which gives the Aztec version of events, includes a portrait of La Malinche from another point of view. It seems that La Malinche was from the coast and spoke Nahuatl and Mayan and that she translated from Nahuatl into Mayan. Then in response to her, Jeronimo de Aguilar, a Spaniard who lived among the Mayas for eight years and one of the two captives Cortés had wanted to ransom, could translate the Mayan into Spanish for Cortés.[115] A cross-cultural relation had begun: the European had crossed the boundary to Native culture and the Native to European culture. Although they worked together, tensions existed between European nations and between Native nations. Both were in conflict.

Cortés is part of another important aspect of the meeting of European and Native. He came upon two Spaniards, Jeronimo de Aguilar and Gonzalo Guerrero, who had been taken captive. The one wanted to return into the Spanish fold while the other wished to remain in Native society. Soon the Spanish and the Aztecs (Mexicas or Nahuas) could communicate. For instance, the Aztec messengers communicated with La Malinche and de Aguilar as she spoke Mayan and Nahuatl and he had learned Mayan over the eight years since his shipwreck in Yucatan in 1511. After La Malinche translated the messengers' Nahuatl into Mayan for de Aguilar, he translated it into Spanish for Cortés. Even during the siege of Tenochtitlán, where apparently hundreds of thousands perished, Cortés used La Malinche and de Aguilar as interpreters.[116] Interpretation is at the heart of cultural exchange between settlers and Natives in the story of empire and colony.

The figure of the Native, especially as a go-between, translator or mediator, is found in many European texts. In examining the relations between cultures in the New World, whether of kidnapping or mediation, the problems of identity, crossing culture, ambivalence and contradiction are themselves full of enigmas and paradoxes. Spaniards and Natives were liminal or threshold figures in a key Spanish text about the conquest of New Spain or Mexico. Guerrero is a striking case because he 'went Native' and fought a war against his former compatriots, the Spanish, with great persistence and resolve. Bernal Díaz has another captive, Aguilar, who returned from the Natives to embrace his Spanish compatriots, reporting that Guerrero had prompted the attack on Cordoba at Cape Catoche.[117] Another Native, Melchior, whom the Spanish had brought from that same place, fled Cortés' expedition to the Indians in the New World in the early years of the sixteenth century, 'advised them that if they attacked us by day and night we should be beaten, for we were few in number. So it turned out that we had brought an enemy with us instead of a friend'.[118] Uprooted, Melchior had nowhere to run: he could not find peace with the Spaniards nor with the Natives. Díaz reported Melchior's fate: Cortés demanded him, and the Natives, who would not turn Melchior in, were reported to have sacrificed him.[119] Aguilar was said to have been so happy to regain the Spanish fold after being enslaved by the Indians. He acted as interpreter on this campaign. As for Guerrero, he remained an elusive enemy for a long time. In about 1534 or 1535, after a battle south of Yucatan, the Spanish surveyed the Indian dead and found among them a tattooed white man: Guerrero.[120] Clearly, this 'White Indian' was unruly and hostile to his European culture.

These liminal figures also suggest that life in the colonies was more complex than one of simple division between the cultures. Cultural mixing and the creation of new cultural practices and groups occurred far from the imperial centre. For instance, Tecuichpotzin or Isabel Moctezuma, daughter to Moctezuma (Montezuma) II, had two Native and three Spanish husbands.[121] Moreover, her children crossed the bounds of race; some of her descendants became titled in Spain; and she was an Aztec princess. Class also mattered: it allowed her to claim the lands Cortés had claimed on behalf of the Spanish Crown. Even though the Spaniards often wanted her to be a symbol of the assimilation of Aztec culture into the new Spanish Mexico, it was not so straightforward a situation. Tecuichpotzin was a Christian: she also became involved in a long lawsuit with the Spanish Crown over her land claims.

The French were also involved in cultural mixing and using Native representatives for their own ends. In sixteenth-century Brazil, the Norman interpreters, or 'trucements de Normandie', moved into the Tupinamba villages, learned their language, and lived with their women and had children with them.[122] Jean de Léry, a Protestant who lived in the French colony in Brazil during the 1550s, reported on the mixing between the Normans and the Tupinamba in the mid-sixteenth century.[123] Like other Europeans, the French often used Native voices as a means of criticizing the decay, corruption or social ills of European society. For instance, Michel de Montaigne told of the three Natives who spoke with Charles IX in Rouen. In his account, Montaigne emphasized their ignorance of how knowledge of French corruption would cost them repose and happiness. Moreover, Montaigne stressed how the commerce would lead to their ruin, which Montaigne assumed was already advanced. Finally, he underscored their misery for having quit their mild air for that of France. Here, Montaigne used these three wise men to expose the French by turning the ethnological glass back on itself. In this recounting of the event, Montaigne recalled the questions of the Natives. Why would strong well-armed men obey a child rather than choosing one among them to assume power, and why do the hungry beggars outside the gates of the well-fed great not seize them by the throats or burn their houses down? The observations of the Natives suggested French corruption even if, by implication, that decay and barbarism might be applied to all of Europe. Montaigne's 'Des Cannibales' ends with the modest celebration of great warriors amongst the Natives and with their near nakedness.[124]

Representations of native peoples became a political act in the textual battles in Europe itself. Natives had become a weapon against Spain. Girolamo Benzoni included a summary that stressed the diverse views of the Natives on the American mainland. He wrote about 'how the King of Spain, from the report and persuasion of a few Monks, by Edict condemned these people of the Continent to perpetual servitude, if they did not want to convert, and has since revoked this Edict and given back liberty to the Indians by the advice of the Pope'.[125] Benzoni's argument showed the Spanish abuse of power but also the king's recognition of the mistake, reversing the enslavement of the Natives and giving them their liberty. This summary condensed the 387 pages of Benzoni's first book into three pages, thereby bringing out the contradiction of Spain as tyrant and reformer. Benzoni also revealed another discrepancy – the wrongs done to the Natives, whose 'mortal enmity' the Spanish had gained, and the description of the superstitious nature of the inhabitants of Hispaniola.[126] The ethnological and the political discourses created a friction that brought out an ambivalence in which neither Spain nor the Natives could be entirely praised. Even in such an ambivalent context, the summary of Benzoni's argument tended to sympathize with the Indians and criticize the Spaniards. Las Casas was a more familiar figure in the polemical assault on the Spanish in their colonies and, typologically, in Europe – the Black Legend of Spain. Still, Le Challeux, Benzoni, Montaigne and others were enlisted in the battle.

Although Native images of the Europeans have not been widely disseminated, they are coming to light more and more. The annals of the Valley of Mexico (1516–25), a Tupi taunt of French missionaries in Brazil (1612) and an Algonkin account of Europeans entering North America (seventeenth century) are three instances that represent a small fraction of the Native texts describing the relations with the Europeans in the first two centuries of contact.[127] Like the texts of Columbus, Native written documents are also fraught with textual uncertainty and mediation. The documents written in Nahuatl about the first exchanges with the Spanish and gathered together by Miguel Leon-Portilla as *Broken Spears* are problematic.[128] In 1959, Leon-Portilla collected various of Angel Maria Garibay K.'s translations into Spanish of Nahuatl oral accounts of this conquest.[129] From about 1524, the Franciscans trained some of the Nahua noblemen to read and write Nahuatl, presumably in a way that owed a debt to Latin and Spanish writing and grammar. Temporal and textual medication characterizes these accounts. For instance, the *Codex Ramirez* preserved a few Spanish fragments of an older indigenous text in Nahuatl about the Spanish March to Tezcoco, including Cortés' visit there.[130] The text was already a hybrid. From these Native and alternative voices in the New World, it is important to move to a more global context in order to gain yet another perspective, this one less to do with individuals and more to do with patterns and general situations and trends.

The Rise of Europe in a Wider Context

Western European innovation was not yet something that gave its nations strength above others. The Ottomans took Constantinople in 1453 partly because many of its fortifications dated back to Justinian's rule in the sixth century. While one Rome fell, another was raised to the east. The Russians curtailed Mongol power in the fourteenth century and Ivan III (r. 1462–1505) was the first to claim the imperial title tsar or czar from Caesar. After the fall of Constantinople, the tsar was proclaimed as a caesar ruling over Moscow or the Third Rome (Constantinople being the second Rome), but, besides this mythology, this only defender of the orthodox church in the face of Islam and Catholicism also drew on the autocratic traditions of the Mongol empire. It succeeded two empires, the one Byzantine and the other Mongolian.[131]

Europe had generally, despite the attempts at various unified empires, been fragmented politically partly because of its lack of large plains.[132]

Superior military technology might have concentrated power in a single prince in Europe as it did in Mogul India, Tokugawa Japan and Muscovy, but even Emperor Charles V, about 1550, could not achieve that in the highly innovative and competitive world of Europe.

The existence of a number of decentralized centres of power meant that no one ruler could dominate. This rivalry was complicated with the Reformation. Arms manufacturing, shipbuilding and mercenaries could be found in many places. Paid armies in Europe were hired and supervised with the expectation that they would produce value for money. Europeans continued to make innovations in the manufacture of gunpowder and arms and an inventor no less than Leonardo Da Vinci filled his notebooks with sketches of war machines and weapons, some that had to await the future: a tank, machine gun and steam-powered cannon. The very innovations of the French with their bronze guns in 1494 demanded Italian counters in the war of innovation – something that did not seem to happen as much in other parts of the world. The Italians, and later the Dutch in their revolt against Spain, realized that raised earthworks within city walls could much reduce the effectiveness of bombardment by artillery. European guns on land and on ships improved greatly after 1500. The Europeans reached outwards in a systematic way: in a repeated framework the Portuguese collected geographical data, the Genoese funded voyages into the Atlantic, the various countries fished the cod fisheries off Newfoundland.

This arms race produced many polities in a balance of power in Europe and led to mastery of the seas of the world. The ships of the powers of the Atlantic seaboard of western Europe developed three-masted ships (galleons and caravels) that slowly became the most versatile and reliable on the seas. The Dutch made great improvements over the small ships the Portuguese sailed to India in the 1490s. The other great powers did not fold before the Europeans: the Chinese, Japanese and Ottomans did more than stand their ground in the sixteenth and seventeenth centuries. From the Portuguese onwards, the Europeans did begin to control the seas, something that led to control of an important aspect of global trade, whether the emperor of China thought this was significant or not. The Portuguese artillery on ships threw the fleets of Arab dhows into disarray. The Spaniards sent home from their New World colonies cochineal, hides, silver and sugar: from 1500 to 1550 this transatlantic trade grew eight times and from 1550 to 1610 threefold again. This Iberian imperialism was organized to be permanent. Personal courage and terrible cruelty, as Kennedy and many before have observed, complicated the ambivalent nature of European expansion to Africa, Asia and the New World.

Fish, whale and sea oil, indigo, sugar, tobacco, rice, maize, potatoes, furs, silver, gold, spices and a plethora of other foodstuffs and valuables flooded into Europe and helped to create or expand European industries. To speak of Europeans as a whole, as if they were unified, would also be to forget their rivalries. Even the Iberian nations experienced conflicts with each other overseas. After the Revolt of the Netherlands and the decline in the English cloth trade, the French, Dutch and English intensified their challenge to the Portuguese and Spanish in the Atlantic. Religious division between Catholics and Protestants complicated this rivalry. In Europe there was a revolution in knowledge. This meant its dissemination and the development of market economies in which variety, openness and competition were increasingly valued and inquiry, experimentation, disputation and improvement were tolerated, allowed or encouraged. Over the course of the book we will need to ask how trade, resources and technology were in the expansion of western Europe.

It might well be that scholars in open democracies, especially in those of the English-speaking countries that have had so much influence in the past three centuries, might well use a kind of reverse teleological argument in which the apparent virtues and successes of the recent past or present are made to be the aims of those who came well before, as if the future could determine the past. Historians have a critical distance to see what others alive could not see at their time (equally, of course, scholars miss documents and events that might be available or obvious to those in the past). A tension between potential hubris and blindness catches the historian in pursuit of a theme or topic. In trying to come to terms with the intricacies of European empires and colonies, we face challenges that change over time. The Portuguese began something, even if we cannot say definitely why, or why other western European seaborne empires took up where they left off and effected a sea-change on the world for better and worse.

For a brief moment only did the Chinese fleet revive enough in the 1590s to help the Koreans to resist two attempted Japanese invasions. It seems that the Mongolian changes to the bureaucracy caused resentment among the civil servants, particularly in the Ming period, so that a nostalgia and a preservation of tradition were foremost in their plans. An admirable tendency in the Confucian code to view war and armed forces as deplorable but necessary for defence against barbarians or rebels and a suspicion of private capital trade (especially trade with foreigners) may have weakened the empire against new external threats. Technological innovations – and the Chinese were early masters of these – were really at the service of and pleasure of the emperor, so that canals, armies, clocks, ironworks could all, albeit gradually, fall into desuetude or decay. The bureaucracy also restricted printing to the works of scholars, discontinued paper currency and banned overseas trade and fishing. Chinese cities lacked autonomy, and merchants, in this cultural milieu, spent their money more on education and land than in industrial innovation. Ming China, despite its great accomplishments (including those in agriculture), was less dynamic than the Sung dynasty 400 years before. After 1644, the Manchus could not slow the relative decline.

Just when the ironworks in England were starting to boom in 1736 – to jump ahead of the 1608 end date for this chapter – the Chinese were abandoning the coke ovens and furnaces that had been booming 700 years before. The Europeans, on the other hand, continued to try to learn about China. Marco Polo had interested many, like Columbus, and later writers continued to describe China and the East. A critical tradition developed among European humanists. Paolo Giovio (1448–1552) was apparently the first to mention that printing had originated in China. João III of Portugal (ruled 1521–57) had himself received a humanist education, invited humanists to his court and appointed an official historian – João de Barros (1496–1570) – who wrote about the Portuguese in Asia (Persia, India and China). The chroniclers – Gaspar Correia, Fernão de Castanheda, Diogo do Couto and Barros himself – concentrated most on the deeds of the vassals of the Portuguese Crown in Asia, and even Correia and Couto, although less sympathetic to matters of rank, did not leave us with a full view of the marginalized, more particularly of exiles and renegades, those go-betweens who moved from one culture to the other.[133] For China, Barros used Chinese sources and bought a Chinese slave to interpret them. Collections also reflect a receptiveness as well as a wide-ranging consumption: for instance, Emperor Rudolf II (ruled 1576–1612) collected objects from China, India, Persia, the Ottoman empire and the New World.[134] The Ming views of the Portuguese were split after the Portuguese arrival in China in 1513, some wanting regulated trade and some who did not. Like westerners, the Chinese misrepresented these 'others'; they did so, according to K. C. Fok, because of the casual nature of their exposure to the newcomers and of the assumption that their own customs were the most human.[135] Some early images represented the Portuguese as a kind of goblin with cannibals for ancestors.[136]

The Persian and Ottoman empires were strong for much of the sixteenth and seventeenth centuries. The Turks had built up sea power and had taken Constantinople in 1453 and threatened Genoese, Venetian and Habsburg fleets in the Mediterranean, taking Cyprus in 1570–1, before suffering defeat at the Battle of Lepanto in 1571. A number of epic poets, such as Don Alonso de Ercilla y Zuñiga, Juan Latino and Juan Rufo, narrated and represented the causes of the victory at Lepanto as the superiority of western artillery and small arms and the confidence that the general, Don Juan, instilled.[137] The Turks would besiege Vienna in 1529 and in 1683. The Ottoman empire, suing a conquering elite like the Manchus in China, attempted an official unity of language, culture and religion over an area greater than the Roman empire. Orthodox Christians and prosperous Jewish communities (augmented by Jews expelled from Spain) found relative tolerance in the Ottoman empire. After 1566, thirteen sultans of uncertain talents reigned in succession, so that there was a crisis of leadership at a critical time in the Ottoman empire. Like the system in Ming China, the one among the Ottomans increasingly stifled dissent, initiative and commerce. Owing to poor leadership, plundering janissaries, soldiers and civilian officials, the merchants and entrepreneurs (many of whom were foreign) as well as peasants found themselves subject to heavy and unpredictable taxes. The Persian war had meant a loss in the trade with Asia and censorship of the Shi'ites helped to contribute towards a wider censorship and the forbidding of the printing press. The janissaries were slow to respond to European advances in military technology, and medical innovation was neglected and exports discouraged.

Japan and Russia were expanding powers, so that while the western European states were establishing vast empires, it is important not to forget the growth of other states. Although not as large or populous as the Ming, Ottoman and Mogul Empires, Japan and Russia experienced political and economic expansion in the sixteenth century. Whereas a centralized bureaucracy under the watch of the emperor governed China, feudal lords and their clans, not the emperor, were the powers in Japan for most of the sixteenth century.[138] European armaments affected Japan and other countries in the world, so that warlords, like Hideyoshi (died 1598) and later Ieyasu and other shoguns of the Tokugawa clan, centralized military rule. This centralizing monarchy of the Tokugawa differed from those in Europe in that it abjured overseas expansion and almost all contact with the outside world, so that, in 1636, the year Harvard was founded in the Massachusetts Bay Colony, the court in Japan ordered the halt of seafaring vessels and forbade the Japanese to sail the high seas. Over 700 years before, the anonymous poem 412 from the *Kokinshu* offered a mediation on travel, the haunting cry of one of the northbound geese in the night who in autumn flew this way but did not come home with them. Now travel in a country built on those who migrated to its shores and that traded in goods and ideas with China and Korea had become something not left to choice. A different kind of elegiac to loss and isolation came to Japan.

Russia, despite the disruptions of trading routes with the lands to the west by the Ottoman empire, Sweden, Lithuania and Poland, found that European muskets and cannon allowed it to use gunpowder to defeat the Asian horsemen that threatened it.[139] Eastern and southern expansion was easier because the new western technology in armaments was lacking there. Russian troops reached the Caspian Sea by 1556, although the troops of the Tartar khanate of the Crimea sacked Moscow in 1571 and remained independent until the late 1700s.

Japan and Russia also experienced the uneven development of power and expansion. Like the European powers, their growth was not linear. Setbacks were known to them. The Poles would occupy Moscow in 1608.

Transitions

Some states were waxing and waning in the greater world beyond Europe. In western Europe itself, rivalries and alliances were shifting. Just as the English and French were establishing colonies that might endure in North America, which the Huguenots (De Mornay, Coligny and others) and the English (Gilbert, Hakluyt and others) advocated, the Dutch were on the verge of empire and Portugal and Spain began their decline in Europe. Overseas, however, especially in the New World, Spain remained strong. The Netherlands began to prey on Portuguese possessions as a means to find a ready-made colonial network. The next century, to the peace that ended the War of Spanish Succession, France was on the mend and became the great Continental power, and now, as the leading Catholic state, came into friction with the Netherlands and England (Britain). If members of other states were afraid that the union of Portugal and Spain in 1580 would lead to Iberian domination in Europe and the world, they were concerned in 1700 with the possible union of France and Spain under a Bourbon crown. In the wake of the war that was fought over that prospect, rivalries between western European states and empires did not cease. In the seventeenth century France and England would fight in Europe and overseas while Portugal, Spain, the Netherlands and others were key players in the contest of empires and colonies.

Once more ambivalence and contradictions occurred in exploration, settlement and the exploitation of the new lands and indigenous peoples. The great economic and political forces of European expansion, the biological destruction of indigenous peoples and the exploitation of slaves qualify the story of overcoming odds, obstacles and hardships among the settlers. The meeting of cultures modifies and complicates the inter-European rivalry for the prestige and power of empires and colonies. The French, English and Dutch would expand in the seventeenth century, which added to the pressures on aboriginal peoples and African slaves and increased the intensity of rivalrous European empires.

3

The Relative Decline of Portugal and Spain: 1608–1713

〇〇

Into the first years of the seventeenth century, the Iberian states led the way in expansion. They were not as populous or as economically powerful as the states in and about India and China and, even at the height of their power, they were not fully dominant in Europe or in the world. Islam had continued to expand, and powers like the Ottomon empire were forces to be reckoned with. We also saw that although Portugal and Spain were united under one crown, they had begun to work more alike before that while still maintaining some differences. The violence of this expansion, as well as the ecological wreckage (which could be seen especially in the Spanish exploitation and settlement of the Caribbean), was something peoples, particularly indigenous peoples in the New World, who seem not to have had the technology of written communication and warfare to resist effectively, suffered over a long period. In time the Europeans allied themselves with other peoples to fight their European rivals, for instance the Portuguese and the Venetians did that and later the Portuguese and Dutch and others continued that trend. In all this, a quasi-legal and religious framework set out the parameters for the expansion, and such a frame was in place long before Ceuta in 1415. European rivalries intensified and became more complex with the Reformation. We have been able to glimpse the intricacies of each empire and the peoples they encountered without having the space to be exhaustive.

In each phase of expansion, ambivalence and contradiction often characterized individual motives and group dynamics within and among states. To speak about 'Portugal' and 'Spain' as unities with a single purpose has been, as we have seen, problematic, and such personifications of a nation or empire have a mythical urge, a kind of necessary shorthand that can get us all into trouble with hasty generalization and stereotyping. That is one reason I have chosen alternative voices and contradictory motives and actions to complicate this narrative of the centralization of state power in the Iberian and western European states and in the encounter with other peoples, whose cultures and states were also shifting economically, politically, socially and religiously. This is a relative motion.

England, France and the Netherlands, as well as the German and Italian states, had much to do with European expansion, but the prime political and religious roles were those of Portugal, Spain and the papacy until 1517. After that, as within Islam, a further division between sects of Christianity, that is Catholic and Protestant as opposed to Eastern Orthodox and Roman Catholic, would affect the notion of the spread of religion. Western European expansion was full of examples of multinational cooperation but was also rivalrous. Other peoples fought one another and formed alliances, so this is why it is important to remember the moving nature of the theme of empires and colonies.

This period of about 1608 to 1713 marks the decline of Spain as a great European power, although its influence in the New World remained strong. The struggle with England and France and in the Netherlands took its toll. Even the peace of 1604 did not stop the loss of the Netherlands in 1609 and the bankruptcy of its treasury in that year. By 1640, Portugal was lost and by 1700 a war broke out over the succession for the Spanish throne. From the founding of permanent English and French colonies in North America to the Treaty of Utrecht at the end of the War of the Spanish Succession, Spain and its empire faced challenges that, increasingly, could not be met. This war would ultimately prevent France and Spain uniting under one Bourbon monarch. Still, in 1608–9, it would have been hard to see this fate for Spain and the tensions that would be caused between a weak imperial centre and some strong colonies, particularly in Central and South America.

Portugal and Spain

Since Portugal began our story of expansion, it is best to begin with its relative decline before discussing the falling off of Spain. Portugal was a strong empire that did not collapse under the weight of its own fatigue or corruption. External elements impinged on the Portuguese empire, the most important of which was Dutch military strength. The conflict was multi-polar and involved parties such as the Sultan of Makassar, the Nayaka rulers of Madurai and Tanjavur and the Safavid Shah. Moreover, the Portuguese suffered these significant losses without any involvement of the Dutch: the first Syriam (1612), the Hurmuz (1622), Hughli (1632), the trade with Japan (1638), and the Kanara ports (1654). The Portuguese fought the Ottomans (who had expanded into Egypt and the Red Sea), tried diplomacy with the Vijayanagara of southern India (who were defeated by the rulers of Bijapur in 1565), and kept a respectful distance from the Ming dynasty in China. From the 1570s, the Mughal state, controlled by a central Asian dynasty, expanded from the Ganges to become a maritime power that reached into the western Indian Ocean and the Bay of Bengal, something that endured into the eighteenth century. It seems as though the rivalry between the Mughals, ruled by Akbar (r. 1565–1605), and the Ottomans was a main reason the Mughal state did not challenge the Portuguese at sea. The Ottoman empire fought Portugal in maritime battles. The Safavid rulers of Iran, who had established trade with Moscow, posed another balance or threat to Portuguese and Ottoman power. Shah Abbas (1587–1629) had to decide which he would strike, the Turk or the Portuguese, and in 1616, an Anglo-Iranian alliance against the Portuguese began. In Japan, the fruitful trade alliance with Toyotomi Hideyoshi began to have sticking points, particularly religion and politics. Conversion was so successful that significant Christian *daimyo* destroyed Japanese shrines and forced the conversion of peasants. In 1587, Hideyoshi curtailed the power of the Jesuits who had taken on an armed presence, confiscated their post at Nagasaki and pressured Christian *daimyo* to return to their original religions. Frustrated by the lack of success with his invasion of Korea, Hideyoshi, who died in 1598, turned his wrath towards Europeans and Japanese Christians, executing twenty-six (including three Jesuits and six Franciscans) in February 1597. In 1614, Tokugawa Ieyasu and his more centralized government ordered the expulsion of all missionaries.

Other problems mounted. The Dutch took Ambon in 1605. Burma captured Syriam, a key to the Bay of Bengal, in 1612, impaling its leader Felipe de Brito on an iron stake, and this event allowed Burma and Masulipatnam to expand their trade. At the same time, Philip III was trying to give control of the administration of Portugal to Spaniards. Portuguese Asia was being starved financially. The alliance between Shah Abbas and the English led to the fall of Hurmuz in 1622, which cut into Portuguese revenues in the Persian Gulf. The English East India Company (1600), the United East India Company (VOC), formed by the Dutch in 1602, and the company created by the Danish in 1616 did come to challenge the Portuguese in Asia. In reaction, the Portuguese East India Company was created, but to little effect. Despite the defeat of Aceh in 1629 and an Anglo-Portuguese agreement in 1630, Portuguese power continued to decline. During the 1630s, the Dutch made incursions into Sri Lanka and the Mughals took Hughli and other posts from the Portuguese. Portugal's share of the silver trade with Japan began to fall as the Japanese had established traders in Taiwan, Macau and elsewhere. The Japanese expelled the Portuguese in 1639 (the Spaniards were banished in 1625): Japan executed European merchants and priests in the 1620s and 1630s. Violence went both ways in the western European encounter with other nations. The Japanese violently put down the Shimbara Revolt of Japanese Christian peasants. The Portuguese sent an embassy to Nagasaki in 1640: as a warning, the Japanese beheaded sixty-one of the seventy-four representatives. That was the end of the lucrative trade between Japan and Macau.

Significant portions of the Portuguese aristocracy and merchants had had enough of Spanish attempts to control the government of Portugal and to neglect the Portuguese empire. The revolt in Catalonia allowed the Portuguese space to act. With this internal support as well as with that of the Jesuits and of Cardinal Richelieu in France, the Duke of Bragança declared himself King of Portugal (João IV) in December 1640. Despite establishing a peace with the Netherlands, the Portuguese found the Dutch aggressive in Asia. With the help of the Johorese, the Dutch took Melaka in January 1641. The Netherlands had also taken Pernambuco in Brazil in 1637. The Portuguese were besieged before and after the restoration. From 1641 to 1680, the Dutch were at the height of their powers in the seas of Asia. The Dutch controlled much of the trade of Makassar and were involved in trade with Japan. The Portuguese trade still stretched from Macau to east Africa, but Portugal had lost many important posts between, such as Kanara, Malabar, Sri Lanka, Hurmuz and Melaka. As Native and Dutch opposition curbed Portuguese power in Asia, it is important to avoid overestimating the power and influence of an empire or underestimating that of its rivals and of the local peoples. When the Portuguese and English-Scottish monarchies established a marriage between Catherine (Catarina) and Charles Stuart, part of the dowry from Portugal, much against the protests of certain Portuguese administrators, was the island of Bombaím.[1]

Before turning to Spain, it is important to trace the continuing pattern of Portugal in the last three or four decades of the seventeenth century. It seems that the Portuguese defended the Atlantic empire of west Africa and Brazil more effectively than their empire in Asia. Portugal had driven the Dutch out of Brazil in January 1654 (Recife). Persecution of New Christians involved in overseas trade was on the rise again in Portugal, and this complicated an effective policy for the empire. In the 1690s, gold-mines were found in Minais Gerais in Brazil, and Portugal used this gold in its trade with England. In the 1690s, after some tenuous moments, the position of Goa in India seemed stable. The Portuguese stronghold of Mozambique faced a new threat. Colbert formed the Compagnie des

Indies and the French had established a presence in Madagascar, so the Portuguese feared for their gold trade. The Portuguese were able to keep up their strength with local populations and in the trade. Further, the Portuguese were able to maintain trade in the Bay of Bengal despite the shifting of power in the region. The French were, however, to take Coromandel and, in 1749, the British were to seize São Tomé. In Macau and Timor, the Portuguese survived. Like the Dutch, they had to keep close and careful watch over trade with China and the politics of that state, without which their settlement at Macau would probably have been unable to persist. Even so, the trade was much lighter at the end than at the beginning of the seventeenth century. The Portuguese were, however, able to make a comeback as the Dutch trading power in the region began to decline in the early eighteenth century and as the opium trade developed between Bengal and China. When the Portuguese first came to Asia, pepper and spices drove the trade, but in 1700 it was textiles and soon would be coffee and tea as well. Textiles and spices were the lures of Asia for Europeans, and they had to find a way to pay for these. There was a shift from seigneurial to capitalist modes in the European trade with Asia, but the same shipping services among Japan, the Spice Islands and India informed the Dutch as it did the Portuguese.

The Dutch became fortunate in the seventeenth century to be granted privileges under the Tokugawa government, which allowed them to profit so much from Japanese copper and bullion as well as Indonesian spices. The Dutch relied on diplomacy in this case and force in others to achieve financial success. The VOC was a quasi state authority and not simply a capitalist company. The English company was undercapitalized and did not have the support at home the VOC did. It also lacked military power. Consequently, the English concentrated on trade between India and Europe, especially in textiles, which began to pay off in the last half of the seventeenth century. The English company also drew on the long English tradition of force and piracy. It even picked an ill-advised fight with the Mughal empire between 1687 and 1689. During the eighteenth century, the English would take over from the Dutch as the leading European traders in Asia. They did so partly by leaving intra-Asian trade to private hands, and they made great profits from the trade between Asia and Europe. Local conditions in Asia affected how all these European empires changed goods and strategies over time, so that while Portugal provided a model to the Netherlands, which was an example to the English (if we take one strand), the flux in Asia in trade, religion and politics governed what happened in the vast extent of Asian trade.[2] But before getting too far ahead of ourselves, let us return to the other Iberian state: Spain. It, too, was having its own difficulties even above and beyond losing Portugal in 1640.

The strain of maintaining an empire on the Habsburg coffers and the economy of Spain was heavy. From 30,000 troops in the 1520s the Spanish empire had at least 300,000 in the 1620s. The Anglo-Spanish peace of 1604 meant that Spain had to contend now mainly with the Dutch, but this commitment was increasingly costly because warships were more and more heavily armed. Whereas from 1500 to 1630 industrial prices went up 300 per cent and food prices rose 500 per cent, the cost of warfare, given the doubling and redoubling of armies, was even greater. Protecting an empire in America and the Philippines was also costly. In 1618 the outbreak of the Thirty Years War involved the deployment of troops and money in Germany and Flanders: increased bullion deliveries from the New World helped to finance Spanish victories. Despite the alliance with the emperor, Spain began a critical period; its revenues declined from 1628; the Dutch seized the silver fleet in 1628 and this cost Spain an amount estimated as high as 10,000,000 ducats.[3] After the Catalan and Portuguese revolts and the reduction, by the 1640s Spain had begun its decline. Unlike France, Sweden, the Ottoman Empire and England, Spain did not have much rest from war and so was unable to recover under the shelter of peace. Although after the retirement of Charles V the Holy Roman empire did not always support Spain in its wars in western Europe and overseas, Spain did aid that empire. Without wealth from the New World, Spain would not have been able to maintain that and other military commitments.[4] As Spain declined, the power of France was on the rise.

The Spanish empire, as we have seen, suffered a revolt in Catalonia then another in Portugal. John Elliott has said that the dissolution of Spanish power during the 1640s was irrevocable, absolute and, therefore, inevitable.[5] Between 1621 and 1643, Count Olivares attempted to construct a foreign policy, based on that of Philip II in the 1580s and 1590s, that attempted to quash heresy and to establish Spanish hegemony over Europe and, by extension, over rivals overseas. This policy taxed the Spanish treasury to exhaustion.[6] In 1630, Olivares commented on the 'barbarism' of internal transport and engineering in Spain.[7] The revolt of the Portuguese in 1640, after having been joined with Spain since 1580, diverted Spanish troops, while the Dutch came to attack Ceylon, Angola and Brazil. António Vieira, a Jesuit father, played a major role at a key point of Iberian and colonial history – the separation of Portugal from Spain in 1640 (they had been joined in 1580) and the expulsion of the Dutch from Brazil in 1654.[8] Two important factors in the globalization of trade in the sixteenth century were the importation of American silver into Spain and the discovery of the route round the Cape to the East Indies.

Other reasons for the decline of Spanish power have been outlined. Paul Kennedy, like Elliott, weighs them well in the balance. The Spanish government failed to recognize or at least implement economic policies that provided the prosperity necessary to underpin the military. Spain also expelled the Jews and then the Moriscos. It closed contacts with foreign universities, did not allow the shipyards to produce enough small commercial vessels in addition to large warships, sold monopolies, taxed wool exports heavily, and maintained burdensome internal customs.[9] In short, it stifled its economy and so could not finance its central role in Europe and overseas.

The governments of European states were finding themselves increasingly entwined politically and economically with other places in Asia and not simply worrying about trade and the balance of power in Europe. Still, statecraft and interests cut across religious lines in Europe. Cardinal Mazarin allied France with Cromwell's England against Spain, so that religion was not always the motive in these alliances and wars. Spain had formally recognized the independence of the Netherlands in 1648 and of Portugal in 1668; by the Treaty of the Pyrenees in 1659, the Habsburgs were no longer the predominant economic and political force in Europe.[10]

The Struggle for Brazil

The Portuguese found rivals in the land of the True Cross (as they first called Brazil), first in the French in the sixteenth century and then in the Dutch in the seventeenth. Amid this rivalry, there were connections between the Portuguese and the Dutch there. Other frictions within the Iberian world meant that the Portuguese officials helped to break the laws of the king of Spain. As a result, the Dutch had somewhere between a third and two-thirds of the carrying-trade between Brazil and Europe. In May 1624 the Dutch captured Bahia, a key to Brazil, but in 1625 an Iberian force defeated the Dutch at Bahia, Puerto Rico and Elmina (São Jorge da Mina in western Africa).[11] There was a struggle with the Dutch over Pernambuco, in the northeast of Brazil and the richest region in the world for the production of sugar and the most prosperous part of Portugal's colonial empire. The Dutch inflicted heavy losses to the Iberian fleets from the New World between 1630 and 1636. The Spanish and Portuguese could not work together to send an Iberian armada to Brazil and blamed each other for this situation. Fearing that Brazil was a launch for Dutch ambitions in Spanish America, the Spaniards complained that the Portuguese were relying too much on Spain and the Portuguese maintained that they were overtaxed and that their union with Spain had drawn them into a conflict with the Dutch. Having contributed a great deal to this struggle, the Spanish Crown was willing to sacrifice some of the interests of its subjects in Flanders to those in Portugal. Even though the Dutch were prevailing, the West India Company was bearing great financial burdens despite the booty from the 547 Iberian ships taken between 1623 and 1636.[12] A friction between the public sphere of politics and the private realm of finance made it more difficult for the Dutch to succeed even though their navy was powerful and their economic clout was substantial.

For a while, the Netherlands looked as though it would come to rule Brazil. Between 1637 and 1641 Johan Mauretis, the Dutch governor-general in Brazil, proved successful in expanding Dutch holdings and influence. Subject to Roman-Dutch law, the local Portuguese were guaranteed equal rights with the subjects of the United Provinces. Moreover, Mauretis permitted Jews and Roman Catholics freedom of conscience and worship and allowed some French Capuchin friars to enter the colony. Early on, the Dutch had also been weary of or had opposed the slave trade with Africa. In 1596 the city fathers in Middleburg had freed a hundred slaves brought as cargo there and in 1608 Usselincx had opposed the use of black slaves in Dutch America. Soon, however, the demand for slaves after the Dutch capture of Paraíba and Pernambuco in 1634 to 1636 changed the Dutch position. Rather than opt for German labour, Mauretis chose to go the route of African slaves in the sugar-mills. As with all such decisions, the conflict between an immediate economic fix and the longer ethical view divided people from themselves or from their neighbours.

Even though the rule of the Netherlands in Brazil was tolerant (to use that Lockean term from later in the century), it met with resistance. The Portuguese did not wholeheartedly accept Dutch rule and were sometimes bitterly opposed to it. On the eve of the Portuguese Revolution, Antonio Vieira preached an anti-Dutch sermon. In Brazil, Mauretis surrounded himself with forty-six artists, scholars, scientists and craftsmen from the Netherlands, and their work, some of it published, was influential. He also established a legislative assembly. In spite of wealth and sea power, the Netherlands lost Brazil to Portugal, one of the poorest countries in western Europe. The weakness and unfocused efforts of the Dutch West India Company and the States General from 1645 to 1650 mishandled policies towards Brazil. This vulnerability amid government and business was owing, as Charles Boxer has maintained, to the lack of will in Amsterdam to find the money for the proper blockades before war broke out with England. Delay did not help because the other rivals of the Netherlands found themselves strengthened. By 1657, France and England were strong enough to resist the tough policies of the States General because they had their own designs on the Brazilian trade. Portugal, on the other hand, united under John IV. In 1664, George Downing wrote home to his government in England that it was the divided and shattered government of the Netherlands that contributed to its problems, and Cromwell's government in the late 1650s and that of Charles II in the 1660s were glad to see it that way. Charles was now married into the House of Braganza, which had helped him so much. He came to broker Luso-Dutch negotiations, but did not want to give the Dutch equal access to the Luso-Brazilian trade. Just as the Netherlands had wished to succeed Portugal, now England wanted to displace the Netherlands in America and Asia.[13] No empire was exempt from such dynamics.

The Netherlands and Its Neighbours and Rivals

One of the themes or paradoxes for the expanding states of western Europe is that their weakness, deficiencies and adversity often encouraged them to unify and look outward. It is not as though Portugal, Spain and the Netherlands were all so large and powerful that they inevitably expanded. In 1555, when Charles V abdicated, he handed over to his son, Philip II of Spain, seventeen provinces of the Netherlands, three of which Charles, born at Ghent, had acquired during his reign. At this time, the Netherlands then covered what is now a northern part of France as well as Belgium, Luxembourg and the Netherlands. In a few years, the Netherlands were in revolt against Philip. This hardly looked like a state on the verge of power.

This rebellion was not simply a Protestant rebellion against a Catholic king of Catholic Spain. In the early years, the mainly Catholic nobles rebelled against Philip's desire to centralize and bureaucratize the Netherlands. Even the leaders of the church opposed these changes to the ecclesiastical and civil administration. Protestantism was actually stronger in the south than in the north and Calvinism had taken off in the textile industry in Flanders, especially Ghent. The Duke of Alba directed his fury against the Protestants and that is why the concentration on religious difference often occurs. Alba's excise tax caused opposition among merchants of all religious persuasions. Some of the lesser nobility and gentry began to convert to Calvinism, which complicated matters further. The violence and losses were huge on both sides.

In 1609 there was a truce, which was a de facto division of the Netherlands into the Dutch Republic (the seven northern provinces) and the Spanish Netherlands (the ten southern provinces), which was recognized formally by a treaty in 1648 at the end of the Thirty Years War. As a reminder that all is not inevitable, somehow the richer southern part, which had more Calvinists and nobles (often French-speaking Walloons), remained under the aegis of Spain. Perhaps, as Peter Geyl and Charles

Wilson have suggested, the geography of the north made it more defensible, although Wilson notes as well that the Dutch Republic may have been born because Alba and his successor, the Duke of Parma, had not had to contend with France.[14] The English defeat of the Spanish armada and the rise of William of Orange (a noble of German background who was also called William the Silent) were other factors that kept the Spanish from maintaining all its territory in the Netherlands. Many other aspects of good fortune had to obtain for the fledgling state to prevail. William himself converted from Catholicism to Calvinism in 1573, but even before his assassination in 1584, the nobles in the south were moving back to the side of Spain. There were also tensions between the great liberal merchants and the Calvinists. Calvinism had international friendships and connections in places like France, the Netherlands, England and Scotland. Duplessis-Mornay and William of Orange were close friends, and William's fourth wife was Coligny's daughter, so the tie with Protestant France was especially strong. The Netherlands before and after division was full of frictions and divides.

The revolt brought skilled migrants and capital into the north, transforming Amsterdam, which was not as developed a commercial centre as Ghent and Antwerp, into a great trading city. This change began to happen when there was a purging of its Catholic elite in 1578. Amsterdam became a great entrepôt for Europe and, to some extent, for the world. The Netherlands or Dutch Republic became the great commercial shipping nation, fashioned banks on the Italian model, developed a bourse or stock market, attracted a community of Portuguese and Spanish Jews (often as refuges from Antwerp), became a polyglot place of trade, drew immigrants from the southern Netherlands and was the centre of a great network, which included sugar from Brazil and the West Indies and textiles, spices and silks from Asia. Ironically, the Spanish colonies had to send silver to Amsterdam to have food and goods, so that the Spanish empire depended on one of its former possessions. Still, the Dutch fought for their survival in the Eighty Years War (1567–1648) and against French hegemony in wars from 1664 to 1714. The English and the French put pressure on the Netherlands through propaganda and war through the last half of the seventeenth century. Another part of our argument is that so-called great powers are often most vulnerable at the time of their greatest strength. This was true for Portugal, Spain and the Netherlands and would also be true for England and France. Local conditions, as Portugal and Spain learned, in Europe and around the world affected what happened, and sometimes no number of abstract policies could remedy problems. Circumstance and context, as we have seen and will see, can seldom be overrated.

Some specific changes occurred to Dutch society in the wake of the successful revolt against Spain. The government of the cities passed from

Catholic oligarchies to Protestant merchant elites. The States General sometimes moved slowly or could not reach an agreement, which made it difficult to resolve colonial disputes with England. This inability to agree on orders to the officials that served the States General meant that in 1651 a treaty of alliance with England collapsed. The first Anglo-Dutch War (1652–4) showed how difficult it was to have rivalries between local authorities, such as five different admiralties being responsible for the war at sea. Conflicts also occurred between the ruling elite and the less tolerant representatives of Calvinism. Internal and external tensions were part of the life of this most prosperous new state.

The conflict with England helped to develop international law, especially the law of the seas, as they were both maritime powers. Hugo Grotius (Hugo de Groot), a Dutch jurist, was a key figure who argued that every state had equal rights to fish and navigate on the high seas, something that Portugal, Spain and England opposed in the early seventeenth century.[15] This doctrine was important for the Netherlands, which had become the leading maritime and trading colonial power in western Europe. As the Netherlands had an advantage in trade, it did not benefit from restrictions. Grotius visited England to mediate disputes between the Dutch and English East India Companies. While there, he discussed Calvinism with James I and with the Archbishop of Canterbury, and his favouring of the more tolerant views of Arminius, as opposed to the more orthodox ideas of Gomarus, got him into trouble at home. He was later imprisoned and escaped in a trunk, ending his days in the service of Sweden.

Grotius' contribution is that he argued for a freedom of the seas, which went against all protective practices and doctrines by western European states in the seas at home and surrounding or joining their colonies. The Dutch challenged this exclusion of foreigners from the Portuguese and Spanish territories as defined through the papal donations. The Dutch sailed about Africa and then to Mauritius, Java and the Moluccas. In 1602, a ship of the Dutch East Indies Company captured the *Catherine*, a Portuguese galleon, in the straits of Malacca. The VOC retained Grotius, who argued successfully before the Amsterdam Court of the Admiralty, that they could keep the confiscated Portuguese goods. He also helped the Dutch to ignore the Spanish demand that the Netherlands not trade in the West and East Indies. In *Mare Liberum* (*The Freedom of the Seas*) (1608), Grotius argued against any one nation's right to the seas and claimed that fishing, sailing and trading on the seas was the right of every nation, something the Netherlands would have to fight for if necessary. The Dutch also fished off the eastern coasts of Scotland and England under the guard of warships and made a large profit in salting, packaging and exporting herring. Grotius said that James I could tax English, but not Dutch, fishermen. William Welwood, a Scottish lawyer, wrote the *Abridgement of all the Sea-Lawes* (1613) in which he argued that the seas by Scotland were part of its domain, and John Selden defended the seas of the British empire in *Mare Clausum* (1635; written 1617). The English forced the Dutch to take out fishing licences to fish off the coast of England and to accord honours of the flag. By 1667, the colonial disputes between the Netherlands and England were mainly resolved, and from 1689, under William III, Marlborough and Heinsius, an alliance occurred between the two nations. As England, then Britain, grew as a maritime and commercial power, it, too, followed the Netherlands in the doctrine of the freedom of the seas. Liberty, as John Locke had argued, was now the idea of a rising middle class and nations and empires of trade. In *De Jure Belli ac Pacis*, Grotius attempted to subject nations to a law of nations based on a law of nature, just like the individual, putting the good of the nation first.

The Dutch mainly built a trading empire between the truce with Spain (1609) and the Treaty of Breda with England (1667). The East India Company used Dutch navigators who had sailed for Portugal. Those voyages by Drake and Cavendish inspired the merchants of Amsterdam who backed Cornelius Houtman's first voyage of 1595. The experienced English seamen, John Davis and James Lancaster, sailed on Houtman's voyage. Although an economic power, the VOC did little to affect the societies of the local peoples in Java, Sri Lanka, India, China, Japan and elsewhere, whether or not they had brought military conquest. In 1606, Willem Janszoon, sailing from Bantam, came upon north-eastern Australia in 1606, and the Dutch sailed to western Australia in 1616. The governor-general of the East Indies, Antony van Diemen, was the patron for Abel Tasman and his chief pilot, Frans Visscher, and hoped that they would find a southern passage to South America. He came upon Tasmania and New Zealand. The Dutch were more interested in trade and spices, so they did not put much effort into settler communities of farmers and paid less attention to self-government. When their chief rivals, Portugal and England, did not occupy the Cape of Good Hope, no matter what claims the English had made in 1620, and the proximity of Mozambique, the Dutch claimed it in 1652 and made it a stopping place. Differences occurred between the settlers or farmers (*boeren*) and the merchants and administrators of the company. Unlike the VOC, the West India Company, most of whose directors were Calvinists from the south, mixed trade and religion. Chasing away Catholicism was a goal of the company. The campaign against the Portuguese in Brazil began well, but got lost in the fluctuations of the sugar trade, which ate up the profits of the west African trade. The company went into the illegal slave trade to the Spanish American colonies. It also established New Netherlands (in the area of what is now New York). Henry

Hudson, an Englishman in the service of VOC, sought a northwest passage and also noted the potential for a fur trade. In New Netherlands, the colonists also had their frictions with the company, especially over having a say in local affairs. The company probably did not encourage immigration enough. In 1664, New Amsterdam became New York. Commerce and profit, the very strength of Dutch innovation, might also have caused the Dutch empire not to seek to develop colonies based on farming and settlement. It may be that it was difficult to find emigrants from the prosperous land of tolerance. The internal pressures in the Netherlands over class, religion, economics and kind of government also affected the colonies and the relations with peoples beyond the empire. Colony and empire affected each the other.[16]

One of the neighbours of the Netherlands that was expanding was England. Elizabeth I, as we have seen, used a double strategy of resisting Philip II in Europe and disrupting his empire at sea. After the peace of 1604 with Spain that James I agreed, it was not until 1652 to 1654, when the English fought the Dutch in a commercial war, that England got involved in a continental war.

Rivalries between the Netherlands and England occurred in Asia and the New World.[17] The English sailed the first English ships to India in 1608, but the Mughal governor at Surat, anxious not to anger the Portuguese, ordered the departure of an English fleet in 1610. This action caused Sir Henry Middleton to intercept the annual Haj pilgrimage ships from Surat in the entrance to the Red Sea. In order to avoid the name of pirate, he forced an exchange of Indian cloth for broadcloth. In 1611, other ships opened relations with the other coast of India which was outside the Mughal (Moghul) empire. The East India Company opened a factory at Hirado in Japan and in 1613 the Mughal empire, which covered the northern two-thirds of the Indian subcontinent, was the dominant power in the region. The Taj Mahal, the Red Fort at Delhi and the Muslim rulers' attempt at conciliation with the Hindu majority were products of this time. Whereas the Mughals would keep the peace for traders, the East India Company would come to please the emperor by arming its ships and holding the sea against pirates and the Portuguese. An Englishman, William Adams, helped the Dutch set up in Japan in 1609.[18]

England pressed the Netherlands and others on many fronts. The army under Cromwell and particularly the navy began to close the gap between the militaries of England and the Continent. Despite setbacks, the English navy fought the great Dutch navy and, after 1655, seized Acadia from France, Jamaica from Spain, part of the Spanish treasury fleet in 1656 and blockaded Cádiz and destroyed the *flota* in Santa Cruz following year. The Dutch remained neutral and gained the trade with Spain. Cromwell was spending four times what Charles I had. The overseas colonies and a market economy like that in the Netherlands helped to spare England from hardship.[19] Overseas colonies were now changing the face of all the powers in western Europe, from the greatness of Spain to small but growing powers like England. Another state that had gained in wealth, trade and influence was the Netherlands, which, in some ways, became a harbinger for the Thirteen Colonies: it won its independence from a great empire and itself became a formidable power.

The relation between France and Spain also affected England and the Netherlands. Philip II of Spain would not put into the Treaty of Vervins (1598) a provision that would allow the prosecution of French ships in American waters because that would acknowledge their existence there, so that prosecution was avoidable for offending ships from both sides.[20] The assassination of Henry IV, aristocratic factions and religious tensions all weakened France, which may have gained on Spain with the Treaty of the Pyrenees in 1659 but still had a long way to go.[21]

The Netherlands balanced its interests in the East and West. Between 1609 and 1621, the Dutch concentrated most of their efforts in Asia, although trading posts were expanded in Guiana and founded at Fort Orange on the Hudson River in 1614. From 1623 to 1630, Portugal destroyed all the trading-posts where the Dutch, Irish and English traded in the Amazon region. In coastal Brazil and in the Gulf and Guinea in west Africa the Dutch had their greatest success. By 1621 the Dutch, who maintained low prices for trade goods, had supplanted the Portuguese as the main traders in gold and ivory on the Gold Coast. At the end of the truce with Spain in 1621, the war between the Dutch and the Spanish was renewed, and in June 1621 the West India Company was incorporated. Although modelled on the East India Company, this company subordinated its commercial activities to naval and military functions, which was opposite to its prototype venture in Asia. Both companies divided the world in two spheres for the influence and trade of the Netherlands.[22]

How did the Netherlands arrive at a position where it was able to displace Portugal? The Dutch often followed the Portuguese overseas and could use that situation to their advantage. They also studied the positive and negative precedent of Portugal. For example, François Valentijn's work, which is more like a chronicle, noted the arrival of the Portuguese in Ceylon. Emanuel, king of Portugal, had as his representative Payo de Sousa [Lelagius Sousa], who was to ask for an annual tribute of 250,000 pounds of cinnamon in exchange for protection. The king or emperor regretted this treaty and slew some Portuguese, and the violence continued for some years.[23] By studying the relations between Portugal and local populations in terms of trade, culture and politics, the Dutch could try to use this information against Portugal and as a means of creating their own policy for economic and, later on, political expansion. Emulation and displacement were part of a familiar double movement in the history of empire.

In the seventeenth century, the Dutch challenged the Portuguese in trade and empire. In order to exploit the sugar production of Pernambuco and the region as a whole, the Dutch West India Company had captured the northeast of Brazil in 1630. The Company granted religious freedom and offered good conditions for work and trade to the Portuguese on whom the Dutch relied in the specialized world of sugar plantations. A physician to the governor of Dutch Brazil from 1638 to 1644, Willem Piso, edited a key book from this brief Dutch sojourn in this area of Portuguese influence.[24] Portugal traded with Brazil and Africa, where it found gold, ivory and slaves. In the 1630s, the Dutch, who employed many Germans in the Dutch West India Company, attacked the Portuguese slaving stations on the Atlantic coast of Africa as well as their posts in Brazil. Michael Hemmersam was one such German employee: he was in Brazil from 1639 to 1644 and described the slave trade and the peoples of west Africa.[25] The multinational aspect of trade and empire recurred time and time again. Usselincx advocated free rather than slave labour. This issue of slavery would be a crucial one in the Netherlands as profit and labour overcame early opposition to the trading and holding of slaves.

In Asia the rivalries persisted. The Dutch East India Company played a key role in Mughal Bengal from about 1630 and into the first decades of the eighteenth century. Although the East India companies of the Dutch and the English had started out in search of spices like pepper, they came to see other potential in India, which produced manufactured goods such as cloth and agricultural produce.[26] Sometimes Dutch and Indian merchants collaborated in financing voyages, as did the French and Bengali investors. At the end of the seventeenth century, the Dutch silk industry depended on the raw material from Bengal, the kind of relation, as Om Prakash suggested, which was a harbinger of the relation between Europe and Asia in the nineteenth century.[27]

To control the fine spice trade in Asia, the Dutch offered, through treaties, protection in exchange for a monopoly over the spices. The Dutch imitated the Portuguese example of Goa in India by establishing Batavia (now Jakarta) as a hub or rendezvous for its trade. The English and Dutch cooperated for a few years, but in February 1623 the Dutch governor, Herman van Speult, put to death Gabriel Towerson, the English leader on Amboina, nine other Company employees, nine Japanese samurai, and a Portuguese. A propaganda battle broke out between London and Amsterdam. In England something akin to the Black Legend of the Netherlands developed for fifty years or more. Works like *A True Relation of the Unjust, Cruell and Barbarous Proceeding against the*

English reflected this anti-Dutch attitude. A series of events reflected the negotiations and rivalry between England and the Netherlands. The English gave up Run in exchange for New Netherlands, which included Manhattan. There were Anglo-Dutch Wars of 1652–4, 1665–7, 1672–4 and 1780–4. France invaded the Netherlands during the French Revolution. A consequence of this invasion was that, on 31 December 1795, the Dutch East India Company was dissolved. For most of the seventeenth century, it had been the European commercial power in east Asia.[28]

But this is getting ahead of the period in question: the vicissitudes of empire depended on time, place and point of view. If at this time the Dutch were challenging the Portuguese in east Asia, then the British were taking over from Portugal in India. On the west coast of India the Portuguese had been present before Mughal control of the area. Bombay, 160 miles south of Surat, which the sultan of Gujarat ceded to the Portuguese in 1534, was part of the dowry Catherine of Braganza brought to Charles II in 1661. The king handed it over to the East India Company, which made it its headquarters in 1674. In 1700 the English had three strongholds – Madras, Bombay and Calcutta – amid their factories in India.

By the 1680s the English empire was much less tentative that at the turn of the century when it did not have one permanent settlement in North America. In 1685, R.B., most probably Nathaniel Crouch, wrote the *English Empire* which discussed many aspects of imperial expansion, including technology, resources and economics. No longer the leading power, Spain was still there as an example of empire: 'Nothing more pleased the Spaniards than the Gold, which the Innocent Inhabitants exchanged with them for Bells, Glasses, Points, and other Trifles. Columbus got leave of the King of Hispaniola to build a Fort.'[29] The English past was also part of the lesson. R.B. also spoke of Frobisher's attempt in the 1570s to bring gold back from the northern reaches of North America.[30] Riches were an allure to the English as they were to the Spanish. This desire for gold, as if to emulate the success of the Spanish, also came to haunt Walter Ralegh. At about the same time as Frobisher, Francis Drake was sailing for England, but he seemed to be like the French pirates that preceded him in the attack on the Spaniards. Moreover, R.B. called attention to Drake's voyage about the world in 1577, which, unlike Magellan, he had completed himself.[31] Drake also plundered the Spaniards, taking wine, gold, animals, silver, silks, linens and precious stones, and arrived back in Plymouth on 3 November 1580.[32] The economics of piracy were, as they had been for the Vikings, part of a larger economy of expansion for the French and English.

Origins were also important to R.B., who returned to the Cabot voyage to Newfoundland.[33] This later English effort is something R.B. stressed. By commission of Queen Elizabeth, Humphrey Gilbert took possession, so no one else could fish there: he wanted to establish a colony there. It was not until John Guy established a colony there in 1608 that the English claim started to take hold. They gradually built a strong position in the northern reaches of America.

Even though England was by no means a dominant power in the late sixteenth and early seventeenth centuries, it began to build the foundations for later power and influence. Between the 1550s and 1640s the English government set out a model for their future colonization overseas: it built a strong navy. Although created for empire, the navy bore henceforth on all policy in England. Early on, England did not centralize and micromanage its colonies. The government of an English colony had to raise enough funds to pay its bills. The English founded colonies in locales that were either sparsely peopled or had disintegrated politically, as in India. In the late 1800s and early 1900s, the British took advantage of a situation in which they possessed greater technology than the African territories they came to control.[34]

England was subject to economic, technological and political factors in Europe and overseas. The balance of power was delicate and mutable. Trade continued to shift from centre to centre. The first international Bourse of European commerce (exchange) was created in 1460. Philipe de Bon created complete economic liberty. From the beginning of the sixteenth century, Anvers appeared as the principal port of the western world. The port of l'Escault grew owing to the extraordinary development of the marine and transoceanic commerce and came to be in the sixteenth century the principal market of spices and the confluence of commercial currents coming from the Indies and America.[35] This story of economics, then, can only be artificially divided into states because as much as regional and national economies existed, they could not exist in isolation. Here are but a few of these connections in areas of economic interest to the English (later the British) not simply in the New World but in a number of key places.

The English then British empire, like others, was not monolithic. It changed over time according to circumstances. This was true in south Asia but also applied to the east. In east Asia the English found that the Chinese dominated maritime trade from Sumatra and Java to Japan. The English also saw that the Dutch were allowed to stay in Japan after the Portuguese were expelled and that after 1644 the Manchu invaders captured Beijing and established the Ch'ing dynasty. In resistance and flight, Cheng Ch'eng-kung (Koxinga) drove the Dutch out of their stronghold of Fort Zeelandia in Taiwan. English ships traded in Canton from 1699 and were later joined by Dutch, French, Danish, Austrian, Swedish, Indian and (after the War of Independence) American ships. The language of trade there was first Portuguese and then pidgin: a British embassy to the emperor in 1793 had both sides communicating by writing in Latin.[36] Just as the Portuguese had adapted to different circumstances in various parts of the world, so too did the English. The daily practices of empire took unexpected turns.

England in America

The work of Robert Johnson, John Smith, Samuel Purchas, and Thomas Scott, the first the author of promotional tracts, the second a governor, promoter and historian of Virginia, the third a collector and editor, heir literally to Hakluyt, and someone who never travelled to America, and the fourth a Protestant propagandist of the 1620s who was bent on creating opposition to the royal marriage between Spain and England, demonstrated the differences and divisions within English views of Spain, but none of them could think about the establishment of a permanent settlement in Virginia without considering Spanish America. In Johnson's *Nova Britannia* (1609), a promotional tract about Virginia, he had much to say about the Spanish. This work was dedicated to Thomas Smith, a member of the king's council for Virginia, treasurer of the colony, and governor of the Moscovy and East India companies.[37] For Johnson, the papal donations were 'legendary fables'.[38] Johnson's *The New Life of Virginea* (1612) also used the ideas of *translatio imperii* and the example of Spain.[39] Johnson expressed his mixed feelings towards the example of Spain.[40] William Strachey's *The Historie of Travell into Virginia Britannia* (1612) was also an important document in setting out English colonial aspirations in a New World dominated by the Spaniards. Moreover, Strachey's unvarnished view and the Virginia Company's defensiveness suggest the fragility and precariousness of the English colonies in the Americas, something like the instability of the French colonies there. One of the justifications that recurred in these narratives was religion. For Strachey, the aim was 'to endeavour the conversion of the natiues, to the knowledg and worshippe of the true God, and the world's-Redeemer Christ Iesus'.[41] Strachey warned his English readers about Spain, more specifically about how the Spaniards killed Huguenots in Florida and how the French had their revenge.[42] In building colonies in North America, the English should resist Spanish cruelty by learning about the example of the French in Florida.

Virginia was also a key to English colonization in T.A.'s dedication of John Smith's *A Map of Virginia* (1612).[43] Criticizing the Spanish treatment of the Natives during the conquest of the New World became problematic because the English now found themselves in conflict with the inhabitants of America. Such English narratives constructed the Natives as desiring to surrender their sovereignty to England. Another example was 'The Proceedings of the English Colonie in Virginia . . .' by William Symonds, which was appended to Smith's work in one volume. It portrayed the Natives and the Dutch as treacherous in their dealings with the English. The Dutch were said to have supported Powhatan, a chief, in the betrayal and attempted murder of John Smith.[44] Smith, who portrayed Columbus as a bold visionary, called attention to the notion of imitation.[45] For Smith, a personal and national model could be found in class mobility, skill as soldiers and captains and the memory of their great glory as servants to the king of Spain. This New World allowed for merit and daring. The Dutch, like the Spanish, continued to be a topic of discussion in English texts. Samuel Purchas translated or reworked translations of Spanish works in Hakluyt's papers.[46] Purchas included 'A Note touching the Dutch' in his prefatory matter, where he 'related such abuses of some of that Nation in the East Indies and Greenland to the English there.'[47] Some writers, like Thomas Scott, were far more direct and one-sided in their depiction of Spain than Purchas was. Anti-Spanish sentiment in England persisted and coincided with the Pilgrims' voyage to the New World. One of the best instances of this negative use of the example of Spain was the work of the prolific Scott during the 1620s. His anti-Spanish and anti-Catholic propaganda included *An Experimentall Discoverie of Spanish Practises or the Counsell of a Well-Wishing Souldier* ([London], 1623).

Spain continued as a preoccupation in the 1630s, 1640s and beyond. The supporters of the commonwealth or republic in England were not any kinder to Spain than were their royalist opponents. In the middle of the English Civil War, Thomas Gage produced a work that would become popular and would catch the attention of Oliver Cromwell and be used in his 'Western Design', the attempt to attack and supplant Spain in the West Indies.[48] Gage's work became politically instrumental.[49] His knowledge of New Spain would give England an advantage in trying to displace the Spaniards in America.

There was a French angle to this text, so that intertextuality continued to play an important role in colonization. Gage's work was translated into French and served the interests of Colbert, who saw Spain as a rival to France.[50] As Spain and Holland were allied against France in the Dutch War (1672–8), this was one reason Colbert sponsored the translation of Gage. His text was supposed to reveal Spanish secrets about its American colonies.[51] About two decades before, Cardinal Mazarin had focused on the war with Spain and, to gain Cromwell's support, he gave him free run of the Atlantic.[52] The war between France and Spain ended in 1658.

Virginia continued to have problems under the English republic, and soon the Caribbean would create obstacles for the English who had designs on the Spanish colonies there.[53] On 19 April 1654, peace with Holland was proclaimed. Soon the Western Design against Spanish America was begun. John Cotton saw a typology between the expulsion of the Spanish from America and the drying up of the Euphrates in Revelation.[54] In 1654 Thomas Gage, who became chaplain to the expedition to the West Indies, wrote a government report on the proposed attack, and the next year his work, *The English American his Travail by Sea and Land* (1648), was reprinted under another title. In 1655 Roger Williams wrote to John Winthrop about the expedition and connected Cotton's interpretation with the Protector's 'strong thoughts of Hispaniola and Cuba'.[55] Moreover, a revival of Las Casas was an aspect of this republican propaganda against Spain. In 1656 John Phillips' translation of Las Casas, *The Tears of the Indians*, had an extended title that appealed even more to the victims of Spanish cruelty and to the emotions of the English reader. Phillips addressed to the Lord Protector in dramatic fashion.[56] He represented Cromwell as the arm of God's revenge, the advancer of his glory: God would recompense the Protector, crowning him with fame.[57] Against the facts, Phillips celebrated Cromwell's victory over the Spanish, when there was not great triumph.[58] The Western Design, largely a failure, was an embarrassment and a defeat to Cromwell and England. Spain was not a straw man in a propagandist's pamphlet: the discourse of Gage and the expansionist party in England came up against the wall of actuality.[59] The decline of Spain was more apparent in Europe: in America it was still strong.

Another English translation of Las Casas came out in 1689. The same old charges of the Black Legend appeared here. Las Casas' text was translated again during the build-up to the War of the Spanish Succession.[60] This book was translated from the French version of J. B. Morvan de Belle-Garde, *La découverte des Indes Occidentales, par les Espanols* (Paris, 1697).[61] Once more, the intertextuality of French and English editions of Las Casas extended to the Netherlands and beyond.

John Harris's two-volume folios of 1705 announced its debt to Hakluyt, Ramusio and others and that the volumes included original papers, such as '*the Pope's Bull, to Dispose of the West-Indies to the King of Spain*', and emphasized that the histories and other allied works related to the four parts of the world, especially America.[62] Melchisédech Thévenot had borrowed from Hakluyt and Purchas: Harris used Thévenot.[63] Although English anxieties about rivalry in the New World shifted in part from Spain to Holland and France, the Spanish origins to colonization of the New World and worry about Catholicism remained in England into the eighteenth century. A triumphalism also arose that was based on the Protestant victory in the Glorious Revolution of 1688, successful wars with rivals, and the decline of Spain.[64] The myth was stressed, here and elsewhere, that England ruled out of duty and against its will.

In the War of the Spanish Succession or Queen Anne's War, British writers would be concerned with Spain's role in Europe and America. Like Harris, John Oldmixon discussed the Spanish. In *The British Empire in America* . . . (1708) Oldmixon recalled the Romans, Columbus, the preoccupation with Spain and the origins of European settlement in the Americas, and the developing rivalry with the Netherlands. The war with Spain and the contention with the Spanish in the West Indies proved the significance of colonies in the New World to the Spanish and British.[65] The decline of Spain was not a simple and direct narrative for a Britain on the rise. The relation was triangulated with other states, such as the Netherlands and France.

France and Its Colonies in the New World

France began to establish enduring colonies in the Americas in the seventeenth century. One of the key figures in the colonization of New France was Samuel de Champlain, who was an associate of Sieur de Monts and who had experience in the Spanish West Indies before he founded Québec in 1608. The work of Champlain, Marc Lescarbot and Pierre d'Avity embodied ambivalent attitudes to the Spanish empire. As France was on the verge of establishing permanent settlements in North America, its colonizers and writers were learning from, and posing a threat to, Spain. The French still seemed closer to the Spanish than the English despite James I's policy of peace with Spain. As Marcel Trudel suggests, Champlain was quiet about his private life, might have converted from Protestantism to Catholicism, and crossed the Atlantic twenty-one times.[66]

Marc Lescarbot was a lawyer, poet and humanist. He lived in the Port-Royal colony from July 1606 to the next summer when de Monts' licence expired and the entire colony was returned to the Crown. Lescarbot became the chronicler of Acadia, was apt to comment on Spain and was a Catholic who maintained friendships with Protestants.[67] He concentrated on French discoveries in the New World.[68] Lescarbot presented paeans to France and expatiated on the greatness of his country that would have the Orient and south equate 'Christian' with 'French'.[69] Lescarbot was defensive about the relation of Spain to France.[70] Besides cruelty, another element of the Black Legend appeared here: greed.[71] Lescarbot envisaged discontents and unemployed tradesmen going to the colonies rather than being lost to foreign lands.[72] He told the story of French failures in the New World.[73] Whereas Lescarbot mostly borrowed

from Jean de Léry (ten chapters), he did defend André Thevet's imaginative Brazil as a means of inciting others to support and transform the
colony (which drew so much sarcasm in François de Belleforest).[74]
Lescarbot used the language of Christian republicanism and of a French
preoccupation – 'la gloire' – a glory that involved honour, courage, civilization and evangelization in a way that only France could produce.[75]

Pierre d'Avity, sieur de Montmartin, collected information about the
New World. He was interested in Catholicism as a key factor in colonial
policy and relations with Spain. While assuming an ideology of a united
Catholicism, d'Avity concentrated most on geographical information and
described America in his *Les Estats, empires et principavtez dv monde . . .*
(1613).[76] The sheer bulk in d'Avity devoted to the description of the
Spanish empire attested to its pre-eminence. Two years later an English
edition of d'Avity appeared in London.[77] In d'Avity's scheme the New
World received almost as much space as France.[78] D'Avity noted that the
depopulation of the Natives in Peru occurred because of disease and civil
war among the Spaniards, who moved the 'Indians' from place to place
far from their country and worked them excessively.[79] Grimeston's
English translation was more explicit about Spanish cruelty.[80] D'Avity
also presented colonization positively.[81] He saw America in religious
terms: Spain kept the Muslims from taking the Philippines and the English
from seizing America.[82] This Frenchman's Spain as a providential leader
was not the Spain that destroyed the Huguenots' colonies.

The question of religion continued to divide France at home and in its
colonies, sometimes in strange ways. At Port Royal, some of the settlers
were Catholic and some Protestant.[83] Sieur de Monts and Samuel de
Champlain were the founders of New France, which was, in 1627, to
become for Catholics only or for those who wished to convert to
Catholicism. After the Peace of Alais in 1629, which took away the political privileges of the Huguenots, Richelieu's adversarial policy towards
them changed and he protected them, whereas the Cardinal was no longer
on good terms with the 'ultra-Catholics' because they were allies with
Spain, a country Richelieu was wary of and a part of the Habsburg lands
that surrounded France.[84] The religious missionary work in the New
World interested the French clergy, but was something the French
Protestants could no longer approach officially. In this respect, Cardinal
Richelieu made French America more like Spanish America. As the
French did not seem to emigrate in large numbers, Cardinal Richelieu also
encouraged the Flemish and Dutch to emigrate as long as they were
Catholics or converted to Catholicism. In building the power and glory
of a centralized monarchy, he did not like the privileges, especially control
of fortresses like La Rochelle, that the Edict of Nantes had granted to
Protestants in 1598.

In May 1628, before La Rochelle, which had been subdued after a long siege, a charter was signed creating *La Compaignie des 100 Associés*, a provision of which specified that the company people New France with Catholics only. Another article of the new charter declared that converted Natives would be considered French subjects and could settle in France with full rights. This new company was to replace *La Compaignie de Caen*, whose directors were Huguenots and who were suspected of planning to make Canada Protestant in order to secede from France and to ally itself with the Netherlands and England. Like the Dutch, the French first commissioned companies to trade with its colonies in 1602, but the French companies, seventy-five of which were chartered from 1599 to 1789, were undercapitalized. The Levantine trade was still too profitable to attract much financing for New France.[85] The Jesuits and Capucins had concentrated on bringing back French Protestants to Catholicism, but they began to look overseas.[86]

During the 1630s and 1640s, religious concerns intensified once again in the colonization of the New World. After the English and French were establishing permanent colonies in North America and were trying to maintain them and to encourage their growth, England and France became rivals and focused their attention on each other as well as on the power of Spain. An example of the French preoccupation with the English in North America can be observed in Gabriel Sagard's *History of Canada . . .* (1636).[87] Conversion became a central goal of New France in its first decades, which was one of the pretexts, as well as the occupation of the land, that France used from the early sixteenth century to challenge the right of Portugal and Spain to the New World. Another example that raised expectations amongst the French was the riches of Peru. Sagard described it as perhaps having the richest deposits of gold and silver in the world as a means of talking about the Spanish possession of that country and the ransom king Atabaliba offered the Spaniards. The anxiety Sagard anticipated in his readers was the inadequacy of New France beside the Spanish colonies.[88] The success of Spanish Recollets, real and imagined, in conversion in America and the Far East became a model that the French amongst the Hurons in Canada sought to imitate.[89]

French religious writing in and about the New World was also indebted to Spanish influences even as, in some instances, the writers resisted Spain or felt ambivalent about its colonization, particularly in its treatment of the Natives. In France, collections also helped to promote colonies in the New World, and between 1632 and 1672, the Jesuits published their annual relations, partly in order to promote their mission to the Natives to patrons from the upper class.[90] Occasionally, the Jesuits in New France found themselves commenting on more temporal and political matters. Francisco Bressani, an Italian, wrote a relation or account from New

France in 1653 that set out a brief history of the relations between the French and the English and other Europeans. Here, he said that although some had supposed that the Spanish had discovered and named Canada, the French had taken possession in 1504.[91] In the missions of French priests to the New World, there was a double movement of French colonial thought on policy and the transnational nature of religious orders or sects.

Accounts of America in French in the sixteenth century had been overwhelmingly Protestant, but in the seventeenth century they were Catholic. The French Franciscans, who, from 1612 to 1614, were part of the colony of Maragnan in the Amazon delta that usurped what was called Maranhoa, seemed to have had a closer connection with Franciscans in Iberian colonies.[92] Sometimes the French priests, such as the Dominican Jean Baptiste Du Tertre, who wrote *Histoire générale des isles de S. Christophe* . . . (1654), could take a sympathetic view of Natives and try to disabuse people in France of misconceptions.[93] He also noted the way the French watched the English colony flourish with a large population while the French one diminished.[94]

In the seventeenth century, France often shifted its policy on religion in the New World, sometimes resembling Spain's religious politics and sometimes not. Religious directives also had racial and economic dimensions. In order to encourage the growth of the white population in the islands, like Martinique, during the 1660s, Colbert advocated the toleration of Jews and Huguenots, a divergence from the Catholic-only policy that Spain had followed and that France had considered when Richelieu assumed power in the 1620s, but he repealed this tolerance and the liberal conditions for African slaves, Huguenots and Jews in the 'Code noir' (1685), which was instituted under his son, Seignelay.[95]

The French, like the English, had designs on the Spanish colonies in the West Indies. Las Casas was still used for political ends, as in the role of the English translation of 1656 in Cromwell's Western Design. It is also possible that Comte de Pagan's *Relation* (1655), a translation of Spanish texts on the Amazon, was part of French plans for an assault on the Spanish colonies in South America, a kind of French counterpart to the Western Design.[96] In the 'Epistle Dedicatory' of the English translation of 1661, the translator, William Hamilton, explained to Charles II that the work was first addressed to 'Cardinal *Mazarine*, in order to have set his Majesty of *France* on conquest of the great Kingdome of the *Amazone* to himself'.[97] Hamilton exhorted the king to seek out this land unpossessed by the Portuguese and Spanish, 'For it is possest by the barbarous Natives only'.[98]

The glory of France and French expansion was a theme in many texts. In his *Description of Louisiana* . . . (1683), Louis Hennepin, a Recollet father, wrote a record of the La Salle expedition, which he dedicated to Louis XIV.[99] Hennepin said that he would never have dared to offer the king a relation of the new discovery if the author had not had the glory of obeying such a glorious monarch, in 'the conversion of the Infidels'.[100]]The second expedition of 1684 was recounted in Henri Joutel, *Journal Historique du dernier voyage que feu M. de la Sale fit* (Paris, 1713), which also sought to refute Hennepin.[101] This account recalled the deaths of Jean de Brébeuf and his fellow missionaries at the hands of the Iroquois in New France during the 1640s. The Natives were to be tamed and won over as friends in part with an account of the heroic virtues of the French king. Ambivalence and contradiction inhabited the French texts of the New World.

The spectre of England haunted France in the New World. Both Pierre Boucher's and Baron de Lahontan's accounts revealed that the French in North America were now often more concerned about the English than the Spanish. This shift was, in part, a sign that the balance of power was shifting and that concerns about the closest threats often won out over distant theoretical problems. The writing by French authors was varied over this period in which France itself rose to become a power in Europe and a force in empire. This rise is a significant aspect of the last four decades of the seventeenth and the first fifteen years of the eighteenth century. The years in which Louis XIV reigned with the full power of his monarchy were a time of growing French power at home and abroad.

The Rise of France

The reign of Louis XIV (1643–1715) marked a time when its neighbours left a vacuum for French power to grow. Spain tried to gain back Portugal to no avail. England was involved in a civil war, the killing of its king, the restoration of Charles II, the Glorious Revolution of 1688 and other conflicts that prevented it from gaining its full potential economically in overseas influence. The Netherlands faced the rivalry of the English. In March 1661, when Louis XIV took up his full duties, Sweden and Denmark were weakened by war, the Austrians faced a threat from the Ottoman empire, the Protestant princes in Germany were preoccupied with the Catholic Habsburgs, and the Poles were squeezed between Sweden and Russia. The French could play one side off against the other and have the peace for Louis, with the support of minister like Colbert, to revamp the administration and fund the military. All this allowed Louis to pursue that great object that his predecessors sought, but under much more divided circumstances – 'la gloire', or glory.[102]

While England and the Netherlands were engaged in their second war in 1665, the French, who were supposed to support the Dutch, were more inclined to expand into the southern Low Countries, which were still under the aegis of a weakened Spain. In May 1667, the French invaded and took possession of many towns in the southern Netherlands. The Europeans were every bit as fickle in their alliances in Europe as they were overseas. The English and the Dutch soon made peace and, with Sweden, checked Louis' ambitions with the Treaty of Aix-La-Chapelle in 1668. Louis was not pleased with the Dutch. Colbert hit the Netherlands with tariffs while France built up its military until it invaded in 1672. The English fought against the Dutch in the third Anglo-Dutch War (1672–4), but withdrew as the Dutch contained them at sea and the war became unpopular. Louis' growing power raised concerns in Europe, and soon France was fighting German states, the Habsburg Empire, Spain and Denmark in addition to the Netherlands, led by William of Orange. French and Dutch commerce suffered to the benefit of England, so, in 1678, the merchants of Amsterdam pressed the government to seek peace with France, which occurred under the peace treaties of 1678–9. As the Germans relied on Dutch and French subsidies and the English on the French, so the keys to the struggle in the second half of the seventeenth century were the Netherlands and France. The French took Luxembourg from Spain in 1683. But France soon faced resistance. Its mistreatment of the Huguenots under the revocation in 1685 of the Edict of Nantes alarmed Protestant states in Europe. The Austrians drove out the Ottomans from near Vienna in 1687, and William of Orange became King of England in 1688 (deposing James II, who was the last Catholic king of England or Britain), while France was invading Germany. France stood alone against Catholic and Protestant powers. This was a trade war and a military contest in Europe and overseas. Fighting occurred globally – in Pondicherry, the West Indies, Newfoundland and Acadia. Famine in France and exhausting taxes in the Netherlands and England helped bring the two parties to peace, after nine years of war, under the Treaty of Ryswick in 1697. More or less, the English, Dutch and Germans had kept France out of Flanders. But this was not to last. One of Louis' grandsons was offered the throne of Spain in 1700, which gave him a pretext to occupy the southern Netherlands for his grandson, Philip V, in return for monopolies for French traders in the Spanish empire. In 1701, Austria, Britain and the Netherlands entered into what came to be known as the War of the Spanish Succession in an attempt to curb Bourbon ambitions in Europe and the world. Spanish silver from the American colonies and French might combined. None the less, Austria was strong, and England (soon to be Britain in the middle of this war) had a great general in Marlborough, paid great subsidies to German allies, and built up a vast fleet and army.

The Grand Alliance was a worthy force to check Louis. Marlborough's victory at Blenheim in 1704 kept France and their Bavarian allies from invading Austria while the battle of Ramilles in 1706 allowed the English and Dutch to take most of the southern Netherlands. The Royal Navy, which was now eclipsing the Dutch navy, worked with this ally to maintain Portugal, a new ally against France and Spain, and a source of Brazilian gold. The Grand Alliance attacked the French possessions in North America and the West Indies. Wars continued to be global in the world of these empires. The Royal Navy seized Gibraltar and thereby divided the Spanish and French fleets by controlling the entrance to the Mediterranean. The French returned to piracy with attacks on commercial ships. In 1712, Britain left the war, the Dutch followed suit, and Archduke Charles of Austria, who had become the Holy Roman emperor, realizing that he could not become king of Spain and be emperor, also exited the conflict.[103]

The War of the Spanish Succession ended with the treaties of Utrecht in 1713 and of Rastadt in 1714. The power of France came to be challenged by the British. Britain gained Gibraltar, Minorca, Newfoundland, Nova Scotia, the lands surrounding Hudson Bay, and trade concessions on the Spanish colonies of the New World. The Habsburg empires received Milan, Naples, Sardinia and the southern Netherlands, but the United Provinces (the Dutch) began to decline and had to guard its southern boundary in the years to come. France, as Kennedy has noted, suffered seven times the government debt.[104] So when George of Hanover became George I in 1714 and Louis XIV died in 1715, the balance of power had shifted. The great empire now was the British empire, but Napoleon I, Kaiser Wilhelm and Adolf Hitler would challenge it in Europe and, as always in this typology, overseas. Ultimately, Britain was the first great colonial power from 1713 to 1815, and an even greater imperial power from 1815 to 1914. Nevertheless, Britain, like any great power before or after, could not be assured supremacy. France and others had learned that lesson. Others, like the Soviet Union and the United States since 1945, have gathered as much. And each empire had internal injustices or tensions. For instance, even amid the tolerance of the Netherlands, the Dutch empire tolerated slavery. Ambivalence and contradiction surrounded a political economy based in part on enforced labour and the slave trade and institution of slavery.

Slavery: the Dutch in Context

The slave trade in the English, Dutch and French colonies had ambivalent beginnings. For instance, the Dutch had been weary of or had opposed the slave trade with Africa. In 1596 the city fathers in Middleburg had freed a hundred slaves brought as cargo there. In 1608, Willem Usselincx had opposed the use of black slaves in Dutch America. A Dutch ship brought twenty black slaves to Virginia in 1619: it may have captured them through piracy from a Portuguese slaving ship. Commodities depended on slave labour. Like sugar before it and cotton afterwards, tobacco came to rely on enforced work. After the Dutch capture of Paraíba and Pernambuco in 1634 to 1636, the demand for slaves changed the Dutch position. Rather than use German labour, Johan Mauretis chose to go the route of African slaves in the sugar-mills. The conflict between a quick financial fix and the longer ethical view divided people from themselves or from their neighbours.[105] Piracy was another form of economic opportunism in the face of legitimate commerce.[106] The Dutch navy was powerful and its economic clout was substantial, but a friction between the public sphere of politics and the private realm of finance made it more difficult for the Netherlands to succeed in this struggle in the southern part of the New World.

Long after Columbus, the Spaniards had understood the importance of black slaves to their imperial wealth. In Lima in 1646, for example, José de los Ríos complained that a shortage of black slaves would ruin Peru because the riches of the hacienda and kingdom were based on the labour of those Africans. The Netherlands also understood how important the links were among their various spheres of influence. In 1652 the Dutch East India Company founded a refreshment station at Table Bay for crews fighting scurvy in their journeys between Europe and Asia and in 1657 they began to encourage permanent settlement. This would be the basis for the future of the southern tip of Africa.

Opposition to slavery was there from the beginning. The groundwork for a movement against slavery had been laid as early as the fifteenth century. In the seventeenth century more examples of anti-slavery voices arose. Pope Urban VIII had condemned slavery in a letter of 1639 and threatened excommunication to those who practised it; Richard Baxter insulted slave-holders by comparing them to conquistadores; in 1688 Aphra Behn published a novel, *Oronooko*, which exposed the inhumanity of slavery.

During the 1680s, when *Oronooko* had appeared, the French were codifying slavery in their Caribbean colonies. The first Code Noir was promulgated under Louis XIV (r. 1643–1715) under the influence of Jean-Baptiste Colbert (1616–83), and the second under Louis XV in 1724. This later version shed Articles 5, 7, 8, 18 and 25 of the version of the Code Noir of 1685. The two codes insisted on the humanity of slaves, but codified slavery and linked blackness to it. For instance, the code of 1685 opened with a declaration of a paternalistic and providential view of the king's role in the French empire. The document stated that it is the king's duty to extend his care or protection to 'all the peoples that Divine Providence has placed under our obeisance' and regulated slaves.[107] Although some important protections existed in this code, it also allowed masters to treat their slaves with great severity in the face of violence, insubordination or any strong challenge to their authority and the hierarchy that sustained it. Article 1 prohibited Jews unless they converted. Article 2 set out that slaves were to be baptized and instructed as Catholics. Moreover, Article 3 interdicted the practice of any religion except Catholicism. Article 13 regulated marriages so that, whether free or enslaved, black children would inherit the legal status of their mothers. Article 15 forbade that slaves be in possession of offensive arms.[108] The brutality and violence of such a code had glimpses of humane treatment of slaves, but still underpinned a cold and deadly institution.

Although the permanent population grew slowly in southern Africa, German, Dutch and, to a lesser extent, French Huguenot settlers – some freeburgers and others not – helped the population grow. In 1707 the Dutch ceased to grant free passage and afterwards natural increase was responsible for demographic increase. There were some former Asian and African slaves, and some of them came to own land. Moreover, some of the white settlers married former slave women. Their children were assimilated into the white community.[109] Complications occurred in relations between those who were settlers and who were not and between black and white populations in South Africa. These connections became even more so over time. The Dutch are but one instance in this wide network of slavery, including in Brazil, which has not been included here because of the section on Brazil itself, which also discusses slavery. And dominance occurred in other forms. Some Natives sought to be equals or partners in cultural and other forms of mediation.

Native Voices: the Case of Squanto

In the early period, Native voices were often reported, represented or ventriloquized in European texts. An example from New England also shows the ambivalence and contradictions within and between European and Native people. Even though Squanto suffered badly at the hands of the English and had witnessed the decimation of his nation through pestilence, he chose mediation over revenge. In this he differed from Don Luis de Velasco, a Native kidnapped by the Spanish. Squanto was a male Patuxent Indian who acted as a translator and interpreter for the Pilgrims at Plymouth. John Smith left Thomas Hunt in charge of the fisheries in 1614. That had dire consequences for Squanto.

Discord happened among the English, with consequences for the Natives. Freedom and slavery divided. Acting against his superiors' wishes, Hunt captured Squanto and about twenty other Natives. He took them to Malaga in Spain to sell them into slavery, but most were saved by friars. In 1617, Squanto was in London and then travelled to Newfoundland. By 1619, he was back home and convinced his English hosts of his value as a go-between. He found his people gone, victims of disease. He was taken captive several times by different anti-English Native nations. Eventually, as his position as a mediator weakened, Squanto seems to have made trouble to ensure the necessity of his mediation.[110] Being a mediator meant potential mistrust on both sides. Identities in the New World and other colonies, for European and Native, were in flux from the start.

William Bradford is a major source for the story of Squanto. In *Of Plymouth Plantation: 1620–1647* (published 1847) Bradford represented Squanto's ambivalent situation. As Bradford's papers were not published for more than another two hundred years, the immediate effect of his representation did not have a public. Bradford's work could not, at least through a written record, affect his immediate successors and their children. Bradford viewed this mediator as a divine gift to the Pilgrims.[111] In *A Briefe Relation of the Discovery and Plantation of New England* (1622), Thomas Dermer related more about how he was nearly killed when the Nausets took him prisoner. He also described how, in 1619, he seized some of them in order to escape, which shows how tense the region was at the time Squanto was acting as a mediator.[112] In fact, Bradford reported that while Dermer was going ashore to trade in what is now called Martha's Vineyard, with Squanto at his side, 'he was betrayed and assaulted' by the Natives, his usual trading partners, so that all but Squanto, a boatman and Dermer were killed.[113] Dermer later died of his wounds. Bradford did not say who betrayed Dermer, but while the Natives are blamed, no censure is attached to Squanto.[114] The governor saw the subtleties and difficulties in this situation and, more generally, in the contact between the English and the indigenous peoples.

The relations among the Natives and Europeans were strained. Bradford reported that the Natives kept aloof from the English because they had killed French castaways on Cape Cod and enslaved the three or four survivors, of whom Dermer redeemed two. Bradford noted that the Natives confessed all this and that they thought that the *Mayflower* was coming to revenge their act against the French.[115] Squanto's help was indispensable. In 1621, after the *Mayflower* departed, many of the Pilgrims benefited from Squanto's help.[116] He became necessary for the very survival of the English.[117] Squanto never got to tell his side of the story.

Another well-known New England colonist, Captain Miles Standish, continued to use Squanto as a guide and interpreter after the controversy over whether this Native was reliable. On one expedition, Standish became ill and Bradford had to take over, and Squanto died.[118] Bradford represented Squanto, even in death, as being between Native and English: his sickness is Indian and the heaven he hopes for, English. The reader hears of Squanto's mediation through Bradford's mediation, his acculturation through the Governor's culture. In this account, there are, however, glimpses of the struggle and the predicament in which Squanto found himself. Bradford displayed affection for Squanto, but the voice of the Native dwelt and dwells in the occasional detail and in the silence of what he did not say in a text written in English for the English. It is still important to take into account many Native points of view in the colonies, and this is but one such example. It is a sounding. Other experiences, beyond the New World, place the European view in context, such as those in eastern Europe and east Asia. In this book personal voices and impersonal trends and structures qualify one another. And these contexts occur in a comparative and relational context.

Japan and Russia

The western Europeans were not alone in their aspirations and experiences in expansion. Although not as large or populous as the Ming, Ottoman and Mogul empires, Japan and Russia experienced political and economic expansion in the sixteenth century. Whereas a centralized bureaucracy under the watch of the emperor governed China, feudal lords and their clans, not the emperor, were the powers in Japan for most of the sixteenth century.[119] European armaments affected Japan and other countries in the world, so that warlords, like Hideyoshi (died 1598) and later Ieyasu and other shogans of the Tokugawa clan, centralized military rule. The Japanese government expelled the Portuguese in 1639 and the Portuguese mission for readmission to Japan failed in 1647. The imperial and commercial enterprise of the Portuguese in Asia, according to Sanjay Subrahmanyam, evolved markedly between 1500 and 1700 as a result of changes in South America, Africa and east Asia as well as in the metropolis and involved the Society of Jesus and Japanese silver among its key factors.[120] The only trade with Europeans was restricted to a Dutch ship permitted to call at Deshima in Nagasaki harbour. Christians (native and foreign) were murdered and other feudal lords and their families were watched closely and were often controlled as though hostages. Although Japan grew more populous and prosperous under this reign of relative peace, it was also like China in one important regard: it did not adopt industrial and technological developments from other countries. Even though the Japanese elite was more open to foreigners than its Chinese counterpart, it still fell behind the western powers in technology.

Russia, despite the disruptions of trading routes with the lands to the west by the Ottoman empire, Sweden, Lithuania and Poland, found that European muskets and cannon allowed it to use gunpowder to defeat the Asian horsemen that threatened it.[121] Eastern and southern expansion was easier because the new western technology in armaments was lacking there. The Poles occupied Moscow between 1608 and 1613. Pioneers and explorers pushed beyond the Urals through Siberia to the Pacific in 1638. The Russians ruled over a multicultural empire that was a resource and a potential source of division. In 1500 – as opposed to 1900 or 1950 – Russia did not appear to be a great power. In its expansion, as rapid and far-reaching as that was, Russia faced many challenges that made it lag behind the western European powers and, later, the United States: extremes in climate, great distances and poor communications; military absolutism; serfdom and consequent static agriculture; the Orthodox church's monopoly in education; resistance to foreigners (who were segregated); resistance to modernization. Under Peter I (Peter the Great: ruled 1689–1725), Russia emerged as a European power, being opened to Westernization in education, culture, the military and industry. Between 1703 and 1725, Peter had even erected on a site in a Baltic province conquered from Sweden the new capital city of St Petersburg, which had grown from scratch to 40,000 inhabitants. This was Peter the Great's window on the west.[122] Peter I's reforms did not always hold or progress after his death, when a period of instability and rapid changes in rulers ensued.

Transitions

In the story of empire and colony it does not take long for one empire to decline and fall while another rises. These patterns are a little more uneven and intricate than this simple shape, now so ingrained in the language of empire, especially since Gibbon. As Spain declined, so did the Netherlands rise, and in turn as the Netherlands declined, so did France rise. But with the end of the War of the Spanish Succession in 1713 and with the death of Louis XIV in 1715, the French were already feeling the growth of British power. London would be a centre among centres from 1713 to 1945, but not without struggles with France and Germany, which had their own imperial longings. The British empire would dissolve even faster than it took to assemble as the world power. But that is getting too far ahead. The story of the eighteenth and early nineteenth centuries is one of revolution and freedom building on the Dutch Revolt and the English Revolution of the sixteenth and seventeenth centuries. Some key groups did not share in these evolving liberties.

But there was not necessarily liberty for all, such as for the indigenous peoples and slaves. There might be, as Thomas Jefferson later hoped, a pursuit of happiness, but violence and injustice were in the worlds of empire, decolonization and beyond. The eighteenth century was also an age in which industrialization first occurred and in which women and children at home and overseas were exploited, and a time when the economy developed energy sources beyond the one in the biological order of an agrarian or hunting economy. This meant that nature was increasingly under stress.[123] The late eighteenth and early nineteenth centuries were when the French and then the British lost their key colonies in North America and when the Spanish lost theirs in the New World. Flux is the story of empire. And colonies will not remain colonies for ever. And some even become their own empires. And that is the part of the story of empires and colonies to which we now turn.

4

The Rise of Britain and France: 1713–1830

⟡

Even after such a long time since Portugal pushed south into Africa and Columbus landed in the New World, the English, French and Dutch found themselves facing some similar quandaries to those that the Portuguese and Spanish faced. Would they use cheap labour or slavery to fuel their empires and how would ideas from the Enlightenment or revolutions affect their colonies and inhabitants, indigenous and settler? What would be the effect of the Industrial Revolution and of the beginnings of European military and economic pre-eminence in the world? By continuing this comparative discussion of the western European empires, Russia and the new independent states in the Americas, including the United States, I hope to show the ambivalence in, between and among empires and colonies (and former colonies) and the stresses on lands and peoples that this radical departure from earlier economies – agricultural and commercial – produced. Once again a tension within individuals and between them and systems suggests some of the pressures that this change had on Europeans and other peoples.

Military and economic changes, although seemingly abstract, had material consequences in the daily lives and the practical experience of cultures. The very contention of Europe, its fractiousness and division, created rivalries that the larger and more populous and developed empires of India and China did not. The pain and violence of competition and innovation led the Europeans and those who were in their empires or who came into contact with them to feel the brunt of expansion and economic growth. Disease and death continued to affect how that history unfolded and how much shock occurred to those who lived through it. Part of the function of the sections on other voices and on slavery is to serve as a reminder of individuals, and often those whose voices were often not from the group that was driving this expansion – that is, the men from elites or who served elites in Europe and the cities of its colonies or former colonies. Many of these institutions, such as slavery, and practices, such as the wars with, or pushing aside of, indigenous peoples, persisted for centuries.

The eighteenth century involved a rivalry between the French and British empires. Revolts and revolutions, based on claims for rights, actually occurred on and off from the Revolt of the Netherlands in the late sixteenth century to the revolutions of the nineteenth century in 1830 and 1848. As the power of the Netherlands subsided, that of France and Britain grew. From the death of Louis XIV to the last exile of Napoleon, France was a world power with which to be reckoned. Still, despite the setback of the American War of Independence, the British empire came to be the dominant force in the world, which was especially true from 1815 to 1914. How did that happen? It is always important to remember that even dominant states and empires have less power than their leaders think. In the details of accounting, economics and war, the story of empire played out.

Finances, Warfare and Revolt: the Balance of Empires

Britain and France followed Portugal into India and were rivals there. British power gathered in the Indian subcontinent. Aurungzeb, the last of the powerful Mughal emperors, died in 1707. Subsequently, divisions occurred, and his successors weakened the imperial government, its viceroys setting themselves up as independent rulers in Hyderabad, Ouhd and Bengal. In 1709, the Old and New East India Companies united and increased profits from their centres in Bombay (Mumbai), Madras and Calcutta. In 1739, from the northwest, Nadir Shah of Persia invaded India, defeated the emperor and sacked his capital, Delhi. By 1740 Britain was importing from India over £1 million annually of saltpetre, sugar, spices, indigo cotton yarn, calicoes and raw silk. A league of Hindi princes of central and western India, the Marathas warred and raided, collecting taxes and defying the emperor. Although the Marathas were routed in 1761, the Mughal empire was declining. In time the French and English, who fought each other on and off between 1744 and 1760 – François Dupleix and Robert Clive being among the key figures – came to fill that vacuum.[1] Ultimately, the British would prevail, replacing another empire and formalizing that about a hundred years later. For many in Britain in the late eighteenth century or during the Napoleonic Wars, India at this time was not a colony because the British there were administrators and soldiers and not planters or colonists: later, India would be perceived in

Britain as the prototype of colonies in the empire that were not settler states.[2]

The American War of Independence was a significant conflict in the rivalry because France had lost Canada in the Seven Years War (1756–63) and now Britain would lose its most important colonies in northern America.[3] Both countries suffered financially. The loss of Britain's largest colony raised its debt to £220 million and the conflict with Britain cost a billion livres (the servicing of which cost both states about half their expenditures). The difference was that the British paid 3 per cent and the French paid at least that. While Britain consolidated its position by stabilizing the debt and strengthening its credit, France floated new loans annually, thereby increasing its deficit and lowering its credit rating. Although Britain lost the Thirteen Colonies, France was itself lost. The financial crisis – which included proposed tax reforms, the suspension of the treasury's payments and the calling of the States General in 1789 (the first time since 1614) – set off the collapse of the *ancien régime* in France. This led to reforms in administration and finance, but France fell further behind its rival of over at least a hundred years and a territory with whose history its own had been intertwined for more than seven hundred years – Britain. War had put a strain on the Netherlands, France and Britain – the richest states in Europe from the middle of the seventeenth century. Prussia relied after 1757 on subsidies from Britain. The Habsburg empire, Russia and Spain had great difficulties raising monies to pay for warfare.[4]

Amsterdam was the greatest financial centre in the world, but the United Provinces declined as a power. In the seventeenth century, the Netherlands had a strong economy and a stable social order as well as a strong navy and army. Over time, British sea power had eroded the Netherlands' trade with America and the Indies while the Swedes had lessened its hold on the Baltic trade. The Dutch also had to spend a great deal buttressing themselves against the threat of Louis XIV's France. This debt caused a weakening of the economy, and the loss of life was especially hard on a country with such a small population. After the alliance with England in 1689, the Netherlands came to rely on British power, especially at sea, as the Dutch had to spend 75 per cent of their defence budget on land.[5] France weakened the Netherlands and Britain tried to dictate its terms of trade from the end of the seventeenth century onwards. These two factors helped the decline of Dutch power in Europe and overseas.

France was a great power in this period, but, as is so often the case for states in history as for protagonists in tragedies, the time of greatest strength is also that of greatest vulnerability. As late as the period between the world wars, a French study (probably not too different from its counterparts in other European centres of empire) described the history of French colonization in terms of the unerasable (ineffaçables) civilizing

instincts and reflexes that the genius of the race ('la génie de la race') man-
ifested and described 'the phases of this great adventure'.[6] France was
caught between continental and colonial ambitions. Louis increased his
army from 30,000 in 1659 to 350,000 by 1710: he took advantage of the
exhaustion of Spain and the distraction of Austria. Although the Turks
caused the Austrians trouble and Spain had declined, Louis XIV could not
take full advantage. When the Turks were at the gates of Vienna in 1683,
Leopold I had more on his mind than Louis' designs on Alsace and
Luxembourg. Neither the Habsburgs nor the United Provinces and
England wanted to see France expand into the southern Netherlands
or Germany. Although the Habsburgs often opposed France through
alliances, Vienna later called on France and Russia after 1740 when
Prussia seized Silesia. France also found that as the eighteenth century
went on, one of the German powers, Prussia or Austria, tried to enlist
England or Russia to balance French ambitions. The pattern of diplomacy
was intricate and sometimes because Austria could not rely on France, it
checked French interests with an alliance with Britain, for instance
between 1744 and 1748. The Austrian empire also had designs on the
Balkans and so was sometimes ambivalent or opposed to Russia, which
also sought expansion there. France, Britain and Russia seemed satisfied
in keeping a divided Germany and a balance of power within the German-
speaking lands between Austria and Prussia. The French, who faced
various alliances to balance against the strength of France, were also
divided between land and sea, metropolitan and colonial expansion,
thereby making it unable to concentrate on the army and navy in its struggles with England then Britain. Fighting on its borders in Italy, Germany
and Flanders, France also fought in Canada, the West Indies and India.
Only from 1778 to 1783, when it supported the rebellion in the Thirteen
Colonies and abstained from conflict in Germany, did France bring
Britain low. Although France was large, populous and rich, it could not
dominate Europe or the colonial world. Only under Napoleon, after the
transformation of the Revolution, could France impose its will on much
of western and central Europe and then only briefly. Many powers joined
to oppose this French hegemony. The Austrian empire, although not as
powerful as it once was, did not decline as fast as Spain or Sweden and
was impressive in its resistance to French imperialism from 1792 to 1815.
The Prussians, between about 1640 and 1786, had expanded and had
taken advantage of the Austrian preoccupation with the Turks and the
Turkish concentration on the Russians, the decline of Sweden and the fall
of Poland. For all the advances made in Prussia because of great military
leaders, fiscal stability and reliable taxation, the encouragement of industry and trade, and bureaucratic competency, its relative weakness showed
during the Seven Years War (1756–63) and under the diplomatic pressure

of Russia and the attack by Napoleon in 1806. Only after transforming its military and industry from the 1860s could Prussia lead a challenge to France, Britain and the greatest powers.[7]

In Britain there were some important voices against the economics of colonialism. Adam Smith, writing at the time of the tensions between Britain and its American colonies, wrote about the expense of establishing peace before 'the present disturbances' in these territories being 'very considerable' and, 'if no revenue can be drawn from them, ought certainly to be saved altogether'.[8] Although the peace cost Britain a great deal, war was even more expensive. Smith stressed the colonies as the cause of wars that began in 1739 and 1756:

> The last war, which was undertaken altogether on account of the colonies, cost Great Britain . . . upwards of ninety millions. The Spanish war of 1739 was principally undertaken on their account, in which, and in the French war that was the consequence of it, Great Britain spent upwards of forty millions, a great part of which ought justly to be charged to the colonies.

In case there was any doubt about the size of this burden, Smith specified just how large a debt this incurred: 'In those two wars the colonies cost Great Britain much more than double the sum which the national debt amounted to before the commencement of the first of them.' This is a very different story from the one the American colonists were telling in the political (legal) documents they were producing. When the British defeated the French at Quebec, Boston held a day of thanksgiving on 25 October 1759. Jonathan Mayhew preached that day and sent his praise for the British to be published in London. In his *Two Discourses* (1760) he predicted that the American colonies 'would by the continuous blessing of heaven in another century or two become a mighty empire' and predicted that this state, now that the French threat was gone and it could expand into Canada, would be 'in numbers little inferior perhaps to the greatest in Europe, and in felicity to none.'[9] This mood would change and the euphoria would turn to self-interest, self-determination and independence. The foreign threat being gone, domestic liberty could be established on its own terms, by Americans and for Americans, a new nationality that was forged from the welter of colonies and in the midst of change and chaos. The Americans, with the help of the French, Dutch and Spaniards, won the war, which was an even greater cost to Britain as Smith was implying. As soon as the War of Independence was over the United States found itself contesting its southern border.[10] Shifts in the balance of power occurred over the course of the eighteenth century.

Alexis de Tocqueville, writing in the nineteenth century, after the period we are discussing here, saw two powers on the horizon. These powers were not France and Britain. He predicted that the Anglo-Americans and

Russians would be the influential powers of the future: 'Both have grown in obscurity, and while the world's attention was occupied elsewhere, they have suddenly taken their place among the leading nations, making the world take note of their birth and of their greatness almost at the same instant.'[11] In predicting that each of these nations would hold the destiny of half the globe, de Toqueville distinguishes how. The American nation is based on freedom and equality, the Russian state on servitude to one man. Although the North American colonies and Russia were pushing ahead in the first decades of the seventeenth century, they were not much developed compared to western Europe during much of that century. Both produced raw materials and consumed manufactured goods from the Netherlands and Britain. Muscovy developed more under Peter the Great (1689–1725). The Russian defeat of Sweden at Poltava in 1709 ushered in a new power in the affairs of central and western Europe. The Russians also overran the Poles and Turks, so that by the time Catherine the Great died in 1796, Russia had added 200,000 square miles to its vast empire. Russia occupied Berlin in 1760, participated in the campaigns in Italy and the Alps from 1798 to 1802 and advanced from Moscow to Paris from 1812 to 1814. With the eclipse of France as the dominant power (although still strong), the empires of Russia and Britain came to dominate their respective spheres of eastern and western Europe, not necessarily by occupying territory but by their potential and ready power at the margins of Europe. Unlike Britain, however, Russia, as impressive as its power was and as vast as its empire was, did not develop economic and financial institutions and practices that allowed for adequate development vis-à-vis rival powers. Like Prussia, Russia sometimes relied on British subsidies in war. Once Britain expelled France from Canada and Acadia and excluded Spain from the west of Florida, the American colonists were freed from foreign incursions and did not need the connection with Britain. The North American colonies had a population of about two million in 1776 (at least thirty times more than New France at the end of the Seven Years War), which was doubling every thirty years, and were self-sufficient in food and other key commodities, so that such a population with such provisions could not be defeated by naval blockade or land forces supplied from across the Atlantic.[12]

Even though, in the twentieth century, Germany, the United States and Russia would challenge British supremacy as the dominant world power, Britain was establishing itself in that position during the last half of the eighteenth century. From about 1814 to 1914, it was the first among the great powers. From 1660 to 1815 Britain made the most advances among the European powers and empires, thereby supplanting France as the leading nation. One of the reasons that Britain prospered was that it was well placed to take advantage of the shift from the Mediterranean to the

Atlantic, from land routes to Asia to sea routes connecting Europe with east and south Asia, the West Indies and the Americas. Sea power underwrote national wealth and political clout. Overseas trade bolstered metropolitan centre and colonies. The navy supported trade and the colonies, but, as Paul Kennedy has noted, agriculture was still the basis of the British economy in the eighteenth century and British trade with the Baltic, Germany and the Mediterranean was important even as the colonial trade in sugar, spices and slaves was growing more rapidly.[13]

On and off for about thirty-five years before the Glorious Revolution of 1688, Britain was engaged in wars with a naval power. However, after William of Orange ascended the English throne until the final defeat of Napoleon, the chief opponent in war was France, which, although a naval power, concentrated many of its resources on land and much of its ambition in continental Europe. Britain and its allies did fight France from India to America, but it had to watch what France was doing in its own backyard. While during the war of 1689 to 1697 military campaigns occurred in Newfoundland, Acadia and Pondicherry, the Anglo-Dutch-German allies also worked to keep France out of the Rhineland and Flanders. The old state rivalries played at least as much a role in Anglo-French relations as the role of empire and colonies. The War of the Spanish Succession (1702–13) involved an effort to keep Louis XIV's grandson off the Spanish throne. Louis occupied the southern Netherlands and established a monopoly for French traders in Spanish America, moves that caused the British, Dutch and Austrians to form an alliance. Britain benefited most from this war, gaining trade concessions in the Spanish colonies in the New World as well as territories like Minorca, Newfoundland, Nova Scotia and the lands surrounding Hudson Bay. France and Spain were not permitted to be united under the Bourbons. In the Anglo-Spanish war of 1739, Spain, with the aid of France, resisted British attacks in the Caribbean. As late as 1744, Pierre Charlevoix, a Jesuit and thus another part of the representation of the New World (although Le Jeune had made recommendations on military action), claimed that the French, unlike the Spanish, had no conquerors like Cortés and Pizarro on the stage of the New World. This statement was true if measured by his term *éclat* but was not accurate if the would-be conquerors, pirates and lords of the French (and often Norman) in the Caribbean were taken into consideration.[14] The term *éclat* can mean a burst of noise, the glitter of a gem, or brilliance, all appropriate for the conquerors whether or not Charlevoix intended all these meanings. In the 'Advertisement' Charlevoix said that some people thought that he should have included the Spanish conquerors, like Cortés and Pizarro, as part of his description of San Domingo, so that 'the History of Saint Domingue would have been that of nearly all the Spanish Empire in the new World'.[15] The ghost of Spain haunted French and English texts about the New

World. The British and French settled their differences at the Treaty of Aix-la-Chapelle in 1748 as France threatened to take the Netherlands and Britain had seized the strategic fortress of Louisbourg in Cape Breton. This peace was more of an illusion as British and French settlers clashed with each other in North America and used Native allies in this conflict.

Spain and the Netherlands remained neutral while France and Britain entered the Seven Years War for imperial control of the world of colonies beyond Europe. France sought to attack Hanover, which had dynastic connections with Britain, in order to have the British embroiled in a costly European conflict. The Anglo-Prussian alliance and the Franco-Austrian-Russian alliance constituted new configurations in the balance of power in this conflict. Britain and France would be required to subsidize their allies. British sea power and the trade it engendered and protected in the West Indies helped to pay the large subsidies to Prussia. Colonies were helping to pay for the imperial centre. The Royal Navy blockaded the ports of the French Atlantic and sought to be supreme in the Mediterranean, thereby stifling French maritime trade, defending Britain and enhancing British trade. As a result, while in 1759 the Anglo-German troops were defeating the French in Europe, the British were also capturing French colonies in Canada, the West Indies and India. Spain entered the war in 1762 and soon lost colonies in the Philippines and the Caribbean. Britain was the main beneficiary of the peace of 1763. It gained in west Africa and the West Indies, curtailed France in India and drove the French from North America. The Seven Years Wars left many of the continental powers with high casualties and in financial exhaustion. The high debt helped to lead the British Crown and government to seek new revenues: the American colonists rebelled over taxation and the Acts of Trade and navigation. France, despite its dire financial situation, decided to respond to its defeat in the Seven Years War by spending great sums to build up its navy. Meanwhile the British economy and navy eroded after this war, and the factions and lack of coherent leadership weakened Britain. The errors in naval policy were solved too late – the American colonies had all but formally won their independence by the time the Royal Navy was once more dominant.

Portuguese Decline and the French Enlightenment: Raynal's Analysis

By the eighteenth century the example of Portugal was one of decline. Enlightenment *philosophes*, like Abbé Raynal, saw much to admire in Portugal's past expansion but considered its recent and present state as a cautionary tale.[16] Raynal asserted that although this 'little nation sound itself at once the mistress of the richest and most widespread commerce on earth, . . . she lost the foundation of all real power, agriculture, national industry and population'.[17] He looked back and found that the Portuguese of that time did not understand the expansion in which they were involved and they allowed their customs (morals; 'moeurs') to become depraved, so their 'soldiers and officers were without discipline, without subordination, without love of glory' ('la gloire' being a prominent interest of the French).[18] This was, then, a story of the decline of an empire.

What the reasons were for this dwindling of empire Raynal set out to amplify. In his view, the corrupt Portuguese leaders could not suppress these vices, so what began, after the route round Africa to India, as 'the emulation of the Portuguese', that is the instance of Portugal, ended with a shift in worldview and in the business of empire:

> The Portuguese finally lost their grandeur, when a free, enlightened and tolerant nation, showed itself in India, and disputed the empire with them. It appeared that in the time of the discoveries of the Portuguese, the political principles on commerce, on the real power of states, on the advantages of conquests, on the manner of establishing and maintaining colonies, and on the utility drawn from the metropole, were not then known.[19]

Although Portugal wanted to conquer, it did not have the means and population to carry this out because it 'embraced an expanse of territory that no nation in Europe could maintain without weakening itself'.[20] Overextension was and would be a theme of great powers and empires. Using progressive views of tolerance as a measure, Raynal explained the demise of the Portuguese empire in terms of intolerance, indifference to commerce and the submission to Spain, which contrasted to 'the measured and reflective conduct of the Dutch'.[21] Examples of leaders in Europe and empire came to be translated from one power to the next. In the Netherlands, Raynal saw the virtues needed for the kind of empire that he described as a successor to that of Portugal, whose eschewing of commerce led the Portuguese to change 'projects of commerce into projects of conquest, [and] the nation that never had a spirit of commerce, took that of brigandage'.[22] What was required to be a successful state or empire changed over time. Failing to adapt would lead to decline or failure. The new way of operation required peace, prosperity, skilled labour and tolerance, all of which Portugal, a country of extremes of wealth and poverty, lacked: 'Its intolerance does not allow it to admit to the rank of its citizens the peoples of the Orient and of Africa, and it must everywhere and all times combat its new subjects.'[23] A contrast of the old empire, Portugal, and the new, the Netherlands, would be instructive.

Whereas the Portuguese used force, the 'Dutch were animated by the hope of founding a great commerce on the ruins of the commerce of their enemies. They conducted themselves with speed, with firmness. Their mildness and their good faith reconciled them to peoples. Soon several declared themselves against their ancient oppressors'.[24] The present could view the past as a negative example and not simply a source of nostalgia or inspiration. Raynal was creating, by design or not, a Black Legend of Portugal, but part of that legendary apparatus was also complicated by the attitude of Spain, 'to which Portugal had then submitted, in desiring its debasement, and rejoicing in its defeats, as if they had not augmented the means of its enemies the Dutch' and sent men – as if to spite the Portuguese and in fear that if Portugal lacked the resources itself, Spain would have to fight its neighbour's wars – to battle in Italy, Flanders and elsewhere in Europe to make war.[25] Although the Portuguese empire came under criticism, the Spanish empire was subject to a much more pervasive and enduring Black Legend. Raynal's France and the British Isles off its coast were now the states that had to be modern to change with the times if they wanted to succeed in the imperial theme or the business of empire.

Taxes, Finances and French and English Rivalries

In the eighteenth century France seemed to have greater resources than Britain, although its per capita income was lower. The government revenues and army of France dwarfed those of any rival in western Europe. Britain relied more on indirect taxes than France did, but its regressive tax system had fewer tax collectors and appeared less visible in its excise duties. Having higher incomes, Britons seemed more willing, or at least able, than their French counterparts to pay higher taxes. Those with the highest incomes in Britain could save because they had fewer direct taxes than those in a similar situation in France. By the Napoleonic War, Britain, with a population less than half of that of France, was able to raise more taxes in absolute terms than its neighbour. A stable financial system gave Britain an advantage over France and other western European states. Long-term loans, the creation of the Bank of England in 1694, a flourishing stock exchange, the increase of paper money without severe inflation, good government and guarantees of such finance by Parliament, expansion of industry and trade, and protection of overseas trade by the Royal Navy all gave Britain an advantage over France in Europe and overseas, especially in times of war. The Dutch found the British government a good place to invest and Anglo-Dutch financial and commercial connections flourished. In one conflict, however, the weaknesses of Britain – in its army, navy, diplomacy and trade – caused Dutch funds to subside: the American War of Independence. The Dutch, despite higher interest rates being offered in London, thought that this time British credit was a poor risk. When in 1780 the Netherlands entered into the war on the side of France, Britain discovered that its own investors had great domestic capacity to absorb its loans. Loans allowed Britain to wage war on a scale that its tax revenues would never have allowed. Credit gave Britain an advantage over France, which lacked a developed system of public finance. The various tax collectors took a cut of the taxes collected. Until the reforms of the 1770s, France had no proper national accounting, so that national debt was not thought important. Unlike the British, those in France with surplus capital tended to avoid investments in business.[26] But leaving off for a moment before getting too far ahead, I turn now to England and its overseas expansion.

The Spanish, British, French and Other Colonizers

Technology and economics affected how people lived and were governed. The greatest change was a move from the power of trade to that of political dominion. As the Mughal empire was collapsing in the 1750s, the Europeans fought their wars beyond the bounds of Europe. In 1664 France had founded the Compagnie des Indes and was a rival of Britain from the 1720s. In North America, the Indian Ocean and India, France and England (Britain) battled. During the Seven Years War, Clive began a string of victories for the British in India against the French and local rulers. In 1773 the British East India Company assumed the monopoly for growing opium in Bengal, and when France invaded the Netherlands, the company took Ceylon in 1796 and Java in 1811. France invaded the Netherlands during the French Revolution, which, as we saw, caused the dissolution of the Dutch East India Company on the last day of 1795.[27]

The Chinese had prohibited the sale of opium in 1729, but by 1840 the Chinese state, trying to stem this drug trade, suffered a defeat and the British seized Hong Kong.[28] The internal weaknesses of the Indian subcontinent and China left a vacuum for British power. Other Europeans and later the Americans continued to share in this Asian trade, some of it of dubious moral value. Three major empires fought in Spain during the Napoleonic Wars – France, Britain and Spain itself. On 19 March 1812, the Cortes of Cadiz promulgated a constitution, based on universal suffrage for men, a responsible executive and a representative legislature. When, after the defeat of the French, who had occupied much of Spain at this time of promulgation, Ferdinand VII returned in March 1814, he restored absolutism by declaring null and void all the acts of the Cortes and abolishing the Constitution. After revolts, on 6 March 1820 the king agreed to call the Cortes and, on the next day, restored the Constitution. In this period, Jeremy Bentham wrote 'Rid Yourselves of Ultramaria', an appeal to Spaniards to rid itself of its empire and grant independence to the colonies because they were a threat to the progressive government now in effect in Spain itself.[29] Bentham appealed to Spaniards to be an example to Britain and the world: 'More than forty years have elapsed since the men of the Anglo-American United States shook off the yoke of our Kings: the yoke – the fouler yoke – of our lawyers, is even hugged by them, and remains still upon their necks. Ridding themselves of this Nightmare, what a lesson will you thus read to England!'[30] Besides matters of yoking kings and lawyers, but by ridding itself of its empire, Spain would be the greatest and highest example in the world with regard to slavery. Spain would be above what Bentham liked to call 'the Anglo-American United States', a country he clearly admires as a leader in liberty: 'In the endeavour to stop the traffic, they were, it is true, the first. Yet still has the poison maintained possession of their veins.'[31] The shedding of empire, for Bentham, would bring economic, political and moral benefits. That was true for Britain, Spain or any other European empire. Despite not having shed itself and its colonies entirely of the scourge of slavery, Britain was on the threshold of being the dominant world power for 100 years. Soon after the defeat of Napoleon, Spain would lose most of its empire and France, although building up great territories as part of its imperial expansion, would never quite match the British colossus. What marks the years after the defeat of Napoleon is the development of global trade centred in Europe and, more particularly, on Britain. Industrialization grew in the period of the Great War of 1793–1815.

Revolution and Its Aftermath

Perhaps no amount of military power could have subdued the rebellious British colonies once the threat of France in North America had been removed. French and Spanish military support was also important for the winning of American independence.[32] The balancing of military alliances had now been applied in colonial America as they had been for some time in Europe. Britain was isolated in Europe, partly because the French had, for once, not attacked British allies in the Netherlands or Hanover. France and Spain – through the Bourbon connection – could concentrate on an overseas and colonial war with Britain. If France devoted its resources to struggles on land in Europe with inconclusive results, then it would not have its resources freed up to spend on its navy and to rival the Royal Navy. A year after the British lost control of the English Channel (perhaps it was more now *La Manche*) in 1779, the Dutch intervened on the American side as well in 1780.[33] The French fleet was able to keep the British navy from aiding Cornwallis, who surrendered at Yorktown in 1781 and thus ended, all but formally, the conflict between Britain and its principal colonies in North America. The Royal Navy had to face the increased and great sea power of France, Spain and the Netherlands and could not build itself back up until it was too late. France, although militarily successful as a result of the rejuvenation of its navy, was in serious financial difficulties. Like the French, the Spanish and Dutch hoped for an early peace between Britain and its American colonies, so that there might not be some reconciliation between them. The tension between empire and colony, which was to become so crucial in all the European overseas empires, was being aggravated here for the benefit of Britain's rivals in Europe. Britain's regained power in 1782 meant that the bargain driven at the Treaty of Versailles in 1783 was not as much to France's benefit as it could have been. Despite victory against Britain, increased trade with the West Indies and the Levant and a fast-growing economy, France faltered.[34]

The cost of the war of 1778 to 1783 cost three times more than the previous three wars and the failure to reform national finances helped to bring about a collapse of the *ancien regime*. The downward spiral into crisis worsened from 1787 onwards as France's internal problems meant that it abandoned its Dutch and Spanish allies at key moments. From 1792 onwards, the battle between France and foreign powers came to dominate the European military, political, social and economic landscapes from revolutionary through Napoleonic times. France overran other territories with a massive army and soon the other nations bore the costs of the French military force. Russia was busy undermining Polish independence, thereby causing Prussia to concentrate its forces more on the Vistula than on the Rhine, which in turn caused Austria to focus on a possible Russian and Prussian attack on what remained of Poland. France overran the Netherlands and converted it to the Batavian Republic. The Habsburg empire and Britain, on the defensive, were alone left to fight France and to regroup. The repercussions of a colonial war – the American War of Independence – were turning Europe on its ear. This pattern would be repeated on and off until the 1970s when most territories had won their independence from the seaborne European empires and their successors. Britain used its naval power to blockade France and to fight in the colonies. None the less, this strategy, while successful, did not counter the French successes on the Continent in the 1790s. For instance, between 1793 and 1796, disease and war in the West Indies killed 40,000 British troops and disabled many others and the British campaigns cost in excess of £16,000,000. The British faltered as the Bank of England suspended cash payments and there were naval mutinies, and, in 1797, the Austrians, exhausted, sued for peace with France, recognizing its dominance on the Continent. Even at this nadir, British finance was the key to the defeat of France. Pitt the Younger introduced income tax. France was readying for an invasion of Britain, so British resolve was as much about the survival of the nation as about imperial expansion. The Netherlands and Spain, however, did contribute to that expansion because they fought on the side of France. The British took key colonies from both in the West and East Indies, the Cape of Good Hope, Colombo and Malacca. Britain was dominant at sea and France on land. The expansion of British trade and commerce could finance its sizable subsidies to its continental allies in its wars with France.

Changes were not happening in the British colonies alone. The colonies tended to reproduce, as D. K. Fieldhouse has observed, the traditions of their parent states. This emulation could be positive and negative. By 1700, the Dutch West India Company lost most of what it had gained from the Swedish, Portuguese and Spanish. The Dutch had, except in colonies with a large number of settlers, thought about colonies in terms of commerce and war and not of emigration and settlement.[35] The Dutch colonies in America remained under the control of the West India Company until 1791. By the end of the eighteenth century, most Dutch colonies possessed representative political institutions.

By 1798 Turkey, Russia, Austria, Naples and Portugal had joined Britain in its fight with France, but without success. The French punished the Russians and Austrians while Spain invaded Portugal and Prussia and Denmark took that continental link with the British monarchy: Hanover. Once more, in 1801, Britain stood alone. The British captured Malta, smashed the Danish fleet, defeated the French at Alexandria in Egypt, overcame French-sponsored clients in India, and seized French, Danish, Swedish and Dutch territories in the West Indies. The Peace of Amiens in 1802 did not last long and Britain and France were back at war in 1803. This final of the seven wars between France and England between 1689 and 1815 would last twelve years. During this period Britain would capture the following colonies (returning some of them): St Pierre and Miquelon, Tobago, St Lucia, Curaçao, the Danish West Indies, French Guiana, San Domingo, Guadaloupe, Martinique and Dutch Guiana in the Americas; Senegal and the Cape in Africa; and some of the Moluccas, Mauritius, Banda, Amboina and Java (as well as expansion in India) in Asia. The Royal Navy was an extraordinary force. Pitt died late in 1806 and, in 1806–7, France was strong and crushed the Prussian, Russian, Austrian and other allies Britain helped to finance and had brought the Holy Roman empire to an end. Napoleon tried to crush mercantile Britain by banning its exports to Europe and keeping Baltic timber away from the Royal Navy. Britain had to turn to its colonies like Canada for masts for its ships even as Napoleon's Continental System and worsening relations with the United States were increasing pressures on British finances and labour. This pattern of seeking out the resources, trade, markets, labour and troops of its colonies would be repeated in Britain to at least the end of the Second World War. In 1808, Spain rebelled against France, and Russia broke with Napoleon in 1811–12. British goods, whether manufactures from Britain or colonial re-exports, could not be kept entirely from Europe. In 1813 alone, Britain subsidized about 450,000 allied troops. Britain looked outward to its colonies and inward towards Europe, the one as a means of expansion and the creation of wealth and the other as a means of maintaining a balance of power that would ensure national security. During the Anglo-American War of 1812–14, goods travelled between Canada and New England.

Seeking new markets in Latin America, the West Indies, Africa and Asia, British trade more than doubled between 1794 and 1816. Cotton was now Britain's largest industry: slavery underpinned that business as it had sugar.[36] This meant that the United States and the West Indian colonies were still tied in to the British economic sphere. Britain was also experiencing the Industrial Revolution, so that British wealth and productivity were still on a rapid rise. British debt tripled but its increased wealth was able to bear that weight. The economy of France grew in this period as well, but not as much as Britain's, and became less competitive. Atlantic France was hit especially hard. Plunder helped to pay for the wars of the French empire under Napoleon. Conquest led to indemnity payments as well, but, as Napoleon himself knew, victory after victory was the only way to keep up these war profits. But campaigns in Spain and Russia were the ruin of this logic of plunder and occupation that was begun by a revolutionary power in the face of invading armies bent on restoring the monarchy. For some reason, France, with all its resources, did not rebuild its navy in order to overwhelm the Royal Navy, which it might well have done. The British and their allies had brought the fight back to French soil and by April 1814, Napoleon, despite his brilliant military career, had abdicated. The war with the United States, which was a dispute over blockade and impressment, was neither won nor lost: merchants in New England were often not enthusiastic about fighting with its major trading partner. For Britain, Canada and India strengthened its power and commerce but could seem like a distraction from Europe in times of crisis. When Napoleon had occupied Portugal and Spain, he weakened their hold on their colonies in the Americas.

Although a restoration of Portuguese and Spanish rulers occurred in 1814, most of their colonies waged a series of successful rebellions from

1811 to 1830. A revolt in Spain itself from 1820 to 1823 led to a constitutional government and contributed to Mexico's independence directly because the Spanish general who was sent to put down the revolution in Mexico actually joined the rebels and helped them to gain independence in 1821. Napoleon's campaign from March to June 1815 helped to demonstrate Britain's primary, although not dominant, place in Europe, something that would last for a hundred years, something also underwritten by expansion and plunder in India. By 1815, Britain was becoming the greatest economy in the world and the primary power worldwide. It controlled most of Europe's colonies by 1815: for instance, its seizure of Santo Domingo, which made up 75 per cent of France's colonial trade before the French Revolution, was by the end of the 1790s a market for British goods and a source of British re-export goods. Contemporaries could often see that Napoleon's fall was to the benefit of Britain. He could not halt that rise.[37]

First Decolonization: Revolution and Breaking Away

The American Revolution was the first great moment of decolonization as the Thirteen Colonies broke away from Britain with the help of other European states and empires, principally the French and Spanish. This movement reoriented the primary European imperial focus on the Americas to one on Africa and Asia. The French empire in America started to disintegrate in 1763 and the British empire there a few years later, until from 1775 to 1783, the break was confirmed in British civil war and by treaty. Britain had concentrated on defeating its chief rival, France, and had been more interested in an informal empire within the Spanish empire and not in wresting territories from Spain. When the Latin American colonies became independent states, Britain could develop more economic ties.[38] By 1830, Europe had lost direct imperial control over the continental Americas and had to try to exercise indirect influence.

An ambivalence occurred among settlers in all American states in all the empires. For many generations, there was, as D. K. Fieldhouse notes, a balance between imperial restrictions and the ability of the colonists to evade them.[39] The Seven Years War defeated France, and took away the chief threat to the British colonies in North America. Some among the British colonists rebelled against changes to the way the metropole was managing the colonies. Even in 1754, the colonists had refused a federal authority to coordinate troops. After the defeat of the French, the British wanted to maintain an army in North America in order to guard against any potential French threat and against any friction there might be between the expanding colonies and the Natives. Pontiac, an Amerindian chief, had led resistance in 1763. The colonists did not want to supply troops themselves. The British wished to establish a series of western forts and sought a way to pay for them. First, they would start by trying to convince colonial assemblies to provide money for this defence. If they could not, Parliament would have to impose new customs duties on colonial trade, which happened in 1764 and was followed by the Stamp Act of 1765, which levied a duty on legal documents. In 1768, import duties were imposed. The colonists saw no reason for a British regular army in America and had never been taxed by the British Parliament before. The British also cracked down on smuggling and trading with the enemy. The sheer number of changes seemed to be an assault on the colonists' English liberties. Even though many of the taxes had been repealed, a conflict occurred in 1775. Some of these British subjects in America were considering their identity and political and legal rights in relation to how Britain saw them. The colonial upper and professional classes lost a good deal of control of the American colonies from 1763 to 1775. The Loyalists (Tories in American parlance) lost their influence, and British military strategy did little to strengthen their cause in the colonies. While the British made concessions, they were not enough for those who were thinking of themselves more and more as Americans. France in February 1778, Spain in April 1779, and the Netherlands in 1780 joined in the war and helped the British colonists to independence, which was ratified in 1783. None of this was inevitable, but a series of domestic and international events sealed the fate for this first great example of decolonization.

The Latin American colonies sought independence for reasons that, like those in North America, were intricate and sometimes almost inscrutable. When Napoleon occupied Spain in 1808 and when Charles IV abdicated in favour of Joseph Bonaparte, a crisis occurred in the colonies. The elites did not want to swear allegiance to this foreign king, but they did not choose independence. When Charles's son, Ferdinand VII, acceded to the throne, every American province recognized him. None the less, the American provinces had been like republics for six years and were voluntarily choosing Ferdinand rather than recognizing his right to rule over them. They had a taste of self-government, which relied on local *juntas*, something that divided and thus reduced the influence of the upper classes of Creoles. Republican and royalist sympathies cut across class lines, as Simon Bolívar was from an affluent Creole family and some of the royalist army in Venezuela were *Mestizo* herdsmen and Natives from the back country. The divisions within the colonies became apparent in these years. The restoration of the king could not cover up these rivalries.

Although the *cortes* or legislature in Cadiz was liberal and appointed colonial representatives to itself, it took a centralizing view and refused to legalize trade with foreigners when the Spanish colonies were busy trading with Britain and the United States. The restored monarch understood even less how conditions had changed after Napoleon had taken Spain and the colonies were on their own. Still, in 1814 royalist parties won throughout the colonies, but ten years later all the continental colonies were independent republics. As in the Thirteen Colonies, there was a tension between loyalty to the mother country and the assertion of American identity, rights and interests. When the Spanish monarchy tried to go back to its old ways, to employ commercial monopoly and to favour force over persuasion and diplomacy, it weakened the monarchy and the cause of the royalist parties in the colonies. Unlike Britain, Spain did not have the military power, if used effectively, to assert authority over the rebellious colonists. The navy was especially lacking. Britain prevented the monarchies of Europe from coming to the royalist cause because the British would benefit from having Spanish American ports legally open to trade with Britain. As in the American Revolution, a foreign power helped the rebels. In 1822, Britain recognized the independence of several colonies and supported unofficially the Spanish republicans in the peninsula. In 1823, the British let the French know that the government of Britain considered all the Spanish colonies to be independent. The British navy prevented the French from trying to reassert the power of the Spanish monarchy. It also allowed the United States to assert the Munroe Doctrine.

Argentina had been a key place for rebellion and for helping others toward liberation. Bolívar also represented a strong military force for independence until his death in 1830. But South America broke into various states rather than being united as many of the British American colonies were (except those, like Nova Scotia, that later formed Canada). In the north, Mexico became independent but could not assert its authority over provinces that had been under its control: Costa Rica, San Salvador, Nicaragua and Honduras. New Spain had become independent of Spain by 1824, but it was fractured and not the strong union that would have increased its strength in the face of British economic power and the growth of the United States.[40]

Haiti, which was the French half of San Domingo (originally Hispaniola), was the only Caribbean colony to rebel successfully against European rule. The slave rebellions succeeded there partly because the French had to concentrate on the war with Britain. It was a prosperous colony on the verge of the French Revolution, and the planters did not like the French monopoly market in sugar and were growing tired of French authority. The French Revolution gave the planters the pretext to set up a republic of their own, but it also spurred the mulattoes to ask for rights and to rebel when they were denied. In 1793, in the wake of rumours that the revolution would free slaves, uprisings among the slaves occurred. When the British and Spanish invaded the island, many of the slaves welcomed them. The French commissioner then announced in August 1793 that all the slaves were free (France did not formalize the abolition of slavery until February 1794), and the slaves, under the leadership of Toussaint L'Ouverture, backed the French. Spain ceded its part of the island to France. A British blockade allowed L'Ouverture to preside over the island even if it was nominally connected with France.

The Peace of Amiens in 1802 allowed France the chance to reassert its authority, and Napoleon allowed his empire to slide back in regards to slavery. Governor Leclerc found a way to have the black officers betray L'Ouverture, but when the black population heard that the French were going to bring back slavery, they fought the French and won. Yellow fever struck Leclerc's troops and the survivors were carried off in a British ship. Renewed war with Britain and a blockade in 1803 allowed the Spanish half of the island to overthrow French rule and to delay any French attack on the island until 1815. By 1825, France recognized Haiti as an independent country.[41]

Another colony that gained its independence was Brazil. As in the case of Haiti and the Spanish American colonies, in Brazil the French Revolution and Napoleonic Wars had an impact. When the French were about to occupy Lisbon, Dom John, the regent of Portugal, and his wife, Queen Maria I, left for Rio de Janeiro, which became the capital of the Portuguese empire. The Duke of Wellington liberated Portugal in 1811. Would Brazil or Portugal now become a dependency of the kingdom in which the monarchs chose to remain? In 1815, Brazil was a full kingdom equal to Portugal. Maria died in 1816 and the regent became John VI of Portugal, and he decided to stay in Brazil. Portugal revolted, partly because the Portuguese refused to live in a country reduced to a province of Brazil. John returned to Lisbon in 1821, and left his son, Dom Pedro, as regent. The *cortes* in Lisbon, no matter how liberal it was, tried to turn back the clock and return Brazil to a dependent role. Both the republicans and royalists in a now rebellious Brazil accepted Pedro as emperor in 1822. So Brazil had a monarch and a liberal constitution. By 1823, Brazil had severed its ties with Portugal. Britain brokered formal separation in 1825, having Brazil pay the Portuguese debt to Britain and compensate John VI for his properties in Brazil as well as recognizing Britain's economic privileges to which Portugal had agreed under a treaty and signing a convention against trading in slaves. The monarchy lasted until 1889, when Brazil became a republic.[42] This independent nation had severed its last tie, even if it was sharing the same dynasty, with Portugal. While these developments were taking place among the western European empires, other changes were happening in eastern Europe and especially in Russia, which was expanding in all directions.

The Expansion of Russia in Context

No one empire alone was dynamic and expanding. There was always a balancing of power. Russia expanded as Britain and France did. After the truce of Andrusovo in 1667, Russia's foreign policy was directed south. The acquisition of Kiev meant that Russia could concentrate on expanding along the Dniepr toward the Black Sea. The Turks had been turned back before Vienna in 1683, so the Russians thought they could push them back further, especially with allies, like Austria, in Europe. France was not interested as it was allied to the Ottoman empire, and Austria defeated the Ottomans in 1699 and made their own peace with them. Peter the Great toured Europe in 1697 and 1698 and saw the benefits of wealth from the colonies of other states. Although Charles XII of Sweden won battles against Denmark, Poland and Russia in the Northern War (begun in 1700), he failed to stop the Russians from establishing Petersburg in 1703. At Poldova in Ukraine in July 1709, the Russians crushed Charles XII's army and he had to flee into Ottoman territory to avoid capture. Charles had made the mistake of marching on Moscow and had to turn south, where he was defeated. This signified the collapse of the Swedish empire and the birth of Imperial Russia. Charles had crushed Poland and sacrificed Sweden, which left a vacuum for Russia to establish itself as a western European and Baltic power. The favourable conditions of the Treaty of Nystad established Russia's new influence and territory. Russia exposed the declining power of Sweden. By the Russo-Prussian War of 1756–63, Sweden could not even muster an attack on Prussia. Catherine II (Catherine the Great, 1762 to 1796) consolidated that expansion and growth in power. From Peter I's defeat of the Swedes at Poltava to the late 1760s, Russia had considerable indirect control over Poland.

This informal 'empire' was hard to maintain as Poland was also a client of France and bordered on two other great powers: Prussian and Austria. During the 1550s, the Russians came to control the Volga and access to the Caspian Sea and strategic parts of the coasts of the Baltic and Black Seas in the eighteenth century. In Siberia, the indigenous peoples could offer little effective resistance to the Russians, who came for the furs, and a vacuum to the east of Moscow came into being with the collapse of the Mongol empire and the khanates that succeeded it. The nomadic people of the steppes long terrorized the sedentary peoples of Russia and China. It took until the sixteenth century for the Russians to start to advance into this vast steppe, and it was not until the eighteenth century that Russia controlled the steppes, which stretch 6,000 kilometres, and defeated the slaving and plundering of the nomads. Only then could Russian wealth, population and power grow. The colonist replaced or displaced the nomad in this area and in Siberia. In Asia most of the colonists were peasants whereas in southern and southeast Ukraine ('New Russia') about half the land by the mid-nineteenth century was the large estates of nobles. This region and Siberia were different from the heartland around Moscow. Serfdom did not go far in the New Russia, where most of the farming colonists were Ukrainians. In cities like Odessa, Jews, Italians, Greeks and Armenians had large communities. The peoples the Russians encountered were nomads like the Nogais of the steppe north of the Black Sea, the Bashirs, semi-nomads in the southern Urals, and the Kalmyks, who were Buddhists who lived between them. In 1571, the Nogais and Tatars had burned Moscow and continued to raid into the heart of Russia during the seventeenth century. The fertile lands on the steppes were attractive to the Russians as they pushed south and east. Like other European empires, and especially the British empire, the Russian empire sent out farmers who displaced nomads. The Russians conquered the Bashirs in the 1740s and the Nogais and Kalmyks fled Russia altogether, fleeing to Mongolia but losing two-thirds of the 150,000 people to starvation, cold and battles with the Kazakhs, west Asian nomads also called the Kirghiz by the Russians.[43]

Between 1688 and 1815, France and Britain were rivals that would not unite against Russia. The Ottoman empire, Sweden and Poland were in decline. Between 1740 and 1854, Austria and Prussia were rivals or uneasy allies. Catherine the Great had mediated between the Habsburgs and Hohenzollerns. It seemed that Russia was on the verge of greatness in Europe, and its destruction of Napoleon's army after his invasion of Russia seemed to confirm this point. When the Congress of Vienna awarded Russia most of Poland, this caused Russia some problems. It had to consider the influence of the Polish aristocracy over Ukrainian and Belorussian peasants in the lands on the borders of Russia and Poland and the desire of the Prussians for Polish lands or of the French to use an independent Poland as a balance against Russia. In 1815, Alexander I tried to rule Poland in an alliance with the Polish aristocracy by granting Poles autonomy, rights and an elected parliament. Alexander backtracked, and Nicolas I faced a first Polish revolution in 1831.[44] Russia had expanded west, south and east at a great pace, and that would continue in the years after 1830. This expansion increased Russian power, but not without setbacks and problems.

The Austrian and Russian empires had much in common. Both empires might be said to have begun, as Dominic Lieven has suggested, in the sixteenth century, Russia in the 1550s and Austria in 1526, when Ferdinand of Austria became king of Bohemia and Hungary, or in 1556 when the Habsburg lands were split between the Spanish and Austrian branches of the family. The empires of both monarchies fell during the First World

War. Both were continental, bureaucratic and military empires in which commerce and oceans were not of the utmost importance. Russia possessed until 1867 one overseas colony, Alaska, and Austria had none. These two states expanded and became important powers, but they are not the kinds of overseas powers that are the main focus of this book.

Austria became a great power between 1683 and 1719, when it withstood the Ottomans and then defeated them. The French also felt the growth and enlargement of Austria, which became a rival to the greatest power on the Continent. By 1763, both Austria and Russia were great powers and remained part of the balance of power in Europe until the First World War.[45] These two powers, along with the United States in the next generation, came to balance the power of the western European empires as they expanded.

The Expansion of the United States

In Chicago in 1893 the World Columbian World Exposition was being held, and in that city and year, Frederick Jackson Turner delivered a groundbreaking paper to the American Historical Association entitled 'The Significance of the Frontier in American History'. His frontier thesis was that the 'free land' in the west of North America provided an area of difference in which eastern Americans and immigrants from Europe had to adjust to new circumstances and were thereby made American.[46]

Expansion occurred from the first contacts between Europeans and Natives in North America, first in the fisheries and fur trade and then in settlement. This spreading out involved many groups on both sides and all the early modern European states that would be empires, such as Portugal, Spain, England, France and the Netherlands. In the late seventeenth century, for instance, the Spanish experienced rivalry on their frontiers in North America. The English used Carolina as a base, with their Native allies, to try to destroy Spanish Florida. The Pueblos began to regain autonomy over New Mexico. On the coast of Texas, France established an outpost that the Spanish saw as a threat to Spanish control of Florida, New Mexico, the mines of northern Mexico and the sea-lanes of the Gulf of Mexico.

From 1660 to 1760, the English and Northern European population along the Atlantic seaboard grew from about 72,000 to 1,275,000. In South Carolina, which shared a border with Florida, by 1700 the European population was about 3,800 and by 1745 was about 20,300 and in 1760 about 38,600. The Spanish population of Florida at this time went from about 1,500 to 2,100 to 3,000. In 1700, there were about

2,800 African slaves in South Carolina and in 1760 about 60,000. This population boom meant that the English were spreading south and west and that the Spanish and the English vied, as the English and the French did in the north, for Native allies. Despite setbacks, such as losing Florida for two decades in 1763, Spain, by the time Carlos III died in 1788, had reacquired Florida, started new settlements in California from San Diego to San Francisco and made its claims stronger on the Pacific coast as far as Alaska. Much of this success was owing to Carlos III's confidence in José de Gálvez, who was secretary of the Indies and whose efforts led to the founding of New California in 1769. Spain had also acquired Louisiana in 1762. Gálvez's success and the Spanish defence of the Illinois country, Saint Louis, Natchez and Manchac contributed to the Anglo-American victory in the War of Independence by preventing the British from seizing New Orleans and the Mississippi valley. In the peace accord of 1783, the British recognized that the western boundary of the new United States extended to the Mississippi and that West Florida was a Spanish possession while surrendering to Spain the territory of East Florida, which now consisted mainly of loyal British subjects and 10,000 African slaves. This made the Spanish empire and settlements in North America transcontinental. This territory, along with the Native-held lands and that of Canada, which was British, would constitute a barrier to this rapid Anglo-American expansion.[47] More friction would occur. Other European rivals and their Native allies stood before the growing population of Anglo-America and the land they wanted to fuel that growth. Long before the independence of the United States, the move by Anglo-Americans south, north and west for land had begun.

The movement west had begun centuries before by explorers and fur traders, but there was a great movement of settlers from the 1780s onward after the French had been defeated and the authority of the British overthrown. The settlers could grab lands from the Natives without European interference or the protection of the Natives by the various Crowns. Farmers from adjacent regions were the most likely to take up land to farm in the west.[48] Some moved into contiguous regions in Canada before and after the American Revolution, sometimes as much for land as for any allegiance to the Crown. It took the European invaders some time to realize that the most fertile lands in North America were in the interior and that these regions had the heaviest indigenous populations. The Europeans suffered through extreme conditions in harsh environments and prevailed 'by the brutal displacement of native peoples, who were determined to hold their homelands at all cost'.[49] Until the Seven Years War and the defeat of the French and their Native allies, the Anglo-Americans were hemmed in east of the Appalachians. The British had wanted to keep relations with the Natives peaceful, but once the War of Independence was won, there was little to stop the westward expansion. When the French sold Louisiana in 1803, another barrier to expansion to new lands was lifted.

This movement of frontier settlers began in the Appalachian Plateau country then the Mississippi valley, which was occupied in the first half of the nineteenth century. By 1825, much of this area was carved into states, except Wisconsin and Michigan, which remained territories. Only through a series of terrible wars with various Native peoples did these settlers occupy this land. This was a conquest.[50] If we think of the movement of all the Europeans into the New World from 1492, the greed of soldiers, farmers, plantation and mine owners, and of others drove them forward, eating up Native communities and then slave or indentured labourers or cheap labour in their wake, whether the invaders and settlers were Spaniards, Portuguese or English. There might have been a matter of degree in the violence against Natives, sometimes tempered by those religious people like Las Casas, Roger Williams and John Eliot, but Natives died because of land hunger, gold and silver rushes, and other related economic grabs. Sometimes the Natives were blamed as barbarians for their own problems, as throw-backs to the way the inhabitants of the Old World once were. These indigenous peoples had their complex and varied cultures placed under duress. The diseases from the first contact from the Spaniards, Portuguese, French, Dutch, English and others had spread and weakened the Native groups in North America long before the Anglo-American settlers pushed west. Disease was the one reason that although the Europeans met with resistance, they did not experience an even fiercer struggle. The Mississippian Culture that had endured between 700 and 1600 CE was an intricate agricultural people that probably succumbed to disease.[51]

The indigenous peoples, although weakened by sickness and disease, played a significant role in resisting the expansion of the United States. Alliances between Spanish and Natives helped each other to slow the movement of Americans into the south and west. In 1784, the Spanish had signed a treaty of alliance with the Creek nations, led by Alexander McGillivray, whose mother was French-Creek and whose father was an affluent Scottish Indian trader. Later, the Spanish signed similar treaties with the Alabamas, Choctows and Chickasaws. These treaties were a departure in Spanish policy, and the government sought to secure the friendship of the Seminole and Creek leaders while signing treaties with the Camanches in Texas and New Mexico in 1785 and 1786. These documents, as David Weber has noted, represented a shift from Spain's assumption in the sixteenth century that the Natives owed allegiance to the Crown. This change offered protection and trade with a recognition of cultural and religious difference in the borderlands while the Spanish still used *presidios* and missions to make the coastal peoples of California Hispanic. The Spanish also relied on the French in trade with the Natives and two Scots from the days of British rule to supply British goods to the Natives in Florida. These were moves to stave off American traders. The Natives could sometimes play one side against the other: for instance, McGillivray drew stipends from Spanish and American officials after 1790. In 1793, Governor Carondelet brought together different tribes, including the Creeks, Choctaws, Chickasaws and Cherokees, to sign the Treaty of Nogales, which was an agreement of mutual assistance that would preserve Louisiana and the Floridas (East and West) for Spain and which unified the southeast tribes into a confederation. Carondelet became governor-general of Louisiana from 1791 to 1797. When Spain and France were at war in 1793, there were reports that the Americans would try to seize the Mississippi. In Saint Augustine, Governor Juan Nepomuceno de Quesada put down a rebellion instigated by foreign residents. But Spain's lack of strength in Europe prevented it from sustaining and strengthening its colonies in North America.[52]

The tide of Anglo-Americans over the Appalachians meant that the population there grew rapidly. In 1783, Kentucky may well have had about 12,000 people, 73,000 in 1790 (when the first census was taken) and 221,000 in 1800. When Spain wanted to settled the boundary disputes, the United States balked. Spain tried to stem the flow of Anglo-Americans into the Mississippi valley by allowing Spanish shipping only in the lower Mississippi in 1784. The Spanish government permitted its subjects in the borderlands to trade with their allies, the French, in an attempt to undercut British and American goods. These measures failed. The Spanish government also tried to bring in immigrants, such as Acadians and Canary Islanders, but while this policy was successful, it was unable to find large enough subsidies to attract colonists from Spain and its colonies to settle in this region. Fatefully, from the mid-1780s, the Spanish authorities began to allow immigrants from the United States to settle in Louisiana and the Floridas. The Spanish government knew it could not stop Americans from entering the territories, so it hoped to control the flow. And so these colonies became Americanized before they became part of the United States. In 1800, Louisiana, a colony of Spain, had 50,000 non-Native inhabitants, more of them French, English, American and German than Spanish. New Spain was prosperous in the eighteenth century, but in 1800 the economy of the United States was twice as productive. When Spain went to war with revolutionary France, it had to sue for peace in 1795. Spain switched sides and fought with France against England, which devastated the Spanish fleets at Cape St Vincent in 1798 and at Trafalgar in 1805 and which blockaded Spain's trade with its empire almost continuously until 1808. This situation left the Spanish colonies to drift and gave the Anglo-Americans opportunities. Napoleon's taking of Spain and putting his brother on the Spanish throne meant a crisis in the colonies, which later rebelled and formed independent states. The French Revolution, the Napoleonic Wars and the collapse of Spain left the United States with a protracted opportunity for expansion.[53]

Spain's weakness began to show in ways that would benefit the United States. Captain James Cook visited Nooka Sound on what is now Vancouver Island in 1778, and his report on the potential of the pelts of the sea otter brought other nations to the area. When Spain attempted to enforce its claim in 1789, it already found British and American ships at Nootka. The Spaniards seized two British ships and took them to Mexico and there was a crisis as a result. Revolutionary France was not interested in helping Spain, which capitulated to Britain and agreed in 1790 to share the Pacific Northwest with Britain as well as making reparations. The expedition of Alejandro Malaspina in 1791 and 1792, although a brilliant artistic and intellectual enterprise, did not establish the Spanish strength in the Pacific Northwest. So the Spanish hoped to contain the British and the Russians in the northwest and the Americans in the southeast, but this was not to be. The execution of Louis XVI drew the Spanish and British monarchies into an alliance in 1793, and in 1795 they formalized their agreement to share the northwest. A few months later, in July 1795, Spain made peace with the French revolutionaries and then sought the neutrality of the United States, for fear that without it, the British navy could prey on Spain's American colonies. In Pickney's Treaty (Treaty of San Lorenzo del Escorial), Spain set 31 degrees as the northern boundary of West Florida, thereby abandoning claims to the Ohio River, the Natchez district and elsewhere, and allowed the Americans to navigate the Mississippi to the sea without paying duties. This treaty was the beginning of Spain's retreat from the Mississippi. Ironically, British power opened up to Americans two great regions in which Spain had been resident – the Pacific Northwest and Mississippi. When Napoleon came to power in 1799, he began to pressure Spain for Louisiana and the Floridas, and soon was able to have Carlos IV cede Louisiana. Spain had sought to have Napoleon agree not to relinquish Louisiana to a third party because the Spanish were wary of what neighbours Mexico would have. Within a year, Napoleon had broken the agreement and sold Louisiana to the United States. Napoleon could not crush the rebellion in Haiti and needed the neutrality of the United States so he could fight against Britain unimpeded. Thomas Jefferson was assertive in making claims to Spanish territory adjacent to Louisiana, sending troops to the border with West Florida and then later to the boundary between Texas and Louisiana. He sent out a number of expeditions to explore territory, the most famous of which was that of Meriwether Lewis and William Clark, in 1804–6, as part of a strategy to claim new territory. Despite Spanish efforts, Spain could not protect the northern border of New Spain after 1808, when Napoleon forced Carlos IV and Fernando VII, his son, to abdicate their rights to the Crown. For six years, there was no Spanish king on the throne, so this threw the Spanish colonies into some disarray and weakened them before foreign threats. All continental Spanish American colonies became independent in the decade after the restoration of the monarchy in Spain under Fernando VII. Americans in Baton Rouge in West Florida rose up in 1810, declared independence, and then asked for annexation to the United States, which President James Madison obliged. During the War of 1812 against the British, the Americans seized Mobile. In East Florida, rebellious Spaniards, Americans and the American government all set out to follow the pattern of Baton Rouge, but Congress refused Madison support and free blacks and Seminoles helped to thwart the rebellion. In 1812, Spanish-American revolutionaries and American adventurers also invaded Texas, which was sparsely populated. The rebels assassinated the Spanish governor. The large royalist army of New Spain recaptured Texas in 1813. Andrew Jackson seized Pensacola in 1818, and the secretary of state of the United States blamed the Spanish for not keeping better order in the Floridas. In 1819, the Spaniards ceded East Florida, recognized American control of West Florida and preserved their own right to Texas. In 1819, James Long, an American, invaded Texas and declared it a republic, but the Spanish troops forced him back to Louisiana. In 1821, a successful war of independence began in Mexico, and the northern provinces from California to Texas became provinces of the new country. This was another new angle in the friction among Spanish, American and Native cultures in the American south and west. The Mexicans now had to guard against a land-hungry United States as the Spaniards had in New Spain.[54]

There were legal aspects to the expansion of the United States. The Louisiana Purchase of 1803 doubled the size of the United States, and in 1809, Jefferson wrote to Madison that 'no constitution was ever before so well calculated as ours for extensive empire' and that he expected the United States to acquire Cuba, Canada and East and West Florida, thus showing the world 'such an empire for liberty as she has never surveyed since creation'.[55] Although the United States did not come to encompass Canada and Cuba, it did become a transcontinental state or, to use Jefferson's term, an 'empire' by the end of the nineteenth century, with possessions in the Atlantic and Pacific. The United States absorbed a good portion of Mexico and small parts of Canada (northern Maine, the Alaska Panhandle, the northern part of the Oregon Territory). As Gary Lawson and Guy Seidman observe, there is a constitutional difficulty with the acquisition of territory that is meant to become a state, but there are additional problems with lands that are not intended for statehood. How, for instance, does a federal territory that is not a state, especially if it has its own legal traditions, dovetail with the Anglo-American legal system and the US Constitution? Lawson and Seidman follow Jefferson's view that treaty power is implementational power. In other words, federal treaty makers are able to add territory to the United States, but only as a means of effecting other national powers like maintaining a navy or admitting new states. The Louisiana Purchase met this standard as all the land was intended for statehood. This theory of treaty power shows the ambiguity of other kinds of expansion, such as to Alaska and the Philippines (non-contiguous territory); Oregon (discovery); Texas and Hawaii (statutory annexation). Lawson and Seidman argue that the acquisition of the Philippines was unconstitutional, and that its independence in 1948 helped to remedy that. They also argue that some institutions of territorial self-government are unconstitutional and that federal judges in territories do not meet Article III of the Constitution. Sometimes the executive steps in to fill the void when Congress does not exercise its constitutional power to govern, as in California from 1848 to 1850 when federal military officials governed California without statutory authorization. Whereas the Supreme Court of 1854 ruled this to be constitutional, Lawson and Seidman say that the Constitution does not provide for this. They also argue against the current doctrine that allows Congress to deprive some territorial inhabitants of some constitutional protections.[56] Bartholomew Sparrow discusses internal and external empires and says that the United States has always had territories, making it 'an "empire" in the sense that the domain of political authority exceeds that of representative government'.[57] The constitutional aspects of expansion were and are controversial.

In examining Jefferson's claim about the American Constitution and its relation to 'empire', much depends on what he meant by that word. As we saw in the Introduction, the term is difficult, multifold and changing. When the United States expands to include territory that would become states, the Constitution is accommodating. When the empire includes territories that are not meant to become equal parts of the United States, then the Constitution is not so welcoming. Jefferson, as Lawson and Seidman conclude, was not sympathetic to the United States becoming a traditional European empire, and the Constitution is not ready-made for that kind of empire and does not sanction the building of such an empire. Puerto Rico might have been a state in 1899, but in not being a state for so long, does its status question the legitimacy of its connection with the United States? The Constitution does not stand in the way of colonialism and making a territory a permanent colony, but it enables a wide range of constitutional rights, including some Anglo-American legal procedures, which might conflict with traditions in the territory. So much of this debate depends, as Lawson and Seidman note, on what is also meant by the 'Constitution'. Is it the document ratified by nine states on 21 June 1788 or is it a social practice? They choose the answer – document – and raise the issue of interpretation, that is, what are the original meanings and understandings of the Constitution?[58] Whatever the standard of proof, the legal aspect of the expansion of the United States, which was key in the eighteenth and nineteenth centuries especially, is as important as the bulls and donations were to early Portuguese and Spanish exploration and settlement as they expanded in the fifteenth century and beyond. There are many more elements of expansion, but one to which we need to return is the treatment of Native peoples and the violence and displacement they suffered and how the ecology of their land was changed rapidly.

Ecology and Empire: The Case of New Zealand

Here and in the next chapter, New Zealand will act as an example of how the biological expansion of Europe continued to change the land and peoples of ancient places that became new colonies. Although Charles Darwin has been used by, or associated with, Social Darwinism, he did not embrace with happiness the implication of the analogy of the stronger among varieties of animals and humans extirpating the weaker, for just after making this point, he continued: 'It was melancholy in New Zealand to hear the fine energetic natives saying, that they knew the land was doomed to pass from their children.'[59] Darwin himself showed ambivalence as he was also critical of New Zealand: 'I believe we were all glad to leave New Zealand. It is not a pleasant place. Amongst the natives there is absent that charming simplicity which is found in Tahiti; and the greater part of the English are the very refuse of society. Neither is the country itself attractive. I look back but to one bright spot, and that is Waimate, with its Christian inhabitants.'[60] Here, Darwin prefers the Natives of Tahiti and only thinks well of only a few among the English.

New Zealand has been isolated from Australia for 80 to 100 million years. It has not been inhabited for long.[61] About a thousand years ago, the Polynesians arrived and found only one land mammal – the bat. The meeting of Maori and European happened in a context that had much less history of human settlement behind it, at least in the place of the encounter, than, for instance, in the New World.

In time, the British empire sought to lessen distance and otherness and to impose control and what they considered to be civilization on lands and peoples they considered wild and even barbarous.[62] At first, the British, like other Europeans, explored the south Pacific and were not as interested in settlement. Joseph Banks, who accompanied Captain Cook in 1769, recognized only a few of the plants in New Zealand. About 89 per cent of the flora in New Zealand occurs there alone. The biota is as different from that of Europe as any on earth. The Maori had killed most of the moas or flightless birds and burned out their habitat by the time the Europeans had arrived. These Polynesians grew the kumara, a form of sweet potato, successfully. Certainly, the Maori, as Raewyn Dalziel has noted, were agriculturalists who were settled and had the powers to adapt, negotiate, resist.[63] When Abel Tasman landed there in 1642, the Maori killed four of his men. By the time Cook arrived for half a year in 1769, the Maori had, through farming and hunting, affected some of the North and South Islands by turning forest into fern, scrub and grassland. By the 1790s, after the beginnings of the settlement of Australia, British ships were coming to the northern harbours of New Zealand and loading cargoes of flax and timber. Still, half of New Zealand's surface was still covered with forest as dense as that in the Amazon. When in 1792 the British kidnapped two young men from the families of Maori chiefs and took them to Norfolk Island to teach the convicts there how to dress flax, they found out that this skill belonged to Maori women and so, in November 1793, they returned the Maori pair, Huru and Tuki, home with potatoes, maize and pigs. This helped to increase agriculture amongst the Maori.

Australia was also important to New Zealand. Although Britain did not exercise formal control over New Zealand, it did try to maintain order among its subjects living or operating there. Often this control, however erratic, came through Sydney. In 1805, Te Pahi, a chief, complained about the whalers in the Bay of Islands. Lieutenant-Governor Philip King responded by proclaiming that people would need his permission before they took the Maori off shore. This control was easier in theory than in practice. The government in Sydney could do little when, in 1809, the Maori killed the crew of the *Boyd*, only to find that Te Pahi's own settlement was sacked in revenge. Lachlan Macquarie, Governor of New South Wales, issued an order in which he extended British protection over the Maori. He also required ships calling at New Zealand to post a bond to ensure their good behaviour. In 1814, he appointed a Justice of the Peace and gave Hongi Hika, Ruatara and Korokoro, northern chiefs, the power to enforce his orders. The missionaries thought that the behaviour of convicts, seamen and traders jeopardized their safety and their work. The Church Missionary Society petitioned the secretary of state for the colonies about the situation in New Zealand. They sought the punishment of crimes committed there. In 1817, an Act gave the courts the power to try British subjects for manslaughter and murder committed outside the bounds of British territory. In 1823, the British government authorized the courts in New South Wales to try offences that occurred in New Zealand. The recognition was important, but in practice hard to enforce. In 1830, Te Rauparaha, a Ngati Toa warrior, negotiated that the *Elizabeth* transport a war party to Akaroa in return for a cargo of flax, but Sir Richard Bourke, governor of New South Wales, was unable to try the captain of the ship.[64] Britain and Australia could not exercise the kind of control they desired over their subjects as long as New Zealand was part of their informal empire. Australians also formed part of the trade and commerce in New Zealand. Sealers from Britain and Australia had regular expeditions to New Zealand until the number of seals declined during the 1820s. American and British whalers also hunted whales in the waters of New Zealand and were joined by Australian whalers in the 1820s.[65]

Seals and whales were part of the traditional food of the indigenous inhabitants of New Zealand. The Maori, who practised cannibalism according to Crosby, did not farm grain or raise animals, but relied on eating rats, seals and the occasional beached whale.[66] The seals, after Cook wrote about them, tempted others, about twenty-five years later, to come to New Zealand on expeditions, but their numbers declined by the 1820s. Whaling, too, brought in ships, but by the 1840s the whale population was in decline. The more than hundred thousand Maori also faced a few Europeans who wanted the timber and who used cheap Maori labour for its harvest. Moreover, the flax trade attracted small numbers of Europeans or Pakeha. The missionaries were also few and were not very successful in converting the Maori in the first couple of decades.

James Cook brought metal tools and weapons, cannon and muskets. He also introduced pigs. They helped to produce protein and fat in surplus for the Maori. Plants, weeds and crops also arrived, especially with French expeditions under Marion du Fresne and then Julien Crozet. The Europeans brought a new kind of sweet potato and a white potato. This last crop brought the Maori into surpluses that could become part of trade in a global market. They were isolated and shared with the Guanches, Amerindians and Aborigines a lack of B-type blood. The Maori, who were free of many diseases, were susceptible to new pathogens. The British brought with them many diseases, but most damaging were tuberculosis and venereal disease. Epidemics followed.

From 1814 to about 1840, the European presence started to alter the environment for the Maori. In 1814, the Maori allowed some Anglican missionaries to settle in exchange for axes. Some missions, like that sent in 1809 by Samuel Marsden, chaplain of the conflict settlement of Sydney, had a hard time. It wasn't until 1823, when Reverend Henry and

Marianne Williams began to reorganize the missions according to teaching of the church and the Bible, that some success in conversion was forthcoming. Missions functioned under Maori terms and control until the late 1820s. The Maori fought with guns against one another to avenge losses or insults, and they suffered many diseases. In light of these circumstances, the Maori came to ask the missionaries to become peacemakers and to pray for or treat those who were sick.[67] The Europeans brought wheat, fruit trees, horses, sheep and cattle. The Maori provided food from crops and animals for the whalers and acquired muskets and other commodities in exchange. Chiefs saw that gaining advantage in longstanding economic political rivalries amongst the Maori could come from incorporating European religion, literacy, trade and technology into their cultures.[68] Hongi Hiki, chief of the Ngapuhi, went to England in 1820 for guns, and with these, and chain armour given to him by George IV, campaigned against rivals and enslaved women to offer the whalers. He died in 1828, a year after being wounded, and changed warfare in New Zealand.[69] This exchange between the Maori and the English and other Europeans serves as a reminder of similar patterns but also different local conditions over time in these encounters of cultures. Some Europeans used slavery and others cheap or indentured labour to generate profit, but these patterns changed over the course of the late eighteenth and early nineteenth centuries.

Slaves and the Question of Rights

Slavery was a preoccupation and problem from the start in the exploration and exploitation of the New World.[70] In the eighteenth century any objections and scruples some Europeans had to slavery intensified, so that during the American Revolution, both British and Americans began to abolish the slave trade and ultimately the holding of slaves. In France, there was a notable condemnation: Montesquieu's *L'Esprit des lois* (1748) scorned the slave trade:

> The state of slavery is in its own nature bad. It is neither useful to the master nor to the slave; not to the slave, because he can do nothing through a motive of virtue; nor to the master, because by having an unlimited authority over his slaves he insensibly accustoms himself to the want of all moral virtues, and thence becomes fierce, hasty, severe, choleric, voluptuous, and cruel.[71]

The circumstances were suspect in which Europeans had established slavery in the New World: 'The Europeans, having extirpated the Americans, were obliged to make slaves of the Africans, for clearing such vast tracts of land.'[72] Moreover, Montesquieu also questioned a philosophical argument for enslavement: 'Aristotle endeavors to prove that there are natural slaves; but what he says is far from proving it.'[73] For Montesquieu, history, philosophy or law cannot justify slavery. Antoine Destutt de Tracy (1754–1836), who was a pioneer in discussions of ideology, wrote a commentary on Montesqiueu, and Thomas Jefferson published his translation of de Tracy's work in Philadelphia in 1811. On 26 January 1811, Jefferson wrote to de Tracy from Monticello discussing his translation, praising Montesquieu but de Tracy the more for his commentary because the author on whom he was commenting needed correction.[74] Monsieur de Bovis expatiated on the spirit of the laws in the French colonies in the Caribbean and appealed to the Code Noir of 1685, to argue that slavery did not exist there in an arbitrary form.[75]

The first Code Noir, as we saw in the last chapter, was promulgated under Louis XIV (r. 1643–1715) under the influence of Jean-Baptiste Colbert (1616–83), and the second under Louis XV in 1724, which shed Articles 5, 7, 8, 18 and 25 of the version of the Code Noir of 1685. Both codes, while insisting on the humanity of slaves, codified slavery and linked blackness and slavery. For instance, the code of 1685 opened with a declaration of a paternalistic and providential view of the king's role in the French empire.[76] Although there were some protections in this code, it also permitted masters to treat their slaves with great severity in the face of violence, insubordination or any strong challenge to their authority and the hierarchy that sustained it. The code wavered between protection and punishment, showing ambivalence and contradiction. For instance, Article 16 prohibited slaves belonging to different masters from assembling in groups and recidivists could be given lashes, branded with a fleur-de-lys or, in severe cases, put to death. Article 27 demonstrated a stark contrast to this severity by declaring that masters would nourish and maintain slaves who were infirm, old or sick and, if they abandoned their slaves, would pay 6 sols a day for the hospital to care for them. Article 33 went to the other extreme by condemning to death any slave who hit his master, mistress or children causing 'contusion of blood' or in the face. Article 38 was precise in its punishment and the way it marks and controls the body of the slave according to the nature and frequency of the offence. The first two offences involved branding with fleurs-de-lys and the third meant execution.[77]

In practice, slavery was harder to eliminate. The late eighteenth century and the nineteenth century were crucial to the debate on slavery and to the gradual abolition of the institution – the actual holding of slaves and not simply the first step – and of the slave trade itself. The rhetoric of rights that surrounded the Revolt of the Netherlands, the English Civil

War, the Glorious Revolution of 1688, the American Revolution and the French Revolution also affected debate on slavery, women and reform. These rights go back much farther.

The Europeans worked in competition and concert with themselves and others in the slave trade and the institution of slavery. For so many centuries, the causes of slavery were captivity from war, punishment, poverty, and kidnapping. African monarchs later bought slaves to sell them again to Arabs, Africans and Europeans. Most slaves were obtained by trade, some by war and very few by kidnapping after 1448. In the 1690s, Liverpool entered the slave trade and later grew to be the greatest slave market. In the eighteenth century the African slaves passed from Nantes to Saint-Domingue, which Spain had ceded to France in 1697. By 1710, the British had succeeded the Portuguese, the French and the Dutch as the great transporters of slaves and were transporting about 10,000 slaves a year to the Indies, including the Spanish colonies there. In 1713, Britain took over the *asiento*, or official monopoly, for carrying slaves and a few other goods to the Spanish colonies.

Policies on trade and slavery differed in different empires. France and Britain took different approaches. The French Crown taxed a port like La Rochelle – so important in the trade with the West Indies and west Africa – and the British government encouraged Liverpool and Glasgow. The French government did not protect La Rochelle against the Royal Navy, which seized its merchant ships, disrupted its slave trade and destroyed its markets in Louisiana and Canada. France also allowed its colonists to trade with neutral shipping during wars. The British government picked up the Atlantic trade while its French counterpart neglected the importance of profit and the exchange of goods. The French monarchy, after the reign of Louis XIV, seemed to have trouble raising enough money to direct a full and sustained military effort.[78] Trade, shipping and war were connected intricately and this balance favoured Britain in time. In the eighteenth century, the British stressed commerce. Although at times the French challenged them in this domain, they never overcame the challenge from Britain.[79]

However evident or not slavery was in a locale, the financial effects of slavery were present. Slaves and slaver-owners were of many backgrounds. The City of London made money from slaves as did some of the prominent citizens of colonies like Salem and New York. Newport, Rhode Island, developed into a major port that traded in slaves. The greatest merchant of slavers, taxpayer and benefactor in Newport in 1775 was Aaron Lopez, of Portuguese Jewish origin. Dutch merchants handled the sugar trade from the refineries in and about Nantes to various places in northern Europe, and cotton was also a part of the industry and commerce of this city. Britain intensified the slave trade and other northern

European nations emulated it. Between 1740 and 1750 Britain carried about 200,000 slaves to the Americas and about 250,000 between 1761 and 1770.

The Seven Years War (1756–63) was a key moment in the rise of the British empire. On 4 August 1762, the British capture of Havana strengthened the war party in England while weakening the position of the British cabinet because the British victory placed the French and Spanish colonies in the Caribbean and on the Gulf coast at the mercy of the British fleet and made the peace terms more severe. Although Spain and France had been rivals in North America for two centuries, they would come to an agreement that, along with the British victory in the Seven Years War, would see the end of the French empire on the North American continent. In a complex series of events, Napoleon would later sell Louisiana to the United States in 1803. France under Louis XV was willing to give up Louisiana to compensate Spain for the loss of Florida, which Charles III of Spain gave up for Cuba.[80] Still, the British transformed Cuba from 1762 onwards, importing many more African slaves to fuel the boom in sugar. Britain had also driven the French from west Africa in 1758 and retained most of the French African colonies at the Treaty of Paris in 1763.[81] The French government had much to resent Britain for in the wake of this war. Between 1763 and 1778, when the French entered the American War of Independence, the western European commercial nations as well as British North America prospered in the slave trade. France was beginning to overtake Britain as a sugar producer. And the Portuguese continued sending slaves into Brazil.[82] Slavery was a main part of the economy of Europe and its overseas empires.

There was political support for this practice. Governments backed trade and enabled the trading and holding of slaves. In the seventeenth century the Netherlands, Denmark, Sweden, France, England and Brandenburg tried to establish permanent posts on the Gold Coast of west Africa. By 1719, only the English, Danish and Dutch remained. One of the arguments for slavery was that white men could not survive the tropics and so they had to rely on those – usually Africans – who could. A study of the mortality rates among the Europeans who worked for the Netherlands West India Company from 1719 to 1760 determined that there was a much lower rate than published in earlier studies, so that H. M. Feinburg thought it may be prudent to revise downward these estimates of European mortality there.[83] Moreover, Robin Hallett mapped out the European movement into the interior of Africa in the eighteenth century from a worldwide perspective of European expansion from an earlier period: 'For in the initial contact between peoples of different stages of technological development, power inevitably lay with the more highly organized, and imperialism – whether predatory or paternalistic in form – came to assume the inevitability of a force of nature'.[84] Actual problems were natural and human-made with devastating religious, social, political and economic consequences. Often with terrible effects, disease and other biological factors relating to agriculture also contributed to European ecological imperialism in different parts of the world.[85] Slavery was connected with ecology, demography, economics and politics.

The commerce in slaves was a hard business. European states created companies with rights and privileges to carry slaves from Africa to the Americas. Some merchants and ship captains in these countries became wealthy from trading at least in part in slaves. People of all religious persuasions were involved in human traffic. Some bishops and cardinals of the Catholic Church in Portugal and Spain partook in the fifteenth-century slave traffic. Slave merchants in Bahia in Brazil had their own religious brotherhood. Various Jewish merchants played some part in the slave trade in some western European countries and the Americas. Some of the Quakers in England and British America were engaged in the slave trade. And Freemasons in Bordeaux had a connection to slaving at the end of the eighteenth century. All groups were touched or tainted by this association with slavery.

In more than once sense, there was a political dimension to the trade in slaves. Some members of legislatures in France, Britain and British North America were slave merchants. Moreover, some aristocrats and foreign merchants were also involved, first locating from Florence to Lisbon and Seville. And cargoes changed over the centuries as the European suppliers responded to changing demand in Africa. In 1721, the Royal Africa Company (RAC) asked its agents in Africa about many details of the trade. These questions included whether the slaves were taken in war or traded. The RAC lost almost a quarter of their slaves shipped across the Atlantic between 1680 and 1688. By the 1780s, at the apogee of the slave trade, the death rate had been reduced to under 6 per cent. A violent insurrection probably occurred for every eight or ten European slaving voyages and these accounted for many deaths. By the end of the 1700s, about 80,000 black African slaves crossed the Atlantic each year.[86] This was a vast, forced and wrenching movement of people.

In 1780, largely owing to the work of Quakers, Pennsylvania was the first of the British colonies (soon to be formally a state in the new United States) to outlaw slavery. From 1780 to 1800, most British or former British colonies on the mainland of North America had abolished slavery. The British Caribbean colonies did not. For instance, Jamaica, in 1773 alone, exported five times the combined exports of the Thirteen Colonies. The Convention of Paris declared the emancipation of slaves in February 1794 but without outlawing the trade. Some of the other states abolished the slave trade – Britain in 1807; the United States 1808; Venezuela in

1811; New Granada (Columbia – 1812); Spain, Portugal and the Netherlands, 1818.[87] In practice, slavery persisted.

In 1789 in the capacity of first president of the Pennsylvania Society for Promoting the Abolition of Slavery, Benjamin Franklin was cautious about the abolition of slavery causing problems because of the debased nature of the institution: 'Slavery is such an atrocious debasement of human nature, that its very extirpation, if not performed with solicitous care, may sometimes open a source of serious evils.'[88] Even in the one of the greatest opponents of slavery among the founding fathers of the United States, a certain caution prevailed.

Even for the new Americans, who so recently considered themselves British or British Americans, the break with Europe and the attitude toward slavery were entwined. In the 1792 celebration of Columbus in New England – here was an appropriation for American pride of a new order that had broken the imperial bonds of Europe, Jeremy Belknap celebrated Columbus for his 'genius'.[89] For Belknap, the Spanish were part of the Black Legend and 'the first introduction of the negro slavery into America was occasioned by the previous destruction of the native inhabitants of the West-India islands, by the cruelty of their Spanish conquerors, in exacting of them more labour than they were able to perform', and Belknap even blamed Las Casas in part for being responsible for recommending this slave trade – one of the horrors of the European expansion into the New World.[90]

And the first British empire, even with the loss of its greatest colonies, survived and prospered owing to trade, often still with its former colonies. Seeking new markets in Latin America, the West Indies, Africa and Asia, Britain saw its trade more than doubled between 1794 and 1816.

Slavery is a fulcrum for looking backward and forward to a key underpinning of this imperial and colonial regime. Abolishing slavery was difficult and uneven work. To complicate matters, while states in the union could abolish slavery, the federal state did not, for the Constitution of the United States of 1787 delayed a discussion of the slave trade for the country for twenty years. In 1788, at the Royal Academy in London, George Morland exhibited a painting, now lost but still known from copies, that represented slave traders on the coast of Africa.[91] Slavery and anti-slavery coexisted in a double movement. William Pitt and William Wilberforce were important British leaders who opposed slavery. The National Assembly of France condemned slavery in 1791 but more in principle than in practice. Denmark abolished the slave trade in 1792. Meanwhile the importation of slaves to places like Jamaica and Cuba was thriving. In the early years of the nineteenth century the British economy relied heavily on cotton and sugar produced by slaves. Countries such as Portugal also relied heavily for prosperity on slavery in colonies like Brazil.

C. R. Boxer began his study of the 'golden age' of Brazil (1695–1750) by focusing on 'the interdependence of Brazil and the slave markets of West Africa'.[92] Napoleon revived slavery. On 2 March 1807, Thomas Jefferson signed a bill in favour of the abolition of slavery.[93] In Britain the House of Commons and House of Lords also abolished slavery in 1807. Britain withdrew from the slave trade in about 1808. This withdrawal had a much wider context than the revolutionary age and the Industrial Revolution, as important as they might have been to the institution of slavery and its abolition. Slaves from Africa had transformed the European economy.

A modest illegal slave trade occurred in the United States over the next fifty years or so. The British sometimes supplied, invested or sailed in ships of nations that had not abolished slavery. In 1811, Parliament made slaving a felony with a penalty of fourteen years in an Australian penal colony. That year, the Royal Navy also began to police the waters off western Africa. Each country and its empire embodied contradictions and difficulties.

Elsewhere slavery persisted. The slave trade endured among the French, Spanish and Portuguese merchants, and in Africa itself blacks and Arabs continued in this commerce. Slavery continued in Africa without the British. The Americans and African slave-traders, Europeans, Muslims and others, plied their trade. When the king of Ashanti died in 1824, about a thousand of his slaves were sacrificed. The Spanish empire kept the institution of slavery. By 1810, the only places in it to use black African slaves in great numbers were the territories that are today Cuba and Venezuela, which did so to maintain their sugar and cocoa plantations respectively. Still, owing to a lenient view of manumission, Cuba and Brazil had large populations of free blacks.

Many Latin American colonies had become part of the informal British empire even though they remained part of the Spanish empire. Many relied less and less on slavery in order to encourage trade with Britain and to have its protection. Simon Bolívar freed his own slaves and thought that the abolition of slavery was a key to the independence of Spain's colonies in America. The tensions between the *criollos* (Spaniards born in America) and the *peninsulares*, some of whom were in the slave trade, occurred over the commerce and administration of the colonies. The British abolitionists, like Wilberforce, and even the government began to pressure Spain, Portugal, France and Russia to abolish slavery in their empires. Lord Casterleagh prevailed upon the governments of Russia, Austria, Prussia, Sweden, Portugal, Spain, France and Britain to cooperate by signing a declaration that the African slave trade was 'repugnant to the principles of humanity and universal morality' and those powers with colonies promised to abolish this trade as soon as possible.[94] Tensions within metropolitan centres and within colonies as well as between capital and colonial territories make it hard to distil one attitude towards the practice of slavery.

Natives and Women: Other Voices and Experience

Natives in North America were another group often not included in the circle of rights and benefits. The defeat of the French in North America upset the balance of power, not simply for European settlers but also for the peoples the French called 'Amerindiens' (Amerindians). The French loss was, according to Olive Patricia Dickason, 'a disaster, for Natives from the east coast to the Great Lakes and beyond because they lost their bargaining power between two European rivals, cut off the gift or present system and did not allow for protection against the influx of settlers because colonial governments did little to enforce article 40 of the capitulation of the French in 1760 at Montreal had guaranteed that protection'.[95]

Matters worsened for aboriginal peoples as a new nation was born and the Americans moved west. The case of the Iroquois or Six Nations is instructive. The Americans had appealed to the Six Nations to keep out of the War of Independence, but even the Iroquois were split in this civil war. Mary Brant (Konwatsitsiaié'nni, c.1736–96) and her younger brother chief Joseph Brant (Thayenddanega, 1743–1807) were pro-British; others, especially among the Oneidas and Tuscaroras, were for the Americans; the Seneca and Onondaga were split. The British Americans themselves were divided in like fashion. The Iroquois suffered because of the peace of 1783: the Americans would not agree to an independent nation for the Iroquois and although the British had lost the war, they tried to defend the Natives by not giving up their western trading posts as a means of protecting the indigenous peoples and in 1784 they negotiated with the Ojibwa (Mississaugas) on the north shore of Lake Ontario for the purchase of land along the Grand River (near what is today Brantford, Ontario) for 5,000 Iroquois refugees. The British withdrew from the northwest posts in 1796, thereby ending the buffer they provided for the Natives, who were, with the French and British gone from this territory, face to face with the land-hungry settlers. The Crowns of France and England were no longer there to protect them.

John Brant, son of Joseph Brant, would later lead, along with Major John Norton, the Iroquois to victory over the invading Americans at the Battle of Queenston Heights in 1812. Earlier in the eighteenth century, with the Treaty of Montreal, the Iroquois had decided to remain neutral in conflicts among the settlers. The Quebec Act of 1774 was not well liked in the Thirteen Colonies because it brought under the jurisdiction of

Quebec the lands of the Ohio valley and the Great Lakes region. Although the Quebec Act superseded the Proclamation of 1763, the Canadian Constitution would later embed that proclamation, especially in respect to Native rights. The Thirteen Colonies reacted as if the Quebec Act were a provocation and negotiated with the Penobscots and Mi'kmaq (Micmac), and in 1776 the Mi'kmaq signed a treaty at Watertown. This treaty included an agreement that the Mi'kmaq would send warriors to the American army, although this provision was not popular and the treaty was disavowed. None the less, the commander-in-chief of British forces from 1763–76, Thomas Gage, ordered Guy Carleton, governor of Quebec from 1766 to 1777, to use Natives on the frontier. The Iroquois of Kannawake repulsed the invading American army for two weeks but went home because they thought the British were sacrificing them. So Natives were ambivalent about the British civil war in North America.[96]

Already with the powerful Six Nations, except for the Mohawk, who refused to sign, the newly independent United States was drawing up treaties that would keep the Natives within fixed boundaries and would try to extinguish their claims to lands. For instance, article 1 of the treaty of 1789 stated that

> And the undersigned Indians, as well in their own names as in the name of their respective tribes and nations, their heirs and descendants, for the considerations beforementioned, do release, quit claim, relinquish, and cede, to the United States of America, all the lands west of the said boundary or division line, and between the said line and the strait, from the mouth of Ononwayea and Buffalo Creek, for them, the said United States of America, to have and to hold the same, in true and absolute propriety, forever.[97]

The United States and British North America (later Canada) took different routes.

The Revolution and its aftermath were not necessarily good to the indigenous peoples. Some of the Seneca women in 1791 replied to the emissaries George Washington had sent to the Iroquois to ensure their neutrality: 'we are the owners of this land, AND IT IS OURS!'[98] During the 1790s, Red Jacket (Sagoyewatha), a Seneca leader, responded to attempts to convert his people to Christianity (a long tradition among Europeans that the Americans did not leave behind with independence): about the Bible, he said, why did the Seneca and their ancestors not receive the book? 'We only know what you tell us about it. How shall we know when to believe, being so often deceived by the white people?'[99] This conflict recurred in Native accounts of the arrival and spread of white settlers.

Another concern is the situation of women in empire and colony. Some aspects of the cases of Britain, New Zealand, Canada and the United States should cast some light on the progress of extending what is human beyond

European males of substantial property whether in the imperial centre or in colonial territories or former colonies. None of this was a linear process because women in the late Roman empire had achieved a degree of equality and the right to own property, which was a great movement from the *pater familias* and *patria potestas* of the earlier stages of Roman law.[100] The Salic law, whether women could inherit according to the precedent of Frankish law, was a matter of debate that was used in the conflict over France between the French and English monarchs that Shakespeare represents in *Henry V*. At Tilbury on 9 August 1588, in the face of a possible Spanish invasion, Elizabeth I spoke about herself. Although different versions of the speech survive, here, in the standard one, she proclaimed: 'I know I have the body but of a weak and feeble woman, but I have the heart and stomach of a king, and of a king of England too, and take foul scorn that Parma or any prince of Europe should dare to invade the borders of my realm.'[101] Even if Elizabeth was showing her bravery to be amidst her troops and not afraid of danger or death in the teeth of an invasion, she, the ruler of England, displayed an ambivalence, a double vision of her own gender, a weak woman with a man's stomach for war. When women wanted to take part in the rights of 'man', they had precedents for women playing strong roles in history, but that did not prevent many men and women from resisting this change. Writings for and against women had long been part of a debate on the sexes. One book that argued in Latin for the virtue of women was that by Agrippa von Nettesheim, Heinrich Cornelius (1486?–1535), which, already translated into English prose, in 1652 appeared in verse translation as *The Glory of Women: or, A Looking-Glasse for Ladies*; in the first twenty lines of the poem, the question of equality is stressed: 'Hence from the souls no honour doth exceed / Greater in males, then in the female breed: / No doubt of this, nor scruple can arise, / Because their glory God did equalize.'[102]

Women were also advocates for the abolition of slavery. On 22 September 1774, Abigail Adams had written to her husband, John, about a petition by black slaves to the newly appointed governor of Massachusetts, Thomas Gage, that they would serve him in arms in exchange for their liberty. Abigail also mentioned her position on slavery: 'I wifh moft fincerely there was not a flave in the province – it allways appeard a moft iniquitous fcheme to me.'[103] She saw the irony of fighting for freedom while depriving others of it. The pursuit of happiness, then, long before its expression by Thomas Jefferson in the Declaration of Independence in 1776, was something Aristotle, who had contributed the Athenian Constitution, considered essential to individuals and states. Liberty and slavery were key elements in life and political life.[104] Aristotle, unlike Abigail Adams, had a theory of natural slavery. She did not think women and slaves should avoid freedom and expression.

The age of revolution had different effects on women. Maria De Fleury, born French but living in Britain and contemplating the revolution in her native country in 1789, was much more laudatory of George III than many Americans came to be over the course of the American Revolution, for her preface proclaimed: 'a Congratulatory Address to Britons, from a View of the Privileges they now enjoy, from the excellent Constitution of this Country, and the mild Administration of King George the Third;–an Exhortation to watch over and defend those Privileges;–and an Hymn of Praise to God as the Guardian of England'. Although the poem hailed Britannia as 'thou favour'd Queen of Isles', De Fleury did not emphasize the role of women in this realm of liberty and represented Christ, the Saviour: 'Freedom he sent, to bless this favour'd land; / Britain be free! he said; and Freedom then / Became the darling Right of Englishmen'.[105] In Britain, Mary Wollestonecraft (1759–97) wrote *A Vindication of the Rights of Woman* in 1792, so that the revolutionary spirit of the age was not lost on women. In her discussion of unnatural distinctions, she saw property as the root of problems: 'FROM the respect paid to property flow, as from a poisoned fountain, most of the evils and vices which render this world such a dreary scene to the contemplative mind.' That property and the lack of financial independence prevented women from being the people they could be:

> It is vain to expect virtue from women till they are, in some degree, independent of men; nay, it is vain to expect that strength of natural affection, which would make them good wives and mothers. Whilst they are absolutely dependent on their husbands they will be cunning, mean, and selfish, and the men who can be gratified by the fawning fondness of spaniel-like affection, have not much delicacy, for love is not to be bought, in any sense of the words, its silken wings are instantly shrivelled up when any thing beside a return in kind is sought.[106]

Not everyone shared or shared equally in the rights of 'man', to quote Tom Paine's phrase. Slaves, Natives and women did not as a rule participate fully in the freedoms and benefits of empire and colony. The voice of one slave and his groundbreaking work, which is a talking back to discrimination in the age of European expansion, is what we turn to next.

An Alternative Voice: Equiano

The colonized and enslaved began to speak up and write for themselves. In the crossing of the Atlantic the slaves were crowded and degraded in painful, deadly and unsanitary conditions. An important representation based on that hard experience was that of Olaudah Equiano (Gustavus Vassa). About half the slaves carried to the New World during this period were on British ships. In the year that Britain recognized the independence of the United States, William Pitt estimated that the West India trade, which included a large slavery component, accounted for about 80 per cent of Britain's income from overseas. Yet some ambivalence over slavery occurred in the religious communities and beyond. Despite the declarations and writings against slavery, it was not until the end of the eighteenth century that abolitionists became a significant political force. Anti-slavery activists were often involved in fighting other social ills and in advocating for rights and freedoms.

Diaries and autobiography were key genres in facing the question of slavery. A key autobiography was Olaudah Equiano's *The Life of Olaudah Equiano, or Gustavus Vassa, the African* (1789; rpt. 1814).[107] In the Dedication of 1792, Equiano (*c.*1745–*c.*1797) addressed the House of Lords and the House of Commons. According to Equino, the 'chief design' of the book was 'to excite in august assemblies a sense of compassion for the miseries which the Slave Trade has entailed on my unfortunate countrymen. By the horrors of that trade was I first torn away from all the tender connections that were naturally dear to my heart'.[108] While having suffered the misery of the institution of slavery and his own experience of enslavement and transport, Equiano also emphasized how fortunate he was to be introduced 'to the knowledge of the Christian religion, and of a nation which, by its liberal sentiments, its humanity, the glorious freedom of its government, and its proficiency in arts and sciences, has exalted the dignity of human nature'.[109] And so Equiano presented his book amidst the debate on abolition in the legislature. The Preface to the edition of 1814 noted that the subscription list included the heir to the British throne, his two brothers (princes), the duke of Marlborough and other illustrious people in Britain and said that Equiano would have been gratified 'had he lived to peruse the Bill for the Abolition of the Slave-trade,' which was passed in March 1807.[110]

The book reports that Equiano was an Igbo prince from what is now eastern Nigeria. After the front matter, the narrative, which Equiano/Vassa – the title page gives both names – seems to have worked on in new editions, represented a variety of experiences. The volume ranged from the customs of Equiano's homeland in Africa through kidnapping and slavery under various masters in Africa, England, and the West Indies to manumission and freedom. This narrative involved journeys overland and, even more, by sea. Even though there are some similarities with Aphra Behn's narrative about Oroonoko, Equiano's account, while representing some grim actions, shows much more hope than Behn's does. Equiano uses typology – a technique similar to Montaigne, Léry, Swift, and others. This strategy allows the author, narrator and reader to experience the world with one eye on here and another on there, one on now and another on then.

Abuses of colonization were no longer exposed in texts by Europeans like those of Las Casas and Montaigne. Equiano is an example of an enslaved African writing against the cruel nature of slavery. The word 'cruelty' and its cognates appear throughout the narrative. Equiano's memoir is saturated with slavery even before he is taken from his home and sold as a slave: 'My father, besides many slaves, had a numerous family, of which seven lived to grow up, including myself and a sister, who was the only daughter.'[111] Equiano gave one of the reasons for his despair that was based in a meanness that included but also exceeded the matter of race: 'But still I feared I should be put to death, the white people looked and acted, as I thought, in so savage a manner; for I had never seen among any people such instances of brutal cruelty: and this is not only shewn towards us blacks, but also to some of the whites themselves.'[112] Equiano set out many other instances of cruelty and abuse. For instance, Equiano asked one man who had sold 41,000 black slaves how he as a Christian could cut off a man's leg for running away from slavery and reminded him that Christian doctrine instructed 'to do unto others as we would that others should do unto us'.[113] Equiano reported that the overseers were often tyrants and a problem caused by humane gentlemen acting as absentee landlords, but he then named some humane masters in the West Indies. Nevertheless, Equiano did not keep from lamenting the brutal system that works and abuses slaves to death. Slavery is torture and sadism: Equiano revealed that as a result tens of thousands were needed annually in places like Barbados to replace them.[114] Further, he pointed a moral to the reader and the British and Europeans more generally: 'by changing your conduct, and treating your slaves as men, every cause of fear would be banished'.[115] As with Las Casas, with Equiano repetition and repeating expressions that repeat by denying they are doing so play a part in the building up of a case against cruelty. This narrative of cruelty built on the moral indignation of some early European writers on colonization but had an additional power derived from the victim writing about his or her experience.

The life of Equiano became entwined with the institution of slavery. The conclusion of the narrative expressed indignation over the slave trade. It also recorded that Equiano listened to the debate on slavery in the House of Commons on 2 and 3 April and then went to Soham in Cambridgeshire, where on 7 April he married Miss Cullen, daughter of James and Ann of Ely. An element of romance occurs in this long, hard journey of Equiano from a child kidnapped into slavery in Africa through a slave transported to the New World on a terrible slave ship to a free man married north of London. Throughout the book, Equiano distinguished between those who were show Christians and those who embodied Christian teachings. This distinction seems to have kept him from opposing his new religion to the abolition of slavery or his African roots. The moral takes the shape of a question: 'what makes any event important, unless by its observation we become better and wiser, and to learn to do justly, to love mercy, and to walk humbly before God?'[116] The travels and journey of the hero combined with a moral framework: the example of this life is a lesson against slavery and its injustices. Perhaps the greatest revolution was that of the colonized peoples coming to tell their side of the story of empire. And Phillis Wheatley and Equino helped make the way for others.

Phillis, of Senegal and sold to John Wheatley in Boston in 1761, was another early voice of African slaves. Her work was published in London in 1773 and it was surprising to some readers that an African could write poetry in English. In this framework, Wheatley faced racial discrimination more obliquely than Equiano did. In her poem, 'On being brought from A F R I C A to A M E R I C A', the speaker declares: 'Some view our sable race with scornful eye, / "Their colour is a diabolic die." / Remember, Christians, Negroes, black as Cain, / May be refin'd, and join th' angelic train.'[117] The poem addresses the colour bias in this instance in the Bible. This voice of Christian morality and religious commitment is in itself proof against the discrimination. Like Equiano after her, Wheatley seems to be trying to disarm the prejudice and fear of the British at home and in the empire.

Transitions

And Wheatley and Equiano were not alone. The Haitian Revolution (1794–1803) was part of the French Revolution that betrayed itself over the freeing of slaves. The French colony of San Domingo was the home to much cruelty toward slaves. There, Toussaint L'Ouverture led the African slaves of San Domingo against invasions by French, Spanish and English forces. This success produced the first independent nation in the Caribbean and became a symbol of the liberation of slaves and colonized Africans.[118] Although Toussaint was a general who fought for the French revolutionary government, Napoleon, through his brother-in-law, Charles Leclerc, betrayed the peace with Toussaint, who was seized and taken to France, where he died as a prisoner. John Greenleaf Whittier (1807–92), a Quaker who opposed slavery, wrote a poem, 'Toussaint L'Ouverture'. Whittier, an American of European descent, was like Harriet Beecher Stowe, who wrote about the abuses of slavery.

In the fifty to sixty years from the American Revolution through the Revolution of 1830, tensions arose in Europe, the Americas and elsewhere between liberty and authority, between rights and empire. Expansion seemed to be at its peak, even in the first age of modern decolonization. Once more, slaves, enforced labourers and indigenous peoples did not partake fully in the expanding empires. Their voices, although not often heeded, are part of the record, a counter-balance to the teleology of manifest destiny, patriotic mission, religious undertaking, and technological and economic progress. The ecology of the territories and adjacent waters where the Russian empire, the United States and the western European empires expanded suffered stress. Nevertheless, the age of high imperialism would be from the defeat of Napoleon until the First World War. During the 1830s that expansion intensified even further, as did the rivalries in empires and colonies. Once more, the motives, words, actions and results were mixed. It is this mixture, tension and contradiction or ambivalence, that opens the narrative and analysis to alternatives. In the wake of the Industrial, American and French Revolutions, western Europeans and their descendants in the colonies and the United States often took on an ideology of supremacy and progress that drove them to innovation and growth but also took them into the dark places of racism and entitlement. This double movement of liberty for Europeans, especially for property owners and the privileged, but not for women, workers, peasants, slaves, and indigenous and local peoples, created internal tensions in the metropolitan centres and the colonies.

5

High Imperialism: 1830–1914

෧෨

As imperialism gathered force in this period, it was also opposed by some at home. As European peoples expanded, whether in Russia, the United States or in the western European empires, disease spread and indigenous peoples were pushed aside, exploited or decimated. Cheap labour or slavery helped to underpin the economic growth of these 'white' empires. A tension within and between empires occurred, and amidst the patterns of progress and theories of superiority, some doubts occurred at home and some alternative voices and experiences remain of those who did and did not hold the leading roles or influence the course of empire or colony. In the wake of the revolutionary age, more revolutionary changes occurred. Industrialization and the wars in Europe affected the configuration of the world. And the world and its new decolonized independent states, especially the United States, affected Europe and the globe. But decolonization and recolonization in the Americas happened simultaneously. The British empire made Latin America a part of its informal empire as it was decolonized from the Portuguese and Spanish empires. The United States, which had been an example of decolonization, expanded and took over territory from the British, Spanish, French and Russian empires as well as lands from the newly independent Mexico. In the story of empire and colony, there is no one simple linear narrative, no even development.

This chapter moves from the revolutions in the Americas, which began decolonization in earnest, through to the high imperialism of Europe and its crisis that occurred as part of the First World War and its aftermath. Despite the loss of much of the New World, the western European powers continued their expansion. Britain, in India and elsewhere, was reaching its imperial apogee. At the same time, however, Germany, Japan, the United States and Russia were also gathering power and came to have imperial dimensions. This was a time of modernization and change that began to gather steam in the eighteenth century and has intensified ever since.

Industrialization intensified after 1840 in western Europe. Transportation, technology transfer and manufacturing output grew. There were few major wars until the American Civil War, although technology from the Industrial Revolution had a great impact on warfare. After about 1850, telegraphs, railways, rapid-fire guns, armoured warships and steam power all affected military strategy, influencing the ways in which Europeans and the settler cultures in colonies and former colonies waged wars on indigenous peoples. Industrial and technological change along with the development of bureaucratic systems capable of collecting taxes on a regular basis all had a bearing on warfare.

Asia and Europe had increased their commercial activities from the eleventh to fifteenth centuries and became more linked by trade than before. Until after the middle of the seventeenth century, there were raids from the steppes in eastern Europe and most of Asia. From the fifteenth to the seventeenth centuries, a gunpowder revolution took place. In the Low Countries, from 1465 to 1477, easily dragged wall-destroying cannon were invented. The cannon strengthened central authorities, and Muscovy, China, Japan, the Ottoman, Mughal, Safavid, Portuguese and Spanish empires all used such military might to consolidate and expand their power. Empires consolidated in Asia, but not so much in western Europe, where competition occurred in military innovation. The Ottomans felt that innovation in the 1660s, but this military superiority did not begin to take effect until the eighteenth century in India and the nineteenth in China and Japan. Internal frictions, for example the break-up of the Mughal empire, and growing population put strains on states in Asia, such as India and China. Asian governments had not modernized, so that when they came up against European military power in the second half of the nineteenth century, they had trouble resisting. The Industrial Revolution in Britain and then western Europe meant that Europeans had access to transport powered by machine and rapid-fire weapons that were mass produced. In the Americas, Australia, Oceania and sub-Saharan Africa, the discrepancy grew even more. But only in about 1850, when European medical researchers found a way to keep Europeans from dying of tropical diseases, did European states find full military advantage in Africa. As we have seen, in the Americas, Oceania and Australia diseases had worked in the opposite way – killing the indigenous peoples much more than the Europeans. The Aztec and Incan empires fell largely owing to disease. In addition to epidemiological circumstances, weapons technology from about the mid-nineteenth century made it difficult to resist European expansion. Gunpowder was a Chinese invention, but European competition led to innovation in this and other areas. European miners and metallurgists had developed great skills in Europe, which gave access to large quantities of cheap metals. These metals helped to make European ships safer in storms. The commercial network in western Europe became part of the political structure, especially from the seventeenth century, so that a military-commercial complex preceded what Dwight Eisenhower later called the military-industrial complex. There was more political interdiction in Asia. Many of the western European rulers needed loans to finance their wars and so allowed capitalist entrepreneurs to develop large enterprises largely unseen in other parts of the world. European propensities to violence and war seem also to have developed this industry. After the Reformation, intellectual dissent was easier to preserve in a fractured Europe. Innovation was part of conflict and competition, which also had darker and bloodier sides. This background to European technical and military superiority, from about 1850 to about 1914 or even decades beyond, was a meeting of changes in medicine and technology that were temporary. In this period, theories of race, some of which were awful engines of destruction and death, tried to account for the convergence of circumstances that briefly held in the long reach of pre-history and history.[1]

As in the past, no one empire could dominate long. A balance of power occurred. Pride must have its fall, as an English saying would have it. Paradoxically, at the height of empire, traditional modes of empire were declining. The strength of the British empire was its very weakness.

British Power

Britain's dominance from about 1815 to 1860 arose from its technological and industrial edge, but soon other countries like Germany, Russia and the United States began to gain ground. From 1780 onwards, Britain, and then the world, was able to harness the great Industrial Revolution that allowed steam-powered machines to do the work of people and workhorses and productivity soared to such an extent that the economy could support a vast growth in population. Europe's population grew from about 140,000,000 in 1750 to 187,000,000 in 1800 to 266,000,000 in 1850: Asia's increased from over 400,000,000 in 1750 to more than 700,000,000 in 1850. Britain alone went from 10,500,000 in 1801 to 41,800,000 in 1911. There were many more mouths to feed. Inanimate machinery burned coal but not calories from food, so that this helped to avoid a terrible pressure on the food supply. New World foodstuffs were shipped by steam-power to Europe. The steam engine and the power loom allowed Britain and then Europe, with a much smaller population than Asia, to take up a much greater share of the world's manufacturing output. After the expiry of the trade monopoly of the East India Company in 1813, cotton fabric imports rose from 1,000,000 yards in 1814 to 51,000,000 in 1830 to 995,000,000 in 1870. British manufacturers drove local producers out of business and so helped the de-industrialization of India.[2] Whereas in 1750 the Third World and Europe seem to have had similar per capita levels of industrialization, in 1900 it was one-eighteenth of Europe's (2 per cent to 35 per cent) and one-fiftieth of the United Kingdom's (2 per cent to 100 per cent). In 1800, Europeans controlled or occupied 35 per cent of the world's land; 67 per cent by 1878; over 84 per cent by 1914.[3] Industrialization and technology helped forge this massive expansion.[4]

About 1860, Britain had 2 per cent of the world's population but was responsible for about 20 per cent of the world's trade and 40 per cent of the trade in manufactured goods. Britain was unrivalled in producing wealth through its industry but tended towards a laissez-faire economy based on the notion that peace meant prosperity, so that from about 1815 to 1865 it spent a meagre 2–3 per cent of gross national product (GNP) on its military and its central government took up less than 10 per cent. Britain emphasized economic growth and its navy over military hegemony on land. Its navy was dominant. Despite some anti-imperialism at home, Britain expanded between 1815 and 1865 at a rate of 100,000 square miles a year. French, Russian and American expansion could not come close to this rate. Before about 1850, Britain shifted its colonial policy in many parts of its empire. Britain's tendency to favour a laissez-faire economy stressed commercial benefits from colonies and restrained spending on these territories. As Britain faced more economic and political challenges to its informal empire, it sought different strategies, including the exercise of more direct political rule outside Canada and the settler colonies. It sought to have influence and control and now had to formalize it because others would come into competition in its informal empire.

In concentrating on the growth of economic power, it is possible to forget the political and cultural friction that can complicate the mood of a nation, empire or colony. The British expansion in the mid-nineteenth century was, according to John Gallagher, often reluctant on behalf of the government of Britain and the result of pressures that opposition politicians, businessmen and humanitarians brought to bear on the party in power.[5] Free trade was an important aspect of the British empire in the nineteenth century, and this empire was complex. For instance, just as India passed from the informal to the formal empire from 1830 to 1870, the settler or white colonies were, as a result of the move to responsible government, moving in the opposite way.[6] V. I. Lenin thought that when free competition in Britain was at its zenith between 1840 and 1860, the leading politicians of the British bourgeoisie held the view 'that the liberation of the colonies and their complete separation from Great Britain was inevitable and desirable'.[7]

It is worth looking in more depth at the example of India, which epitomizes the many complexities of empire in this period. After the Seven Years War (1756–63), the government of Britain had exercised control in India through the East India Company, which made commercial agreements with local rulers who maintained their political privileges because of this understanding. When a throne became vacant, the East India Company would often expand its influence and construct railroads through the territories. In the meantime British institutions had grown up in India, favoured by Thomas Macaulay, an influential historian: Indians were to be part of the schools, administration and army and be imbued with British tastes.[8] In 1857, Muslim and Hindu troops in India rebelled against rules that violated their religious tenets: for instance, the Indian soldiers had to use cartridges greased with pig and cow fat. These soldiers conquered Delhi and declared an independent Indian state. This Sepoy Mutiny, along with the Jhansi revolt, was the beginnings of Indian nationalism.

The Sepoy Mutiny in the 1850s caused great debate over India. In the wake of this violence, E. H. Nolan set out how India was a focus nationally and internationally:

> The government of India has long been the theme of party politics in the legislature and throughout the British empire, and recent events have not diminished the tendency to debate the matter, even where the information possessed but little qualified the adventurous disputants. Foreign nations have entered into this discussion, and, prompted by envy or by an adverse policy, have subjected the settlement, progress, and government of the British in India to the most searching, stringent, and severe criticism.[9]

There is a political and diplomatic dimension to colonization that focuses on domestic and foreign policies of the metropolitan centre. Other powers use that relation between one empire and its colonies in a way that affects their connections with their rival. The conditions and the treatment of a colony become a source of political friction between imperial centres. How another power treats its colonies might well become more of a concern diplomatically than how a power looks after its colonies. The result of the turmoil in India was that the British passed the Government of India Act of 1858 that took control of India out of the hands of the East India Company. From about 1839, when photography was invented in France and Britain, world events were being memorialized and disseminated in a radically new way, sometimes to the point of manipulating the truth. The interpretation of events was undergoing a great change.[10]

From 1815 to 1870, Britain's investments overseas went from about £6,000,000 to £75,000,000, an impressive figure even with inflation.[11] In addition to financing the global economy, Britain imported food and raw materials and exported textiles and manufactured goods. Britain invested in its future competitors and developed an economy that relied increasingly on international trade and finance, not to mention foreign imports. Banking, insurance, commodities and investment depended on a world market. This liberal ideology of peace and prosperity, of being the leader and banker of the world, would not hold in perpetuity.

An important cultural dimension of imperial expansion, beyond economic concerns, is religion. The religious of the Christian church were part of an expansion from the beginning, although it is also important to remember that the expansion of Christianity happened long before the first European was converted, spreading as a religion from the Middle East to India and North Africa before coming to Europe. Additionally, as Norman Etherington has highlighted, British missions worked outside the British empire and many missions that were not British worked within the British empire, thus helping to reinforce the notion of the ambivalence, contradiction and intricacy of empire that this study has been setting out. The relation between empire and missionary work was ambiguous. Religion could sometimes run counter to imperial policy, and evangelical Christians did not often make the empire their frame of reference, which was providential. Missionary societies in Asia, Africa and elsewhere frequently needed to establish some relations with the government to enable their work. Conflicts between missionary and secular forces were especially intense between the late 1820s and the mid-1840s, particularly in places like New Zealand, New South Wales and the Cape Colony. Whereas numerous missions criticized settlers for dispossessing and killing the indigenous populations and for getting in the way of the work of emancipating slaves, civilizing and evangelizing, settlers often wanted more regulation of enslaved and indigenous peoples to ensure their material benefit.

Tensions between the imperial government and the settlers, missionaries and land- and slaver-owners showed the intricate forces at work among and within metropole, empire and colony. The anti-slavery movement of Granville Sharpe, Joseph Sturge, William Wilberforce, William Knibb and others had, as Catherine Hall has shown, a religious side that was part of a missionary dream of emancipation, where in places like Jamaica, the 'emancipated Sons of Africa' were part of a monument of the Knibb Baptist Chapel in Falmouth of 1841, and a desire for Christianity for all peoples that was so strong in some of the Nonconformist churches.[12] The Quakers, Wesleyans and Baptists were often active against slavery in Britain, the West Indies and the United States. Knibb, a Baptist, had contrasted the

Africans with the debauched white settlers in Jamaica. Settlers in Jamaica complained about the missionaries stirring up the enslaved against their masters. By the mid-nineteenth century, as Andrew Porter has noted, formal separation between church and state was happening and he also noted that there is no basic causal connection between religious expansion of the reach of British imperialism.[13] In British North America religious questions had related closely to political and constitutional questions even before the establishment of the Society for Promoting Christian Knowledge (1698) and the Society for the Propagation of the Gospel in Foreign Parts (1701) and up to the American Revolution. Religious dissent and political radicalism could have close ties. Even colonial officials could think beyond empire in terms of Christendom. William Bentinck, governor-general of India from 1828 to 1835, wrote to Charles Grant in 1833, saying that 'it is Christianity, the whole Christian Church, whose cause in this heathen country we are to cherish'.[14] The connection among empire, colony and mission was complex. For instance, the missionaries helped make Sierra Leone, a community of mainly liberated slaves from west Africa, work through their contribution to education and religion. In the Caribbean and the Cape, local white communities obstructed missionaries. During the Demerara and Jamaica rebellions of 1823 and 1831 respectively, planters persecuted missionaries, something that showed an alignment of missions with humanitarian and anti-slavery movements, which garnered them respect and empathy in London. At this point, official and commercial imperial interests as well as public opinion came to support the missions, which became part of the informal machinery of empire. Still, the evangelizers placed Providence above empire and civilization, even if they had come to see the British empire as a potential tool of God.

Missions grew in strength from the 1830s. Colonial bishops, like George Selwyn, Bishop of New Zealand in 1841, often melded their colonial, imperial and missionary functions. But this combination did not always work for those who sought to proselytize. For instance, David Livingstone, a missionary explorer, abandoned the connection between Christianity and civilization in central and southern Africa during the 1860s. There was a shift away from commerce and Enlightenment notions of progress and towards adapting to local ways and towards a millennial focus on the second coming of Christ. The great diversity of missions and changing circumstances locally qualify this or any other generalization. The missions detached themselves from empire in the period of high imperialism. One example in Africa was the Society of Missionaries from the Catholic Church (also known as the White Fathers because of the Arab costumes they wore). They faced the violence of the slave trade, colonialism and anti-colonial resistance as well as epidemics and ecological catastrophes and later faced suspicion among the German, English and Belgian colonial administrators owing to their mainly French nationality.[15] The World Missionary Conference in Edinburgh in 1910 shows a pan-national approach, as had the Anti-Slavery Society and the Aborigines Protection Society. The missions also took up causes such as the indigo workers in Bengal during the 1850s, the defence of African land rights against white chartered company rule, and the work of the Congo Reform Association after 1904. Missions lobbied the imperial government to take humanitarian action. The welfare of indigenous peoples, public works, medical missions and famine relief all became part of missionary work, and the central role of women in this movement was of key importance. In the scramble for Africa and the friction in China, the missionaries found themselves still sometimes at odds with the governments of the British and other European empires. A tension between the worldly and the spiritual never resolved even at the height of empire.

The Christian and humanitarian forces did not always have their way. The disappointment of the results of the emancipation of slaves in the West Indies tempered the attitudes of the British public and of the missionaries themselves. Charles Dickens, Matthew Arnold, Thomas Carlyle and others satirized humanitarian and missionary figures during the middle of the nineteenth century.[16] British public opinion was sometimes swayed by the violence between their relatives who had emigrated and the Native populations, such as in the intense indigenous resistance in New Zealand during 1845–6 and 1863–4, the eastern Cape during 1847–8 and 1850–2, and in India in 1857. The metropolitan media and the private correspondence of friends and family could often represent the Natives as savage and barbarous and the British as innocents suffering as they brought civilization of the lands they settled. Racism also played its part. And the American Revolution had something to do with this more than two generations after Britain recognized the independence of the United States. The debate on representative government in the English colonies in North America began early in the seventeenth century and the Revolution did not resolve the debate in the colonies that remained in the empire. Despite remaining with Britain, the colonies of British North America still had tensions over this question of representation. The rebellions in Lower Canada and Upper Canada in 1837 led to Lord Durham's *Report* in 1839, written only two years after the Aborigines Committee Report. Durham advocated the granting of self-government to the colonies in Canada as a way of securing their continued loyalty and, contrary to the Aborigines Committee Report, placed the fate of the indigenous peoples mainly in the hands of the local legislatures, which were controlled by settlers. The example of Canada was strong in other settler colonies. British public opinion had much less effect on settler institutions. Missionaries and humanitarians were losing their influence in Britain at a time when they had just secured their victories. The ambivalent and contradictory movement of empire can be seen in the juxtaposition of these two influential reports.

Governments undid the work of the missionaries, who had influenced the government in Britain regarding slavery and indigenous populations. In New Zealand, Governor George Grey, during his first appointment (1845–53), dismissed Clarke and closed down the Protectorate for Aborigines. During this period and during his second appointment (1861–8), Grey fought the sovereignty of the Maori through military force. Between these times, he helped to put down Xhosa resistance in the eastern Cape and to extend British rule to the area that had been restored to the Xhosa. In Australia, the Protectorates of Aborigines were also being abolished or rendered ineffective. There was no pattern of progress. Even with the diminution of the influence of missionaries and humanitarians, they could still – into the twentieth century – restrain the behaviour of the military and of the settler legislatures, but they could no longer control them, as they did for a brief moment up to 1840. Missionaries could rail against British excesses in expansion as well as at African slavers and rival European colonists in places like the Congo, but they never quite had the same influence again.[17] And Britain came up against the expansion of other rival empires, including the Russian empire. Their shared Christianity did not stop war when their interests clashed. Politics and imperial self-interest put great pressure on religious idealism and solidarity. So European states like Russia, Britain and the United States expanded and were rivals economically but also spread Christians and Christianity globally.

The Further Expansion of the United States

The Americans expanded north, south and west from the Atlantic seaboard. A few examples will provide some sense of this expansion, which had many dimensions. When Lewis and Clark reported that the rivers of the Rocky Mountains were full of otter and beaver, trappers and fur traders followed in 1807.[18] Trailblazing was important to the settlement of the west. An American trader, William Becknell, blazed the Sante Fe Trail in 1821, thereby connecting New Mexico to his own country. Sante Fe had been the northern capital of New Spain, and just weeks before Becknell arrived, Mexico declared its independence from Spain.[19] This trail connected the Spanish southwest with the economy of the United States, which would have predictable results given what had happened to the Floridas and Louisiana. By the 1830s, traders had extended the trail to San Diego and Los Angeles. By 1830, the trappers had marked out the trails that would soon lead settlers to California and Oregon, the first in Mexico and the second in territory disputed with Britain and Spain. In the early 1820s, there were about eighty wagons and in the 1850s more than 5,000. As we saw in the last chapter, the events of 1810 to 1821 left a vacuum as Spain lost control of its colonies, and Texas and other lands in the southwest seemed, to some Americans, to be theirs for the taking.

The west was comprised of Spanish territory that changed from New Spain to Mexico when the Mexicans gained independence and of the Pacific Northwest, which was disputed by Spain, Russia, Britain and the United States. In 1822, the Rocky Mountain Fur Company put advertisements in newspapers for white trappers and thus bypassed the long-standing practice of buying furs from Natives. In 1824, the Hudson's Bay Company established a post on the Columbia River in Oregon. The fur trade endured in this area until about 1840 when the numbers of animals had declined and gentlemen were switching from beaver hats to silk hats. During the 1840s, about 12,000 pioneers travelled about 2,000 miles on the Oregon Trail from Independence, Missouri to this territory in the Pacific Northwest. Ultimately, mountain fever, dysentery, typhoid and other diseases meant that 20,000 emigrants were buried along the trail.

The Pacific coast of North America was one Spain had been actively exploring and settling for about three centuries. The Spanish had made a concerted effort to move north when, in the middle of the eighteenth century, they learned that Russian traders and seal hunters were moving down the coast from Alaska. Spain established missions and *presidios* (military posts). From 1769 to 1823, the Spaniards established twenty-one missions in California and, by 1830, 10 per cent of the 300,000 Natives in northwest Mexico worked with crops and herding on those missions. With the independence of Mexico, the mission system was disbanded and their property given or sold to citizens. In 1833–4, the Mexican government expropriated the mission lands and exiled the Franciscan friars. The new owners, the quasi-feudal rancheros, worked the Natives as slaves and, by 1848, helped to cause the deaths of one-fifth of the Natives in California. In 1849, about 80,000 men arrived in California for the gold rush, and only half of these were Americans. The population of San Francisco went up twenty-fold in a short time. By 1848, Americans made up about half of the non-Native population of California. In the summer of 1850, about 55,000 would-be gold-miners followed the trail into California. It was a lawless place under military rule in which the many murders went unpunished and in which cruelty to, and prejudice against, Mexicans, Chinese and Natives were pervasive. Between 1848 and 1882, more than 300,000 Chinese entered the United States, but a law limiting their immigration was passed in 1882. By 1860, the gold rush was done, but California became a larger and more complex society in its wake.[20]

In the same period, the Natives in the east and south suffered the expansion fever of settlers and the policies of the federal government.[21] When Andrew Jackson was elected President in 1828, about 125,000 Natives still lived east of the Mississippi. In the south the Creek, Chickasaw, Cherokee and Choctaw held millions of acres of land. In the years to 1840, Jackson and his successor, Martin van Buren, uprooted the indigenous peoples, with the exception of the Seminoles in Florida and a small number of Natives living on reserves in New York, North Carolina and Michigan, and sent them west of the Mississippi River. Beforehand, the United States had followed both removal and assimilation. The missionaries thought assimilation was the best chance for survival of the Natives given the changes to the lands. Presidents Jefferson and Madison had thought removal would allow settlers to develop the land and permit the Natives to live in their traditional ways on lands far from the harassment of the white population. Until 1830, the government of the United States mixed the policy of encouraging Native Americans to settle on single-family farms and removing 'Indians' who would not. There was opposition to the Indian Removal Act, which was passed by Congress in May 1830. For instance, in the Senate, Theodore Frelinghuysen of New Jersey spoke against the Act, saying:

> Do the obligations of justice change with the color of the skin? Is it one of the prerogatives of the white man, that he may disregard the dictates of moral principles, when an Indian shall be concerned? No, sir. In that severe and impartial scrutiny, which futurity will cast over this subject, the righteous reward will be, that those very causes of equity which are now pleaded for the relaxed enforcement of the rules of equity, urged upon us not only a rigid execution of the highest justice, to the very letter, but claimed at our hands a generous and magnanimous policy.[22]

The shift in 1830 occurred because of a controversy between Georgia and the Cherokee, who had adopted a constitution that asserted sovereignty over their lands. In response, Georgia abolished tribal rule and claimed that the Cherokee were under the jurisdiction of this state. Gold was discovered on Cherokee lands, and the Supreme Court ruled in 1832 that the federal government was obliged to exclude white interlopers from Native lands. Andrew Jackson pressured the Natives to accept lands in Oklahoma and Arkansas.[23] In 1831, the Chocktaw made the journey west without the promised government assistance, and many died from exposure, malnutrition and cholera. In 1836, about a fifth of the Creek died on their march west, and those who resisted removal were chained and marched two by two. The Cherokee tried to resist, and despite government pay-offs, the majority resisted and were evicted from their lands by the army. Over one-quarter of the Cherokee died on the trek west. In

Illinois and Wisconsin, the United States army killed about 500 Fox and Sauk men, women and children during their resistance. The army killed about 1,500 Seminoles in Florida during seven years of resistance, and they kidnapped Osceola, the Seminole leader, during peace talks. Even by 1845, it became apparent that the Natives who moved west could not live safely in their lands. The tide of white settlers was upon them. In 1851, Congress passed the Indian Appropriations Act, which was designed to put Native populations in the west on reservations. Missionaries and humanitarians had agreed that the Natives needed to be moved west. The government could not protect them from the settlers. The Natives were supplied inadequately in their move and the lands they were given were often inadequate. This was part of European expansion in Canada, Russia, South America, Africa, Australia, New Zealand and elsewhere, as part of imperial or national interest and land and resource hunger.[24] Massacres of indigenous peoples occurred, and conflict between armies and local peoples. The Native American victory occurred at Little Big Horn when, on 25 June 1876, Colonel George Custer led 655 soldiers against the Sioux and Cheyenne. It was their contact with the Spanish that brought them horses then guns. These were necessary elements in their triumph. This victory actually harmed the Natives, who, although weakened by disease, were able to prevail. Crazy Horse surrendered in 1877, and Sitting Bull fled to Canada but returned to the reservation in 1881. The destruction of the buffalo herds between 1867 and 1883 left little food for the Natives. Reservations and starvation were the choice. In 1890 and 1891 the Indian wars ended with the death of Sitting Bull and the Massacre at Wounded Knee. In 1883, although he did not take part in the fighting at Little Big Horn, Sitting Bull, or Tatanka Yotanka, reported on the condition of the Sioux, sometimes in personal terms: 'It is your doing that I am here. You sent me here, and advised me to live as you do, and it is not right for me to live in poverty', and he later said, 'I want to tell you that our rations have been reduced to almost nothing, and many of the people have starved to death.'[25]

Texas was another part of the expansion of the United States. During the 1820s, Mexico welcomed American settlers if they converted to Roman Catholicism and became Mexican citizens. These American settlers, as General Manuel de Mier y Terán reported to the Mexican government in 1827, had their own schools, traded mainly with the United States and refused to learn Spanish. The Mexican government reasserted its authority, would not allow slavery (it was banned in the Mexican Constitution) and limited immigration from the United States. In 1832, Antonio López de Santa Anna became president of Mexico, and in 1834 he overthrew the constitutional government, abolished states like Texas, and became dictator. In November 1835, months after Sam Houston and his small force captured the Mexican military headquarters in San Antonio, American colonists in Texas set up a constitution, hoping for support by Mexican liberals, but not declaring their independence. Nearby, in 1836, Santa Anna's troops defeated a small band of Americans, including David Crockett, at the Alamo. Santa Anna mistreated the Americans here and at Goliod, where he broke an agreement and had 350 American prisoners of war shot. Soon, volunteers from the American south joined Houston, and on 22 April 1836, after defeating the Mexicans, Houston captured Santa Anna and forced him to sign a treaty granting independence to Texas. The Mexicans later refused to ratify this treaty because it was signed under duress. The next constitution of Texas denied citizenship and property rights to anyone who did not back the revolution. The Hispanic community was considered in that category, unless members could prove otherwise, and this caused many Mexican landowners to leave. Texas was independent and attracted immigrants. The population grew from 30,000 in 1836 to 140,000 in 1847. Cotton and cattle were the mainstays of the Texan economy. Although Texas immediately voted in a referendum (limited to just over 3,300 of its inhabitants) to join the United States, Andrew Jackson and John Quincy Adams opposed it. Texas became a point of friction between the south and the north over slavery. Sam Houston played up British interest in Texas, even though the British government was not interested in the colony, in order to spur the United States into annexation. British abolitionists were, however, pressing to have slavery outlawed in Texas in exchange for foreign aid. President John Tyler knew there would not be enough votes in the Senate for the two-thirds required for ratification of a treaty, so he proposed the annexation in a resolution that required only a simple majority in Congress. This was narrowly approved in 1845, perhaps because of the fear that Britain would take up Texas. This was the year that John O. Sullivan, editor of the *Democratic Review*, coined the term 'manifest destiny', that is, the providential gift to the American people of a continent that they could settle.[26]

The British ceded parts of present-day North Dakota and Minnesota in 1818 while the United States gave up a small part of what is now Alberta and Saskatchewan on the prairies. Britain also yielded parts of Maine and Minnesota, in the Webster–Ashburton Treaty of 1842. The rebellions of 1837 in Lower and Upper Canada (Ontario and Quebec) raised the hopes of some Americans that British rule would be overthrown and Canada would be annexed. The British and Americans also had a long dispute over the Pacific Northwest. Spain and Russia also claimed rights to the territory. Through the Hudson's Bay Company, the British were the most established there by the 1840s. By the mid-1840s, 6,000 Americans had moved to Oregon. In 1846, Britain and the United States compromised and made the forty-ninth parallel the boundary.[27]

The Natives in the west were a varied group, hunters like the Cheyenne and Sioux on the Great Plains and farmers like the Pueblo, Zuni and Hopi, hunters like the Navajo and Apache and others like the Gosiutes and Paiutes. The United States acquired California in 1848, when there were about 100,000 there, but disease and campaigns of extermination killed 70,000 Natives from 1849 to 1859. The Americans made Native women into concubines and reduced the men to servitude. Trappers shot the Paiutes and Gosiutes for sport. In the west, a war went on between some Native groups, like the Apache, Kiowa, Comanche, Shasta, Cheyenne, and Flathead, and the settlers, with the whites also accusing the indigenous peoples of atrocities. Between 1853 and 1857, the federal government used the army to protect settlers and to attack the Natives in the west while forcing the cession of 147 million acres of tribal lands. Utah was another area that became part of the United States. By 1877, there were 125,000 in Utah. This added half a million square miles to the United States.

Conflict with Mexico continued. Americans once more moved into Spanish and then Mexican territory (after independence in 1821). Within the United States tension over the Mexican War was between those who believed in Manifest Destiny and those who saw it as a trumped-up conflict in order to seize land. Ezekiel Merritt led a rebellion in California and declared it an independent republic in June 1846. General Zachery Taylor took Santa Fe in August 1846 and declared the 80,000 citizens of New Mexico to be citizens of the United States. In 1846 and 1847, the United States navy and army took California. The Mexican government refused to negotiate. The United States forces, under General Winfield Scott, captured Mexico City in September 1847. Ironically, this is the origin of the hymn of the Marine Corps that speaks about the halls of Montezuma, considering what had happened when Cortés invaded over 325 years before. The war was popular and even Walt Whitman supported it, but a vocal minority, like the abolitionist William Lloyd Garrison, as well as influential politicians such as Daniel Webster, Henry Clay, Thomas Corwin and Abraham Lincoln, opposed the war and stuck up for liberty for Mexico. Some saw the forces of pro-slavery behind this war. And the cost of the war to the United States in deaths was harsh: more than one in ten soldiers died from disease and exposure. Newspaper reports about brutality against Mexican civilians qualified public support in the United States. In protest over the war, Henry David Thoreau refused to pay a poll tax and was jailed. In response, he wrote his famous and influential essay, 'Of Civil Disobedience'. This war also raised again the question of slavery. Could this divided democracy solve the question of whether slavery would be allowed in the new American west? The Mexican War was a pretext and prelude not simply for expansion but for the American Civil War.[28]

The Civil War (1861–5) was fought in part over slavery. In the wake of that war Britain urged the British North American colonies to unite as one nation before a United States, a nation that had long shown an appetite for land at and beyond its borders. In 1864, during the Civil War, the British North Americans met, but it was not until July 1867 that four of the colonies formed Canada. Once the Civil War was over, the United States could once again look to matters of expansion. Ulysses S. Grant, a great general in that war and now President, wanted to annex the Dominican Republic, but the Senate rejected his treaty of annexation in June 1870. The United States was moving toward acquiring an overseas empire.

William Henry Seward of New York advocated such an empire when he was secretary of state. He negotiated the purchase of the Danish West Indies (Virgin Islands) from Denmark and of Alaska from Russia as well as the acquisition of the Midway Islands in the Pacific. From 1784, as Arrell Morgan Gibson has pointed out, the Americans explored and expanded trade in the Pacific Basin as far as China, partly to balance out losses in trade with England and Europe.[29] Congress reluctantly ratified the treaty in which the United States bought Alaska for $7.2 million. Anti-imperialists, such as Charles Sumner and Thaddeus Stevens, opposed the plans for expansion. Presidents Benjamin Harrison and Grover Cleveland had a policy of expansion and assertion of the United States as a power. In Samoa, 4,000 miles west of San Francisco, both the Germans and the Americans had interests. Britain, Germany and the United States met in Washington in 1887 but could not solve the impasse. Only a storm in 1889 in Samoa kept the German and American navies from firing on each other. That year the three countries met in Berlin and partitioned the islands; this changed in 1899, when Germany and the United States made official colonies of Samoa, against the will of the inhabitants (as in the case of the partition). In 1875, the United States had a treaty with Hawaii giving it preferential treatment that would allow it to sell its sugar duty free in the United States. In 1884, the United States signed another treaty with Hawaii for the exclusive use of Pearl Harbor by the American navy. Once more the white settlers came to clash with the local population and institutions. In 1891, Liluokalani became queen and proceeded to disenfranchise all white men, except those married to Native women. In January 1893, three days after she dismissed the legislature and proclaimed a new constitution, a rebellion occurred. It took three days for whites to overthrow her government. This pattern happened again and again from the Floridas through Texas to Hawaii.

The American government officials and military supported and helped with this revolution. Harrison tried to annex Hawaii before he left office but could not. Cleveland was an anti-imperialist who had misgivings about what happened in Hawaii. The new president accepted James Blount's report that a majority of Hawaiians were against annexation, and Cleveland wanted the queen back on the throne. She, however, would not give amnesty to the rebels, and Stanford B. Dole, head of a pineapple company, refused to step down as president. On 4 July 1894, the Hawaiian republic was proclaimed: four years later, during the Spanish-American War, the United States annexed it. Cleveland thought he had won a victory when the British finally allowed the United States to arbitrate a border dispute between British Guiana and Venezuela in an area where gold had been discovered in the 1880s. The United States was ready to throw its weight about, as could be seen in the Spanish-American war, which is discussed elsewhere in this chapter. The British government, as Jan Nederveen Pieterse has said, saw that Germany and the United States might well move from being rivals to the British empire and succeed it, so it encouraged the United States in the annexation of Hawaii and in the taking or control of Spain's colonies in 1898. There was, in both countries, a sense of Anglo-Saxondom. For instance, a line from N. Albert Sherman's song from the Spanish-American War illustrates: 'Sing hey! for Britannia, sing ho! For Uncle Sam.' Some key business and government leaders looked the other way in the Boer War and saw the importance for American trade and prosperity of the spread of English by the British empire.[30]

This period was full of shifts. The first insurgent movement in Cuba began in 1868 and there was a brief revolt in the Philippines in 1872. These events would culminate in the Spanish-American War of 1898.[31] Imperialism and colonialism were a matter that split the business and government leaders of the United States. In 1880, Andrew Carnegie, the American industrialist who had been born in Britain, thought that even though Britain had done a good job in introducing technology and institutions into India, it had harmed them by making the populace into colonial subjects. By 1885, he had focused his anti-imperialist position in regard to the United States.

War against Spain was not inevitable.[32] On 20 April 1898, McKinley signed the resolution that Congress had placed before him authorizing him to intervene in Cuba. Americans thereby abandoned isolationism and, along with the events in Hawaii and the Philippines, found themselves with an empire, informal and otherwise.[33] In the United States, the historiography of the Spanish-American War of 1898 has been split from the beginning between denials of imperialism and affirmation of the benefits.[34] In the face of a war against Filipinos themselves, President McKinley still used the rhetoric of the empire of liberty that was not an empire.[35] Others outside the United States attempted at the time of the conflict to understand it and did not always accept the British and American interpretation.[36]

The United States defeated Spain in the war of 1898, thereby taking into its sphere Puerto Rico and the Philippines, effectively ending the Spanish empire which had begun its decline at home in the middle of the seventeenth century and had lost its principal American colonies in the early nineteenth century. Spain itself was in its finale as an empire, so that, as Thomas Hart Baker, Jr has argued, its crisis in government had close relations to decolonization through its war with the United States.[37] On the Spanish stage there were numerous plays produced that represented the insurrections in Cuba and the Philippines.[38] This war between the United States and Spain was also a media or press war in both countries.[39] In 1898, Gonzalo de Quesada, a Cuban diplomat in Washington, and Henry Davenport Northrop published *Cuba's Great Struggle for Freedom*, which began with a rousing typological comparison of Cuba's fight for freedom with that of the incipient United States.[40] As in the translation of Las Casas that became part of the Black Legend of Spain and an aspect of the ambivalent and contradictory use of the example of the Spain by the English, French and others, here the Spaniards are made to be cruel and exploitative.[41] In the debate over the war, Senator White of California raised the question about this design: 'We hear much of our destiny, our *manifest* destiny. What "manifest destiny" can require any man or set of men or any nation to do that which should not be done? Are we destined for turpitude? What is that manifest destiny?'[42] As in Britain, in the United States the question of empire was vexed and divisive. The Spanish-American War was a conflict that allowed those inside and outside the United States to consider whether it was an imperial power as well as other issues such as the decline of Spain. In a report to the Secretary of War of 10 September 1898, Theodore Roosevelt mentioned that 'I was often told by officers who had seen service against the Indians that, relatively to the size of the army, and the character of the country, we had only a small fraction of the transportation always used in the Indian campaigns'.[43] Internal and external conflict and expansion possessed a typology of their own. In *Commonwealth and Empire* (1902), Goldwin Smith, an Oxford don who migrated to University of Toronto and then Cornell University in upstate New York, put the choice for Americans in a clear warning.[44] Smith did not think it a good idea for the republic to slide into empire and was explicit about this choice having serious implications for all of humanity. Imperialism is not worthy of the destiny of the United States. The commonwealth, in his view, has three forces working against it: plutocracy, militarism and imperialism.[45] Smith was specific on the ill consequences of such a partnership between the United States and Britain:

A league between two States in different parts of the globe, bound together merely by origin or language, yet sworn to fight in each other's quarrels,

whatever the cause was, would be a conspiracy against international morality and the independence of all nations such as would soon compel the
world to take arms for its overthrow. Nobody would be cajoled by such
phrases as 'spreading civilization' or 'imposing universal peace.' The world
does not want to have anything imposed on it by an Anglo-Saxon league or
by a combination of any kind.[46]

Smith is as sceptical and dismissive as Carnegie was about this civilizing
mission and ruling subject nations by policing the peace. This critique of
conspiring between the British and Americans sounds a little like Kaiser
Wilhelm II's more rhetorical extreme condemnation of Anglo-American
bandits. The kaiser was half English. Besides these reasons to condemn this
false unity was also the incompatibility of the American constitution and
the 'British game'.[47] There is, then, no one way to characterize the con-
geries of views surrounding empire, colony and imperialism generally, but
that is particularly true of this time of high imperialism.

The expansion of the United States continued, and because it had
always had territories beyond statehood and now possessed colonies not
intended to be states in the union any time soon, there was an imperial
dimension to the United States. Perhaps because it was soon forgotten that
so much of the continental United States had belonged to other empires
and ultimately to Natives before that and perhaps because of the overwhelming size of this soon-to-be heartland of the great republic, the areas
beyond this pale were not considered enough and the imperial dimension
of the United States occluded. Perhaps as a force that fought empire and
was the first great instance of decolonization, the United States was a reluctant imperial democracy. But, amid expansion, there was also a hunger for
land that was the other side of the question. Ambivalence and contradiction were as much a part of the American empire as of those of the older
European empires. These European states were still rivalrous amongst
themselves.

Rival States

Other imperial frictions and conflicts were brewing in these years. In
1898–9 France backed down before Britain over the Fashoda incident on
the Upper Nile. Germany, Italy and Japan were challenging the power of
Britain, France and the Austro-Hungarian empire while the great continental powers, Russia and the United States, continued to grow and
expand. Although the capitalist countries of central and western Europe
had become dominant at the end of the eighteenth century, they did not

translate their economic power into formal annexation, conquest and administration, but between 1880 and 1914 this was to change. The people who triumph, in what seemed to be a kind of Social Darwinist struggle for empire, are, according to Leo Amery, those 'who have the industrial power and the power of invention and science'.[48]

The Continental powers lagged far behind Britain. Only in the 1850s and 1860s did rapid industrial development come to Prussia. From 1812 until German unification in 1871, Berlin avoided provoking Russia, which dominated eastern Europe. The Habsburg empire, spread out from Galicia to northern Italy, balanced French ambitions in western Europe, Russian designs on the Balkans and Prussian dominance of the German states. Prince Klemens von Metternich himself sought alliances that would allow Vienna a central role in the balance of European power, but the Habsburg empire exhausted itself in trying to suppress nationalist causes, which were so central to the nineteenth century. It survived over the centuries the Reformation and the French Revolution and only dissolved from the effects of the First World War.[49] France was still wealthy and powerful, but, after Napoleon, the governments in St Petersburg, Berlin, Vienna and London blocked its ambitions for expansion at its borders. France had sustained huge casualties in the wars from 1793 to 1815 and its population grew more slowly than its rivals. Britain and France had the same manufacturing output at the beginning of the nineteenth century: in 1830, Britain's output was 182.5 per cent of France's and in 1860 it was 251 per cent. France, which had been so powerful during the seventeenth and eighteenth centuries and for the first fifteen years of the nineteenth century, did develop a large empire and a strong economy, but its ancient rival, Britain, had outstripped it in many ways. France also checked Russia most during the Crimean War (1854–6). The French empire was a counterbalance to British influence in Africa and Asia.[50] Russia, which had the dominant army in Europe after it defeated Napoleon, lost ground in industry and technology relative to the other European powers from 1815 to 1880 even though its population doubled to 100 million during that period. By mid-century, with its industry increasingly uncompetitive, its military weakening, and its per capita income slipping even more relative to western Europe and especially Britain, Russia lacked the extensive infrastructure (such as railways) that would serve the United States so well.[51] Russia lost 480,000 people in the Crimean War and the defeat helped to lead to reforms such as the abolition of serfdom. In the nineteenth century Russia had a much greater population than that other continental 'empire' – the United States – but lagged behind it in economic and political reform.

China and Japan were key places in the expansion of formal and informal western influence in the mid-nineteenth century. Christian missionaries from European countries helped to bring about a movement, the

Taiping, or Heavenly Kingdom, whose leader Hung Hsui-ch'uan (Hong Xinquan) thought he was the younger brother of Christ and who preached that the ruling Qing dynasty should end, foreigners should depart China, women should have more equal status, and morals and land distribution should be reformed. The Taiping controlled about half of China by the middle of the 1850s. To combat this challenge to its authority, the Qing government sought aid from Britain and France in exchange for greater political and economic influence. A civil war ensued that endured until 1864 and killed at least 30 million: in comparison, the United States Civil War, fought until 1865, took a toll of about 600,000 dead. This Chinese civil war left China under the indirect but powerful influence of the western powers. Japan fared better. When Matthew Perry declared in 1854 that Japan was open for trade, this intensified an interest in western technology in Japan. The Meiji Restoration of 1868 sought this technological power free from the political control of the west. In different ways and with varying degrees of success, China and Japan tried to resist the hegemony of the European empires and of the United States.[52]

Although the British empire was the leading world power, other countries played key roles. France developed under Napoleon III. Louis-Napoleon Bonaparte staged a coup on 2 December 1851 – the anniversary of the coronation of Napoleon I in 1804 – allowing him to seek a second term of his mandate as president. A year later he declared himself Emperor Napoleon III (r. 1852–70) and proclaimed the Second Empire. This pursuit of glory and grandeur sacrificed liberty. As the Ottoman empire declined, Louis Napoleon declared that France would protect the rights of Orthodox Christians in that empire, something Czar Nicholas I had already done. When war broke out between the Russian and Ottoman empires in October 1853, the British backed the Ottomans in order to protect its Mediterranean sea routes to east Asia while the Habsburg empire remained neutral. When Russia attacked Sinope on the Black Sea, France and Britain became allies and, to protect their interests and fearing Russian expansion, entered the war on the side of the Ottoman empire. The war killed over 750,000 troops and, despite ineptitude on both sides, was the first war to involve some new technologies, for example steamships, shell-firing cannon and the telegraph. The Crimean War checked Russia because with the Peace of Paris it lost the right to base its navy in the Black Sea and the Straits of Dardenelles. This defeat helped to bring reform to Russia. Serfdom had been debated in Russia. In Prussia, serfs had been emancipated in 1810 and in Austria in 1848. In 1852, besides Turgenev's representation of their lot in *A Hunter's Sketches*, a translation of Harriet Beecher Stowe's novel about slavery, *Uncle Tom's Cabin*, appeared. In 1861 Alexander II (r. 1855–81) emancipated 22 million privately owned serfs and, a few years later, freed

25 million publicly owned serfs. Despite the problems, such as the landowners getting the best land, this emancipation, coupled with judicial reform, set out principles of the equality of people before the law. It is quite possible, as Orlando Figes suggests, that had Alexander II implemented Sergei Volkonsky's programme of reforms (similar to those of Pyotr Stolypin between 1906 and 1911), Russia might have been more prosperous.[53] It is also possible that had these further-reaching reforms occurred, some of the subsequent peasant rebellions could have been avoided. The French and British empires had helped to check the expansion of the Russian empire and – something particularly important for the French – to weaken its alliance with the Habsburg empire in Austria. This war had also ushered in modernization in the Russian empire that would help it, however haltingly, become a modern power in the twentieth century. For the French, they were able to work out a free-trade agreement with Britain in 1860. Imperial matters were also a central concern for Napoleon III, who enforced French rule in southeast Asia and in Algeria and tried to make Maximilian, brother to the Habsburg emperor, the ruler of Mexico. Having opposed Russia in the Crimean War, France fought with Austria in the war surrounding the unification of Italy and against Germany in 1870, when Napoleon III's defeat led to his downfall.[54] Bismarck had isolated France and Russia, for Austria and Britain did not oppose Prussia in its war against France. Besides developments in industry, banking and railways since 1850, France's colonial empire expanded in the Pacific, Indochina and west Africa, and its fleet had grown.

More than the Habsburg and French empires, Prussia took advantage of the technological revolution in the 1850s and 1860s that grew out of the Industrial Revolution and that transformed warfare and military forces. Prussia had a long compulsory military service, a large population with a basic education that made good modern soldiers, a systematic study of war strategy and a strong system of logistics. The Prussian command studied its strengths and past mistakes and made improvements. Prussia defeated the Danish in 1864, the Austrians in 1866 and the French in 1870. Another new power was on the rise. In 1870, the German states had a larger population than France, had more miles of railways and its gross national product and iron and steel production were about to overtake that of France. Above all, Prussia and the German states had a more educated general population and better scientific institutions, laboratories and universities than their rivals on the continent. Otto Bismarck made a unified Germany the dominant continental power after 1870. In January 1871, in the Hall of Mirrors at Versailles, King William of Prussia became the kaiser or caesar of the German empire. The translation of empire looked back to the Roman caesars and to Louis XIV, who, as the most powerful monarch in Europe, built Versailles. This gesture, as gratifying as it was to another caesar, Czar Alexander II of Russia, embodied a symbolism and new order that would plague Europe and the world until 1945, with lasting effects to the present. Besides, the French had to give up the rich industrial lands of Alsace and Lorraine to Germany and pay a massive indemnity, a humiliation that set the stage for France to retaliate with terms in kind at the end of the First World War. The Habsburg and French empires were slipping while Germany was rising to challenge all others but, ultimately, the greatest power itself: Britain. Western Europeans could not have known it, but in the summer of European power, the seeds of destruction were being sown. After Bismarck, German ambitions would grow. In the meantime, Bismarck acted as a diplomatic broker between the British and the Russians over Afghanistan, and his treaties achieved peace and delayed war in the 1880s. When the French acquired Tunis, the British intervened in Egypt and the scramble for Africa marked the start of a new wave of imperialism. Writing in 1930, Mary Evelyn Townsend could declare: 'Today Germany stands alone, the only Great Power without a colony' and then proceeded to explain that 'Since 1918 the Allies have partitioned these lands among themselves, and hold them today as mandates under the League of Nations'.[55] The German rise to imperial power would in time lead to a fall that would involve the stripping of its colonies. Germany and the United States began their rise while Britain, still the great power, had peaked in the late 1860s. Before the technological advancements of the 1860s, those powers like the Habsburg, Russian and French empires who did not adapt to the military revolution and those peoples outside of Europe who had not been part of the Industrial Revolution fell behind or before the industrial and military might of those countries that were at the cutting edge of technology.[56]

Profit based on trade or loose control based on trading posts had been an aspect of European imperialism, but more direct control was a hallmark of the new imperialism. During the early 1890s, Max Weber saw this scramble for expansion among these European imperial states as coming down to a matter of power of who would get how much of a share of economic control in the world.[57] The shifts in capitalism and the politics of economic exploitation were and are central to the debate on the roots and ground of imperialism, particularly in this period, and the frictions leading up to the First World War. Competition for economic and political influence within Europe and round the world related to the military build-ups and the Great War. The global economy that had been developing for many centuries had now reached just about every corner of the globe: technology was always a key to imperial expansion.[58] One central key to expansion was that in Africa.

The Scramble for Africa, the Middle East and Asia

North Africa and the Middle East are examples of the increase in European involvement in the political economy of other regions.[59] France and Britain were interested in commercial opportunities in Egypt. Trade with Egypt grew about six times from 1838 to 1880 and threefold from then until the eve of the First World War. The Suez Canal, railroads and telegraphs affected this trade considerably. European bankers charged about 240 per cent more for loans to rulers in Asia and Africa than they did to those in Europe. The British government bought a large share of the Suez Canal in 1875: soon almost nine-tenths of the India trade passed through this canal. Four years later, Britain and France took over the Egyptian treasury to secure their investments. The nationalist response to this incursion on national sovereignty brought about a British military response, despite opposition at home – the bombing of Alexandria and the invasion of Egypt in 1882. Britain controlled the khedive's government indirectly and modernized the Egyptian economy by constructing irrigation systems, introducing agricultural machinery and abolishing forced labour. The British also reduced the country's diverse farming sector, which could feed its populace, to crops necessary to Europe: silk, wheat, rice and cotton. France moved into Tunisia in 1881 and flooded Algeria with settlers. Germany, Britain and France moved into the markets of Asia Minor, their cheap goods affecting local artisans adversely. At home, these powers paid women less than men; in this region they discriminated on the basis of religion and ethnicity. It is no wonder that nationalist movements rose up as imperialism intensified.[60]

European imperialism gathered even greater momentum from about 1870 to 1914. From the 1870s, expansion in Africa intensified, and this brought much of it under direct rule by European powers. This acquisition of territory came with the cost of intense violence and caused discord among and within western European states. In Africa, a shift occurred from the traditional exchange directly or indirectly, which we observed especially in the last chapter, of slaves for manufactured goods. The raw materials of Africa – such as cocoa, cotton, rubber, palm oil and diamonds – attracted the Europeans.[61] As the world's foremost naval and industrial power, Britain wanted to control the eastern and southern coasts of Africa, while controlling the Suez Canal to maintain its empire in India and beyond. European direct political control was coming to Africa. Portugal, which began the expansion into Africa, was still there. France, Belgium, Germany and Italy were all involved in the scramble for Africa. Perhaps the most ruthless colonizer was King Leopold of Belgium (r. 1865–1909), who claimed the area about the Congo river in central

Africa and whose agents – according to missionaries – killed people or amputated hands of those who did not reach targets or quotas and sent them to government officials, who in turn showed them to the king. Germany established control over Cameroon (Kamerun) and part of east Africa and France extended its hold on western Africa. Britain poured its vast financial resources into dominating Africa from Cairo to Cape Town. The Berlin Conference in 1884–5, which included the United States and Russia, involved an attempt to come to terms over trade, boundaries and navigation in the Congo and west Africa and set the framework for the European division of Africa. Britain, France and Germany were the key players in these meetings. As Max Weber suggested, the question of power underlay this imperial expansion; Bismarck called a conference to resolve these problems, but this meeting of fourteen states extended European coastal holdings inland and carved up the continent for the European powers geometrically and with little regard for culture and ethnicity. But despite the banning of the sale of alcohol and guns to Natives, the conference did not stem the imperial tide. Guns, gunboats and quinine (which allowed Europeans to have a much higher survival rate in the face of malaria) all contributed to this continued carving up of Africa. Muslim slave traders and Christians used new types of guns (the machine gun developed after the early 1660s) to subdue and subject the Natives. For instance, the Zulu, Xhosa and neighbouring peoples fought the Boers, or descendents of the Dutch colonists who had settled the area in the seventeenth century, and British immigrants. Gold and diamonds were some of the riches at stake. Racial rationalizations for subjugating peoples were now a part of imperialism. The Europeans dispossessed the Africans culturally, politically and economically. None the less, William Gladstone (1809–98) could become prime minister of Britain, after an election campaign in 1879 in which he appealed to a wider franchise of voters – as more workers and middle-class men could vote after the most recent reforms of 1872 – with a call for more self-determination in Africa and India, much to the dismay of Queen Victoria.[62]

For Britain, by the 1870s, Africa was important for resources, as a base against the slave trade and as a stopover for India and the Far East. Britain was concerned with the decline of the Ottoman empire, which served as a buffer against Russia, and supported the work of missionaries, merchants, administrators and consuls in a way that came to cost much more over the course of the nineteenth century. The British saw that the Suez Canal and the route round the Cape were profitable and strategic but expensive to maintain. Britain sought to find a way for Egypt to pay for its defence and to make the southern African colonies, which had failed to form a self-governing federation, more financially feasible. Part of this move to make colonies more profitable was to bring them under the

Crown. Sometimes this came with violence, as in Sir Garnet Wolsey's campaign to subdue the Transvaal and Natal and to break apart the Zulu kingdom. Cecil Rhodes, who had political and financial clout in the Cape, pressed the British government to extend its imperial reach in Africa. Britain used alliance and clientage more than conquest in southern Africa. German and Portuguese competition did not change the view of the imperial government in London that unless colonies shared costs, Britain was not willing to commit to controlling territory.[63] French and British explorers disputed major trade routes in western Africa. Britain had to react to the different strategies of other European powers who had intensified their interests in Africa. The Anglo-German agreement in 1886 marked spheres of influence for the two states in east Africa. French ambitions in west Africa brought Germany and England closer. In the negotiations with Germany in 1890, Salisbury gave up the corridor from the Cape to Cairo and ceded Heligoland in exchange for recognition of a British sphere from Italian Somaliland to the coast. The agreements with Germany over these years depended on how much the British needed German friendship or how much the Germans needed Britain as a counterbalance because they did not want a war on two fronts with Russia and France.[64] In 1890 Salisbury recognized French Madagascar while the French recognized the British Zanzibar Protectorate. The European powers were apparently bargaining with each other over the division of Africa without African input.

From 1890 to 1914, European control became more centralized. In responding to French military expeditions and as a means of securing territory, Britain, from the early 1890s, made more use of imperial troops, forces on the frontiers and local militias as they had done in South Africa. Britain was moving from diplomacy to political and military control. In Africa, the friction between Portugal and Britain, ancient allies, was partly based on misunderstanding. Raphael Bordallo Pinheiro's cartoons satirized Britain and Portugal, not simply the relation between them.[65] In return for a future share of Portuguese territories, the Germans agreed in August 1898 not to intervene in Transvaal. The groundwork for the Boer War had been set. In Egypt, Lord Cromer controlled the state while the Khedive ruled; something other European states, except France, accepted. France and Germany frustrated the British attempt to use Leopold's Congo as a buffer on the western Nile. Lord Kitchener obtained the withdrawal of the French under Marchand at Fashoda in 1898. Paradoxically, Britain, as Keith Robbins has pointed out, expanded into Africa and Asia because the decades of unchallenged informal control and global supremacy were over.[66] The Anglo-French convention of June 1898 set out the frontiers of Northern Nigeria and the Gold Coast, and an understanding was reached in regard to the boundary with German Togo. Having settled matters with

France, Britain sought settlements with Russia in Asia and concentrated on its naval and industrial race with Germany. The British became more influential in Egypt while the influence of France waned, and the opposite occurred in Morocco. The Anglo-French Entente of 1904 led to British support for France against Germany in the Morocco crises of 1904–6 and 1911. Leopold abandoned claims to the Sudan in 1906.

The Africans offered resistance to this collusion and competition among European states with ambitions in Africa. For instance, there were revolts in Zululand and Asante between 1900 and 1906. Britain and other European states created boundaries that may have resolved conflicts among them but left the Africans torn by artificial political lines through their cultures. The legacy of this carving up of Africa endured long past the outbreak of the Great War in 1914.[67]

There were great episodes of violence. The Maxim gun and European military technology in the second half of the nineteenth century and beyond inflicted great losses on Africans. Occasionally, the underdogs among settlers and tribes won great victories, as the Abyssinians (Ethiopians) did against the Italians and the Boers did against the British, but most inhabitants of Africa were not so fortunate. At Obdurman, the British killed 10,000 Sudanese but made no attempt to save the 15,000 wounded. The Herero, who had suffered an epidemic among their cattle, violence and persistent mistreatment at the hands of some of the settlers, rebelled against the Germans who had come into their lands and taken them as a colony in southwest Africa. In a war against them, General Lothar von Trotha was ruthless. Kaiser Wilhelm II, who had secretly wanted to give the colony to the British because it cost the treasury a great deal, had told him to crush the revolt by fair means or foul. Von Trotha issued an extermination order or *Vernichtungbefehl* against men, women and children of a tribe, driving away about 20,000 of them from wells so they could die in the Omaheke desert. Despite the outcry among some in Germany, when Trotha returned home in 1905 the kaiser awarded him the Order of Merit.

Guns divided up Africa in the final stages of the scramble and would be used again in the movements of independence from the European powers. Sir Roger Casement's report on Leopold's abuses in the Congo received some strong support in the British government, but neither Germany nor France had any intentions of calling a conference on the Congo. For the German government, they backed Leopold for fear that France would get hold of Leopold's private domain in the Congo as this was not an official Belgian colony. Leopold himself had tried to diffuse criticism in the 1890s by having the Native Protection Commission, made up of three Belgian Catholic priests and three British and American Baptist missionaries, look into violence against Natives, but he made sure the commissioners were far from each other and outside the areas that produced rubber, where the abuses were said to have happened.[68]

It is important to remember the violence that all these European states used in their empires. In Africa, the Portuguese had used slave raids in the fifteenth century. All the European powers in the scramble for Africa used terror and violence at one time or another. The Boer War had its own share of ignominy for Britain. The pro-Boer Liberal Members of Parliament had considered as a mistake Kitchener's placing women and children into 'camps of refuge'. Two MPs, John Ellis and C. P. Scott, borrowed from the Spanish *reconcentrado* camps in which they placed Cuban guerrillas the phrase 'concentration camps'.[69] The French and Germans were protesting these abuses. Dame Millicent Fawcett produced a report in which she pointed out the catastrophe of camps in which thousands of white and black people were dying of disease partly because of the medical neglect and lack of support. Lloyd George predicted that this mistreatment of children would be the way the beginning of British rule in South Africa would be remembered.[70] The Janssens Report of 1905 confirmed Casement's and blamed the Catholic missionaries for not making the atrocities public.

Only two African states remained free by 1912 – Liberia, a country populated by ex-slaves from the United States, and Ethiopia, which had doubled the size of its domain. France took most of Morocco, left Spanish west Africa to Spain and gave some of the French Congo to Germany. Italy seized Cyrenica and Tripoli in a war with Turkey and formed Libya.[71] The scramble for Africa was full of contentions, contradictions, indirections and about-faces among and within the European empires. African resistance would pick up later in the twentieth century in reaction to some of the violence, compromises and injustices that Africans suffered during this period. New states, formed by European empires, would use some European techniques and technologies against the Europeans themselves.

The old empire had to cope with the new: power relations made that translation, even among allies, difficult. Later, the United States, which had to put up with British power, later held the power that their mother country, its ally, had to abide. But that was a typology that Britain did not have to face quite yet. The Germans themselves had had organizations for the acquisition of colonies during the 1860s and 1870s, but it was not until between 1883 and 1885 that Bismarck acquired colonies largely as a means to expand German markets and to protect German investments.[72] German rule in southwest Africa, according to Helmut Bley, was not unlike that in other colonies and indeed the Germans borrowed colonial administrative and legal practice from other imperial powers. What did the scramble for Africa have in common with the earlier scramble for America or any of the other colonial scrambles that European expansion wrought and how did it differ from these various expansions? The competition for land, wealth, influence and power pushed each state to expand, sometimes in self-interest, and partly in fear that a competitor would do so.

South and east Asia, too, had long felt the influence of European trade, political pressure and colonies. Imperialism in India often changed the cultural and political landscape. Indians served in the army and civil service, and improved sanitation and medicine helped to contribute to the boom in population. Members of the elite were often subject to British influences and some groups in that upper class could turn on their own traditions, such as the self-immolation of a widow on the funeral pyre of her husband (*sati*), child marriage and infanticide. Paradoxically, the British empire made a united India, which in turn was becoming a national entity that could in turn rebel against that very empire. In 1876, in Westminster, Parliament declared Queen Victoria empress of India. The policymakers in Britain ended the production of finished goods, such as textiles, that would compete against British manufactures and emphasized raw materials such as jute, cotton and wheat to feed Britain and its industries. Mercantilism was not dead and never quite dies. The British civil service in India practised segregation and discriminated against Indians, whose elite founded the Indian National Congress in 1885 in order to challenge British rule. Ultimately, this movement would gain widespread support and would help make India independent.[73] On the borders of India, the British extended their military control, of the Malay peninsula in 1874 and the interior of Burma in 1885. This force secured rice, oil, teak, tin and rubber and allowed the British to build railways and factories in an area that was a gateway to China.

In part, the British might well have been trying to counteract the great expansion of the French and Russian empires. The French, too, were on the doorstep of China, creating the Union of Indochina (Cambodia, Tonkin, Annam and Cochin China) in 1887 and adding Laos to it in 1893. The French, who improved public health and sanitation generally in the region, put in place projects in the Mekong Delta that increased the amount of farmland and food production. As in India, the population grew rapidly owing in part to these developments. The French saw their imperialism as a cultural mission and promoted French literature and architecture in Indochina. Like the Indian elite, that in Indochina used Western culture and ideas against the resident European imperial power. From 1865, Russia absorbed Muslim states in central Asia, for example Turkestan and parts of Afghanistan, and extended into the Ottoman empire, Persia, India and China. Like other imperial states, Russia met resistance from Native populations that did not want to give up their land to the intruders. By building a transcontinental railway, it integrated its own colony – Siberia – into its own polity.[74]

Unlike China, Japan escaped European imperial dominion. Japan modernized so much and had its own imperial agenda, thereby creating enough power to deter European or American hegemony. After 1868, the Japanese government sent officials to study industrial and technological advances in the United States and Europe. Japan had its own sense of national modernization which also developed an imperialist chauvinism that had certain affinities with western imperialism.

Empire created liabilities as well as benefits. The British and Russians had become rivals; the Balkans were explosive; the maintenance of empire was expensive while colonies provided raw materials and a market for manufactured goods; imperial competition might lead to war; Europe itself was undergoing many conflicting changes in belief, thought, culture and economics as it helped to transform the world. This transformation of everyday life and of politics, culture and economics affected villages, towns, cities, nations, colonies and empires.[75] Nationalism and imperialism were in Europe and overseas flipsides of a politics of identity and empowerment. The legacy of the nationalist revolutions of 1848 could not be contained within Europe any more than the American and French revolutions could be in the previous century. Empire and colony could never be separate.

Formalizing Empire

Many of the empires were for a long time a loose set of different kinds of colonies and commercial enterprises, but in the nineteenth century the structures of empire became more formal and often more centralized. This formalization of empire occurred mainly under the aegis of Britain, France, Belgium, Germany, the Netherlands, Belgium, Italy, the United States and Japan, while the pre-industrial empires of Spain and Portugal waned. Spain attempted to exert influence in northwest Africa but lost Cuba, Puerto Rico and the Philippines in its war with the United States in 1898. Portugal held on to its territories in Africa – Mozambique and Angola – which, in E. J. Hobsbawm's view, outlasted other imperialist colonies 'due primarily to the inability of their modern rivals to agree on the exact manner of dividing them among themselves'.[76]

The Portuguese empire was the oldest western European empire, but most of its territory was acquired after 1884. It also endured longer than most in the age of decolonization. After the succession of Brazil in 1822, Portugal lost no colonies until India seized Goa in 1961. Although not unconscious of racial difference, the Portuguese never had a colour bar in its colonies. From the 1580s to 1822, Portugal lost many of its colonies.

In 1832, Portugal incorporated the Azores and Madeira into the metropolis. At this time Portugal had enough colonies to be an imperial power, but not a key one any longer. The partition of, or scramble for, Africa in the late nineteenth century did not demolish what Portugal held there, but actually enlarged its holdings. Balanced between Britain, France, Belgium and Germany, Portugal increased its territory in Portuguese Guinea, Angola and Mozambique. Like France, Portugal aimed for full integration and making the national assembly in the home country the ultimate authority for the empire. The successor to the Council of the Indies, the Overseas Council, which began in 1643, still advised the Ministry of Maritime and Overseas. In 1911, Portugal set up a Colonial Office.[77]

The Dutch kept their profitable ancient colonies in southeast Asia. After 1815, the Dutch empire was a remnant of the territories of the East and West East India Companies, which became defunct by 1800. It was the only western European empire that was no bigger in 1914 than it had been in 1815. The Dutch had lost a good number of colonies by the early nineteenth century. For instance, the Netherlands lost Ceylon (Sri Lanka) and their bases in India to Britain before 1815 and Malacca and Singapore in 1824. Until 1872, the Netherlands held Elmina, a one-time part of the slave trade in west Africa, but transferred it to Britain. The Netherlands did not partake in the scramble for colonies in Africa and elsewhere that other European empires did during the nineteenth century. In the Caribbean, they had the sugar colony of Surinam and the trading islands of Curaçao and St Eustacius. The Dutch had developed their main sphere of colonial influence since the seventeenth century – the East Indies. Indonesia, which was one of the most valuable European colonies, remained under Dutch rule. There, the Dutch government, following the East India Company, made no great attempt to spread Dutch culture, language and religion. When the government took over from the company, they moved away from Native rule and began to annex Native territories, which, by the 1930s, meant that Dutch sovereignty obtained in 93 per cent of Java and more than half of the outer islands. By 1900, with more European immigration, the Dutch hid more centralized government of residents and their European deputies behind indirect rule. Batavia exercised more control. There were some later experiments in decentralization that the Japanese attack in 1941 ended. By that time, the Native States, led by princes, had changed from full protected states to colonial protectorates. The pattern from companies to centralized government in the colonies is a familiar one in the French, English and Dutch colonies. This was a formalization of empire.

Law and land were areas in which the Dutch, while formalizing their empire, maintained some of the practices of the East India Company, for instance of indirect influence and recognition of Native customs while modifying others. The Dutch preserved Dutch-Roman law and Native laws. They had different court systems for both, but most Indonesians came under the jurisdiction of courts staffed by Europeans and administered by the government. These courts applied Dutch-Roman law in criminal cases and Native custom in civil matters. On the whole, the Dutch stuck with the principle that like should try like. The East India Company had forbidden the permanent alienation of Native land to European individuals. The Dutch government allowed for freehold, which took up a good deal of Java between 1800 and 1815, but then reversed the policy. The government then took over in the public domain all the land that the Indonesians did not seem to be using, a policy that, owing to cultural differences about land, led to friction and injustice. The government then leased this land to Europeans for up to seventy-five years. Indonesia became a plantation economy in which Europeans controlled the production of export staples like copra, tin and petroleum and commodities like rubber, tea, coffee, tobacco and sugar. As in most European plantation economies, in the Dutch colonies, labour issues arose. Most Europeans paid for workers in Java, but some exploited the native custom of forced labour, based on a large number of days in lieu of rent. In the Outer Islands, where there was a shortage of labour, the Dutch allowed for the recruitment of contract labourers from Java and elsewhere. One particularly harsh aspect of this practice was that if an indentured labourer broke the contract it was a criminal offence. The Dutch developed a bad reputation with humanitarians about their exploitation of Indonesia for profits for the metropole. The Culture System from 1830 to 1870, which used a system of tribute that the East India Company had employed before 1800, was one of the causes for complaint. The British pressure for reform and free trade reduced trade between the Netherlands and Indonesia radically from 1870 to 1930. Leopold of Belgium had been interested in the Culture System as an example of how profits could be taken from a tropical colony. In the years before 1941, the Dutch took a more paternalistic view and developed social welfare and education. The civil service was open to people of all backgrounds and the population nearly doubled from 1905 to 1940. The economy became diversified.[78] The record, as in most cases in the expansion of western European empires, was mixed.

Other Europeans scrambled for colonies. Leopold II of Belgium was able to have dominion over the Congo as long as he kept it open to the European powers. The Belgian empire consisted of a single territory – the Congo. Later, the German territories of Urundi and Ruanda were added to it. Leopold II acquired the Congo as a private estate that he treated as an investment. His methods of generating profit led to a humanitarian outcry over this and other forms of European colonization. After the

Belgian government took over the colony and thereby formalized it in 1908, the treatment of the Native peoples was more humane. Although the Congo Free State began between 1876 and 1885 with humanitarian objectives, Leopold hid behind the trappings of government to manage the place himself as his private concern. When in 1890 Leopold had no capital left, he sought out the exploitation of natural resources that required little investment: wild rubber, palm oil and ivory. As monopoly had been ruled out by the Berlin Act, Leopold divided the Congo in 1892 into three sectors, two of which he controlled and the third and least profitable he left open to competition. Leopold needed cheap African labour for his scheme to succeed and he turned to something like the Dutch Culture System to achieve this end. There were widespread abuses in this system of contract labour. Foreign observers, including missionaries, complained. By 1905, Leopold's private army consisted of 360 officers from different European countries and 16,000 Africans. Leopold could not control the abuses on the ground by his subordinates and this led to the notoriety of his colony. In 1911, the government of Belgium, three years after taking control of the Congo, itself chronicled the abuses of Africans to force their labour to increase production and make great profits.[79]

Not all colonial empires were ostensibly profitable. The German colonial empire, which was short-lived, lasting from 1884 to 1919, may have generated profits but it also relied heavily on subsidies from the German taxpayer. The Germans, like other Europeans, could mistreat Native peoples. Their colonial empire may not have paid for itself, so part of having such an empire was as much to do with national prestige and glory as with profit. Colonies sometimes look as though they will be profitable when they are not or, if they are, that the profits will be more enduring than they are. Most of the German empire was in Africa: Tanganyika, Kamerun (Cameroon), Togoland and southwest Africa. In the Pacific the Germans held Opulu and Sawaii; the Caroline, Marshall and Mariana Islands; the Bismarck Archipelago; and some of New Guinea. In China, the Germans held the lease of Kiao-Chow. Most of these were colonies of occupation, although some regions of southwest Africa and of Tanganyika attracted German immigrants.

Between 1884 and 1890, Bismarck thought that Germany should have colonies for diplomatic reasons and because of some demand at home. Chartered companies would manage them at no cost to Germany. In practice, the government did have to administer the colonial enterprise as in some cases, such as Togoland and Kamerun, no company could be set up. Except for Kiao-Chow, all others were granted to companies, but the government had to relieve them of administration at different times to about 1900. After Bismarck was relieved of his duties in 1890, disillusionment set in for about fifteen years. Under these circumstances, Wilhelm II still acquired new colonies. Although seen as a liability in Germany, the Germans occupied and pacified colonies, gaining a reputation for brutality in the process. D. K. Fieldhouse attributes some of this violence to administrators and soldiers inexperienced in colonial matters who tended to allow their fear to drive them to excess.[80] The Germans themselves debated the questions of costs and brutality in the Reichstag in 1906. Chancellor von Bülow transferred most of the colonies from the Foreign Office to the *Kolonialamt* or Colonial Office. It tightened up colonial administration, trained administrators and borrowed practices from other empires. The *Kolonialamt* replaced the *Kolonialrat*, a council of experts nominated in 1890 to advise the Foreign Office on colonial matters. This formal reform improved matters. As all German colonies were protectorates, only Germans were subjects of the emperor and had access to German courts. The Natives were protected persons with their own courts. For instance, African chiefs, under European supervision, applied customary law. The Germans paid little attention to Native administration before 1906 and used forced labour. Afterwards, they adapted to local conditions, using chiefs as officials in some jurisdictions and loosely supervising indigenous rules elsewhere. The German government encouraged chiefs to find enforced labour. None the less, the Germans improved medical treatment, leased out Crown land for twenty-five years and prevented Africans from alienating land to individual Europeans for more than fifteen years, which caused resistance in Kamerun (Cameroon) in 1911. The German taxpayers paid subsidies, direct and indirect, of about £100 million in 1914. Germans preferred investment in Europe rather than overseas. By losing its colonies, despite the blow to national pride, Germany did not have to supply these subsidies or to go through the decolonization that occurred in the twentieth century. From 1914, the country would face many other problems, including two devastating world wars and a depression.

The European countries sought new colonies, sometimes for perceived self-interest rather than because of actual benefit. Only Ethiopia, Morocco and Liberia in Africa resisted being carved up, although the empires allowed for buffer states or places under their influence such as Persia, Siam (Thailand) and Afghanistan. Only the Americas were largely in 1914 what they had been in 1875. The Munroe Doctrine of 1823, which kept the Americas free of new formal European colonies, became more formidable with the growth of the power of the United States. Just as the mines in the Americas had given Spain great wealth, modern mines did the same, only in more efficient ways owing to industrialization and the development of railways. Mining was a key to opening the world to imperialism. Oil and rubber were necessary for the internal combustion machine. Copper helped to feed the motor and electrical industries while the demand for precious metals, such as gold and diamonds, led imperial powers far afield. The demand for food, such as grain, meat, tea, sugar, tropical fruit, cocoa and coffee, grew steadily in the metropolitan centres. Chocolate, coffee and tea consumption soared in different countries, Germany and the United States consuming coffee while Britain took to tea from its colonies. Importers, advertising, plantations, farms, traders and financiers all came together to increase this business between imperial centre and colony. Colonies often specialized in products that were produced for the world market in the service of the metropolitan centres. Cuba provided sugar and cigars; Malaya tin and rubber; Chile nitrates; Brazil coffee; Uruguay meat. These economies, especially of those colonies that were not settled by Europeans, became too dependent on the market price of a commodity. Except for the United States, the white settler colonies failed to industrialize much at this stage. Sometimes, as Hobsbawm has pointed out, for white European settlers, colonies such as New Zealand and Australia in this period developed a wider spectrum of political parties (labour and radical) and systems of social security and welfare well before European states did. British foreign investment went primarily to its old settler colonies such as Canada, Australia, New Zealand and South Africa, which, beginning with Canada in 1867, all achieved a measure of independence in this period of high imperialism. Other countries into which British capital flowed were Uruguay, Argentina and the United States. The British investor liked secure investments and found among these that the bulk of investment overseas was in public utilities and railroads (76 per cent in 1913), which yielded 5 per cent as opposed to 3 per cent for instruments of the British government debt. Colonial expansion was partly a search for markets. Colonies took on status. Hobsbawm, who has called empire 'good ideological cement', makes a point that at first excluded the great republic from my study: 'Around 1900 even the USA, whose kind of imperialism has never before or since been particularly associated with the possession of formal colonies, felt obliged to follow the fashion.'[81]

Germany and Italy wanted colonies to keep up with the prestige of Britain and France, but many of their colonies were not economical. Colonies were to complement but not compete with metropolitan economies. Politics and economics were inseparable in the relation between empire and colony. Colonies often depended on the imperial centre for economic survival, but the metropolis would not stand or fall if the bottom fell out of the price of a certain commodity. About 80 per cent of European trade throughout the nineteenth century and of foreign investment was with other developed countries. That is one reason for the title of this book – empires and colonies were joined but not always in balance and their interests could diverge markedly. More than any other country, Britain's prosperity depended on sources for raw materials and overseas markets. In fact, except between 1850 and 1870, British manufactures were not particularly competitive in industrializing economies, so it was crucial for Britain to have access to regions beyond Europe. The Netherlands possessed an empire that was closest to the British empire in relying on areas beyond Europe. By the end of the nineteenth century, the British empire took up 25 per cent of the globe and its informal empire might have extended that reach to 33 per cent. After 1900, more than half of all British savings were invested abroad and in 1914 nearly half of Britain's long-term publicly issued capital was in Australia, Latin America and Canada. Science, manufactures and technology were the triple pillars of the European empires. Whereas the French attempted to transform overseas subjects into being French, the British did not. Emigration between 1880 and 1914 was a ready option. European exports grew more than 400 per cent between 1848 and 1875 and doubled from then to 1915; from 1870 to 1910 the world's merchant shipping doubled; from 1870 to the eve of the First World War the world's railway network expanded about fivefold. Germany and the United States did not depend on colonies as much as Britain did in this world of economic competition and expansion.[82]

Germany was the greatest state in continental Europe and would challenge Britain as the greatest European and world power, but Russia and the United States were beginning to emerge as world powers that would eventually dominate the last half of the twentieth century. At the height of its power, Europe was moving toward inflicting deep wounds on itself and working toward exhaustion. All this was not clear in 1890 or 1908. It is true that the great industrial growth of Germany from unification to 1914 was a topic for discussion throughout Europe, but the extent of the dire consequences of that growth and the rivalry between Britain and Germany – with France caught between – were not foreseen. Germany dominated Europe in innovative industries such as chemicals, optics and electronics. Germany produced 90 per cent of the world's chemicals and its foreign trade tripled between 1890 and 1913. Germany sought colonial expansion and to be the greatest power in Europe, but other countries had imperial ambitions in the two decades that preceded the First World War: Britain, the United States, Russia, Japan, France and Italy. From 1898 to the eve of the war, the German navy surpassed all fleets, except the Royal Navy. From 1910 to 1914, Germany doubled its budget for the army. The German empire was a much greater power now than France and Russia – even if the Russians, by 1914, spent about 75 per cent per cent of what Germany did on its military and more than the French did – but Germany was caught between these eastern and western powers and would have to fight on two fronts if it antagonized Russia and France. Wilhelm II and his advisers lacked Bismarck's diplomacy in which he diffused the concerns of other powers over Germany's rapid rise to power. Germany did not seem to have a coordinated plan within its government, so that contending departments with disparate aims weakened the new colossus. Tensions existed between the agricultural elite or Prussian Junkers and the workers who were organizing. Germany remained strong, none the less. Still, there was a sense among the leadership that it should make up for lost ground. Although Germany was probably no more obsessed with its unique and superior attributes than any of the other imperial powers, it combined, as Paul Kennedy has noted, the industrial strength of the western democracies with the autocracy of the eastern monarchies.[83]

The Habsburg empire (soon to be the Austro-Hungarian empire in 1867), France and Britain were not as strong as they were relative to other powers in the mid-nineteenth century. Despite being the weakest of the imperial powers, Austria had an economy that was growing among the fastest in Europe. Still, the Habsburg empire lagged economically behind Britain and northern Germany. In 1848–50, the Russian army intervened against the revolution in Hungary. The Austrian empire suffered defeat against France in 1859 and Prussia in 1866, and in 1867 Emperor Francis Joseph divided his empire in two between Austria and the Kingdom of Hungary in hopes of maintaining his power over foreign and defence policy. When Prussia defeated France in 1870–1, it absorbed some German states and weakened Habsburg power.[84] There were, however, great economic disparities among the regions of this empire. The population was increasing fastest in the poor and agricultural Slavic regions and not the industrializing Austrian and Czech lands or in Hungary, where farming was becoming more and more efficient. In this empire, fifteen major languages were used to issue the declaration of war in 1914. Nationalism created tensions within and with its neighbours, most particularly with Serbia. The very weakness of this longstanding empire made it look to Germany for military support in the case of a great multinational conflict.[85]

Unlike Germany and Austria-Hungary, France was not in the middle of Europe and was not surrounded on the eve of the Great War by enemies. Its chief enemy had been and would be Prussia/Germany. In the 1880s it had also experienced friction with Britain and Italy over colonial expansion in Africa. Britain and France quarrelled over the Congo in 1884–5 and over west Africa throughout the 1880s and 1890s and almost over Siam in 1893 and the Nile valley in 1898. France had added 3,500,000 million square miles to its empire between 1871 and 1900, thereby creating an empire second in size only to Britain's. From Saigon to Dakar, France established naval bases and had a large colonial army.

Even though the commerce of these lands was not always great, France also had influence in south China and the Levant. Colonial governors, those who lobbied for colonial expansion and bureaucrats all had a great influence on French imperialism at this time. The policies about the French army and navy were not effective. Only in response to the threat of war with Germany after 1911 did the civil and military officials come together in a coordinated effort. France was the largest automobile maker in the world and developed railways, iron and steel industries, canals, engineering, aircraft and other means to improve the economy, including a more vital banking and financial sector. The French had a good deal of mobile capital and had, to Bismarck's surprise, paid off the indemnity Germany imposed on it in 1871. France was second to Britain in investing in other countries and regions: its capital helped to industrialize Italy and Spain. Moreover, France funnelled its loans to China through St Petersburg, invested heavily in the Balkans and Turkey but most massively in Russia, partly as a means of checking Germany, particularly through railroads that could rapidly bring the Russian army west. None the less, between 1890 and 1914, the population of Germany grew by about 18 million, but that of France by just over one million. Germany outstripped France markedly in just about every economic indicator: in 1913, its GNP was almost double that of France and its share of world manufacturing more than double. The Germans could outspend and outgun the French, but France had been successful diplomatically, securing good relations with Italy, Russia and Britain. This was a strategy that allowed for entente with Britain in 1904, so that Germany was surrounded and France would not have to fight this growing power alone. It turned out that this ancient European strategy of alliances, formal and informal, served its purpose, but in a war so bloody that it exhausted Europe, and in which even the winners were losers. If in war there are no victors, only survivors, this conflict made this the more evident than any war before.[86]

Even though the Japanese elite was more open to foreigners than its Chinese counterpart, it still fell behind the western powers in technology. The military system of the samurai (warrior elite) ossified for about 200 years, so when in 1853 Commodore Perry arrived, the Japanese government could do little, in the face of superior technology, but to allow the Americans to put into port. In 1868, the Japanese would begin a great push to modernize and to attend to European and American industry and technology. The Meiji Restoration under the leadership of Satcho Hito and the samurai, who had come to see the virtues of industrial and organizational change, crushed rebellions against modernization. Thus, the elite was able to lead innovations in the culture and economy. During the 1870s, Japanese officials travelled to the United States and Europe to study developments in technology and industry. Western dress became *de rigueur* at the imperial court and a European architect rebuilt Tokyo in western architectural idioms after the fire of 1872. By 1894, the military had used modernization and conscription in conjunction with the samurai spiritual discipline as a means of building such a powerful force that traders had to accept Japan's terms for diplomacy and trade. This power began with a kind of state capitalism and was developed by entrepreneurs. Iwasaki Yataro, the founder of Mitsubishi, for instance, developed heavy industries and gave Japan the economic clout to challenge Russia and China in Asia in the battles arising from nationalism and imperialism.[87] In forty years, Japan had gone from a position of inward weakness to one of strength and expansion. It had lagged but had made the necessary changes to take its place among the world powers, something that it has done in different ways since 1868.

For 400 years, Russia had been expanding east, south and west, reaching a population almost threefold greater than Germany's and fourfold more than Britain's. Russia's army was by far the largest in Europe, as it had been for over a hundred years. Its navy was being rebuilt after the loss to Japan in 1905, and its railways were expanding at a rapid rate before 1914. By then, it had become the fourth industrial power in the world and second in the production of oil. Cola, textiles, steel all grew apace with this industrial juggernaut. Like Italy, however, Russia relied heavily on foreign investment, technology, engineers and entrepreneurs. Food and timber combined constituted almost three-quarters of Russian exports. If Russia's industrial increases were impressive, its actual national product lagged far behind Sweden, Canada, Japan, Germany and the United States. The Russian government seems to have dragged a largely reluctant nation into the modernization needed to make Russia a military power. The peasants suffered and taxes rose to 150 per cent of British levels when the Russian earned about 27 per cent of the Briton's income. Military spending and no way for local governments to raise monies put a strain on education and, especially in the cities, on basics such as providing sewers and housing. Peasant revolts, frequent enough before, grew more frequent and were bloodier, suppressed, as Norman Stone has noted, by 'a force far greater than the army of 1812'.[88] Whereas transcontinental railways were completed in 1869 in the United States and in 1885 in Canada, the Trans-Siberian railway was begun in 1892 and was not completed until 1916. Although this railway was considerably longer than the lines that went from sea to sea in North America, its later date shows the lag in the development of various empires. By 1913, the army was crushing peasant unrest, partly now exacerbated by the breaking up of peasant communes in 1908, as well as discontented minorities – Armenians, Georgians, Poles, Latvians, Estonians and Finns. Yet, there were still important reserves of loyalty to the czar and his realm in many places and a significant mixture of xenophobia and pan-Slavic sympathies in a key portion of the populace. Despite its great industrial growth, Russia was lagging further and further behind Germany. Industrial power would matter more in the war of 1914–18 than it would in any that had preceded it. Russia's difficulty arose in part from its heavy reliance on timber and food exports to pay for its imports and its small percentage of population that worked in industry. In hindsight it is easy to see that Russia, if it could, should have spent more on expertise and efficiency in education, technology and bureaucracy. About 70 per cent of Russians were illiterate and their military lacked an adequate supply of good officers. Many of the railways were too light and the trains did not burn a standard fuel. Serbia and France pressured Russia to get involved in fighting before it was ready to do so. Fodder for horses and food and clothing for the ill-equipped Russian army ate up much of the budget. Russia's sea power, which lacked technical training, was split between the Black Sea and the Baltic. A blind autocracy out of touch with the people, the court's contempt for the Duma (the assembly), a lack of a body of competent civil servants, a tax system that let off the rich and taxed food and vodka, and a lack of communication between the military and the foreign ministry did not help the Russian empire and its preparations for the coming war. The war with Germany came too soon. Germany was simply too strong. The war would break the Russian empire, which would reconstitute itself as the Soviet Union after the revolution of 1917.[89] The expansion of a country or empire did not always lead to success or something enduring.

Europe, Natives and the Last Expansion

Europeans were swallowing up the remainder of the world that they had not controlled since they began expansion in the fifteenth century. By the beginning of the twentieth century, they would come to control directly and indirectly 80 per cent of the world's surface. From 1870, they brought their cultural, economic and political influence to the furthest reaches of Africa and Asia and took advantage of cheap labour in these and other territories. The movements of European peoples were unprecedented whether as members of the colonial administrations or as emigrants to places like Australia or the Americas. The indigenous peoples in these lands suffered. The case of New Zealand is instructive. Two early governors of New Zealand had experience that might have prevented conflict and war in the settlement, but it happened anyway. For example, Robert Fitzroy was a captain of the *Beagle* and had seen the wasting of the Yahgan in Tierra del Fuego; George Grey had become an ethnologist while serving in Australia.[90] This clash over land only intensified a process that began with the Portuguese voyages into Africa and with Columbus's arrival in the western Atlantic.[91] In a history of Canada from the point of view of the first nations, Olive Patricia Dickason observes, 'The imperial civil administration for British North America was dominated by two ideas concerning Amerindians in 1830: that as a people they were disappearing, and that those who remained should either be removed to communities isolated from Euro-Canadians or else be assimilated'.[92]

This was another myth of the savage, of the wild peoples, that the French and other Europeans propagated in the New World from the earliest times.[93] In Canada the mixture of the French and British colonial legacies complicated the cultural, economic and political friction between aboriginal peoples and Europeans. The ideology of empire was used to attempt to create national pride among rural and urban populations of various classes in the metropolitan centres and in their settlers in the colonies overseas. The locomotive, bicycle, camera, telegraph, electricity, telephone, internal combustion engine, automobiles, chemical fertilizer, refrigeration, and other inventions transformed the lives of Europeans as well as other peoples. Coal, iron and steel were centrepieces of this industrial and imperial expansion. Some countries fell far behind Germany. Some spent a fraction of what Germany did on education and science in 1872. Germany and the United States rivalled Britain from 1870 onwards. From 1873, a global recession, which emanated from Europe and was based on industry more than on agriculture for perhaps the first time in history, affected peoples for about three decades. More capital and more consumption were key issues in this new economy. The London Stock Exchange was the centre of this intense private fundraising for enterprises.

After the Civil War ended in 1865, the United States was able to concentrate on its economy. A country blessed with rich farming lands, raw materials and advanced technology, the United States was poised to take up its place as an influential country in the world. It did not have significant threats on its borders, so that it did not have to focus on defence in this period. From the end of the Civil War until the Spanish-American War of 1898, its production of corn rose by over twofold, wheat between two and three times, refined sugar between four and five times, steel rails by over fivefold, miles of railway track almost six times, coal by 18 times, crude petroleum about 18 times, and steel 450-fold. The United States had over five times the miles of railway tracks that Russia had in 1914. This country had a large and developed internal market that all the other industrial powers lacked. By 1914, the national and per capita income of the United States was far above those of every other nation. Its steel production, for instance, was almost equal to the next four countries – Germany,

Britain, Russia and France – and it owned more motor vehicles than the rest of the world combined. The United States put up high tariffs to keep out manufactures and began, after its revolutions in industry and transportation, to export large quantities of finished goods as well as foodstuffs. The great American trade surplus with Europe was also shifting the balance of power. Except for the territorial gains it made with a small empire taken from the remnants of the Spanish empire in 1898, the United States pursued an informal empire built on trade, even more than the Dutch and British had early on. Commercial access to China and Latin America were keys to this strategy. Still, American diplomatic and military intervention was beginning to change the face of the world. By 1914, the United States had the third largest navy in the world after Britain and Germany. Like Britain, the United States did not favour a large standing army. Unlike Russia, the United States preferred to develop industry more for wealth than for war. It was only later in the twentieth century that each of these countries became, in Dwight Eisenhower's memorable and perceptive phrase, a 'military-industrial complex'.[94]

The United States had joined the pursuit of power based on nationalism and imperial pride as well as on economic interests. The Americanization of the world had begun in earnest even as the British empire was the first world power in many ways. The First World War accelerated a process that was already under way: by 1919, the United States overtook Europe as the region with the greatest economic output. At one level, this book could end here, as this was in a sense the end of European colonial domination, but because in many ways the United States became a successor to Europe generally and Britain specifically, it is possible to follow the matter of empire and colony further. Europe would decline relatively but not without influence and convulsions. But that is getting ahead of what anyone could know at that time. After 1900 Britain and the United States experienced a rapprochement: it was with Germany that both countries experienced friction.

Ecology and Imperialism: the Case of New Zealand Continued

The expansion within empires on a local level, what D. K. Fieldhouse termed a sub-imperialist process, took on different forms in different colonies. Whereas non-European colonies of occupation expanded owing to the urge of local governments to address insecurities in the borderlands, European or settler colonies expanded internally because of prospecting, trading, recruitment of labour and the hunger for land. The expansion of western European empires in India, Algeria and Java was therefore different from that in Canada, South Africa, Australia and New Zealand.[95] This last colony is the example under discussion concerning people and land, that is, the effects of European expansion on local demography and ecology.

New Zealand was the first Pacific island to be affected by European colonization. By the 1820s, a colony of Europeans there was engaged in whaling, sealing and selling European goods to the Maori. The Europeans were lawless and sold liquor and guns to the Natives, thereby disrupting their society and politics and helping to cause conflict between the two groups. The British reluctantly asserted jurisdiction over New Zealand, despite some earlier missionary objections to this move, partly to bring order to the British living there, to make colonization methodical and to stave off French interest in the area. At first, the British government envisioned New Zealand as a colony of occupation in which it would rule over a Maori majority and keep some order amongst the British minority. By 1870, with much British immigration and the granting of responsible government, New Zealand became, like Canada, a colony of settlement in which the aboriginal peoples were increasingly marginalized. New Zealand also became the base for British expansion in the Pacific.[96]

In 1830 and 1831, Sydney (Port Jackson) exported guns to New Zealand, where there were only several hundred Europeans, 8,000 muskets and 70,000 pounds of gunpowder. To pay for these firearms, the Maori planted alien crops that altered the native ecosystem. On a visit in 1835, Darwin noticed that the English and French had introduced many European plants. Pigs, horses and cattle arrived in the 1820s and 1830s. Germs killed Maori who went abroad or returned from there more readily than those who remained at home. After 1814, whooping cough, influenza and other diseases started to kill the Maori, young and old, especially in 1827 and 1828. Venereal disease and tuberculosis were rampant. During the 1820s, the missionaries stopped sending Maori to Europe and Australia because of the dangers of infection. Galloping consumption was prevalent, as were the diseases associated with prostitution. In this decade and in the 1830s, respiratory disease caused much sickness and death amongst the Maori. Morbidity and mortality rates increased.

Christianity and literacy followed this disease and cultural pressure. The Protestant missionaries led by example as they created a place with European crops and living patterns. They also learned Maori, rendered an alphabet for it, and translated the New Testament into the language in 1837 and produced many thousands of copies of it. Over half of the Maori were active Christians and could read. Missionaries were key to the changes in New Zealand. Besides this evangelization and their function as teachers, they had political influence. Two hundred missionaries petitioned Britain for protection, and London debated annexation and considered whether it would become a financial burden and whether the Maori, well stocked with guns, might embroil Britain in a costly war. Fifty chiefs signed a treaty and New Zealand became an official part of the British empire. The Maori were not, in their view, giving up their rights as chiefs but were only recognizing William Hobson as governor. The British thought otherwise.[97]

By the 1840s, all sorts of European animals and plants were well ensconced, thereby changing life in, and the landscape of, New Zealand. The 100,000 or more Maori had shrunk to about 56,000 in 1857–8 and to 42,113 in 1896. The Maori did try to do well under this immense pressure. Some seem to have favoured assimilation, which King George Te Waru and John Baptist Kahawai advocated in a letter to Queen Victoria in 1849 that accompanied the flour they sent her from their own mill. They asked to live in peace, grow wheat, breed horses and cows 'in order that we may become assimilated to the white people'.[98] In the 1850s, the Maori tried to put aside tribal rivalry and unite under a single leader. The first Maori king, Te Wherowhero or Potatau I, was installed in 1858. The Maoris started up a press and a newspaper that called for a preservation of the forests and a halt to selling land to Europeans. In 1860, an epidemic, possibly of influenza, killed this first king as well as many others. Before he died, the king called on his people to be good Christians, so even on the brink of war, his mind was divided and his attitude ambivalent. The Maori were still the majority in 1860, but they were losing land and had a very different way of looking at it than being able to be sold fee simple to one person in private ownership. The Maori went to war with the English, but were divided amongst themselves and could not sustain the war. By the mid-1860s, the struggle had become a guerrilla war. The wars of the 1860s did not determine sovereignty for the Maori, and at that time the settler Parliament viewed the Maori as rebels and confiscated about 3.25 million acres on the east coast and in Taranaki and Waikato. Even though about half that land has been returned or purchased, the Maori consider this confiscation unjust. Commissions have addressed this issue, most recently in the Waitangi Tribunal during the 1990s. There was increasing pressure on the Maori lands. During the 1870s, a government drive for immigration helped to double the European population. By 1870, when the last British regiment withdrew, the Maori were at a disadvantage, and the colonists were able to wear them down in an irregular war that ended in 1875. By this time, Britain controlled New Zealand and had left it with over nine million sheep and five times as many British as Maori in the colony. The Maori Parliament met from 1892 to 1901 in order to try to address what they saw as a lack in the observance of the Treaty of Waitangi.[99] The Maori had tried cooperation, negotiation and war in fighting for their people, land and rights.

From the beginning the British had sought material and spiritual control of New Zealand, which conflicted with the desire of the Maori to retain their autonomy and land. Despite the annexation of New Zealand in a period of British liberalism and humanitarianism, this act, along with colonization, involved settlement and possession for the British and dispossession and displacement for the Maori. By 1914, the British had renamed and domesticated New Zealand, exercising control of ownership and over resources and land. By then, the settlers of New Zealand had created grassland, an economy that exported and a state modelled on Britain, but with great cost to the Maori and to harmony between the settler and indigenous peoples.[100] By the 1890s, the Maori had reached their low point demographically, but by 1981, 280,000 New Zealanders identified themselves as Maori. And the indigenous fauna and flora are holding their own. Still, there were ten times more Europeans in New Zealand in 1981 and 70 million sheep.[101] The effects of the encounter between Europeans and Maori had intricate effects on the land and the people, some of which are emphasized here because the isolated state of New Zealand and its relatively short history of human settlement, Maori and European, make it a suggestive example in the debate on ecological imperialism.[102] Throughout the course of this book, we have seen that indigenous peoples facing the Portuguese, Spanish, English, Russians, Americans and others were decimated by disease and violence and that slavery was also present in so many of the lands.

Slavery

Portugal became the principal slaving country and its role in the slave trade endured the longest. Until slavery was abolished, Portugal, including Brazil, would come to transport about 4,650,000 slaves in about 30,000 voyages. Britain would transport about 56 per cent of the number of slaves Portugal would in about 40 per cent of the voyages. Spain (including Cuba) and France (including the West Indies) became major slave-trading empires and the Netherlands, British North America (United States) and Denmark, although much smaller traders, would round off the countries involved in this trade. Brazil would be the destination of about 4,000,000 slaves, the Spanish empire 2,500,000; British West Indies 2,000,000; the French West Indies (including Cayenne) 1,600,000; British North America and the United States 500,000; the Dutch West Indies (including Surinam) 500,000; the Danish West Indies 28,000; Europe 200,000. Historically, then, Portugal and Spain set the example for those who followed and became the largest slaveholders:

sugar plantations would employ more slaves – 6,000,000 of the over 11,000,000 transported – than all the rest of employments.[103] But that was to come; the beginnings of the Portuguese expansion – its economy and its use of slaves – were more modest than in its later empire. Madeira and the Azores in the fifteenth century produced wine and sugar, providing exports for Lisbon and a valuable example for those who would later colonize Brazil.

In 1835, Auguste-François Biard's oil painting, *The Slave Trade*, was shown at a salon in Paris and then at the Royal Academy in London in 1840 and it helped increase opposition to the trade.[104] Lord Palmerston, the British foreign secretary, threatened Portugal in 1838 over the slaving to Brazil. Soon slavers shifted to the American flag as a way of avoiding British enforcement or harassment: because the House of Representatives was full of slave-owners, the United States government did not do much to curtail the slave trade. From 1831 to 1855 about half a million slaves were imported into Brazil and about six million slaves lived in Brazil in 1851, roughly twice as many as in 1793. The curtailing of slavery also encouraged European emigration to the Americas.

In 1859, to fight the slave trade, President James Buchanan sent additional ships to Africa and others off Cuba. The hanging of Nathaniel Gordon, a slaver, on 21 February 1862 – the only North American to be executed for being engaged in the slave trade – became one of many events that showed that the tide was turning against slavery in the United States. Abraham Lincoln needed his ships in the civil war, so he recalled the Cuban and African squadrons that had been operating against slavers. Surprisingly, but perhaps hoping that Britain would side with the north, Lincoln and his secretary of state, William Seward, asked the British to send a force into Cuban waters and both Britain and the United States came to allow warships from one nation to search the merchant vessels of the other country for slaves. The British and Americans also agreed to a mixed court from both countries at New York, Sierra Leone and Cape Town for those accused of trading slaves in Africa or the Americas. Seward himself thought that if Britain and the United States had made such a treaty in 1808 there would have been no civil war. Lincoln's government introduced the Thirteenth Amendment to the Constitution which abolished slavery in the United States. The Spanish colony of Cuba's wealth, as some members of the government of Spain recognized, was based on slaves: in 1863 almost 25,000 slaves entered Cuba.

By the end of the American civil war in 1865, the Africa to Cuba slave route, which had endured for 350 years, was coming to an end. From 1492 to 1820, five times as many Africans went to the New World as white Europeans and even from 1820 to 1870 the numbers of Europeans and Africans were equal. Black slaves had been servants throughout the

Americas, had been crucial to cotton in the Guianas and then North America, rice and indigo in Virginia and South Carolina, gold in Brazil and silver in Mexico and sugar in Brazil and then in the Caribbean. Black Africans had helped to build the New World and often without credit.

The contradictions of imperialism were also apparent because France had invaded Algeria in 1830 and over the next two decades French, Maltese and Italian colonists settled there and often took control of the lands of the Native inhabitants. Although in the wake of the rebellions in Canada during 1837 Britain granted more self-determination there, it annexed New Zealand in 1840 (as it had Singapore in 1819), extended its control of India through the British East India Company and used the same private group of merchants to establish a trade in opium in China against the wishes of the government. In addition to banning the import of opium and forbidding western merchants from going beyond Guangzhou in Canton, the Chinese government prohibited the export of precious metals. British policy in China was not about reform. When the Chinese government expelled British merchants from the south of China, Britain bombarded the cities on the Chinese coast from Hong Kong to Shanghai. In this First Opium War of 1839 to 1842 Britain had China open up four more ports to Europeans, assumed sovereignty over Hong Kong, received indemnity and continued with the opium trade. Opium, which the Portuguese brought from China to Europe in the sixteenth century, was something the British government came to condemn and regulate at home while forcing its use on China. The Revolutions of 1848 in Europe showed a crisis at home while questions of trade, slavery and empire persisted. A second war over opium in China was fought between 1856 and 1858 when concerns over slavery were still pressing in the British government. Reverend George Clayton gave a speech at the opening of the Exhibition of the Works of Industry of All Nations in London in 1851, where the Crystal Palace covered 18 acres, in which he praised Britain and its strength through its colonies.

By the mid-nineteenth century, the slave ports had shifted from Nantes, Amsterdam, Bristol and Liverpool to Pernambuco, Bahia, Rio, Havana, New Orleans and New York. During this phase of the illegal slave trade, the dealers, or 'ebony merchants' as the French called them, partly to avoid detection, shipped slaves in even worse conditions that before, sometimes packing the human cargo into smaller and more horrific spaces. Vile conditions, then, occurred after the British and North American abolition of slavery in 1808, and witnesses to a House of Commons Committee in 1848 testified to that effect. The illegal trade was not always lucrative, for many of the largest merchants transporting slaves to Cuba and Brazil went bankrupt unless they also invested in sugar or coffee plantations. The United States tried to curb the slave trade off the coast of Africa and, to a lesser extent, off the coast of Brazil to deal with slaving under the flag of the United States. Slave-holding Brazilians, like their counterparts in the southern United States, considered the long-time institution of slavery as being natural. Yet there were voices against the slave trade and other unjust practices.

Voices Against Injustice and Slavery

Three voices will suggest resistance to slavery: Mary Prince, Frederick Douglass and Abraham Lincoln. After 1800, the example of Equiano was there for slaves, who published narratives of their own experiences. African women are a significant part of the writing about slavery.[105] In 1831, Mary Prince's book, the first published slave narrative by a woman, appeared in two editions in London. This work transformed the genre because she spoke for herself and claimed authority to speak for other slaves, and helped to gain a voice for black women.[106] Prince, who was born in Bermuda, told of how her master, Mr Williams, was harsh and his wife was kind. Mary was soon sold.[107] For five years, Mary did not escape further beatings. Mary ended her narrative with this warning: 'This is slavery. I tell it, to let English people know the truth; and I hope they will never leave off to pray God, and call loud to the great King of England, till all the poor blacks be given free, and slavery done up for evermore.'[108] The voices of slaves against slavery became an important part of the abolition movement.

What was rooted was a discrimination based on colour. A double standard was applied in the United States and elsewhere to peoples who were not of European background. Frederick Douglass's speech before the American and Foreign Anti-Slavery Society in May 1854 underscored how Americans of African descent were excluded from the rights and freedoms set out by the founders of the United States: 'American humanity hates us, scorns us, disowns and denies, in a thousand ways, our very personality. The outspread wing of American Christianity, apparently broad enough to give shelter to a perishing world, refuses to cover us.'[109] The principles of the republic had been given over to a corruption and selfishness that allowed for racial discrimination. The United States was hardly representative.

President Abraham Lincoln's road to the emancipation of the slaves was not a direct one. His public words did not indicate that he was going to take such a step. For instance, in his inaugural speech of 4 March 1861, he attempted to reassure the south.[110] On 22 September 1862, Lincoln proclaimed the emancipation of slaves to take effect on 1 January 1863.

The whole power of the executive and armed forces was to be marshalled on behalf of the liberty of slaves throughout the United States.[111] Slavery was a topic on Lincoln's mind years before he became President.

In 1855, he had made notes on the history of the slave trade and, while not a member, he had attended and addressed the meetings of the Springfield Colonization Society (he did so on 4 January 1855). In these notes, Lincoln began with the year 1434 – 'A Portuguese captain, on the coast of Guinea, seizes a few Affrican lads, and sells them in the South of Spain' – and moved through Spanish, English and American events and laws and ended in 1816 with the 'Colonization Society is organized – its direct object – history – and present prospects of success – Its colateral objects – Suppression of Slave trade – Commerce – Civilization and religion'.[112] The idea of rights in the United States could not be separable from slavery. In a letter to James N. Brown in 1858, Lincoln had also shown his opposition to slavery and his support for Americans of African descent: 'I have made it equally plain that I believe the negro is included in the word "men" used in the Declaration of Independence.'[113] Freedom and equality, for Lincoln, applied to all men and was the basis of government. Like Africans, Natives wanted to be treated as equals, as people.

Native Experience/Native Voices

Natives in North America did not always benefit from widening protection and human rights. As we saw in the last chapter, the defeat of the French in North America upset the balance of power for Europeans and Natives.[114] The American Revolution had further consequences for the indigenous peoples. Matters worsened for Natives as British Americans spread west.

The United States and British North America (later Canada) took different routes. In the United States, owing to conflicts over land between settlers and Natives, frontier wars were not uncommon, whereas in British North America then Canada treaties were made in order to avoid conflict. Sometimes, as in the Northwest Rebellions of 1869 and 1885, led by Louis Riel, the new Canadian government, although it had made promises to the British Crown and government to do so, did not set out treaties that avoided bloodshed. In the case of those rebellions, the Métis, or people of mixed Native and European origin, felt that their rights and lands were not protected. Dickason summarizes the place of treaties in British North America and Canada until the Hudson's Bay Company ceded the vast western and northern territories of Rupert's Land to Canada in 1870 and beyond:

At Confederation, 123 treaties and land surrenders had already been negotiated in British North America with Amerindians. By the time of the James
Bay Agreement in 1975, the number had approached 500. An important
period had been between 1860 and 1923, when 66 treaties were signed.
Between 1923 and 1973 no new treaties were negotiated because of legis-
lation prohibiting the use of band funds for land claim actions. In acquiring Rupert's Land, to which the terms of the Proclamation of 1763 had not
extended, the Canadian government had promised, on behalf of the imperial monarch, to negotiate with its Amerindians for the extinguishment of
their title and the setting aside of reserves for their exclusive use. An imperial Order-in-Council of 15 July 1870 emphasized the point: 'any claims of
Indians to compensation for lands required for purposes of settlement shall
be disposed of by the Canadian government in communication with the
Imperial government.'[115]

The British government had considered the Proclamation of 1763 a good
vehicle for protecting Native rights. Here is a complication of history, in
which the far-off Crown attempted to protect the indigenous peoples
from the greed and land-hunger of settlers from their European nations
or descendants of these peoples.

The Revolution and its aftermath were not necessarily good to the
indigenous peoples. On 16 June 1870, Red Cloud, a Sioux leader, spoke
to an audience at the Cooper Institute in New York, beginning with 'The
Great Spirit made us both' and reminding them of the history of contact
between Natives and Europeans: 'You came here and we received you like
brothers . . . When you first came, we were very many and you were very
few. You do not know who appears before you to speak. He is a representative of the original American race, the first people of this continent.'[116] This theme of misusing the hospitality of the Native peoples
recurred over the centuries. When Sitting Bull (Tatanka Yotanka), a chief
of the Hunkpapa Sioux, was a prisoner of war between 1881 and 1883
at Fort Randall, he related his views to a journalist, James Creelman.
Sitting Bull reversed notions of American liberty: 'The life of white men
is slavery. They are prisoners in towns or farms. The life my people want
is a life of freedom. I have seen nothing that a white man has, houses or
railways or clothing or food, that is as good as the right to move in open
country, and live in our own fashion.'[117] Freedom was a matter of perspective and the voices of Europeans and settlers of European descent
often defined the terms of debates and discourse. Who was the actual
slave? White men had imposed their way of life on the Natives, and a large
number of White Indians, those of European descent who were captured
by Natives, preferred this free-ranging life, as Benjamin Franklin had
noted in 1753.[118] This idea of injustice for Native people was something
that aboriginal peoples themselves had expressed in speeches and later in

writing. Women were another group occluded in the march for land in the expansion of nation and empire.

The Rights of Women

Over the next 125 years and more, some men and women in Britain worked to effect equality between men and women. For decades, Harriot Taylor and John Stuart Mill worked on questions of society and economics, including on women. Mill published a book on the subjugation of women in 1869. In 'Enfranchisement of Women' Taylor called attention to the groundbreaking work done among Americans to advance the rights of women:

> Most of our readers will probably learn from these pages for the first time, that there has arisen in the United States, and in the most civilized and enlightened portion of them, an organized agitation on a new question – new, not to thinkers, nor to any one by whom the principles of free and popular government are felt as well as acknowledged, but new, and even unheard-of, as a subject for public meetings and practical political action. This question is, the enfranchisement of women; their admission, in law and in fact, to equality in all rights, political, civil, and social, with the male citizens of the community.[119]

Responsible government, one of the key themes of my discussion, needed to be more open and inclusive.

Others pushed as well for a wider franchise in democracy. In Britain, Millicent Fawcett, whose husband, Henry, worked closely with Mill, and Elizabeth Garret Anderson used techniques of passive resistance to try to gain rights for women: these techniques, which may have had their inspiration in part from the life of Christ, were also like the practices of passive resistance that Gandhi and Martin Luther King advocated and embodied. Emmeline Pankhurst and her daughters Sylvia and Christabel attempted, through sabotage and other less peaceful means, to secure the vote for women but they avoided any violence that would threaten lives. Emily Wilding Davison, like other suffragettes who had been arrested, went on hunger strike in Holloway prison. Later, Gandhi and members of the Irish Republican Army, the one pacifist and the other not, came to use the hunger strike as a weapon against British power. In 1913, Davidson, after throwing herself before the king's horse at Epsom, died from her injuries. In 1918, British women won the vote, although with more restrictive terms than men.

Not until 1920 did the United States grant the right to women to vote, even though the country was one of the first to have an active women's movement with that goal. The first Women's Rights Convention in 1848 was a key event in that process.[120] The situations of African-Americans and of women were closely connected in this struggle for human rights. The five women organizers of the First Women's Rights Convention thought of themselves as abolitionists as they were married to prominent abolitionist leaders, worked as leaders of female anti-slavery societies or were friends of the national leaders and thinkers of the abolition movement. The United States Park Service stresses the connection between the abolitionist and women's rights movements, both important in the achievement of human rights. The Park Service also emphasizes Frederick Douglass, who wrote to Kelley, 'in token of my respect and gratitude to you, for having stood forth so nobly in defense of Woman and the Slave'.[121] The Declaration of Sentiments that came out of Seneca Falls in July 1848 was both an echo and a rewriting of the Declaration of Independence.[122] American women and their supporters were willing to declare their resistance to the tyranny ('despotism') of those American men who would oppress them and not give them a voice in responsible government. This new declaration invoked the spirit of 1776 against a country that had not gone far enough in the revolution and the cause of liberty.

Not until 1893, however, in New Zealand, did women achieve suffrage on the national level. Australia followed in 1902, but American, British and Canadian women did not win the same rights until the end of the First World War. New Zealand made progress in the nineteenth century, whereas other countries had to wait. Under the pen-name Femina, the New Zealander Mary Ann Müller had pushed for the vote in 1869, beginning an article with:

> A wise ancient declared that the most perfect popular government was that 'where an injury done to the meanest subject is an insult upon the whole constitution'. What, therefore, can be said for a Government that deliberately inflicts injury upon a great mass of its intelligent and respectable subjects; that virtually ignores their existence in all that can contribute to their happiness as subjects; that takes a special care to strike at the root of their love of country by teaching them that they have no part in forming or maintaining its glory, while it rigidly exerts from them all penalties; even unto death?[123]

Exclusion should no longer be tolerated. A critique of the government, as in Britain, was something those pushing for women's rights and the vote could not avoid. According to a quiz to celebrate Women's Equality Day, the National Women's History Project lists an answer about those countries that won the vote before the United States as 'New Zealand (1893), Australia (1902), Finland (1906), Norway (1913), Denmark (1915), USSR

(1917), Canada (1918), Germany (1918), Poland (1918), Austria (1919), Belgium (1919), Great Britain (1919), Ireland (1919), Luxembourg (1919), the Netherlands (1919), Sweden (1919)'.[124] The Ministry for Culture and Heritage in New Zealand now celebrates the rights extended to women that the government of the day resisted. The change from 1893 to the present is stark: no women were elected in 1893, but today the prime minister, governor-general, attorney-general and chief justice are women.[125] New Zealand is not the only country from the former British empire (the Commonwealth) that is proud of the advancement of women. The rhetoric of rights has been extended and the actual practice of democracy is much more inclusive than before. Empires have not necessarily been democratic and prone to the advocacy of human rights, including equal rights for women and people of colour, so it is important to distinguish empire from liberty and equality. Empires can evolve, as the British empire did and as the United States did, to widen representation and to extend franchise to more and more citizens, but that is not inevitable. Human rights are always fragile.

Transitions

In 1914 it seemed that European expansion would not end. Even up to the end of the Second World War, the illusion of expansion remained. The greatest new power – the United States – would be even more informal in its influence than the British empire and concentrate on economic benefit and outlets for its capital and goods. The United States was on the rise and its leaders and its politicians, policy-makers, scholars and critics saw it variously as a force of decolonization and an implement of neo-colonialism.[126] The tensions of ambivalence and contradiction are once more evident in the story of empire and colony. Once a colony, the United States resisted empires but came to be an empire with its own colonies. From within, it debated for and against expansion. In the twentieth century the emphasis on decolonization or neo-colonialism depended in part on the emphasis on optimism and pessimism for a world in search of equity and on how much people think that the world is now a matter of a new economics or a new economic form for an old politics.

In the twentieth century, no matter how haltingly and unevenly, human rights came, after so many atrocities, to play an important role, sometimes if in theory only, in the international order. The humanitarian movement of the Enlightenment and of the abolitionists and advocates of women's rights and of the rights of workers and all people and peoples bore some fruit, not without struggle, in this century. But it was not without war and terror. Europe in its final phases of hard imperial power tore itself apart in two of the most vicious civil wars in history and brought the globe into these conflagrations. These were wars that the world barely survived and that scarred Europe and all the globe. The world of high imperialism came crashing down, perhaps unexpectedly, but suddenly, in August 1914.

6

European Civil War and World Conflict: 1914–1945

Just when the expansion of empires and the acquisition of colonies were increasing, a cataclysmic war began, and the imperial order would shatter slowly and break down in the second half of the twentieth century. At the peak of power, the western European empires turned on themselves in a civil war that spread to a world conflict on a scale not seen before. It took another world war for the degree of change to sink in. In a generation, these empires were barely holding on, and in a generation after that they were remnants and memories. The United States and Soviet Union (which rose out of the Russian empire) would become, as de Toqueville had predicted, the great states of the world. The ambivalence and contradiction of the imperial theme played out in apparently irrevocable ways. But in January 1914, whatever premonitions the leaders of the empires had, they could not be sure that any of this would happen. Nothing was inevitable. In the human culture of politics and diplomacy, some massive failures were about to occur and a breakdown in civil society amongst the nations that considered themselves to be agents of civilization was about to happen. The arms race became armed conflict. In a kind of death wish, these European states brought one another down low and caused chaos and violence in Europe and in the world. Perhaps, given the level of violence in European expansion from the fifteenth century and the aggressive wars against indigenous peoples and amongst themselves, this European penchant for competitive wars and the seeking of the balance of power should not be surprising. None the less, hindsight was not available to the people in the period in question any more than it is available to us in our present circumstances. This is the irony of time and history. Perspective is something we seek, but we, like them, back into the future.

In Britain the mood among many of those who have left records is a mix or clash of confidence and anxiety. In 1900 the British empire consisted of about 12,000,000 square miles with 25 per cent of the population of the world and had, from 1870, added 4,250,000 square miles and 66,000,000 people. It is quite possible that Britain had upset the balance of world power as much then as the United States would after 1989. Perhaps more. The Royal Navy was twice as large as the next two fleets, and Britain had the largest sectors of any nation in banking, investment, insurance and commodity dealing. In fact, Britain may have been living off the avails of its victory against Napoleon in 1815. British officials often worried, especially after 1870, that the British empire had the most to lose as its Industrial Revolution spread to other countries and thereby modernized their economies and military. The rise of Germany threatened its position in Europe; that of the United States affected it most because it had the greatest presence in the Americas with Canada and the Caribbean and its investments in Latin America; and that of Russia affected its influence in the Near East, the Persian Gulf and potentially in India itself. Even the carving up of China commercially would lessen British influence because it controlled the largest share of that trade and the rise of new power, like Japan, would curtail its great influence in Asia. In Africa as well, there was a scramble for colonies after the 1880s and in this matter, too, Britain was diminished. Generally, as Hobsbawm has said, Britain gave up an informal empire over most of the underdeveloped world for a formal empire over a quarter of it.[1]

As war gathered in 1938, M. J. Bonn, who claimed that Lenin's *Imperialism* could not have been written without J. A. Hobson's *Imperialism*, began his own study by looking back to this moment in Africa: 'The scramble among the Powers for the remaining unclaimed parts of the earth in the last quarter of the nineteenth century had blinded people's eyes to the fact that the age of colonization was over' and 'The Rising of the Nations, moreover, which the Declaration of Independence had set going, was spreading', so that the age of empire-breaking replaced that of empire-building, something witnessed in the crumbling of three vanquished empires in the First World War and continuing thereafter.[2] Here, Bonn asserted that free trade will bring more equality between nations than any 'counter-colonization' can do (Germany, Japan and Italy had been trying that route up to the time Bonn published the book). He also said that democracy and domination will not go together any more. Both assertions represent an interpretation based on a typology in which the end of empire is seen stereoscopically with high imperialism (which turns out ironically to be the beginning of the end, as *hamartia* suggests in Greek tragedy).

East and West: Backgrounds

In the twenty-five years before the First World War, there was a diplomatic challenge in this time of gathering tensions. European and imperial rivalries affected relations among the leading powers. In its empire, Britain had made territorial concessions to France and the United States and had forged an alliance with Japan. France and Britain, allied in Europe in 1904 after years of rivalry after Britain occupied Egypt in 1882, worked hard to avoid being drawn into the war between their allies Russia and Japan in 1905, on different sides, despite what the French and British took to be German attempts to embroil them in a war in the Far East.[3] German diplomacy seems to have waned while its industrial and military power had waxed. Britain also grew close to countries with whom its relations had once been frictional, such as the United States and Russia. In 1907 Britain and Russia put aside their differences on Tibet, Afghanistan and Persia.

A naval race occurred in 1908–9 as the British responded to a German build-up: when over the next three years Britain attempted to alleviate competition, the German government asked that Britain remain neutral in the event of a war in Europe. In 1908–9, Germany backed the Austro-Hungarian annexation of Bosnia-Herzegovina and Russia backed down. From 1909 onwards, diplomacy was caught in a more rigid framework. Britain backed France against Germany in the second crisis over Morocco in 1911 and failed in the diplomatic mission to Berlin. France and Britain forged a naval agreement in 1912, and Italy and states of the Balkan League drove the Ottoman empire out of Europe. The death of the Archduke Ferdinand in July 1914 sparked a war in which Russia feared Austria-Hungary's move against Serbia and the German military backing of the Ottoman empire. The domino effect brought in all the major European powers into a conflict that would have no real winners. Europe would crush itself, its influence waning over the blood moon of its imperial harvest.[4]

The First World War

The war had begun in August 1914. The Anglo-Japanese alliance allowed the Japanese to occupy German possessions in the central Pacific and in China and the decision of the Ottoman empire to enter the war on the side of Germany in November 1914 opened the Near East to much British, and some French, colonial expansion. Like the Germans in Africa, the Japanese came to develop a variety of colonies, so that owing their diverse and incongruous nature, it might be better, in both cases, as Lewis H. Gann has proposed, to speak of each power's empire as empires, although a better strategy would probably be to talk about an empire with diverse kinds of colonies.[5] Britain also had a great diversity of kinds of colonies in its empire. Troops from the self-governing dominions and from India were a great resource, and British wealth and overseas trading ties kept Japan, the United States and Italy neutral or on side. The British helped to finance munitions for Belgium, France, Russia and Italy. In 1914, of the major economic indicators, only in steel production did Germany and Austria-Hungary have an advantage over France, Russia and Britain. This industrial and technological advantage increased in time, but the Allies were unable to win a decisive victory and looked to the United States to tilt the scales in 1917, when the German alliance seemed to have the advantage.

For the most part, the German colonial empire up to 1914 was not significant, so its loss caused little damage and when Germany and Austria-Hungary could not export to the same extent owing to the British naval blockade because of the war, they turned this capacity to domestic advantage in support of the war. The German navy and military technology made it difficult for the British to prevail or to fight peripheral actions as it had in Spain against Napoleon. German U-boats attacked merchant ships rather than take on the Royal Navy. Trench warfare meant that it was difficult for either side to make a breakthrough, and the Germans had seized much of the high ground early in the war. By 1915, however, the Germans had driven the massive Russian army from Lithuania, Poland and Galicia. By 1917, the Germans had forced great losses on the French, and the Russians had all but smashed the Habsburg army. Germany itself, however, was holding its own. In this year, Italy, the Austro-Hungarian empire and Russia were on the verge of financial collapse. Russia was caught between Germany and Turkey and could not be supplied and aided as much as it needed: its transportation system was under great stress from the movement of troops, supplies and munitions and its small and inefficient civil service could not coordinate the war. The Russian government brought on some of its own problems: it abolished the trade in spirits (which constituted about one-third of its revenues), lost heavily on the railways (which had made money for it during the peace), did not raise income taxes on the rich (as Britain had) and printed money to pay for the war and thereby helped to drive the price index up about seven times from June 1914 to June 1917. Despite the Russian defeats of the Turkish and Austro-Hungarian armies, it suffered losses against the Germans. With three to four million dead, the Russians began to call up males who were the only earners in their families and this caused unrest.

Mutinies were occurring in France and were on the verge of happening in Russia, but France was more able to make use of British and American aid (including much-needed grain) and to industrialize where it had to, under difficult conditions. France, like Russia, had lost in excess of three million soldiers, but, unlike Russia, found relief from troops from Britain, the British empire and the United States. Sixty British empire divisions helped in Foch's counteroffensive of September 1918. Britain's strategy of blockade, colonial campaigns and amphibious operations had not worked against the Germans. Lloyd George and his cabinet preferred colonial wars in the Near East, because territorial gains were great with few casualties, to fighting the Germans in Europe, where gains in land were small and losses of troops great. Britain covered the loans for Italy, Russia and France, but it built up a huge trade deficit with the United States, which supplied foodstuffs and munitions to the Allies but not to the Central Powers, owing to the blockade. Britain was forced to borrow for the first time on the money markets in Chicago and New York to pay the munitions dealers in the United States in dollars.

The adaptability of the German command and Germany's ability to mobilize production and the largest fighting force ever, using some of the most advanced technology, while plundering those it had conquered (as Napoleon had), had kept the world at bay and changed it for ever. Germany itself had suffered great casualties, was growing more controlling and authoritarian towards its own population and was printing money and raising inflation. Although Germany seemed to have the upper hand, it too was suffering. Food was scarce in Germany in 1918. Germany had also stepped up its U-boat attacks on the merchant shipping on which the United States and western Europe relied for trade and it had offered Mexico an alliance. These empires would never be the same.

The American intervention, an ancient colony coming to the help of the mother country, was industrial more than military. The United States had mobilized a force that was about 46 per cent of the size of the forces of France, 40 per cent of those of the British empire, just over 29 per cent of those of Russia and just under 29 per cent of those of Germany. The American army was even more unprepared for the First World War than any of the major European armies: there was considerable lag time before its troops could make a difference. The United States had food, destroyers, merchant ships and money aplenty. Psychologically and economically, it filled the void as Russia withdrew and then collapsed into revolution. The British could capture Damascus and Jerusalem from the Turks, but they needed help from their former colony with the Germans. By early June 1918, the Germans, using their new technique of storm-trooper attacks, drove within thirty-seven miles of Paris. By mid-July, the Allies had gained the upper hand. Foch, made the supreme commander as a result of storm-trooper advance, orchestrated a series of offensives by the armies of France, the United States and the British empire that gave the weakened Germans no rest. Revolutions and discontent and military defeats threatened the collapse of Germany and the old imperial order in Europe. Productive forces, as Paul Kennedy has argued, affect the outcome of long coalition wars.[6] Trade and technology underpin warfare and affect the nature of empire specifically and politics generally.

The Aftermath of the Great War

Empires were broken, fell or were transformed because of the Great War. The Treaty of Versailles (28 June 1919) did not settle the issues that arose from the First World War. Not until as late as 1923 were some matters arising from the Russian civil war and the confusion in eastern Europe and Asia Minor resolved. The Ottoman empire expired. Nations such as Lithuania, Latvia, Estonia, Finland, Poland Yugoslavia, Austria, Hungary and Czechoslovakia emerged from the broken remains of the Romanov, Habsburg and Hohenzollern empires. Germany lost its large colonial empire to Britain and some of its empire (the self-governing dominions) to France. The territories of the Ottoman empire in the Near East became French and British mandates under the supervision of the League of Nations. Japan took over some groups of islands north of the equator that Germany had controlled but returned Shantung to China in 1922. In 1921–2 in Washington, Britain, the United States and Japan avoided a naval race by signing an agreement that would restrict the size of their battle fleets. The United States retreated into isolation, despite its great power, and Germany and Russia (the new Soviet Union) were disabled by the First World War. Britain and France continued to have influence beyond their diminishing power and the problem of German war reparations remained. The millions of soldiers and civilians killed in the war and by the influenza epidemic of 1918–19 weakened all of Europe.

The financial costs of the First World War and its aftermath were so enormous that they probably have not been tallied in any way that captures the calamity, but they probably entailed more than a century of all national debt. Colonies, British dominions, and countries not in Europe – such as India, Canada, Australia, South Africa and the United States – out of the direct line of fire experienced growth in the production of food, raw materials and industry. Revolts and protests against British rule occurred in various places. Ireland experienced internal dissension on and off, from the rebellion of Easter 1916 until the declaration of the Irish Free State in 1921. In India in 1919, British troops massacred protesters at Amritsar, and during the 1920s they suppressed revolts in Iran and Egypt. Other empires experienced similar friction in the colonies.[7] While the Dutch put political opponents in gaol, the French punished nationalists in Indochina. New York replaced London during the Great War as the centre of international finance. The United States was the great creditor nation and even Britain and France, to which other European countries owed money for the war, were in debt to the Americans.

The crash of 1929, after the growth of the 1920s, threw countries into a sharp plunge in world trade and industrial output. The United States, and those who owed it money, ended up in a kind of economic war that hurt all sides. The United States, as much as it wanted to do so, could not retreat because isolated countries had not repaid their debts. Nationalists prevailed in many key places, such as Germany and Japan, and democracy retreated there. Scapegoats were sought to explain the Great Depression. France, the British empire and the United States seemed to be going their own ways in the 1930s. Thus, the democracies did not form a strong block, while the Soviet Union, Japan, Italy and Germany chose or furthered totalitarian routes. Both the extreme left and the extreme right that these movements constituted shared a dislike of bourgeois liberalism and laissez-faire capitalism.[8]

Changes in politics and ideology affected trade, finance and technology. Even before the First World War, other regions of the world and the colonies themselves were challenging the European empires. The Russian rebellion of 1905 and the victory of Japan over Russia in 1905 as well as the revolt of Arabic Pasha in Egypt and the breakthrough of the young Turks after 1908 are examples of such challenges to the old imperial order centred in and on Europe. Bal Gangadhar Tilak's attempted radicalization of the Indian Congress movement and Sun Yat-sen's campaign against Western domination in China constitute important anti-colonial actions in the world's two most populous territories. During the war, Allied propaganda for democracy and national self-determination raised hopes not simply for those living in autocratic central European empires and states but for the inhabitants of colonies and dependent nations. German countermoves in the war of propaganda in Ireland, the Maghreb, Egypt and India reinforced such attitudes in the formal and informal British empire.

By 1919, while Europeans were hiding their imperial order behind the League of Nations, Gandhi was bringing together opposition to British rule in India, the May Fourth Movement was developing in China, the Sarehat Islam had between two and three million members in Indonesia, Kemal Ataturk was in the process of launching a renewed Turkey, the Wafd Party was being formed in Egypt and the pan-African Congress had held meetings in Paris. The Soviets under Lenin and the Americans under Wilson were opposed to the old European colonial order. Although the Soviet Union and the United States could not, or chose not to, end that colonial order under the mandate of the League of Nations, the rhetoric

of their governments encouraged nationalists in the colonial world dominated by Europe to oppose that hegemony. The Soviet Union, Japan
and the United States, as well as the Chinese nationalists themselves, came,
by the late 1920s, to curtail European commerce, treaty privileges
and gunboat diplomacy. Colonial unrest caused the western European
empires, especially the British empire, to divert attention from Europe –
including the resurgence of a nationalistic Germany – and to expend valuable resources overseas. Whereas India, Palestine and Singapore worried
the British, the French concentrated on Africa. European armies and military technologies were still powerful after the First World War. For
instance, Britain's force at Amritsar in 1919, the Netherlands' gaoling of
Sukarno and other leaders of the nationalist movement and its smashing
of the trades unions during the late 1920s, and France's response to
Tonkinese unrest at the rapid development of rubber and rice all indicate
the close connection among guns, money and politics. The challenge to
colonialism, despite its mixed results, was a significant force in the political economy of the years between the two world wars. The Italian invasion of Abyssinia and the Japanese incursions into China shifted alliances,
so that these nations or new 'empires' would no longer be allied to the two
great old empires that had dominated Europe and probably the world
since the late seventeenth century: those of France and Britain. Italy and
Japan would help to support a revived Germany, whose industrial and military strength returned in the 1930s as much as its authoritarianism. The
Soviet Union and the United States would come to see that the expansion
of Japan into the Japanese empire and the fascist aggression in Europe constituted a threat to national and world security that was greater than anything that British and French imperialism might throw up in their late
stages. The League of Nations, without the United States and the Soviet
Union, did not succeed. Nor did its exclusion of the defeated countries of
the First World War help the cause. The League also experienced friction
between the French and the British over what its role and machinery would
be. The prosperity and political accord that seemed to have arrived in the
late 1920s dissipated with the Great Depression. Much more than before
the First World War, before the Second World War the democracies of
western Europe and the United States were unprepared for war.[9]

The Crisis of Empire: Loosening Ties and the Challenge to Britain from Nazi Germany

Some colonies did better than others during the economic slump of the
1930s, just as some developed countries did. Britain loosened its imperial

bonds at this time. The textile industry in India became more independent of British cloth.[10] The Statute of Westminster in 1931 gave more political autonomy to British dominions such as Canada, Australia, New Zealand, the Irish Free State and South Africa, but India was excluded from this agreement, which also had trading benefits. Mohandas (or Mahatma) Gandhi (1869–1948), trained in law in Britain, advocated civil disobedience in the face of British rule. The British encouraged Mohammed Ali Jinnah and the Muslim League, using once more its familiar tactic of divide and conquer between Hindus and Muslims. By 1935, Parliament passed the Government of India Act, which granted self-government, except in foreign policy, to much of India. Another instance of tactics built on movements in the West was the reforms of Mustafa Kemal (1881–1938), who led Turks to found a republic in 1923. He moved the capital to Ankara from Constantinople (which was renamed Istanbul in 1930), introduced the Latin alphabet, abolished polygamy and instituted Western dress (as the Japanese had done so long before). Persia became more autonomous, required negotiated oil contracts and, in 1935, changed its name to Iran. After protests in Iraq, Britain ended its mandate there in 1930. Britain had promised self-rule to Egypt in 1922 and ended its military occupation, except for the Suez Canal, in 1936. Britain was caught between protecting the rights of Jewish immigrants and native Arabs in Palestine, but its policies did not prevent conflict. France took another tack and tried to use military force to hold its empire together. It put down nationalists in Algeria and Ho Chi Minh's uprising in the 1930s: this Communist leader would achieve victory in the war against the United States and its allies in Vietnam in the 1970s.

From 1918 to the Second World War, Britain and France were preoccupied in different ways with empire and may have not countered the rise of totalitarianism enough on the Continent. Fascists, Nazis and Communists all waged war on their own citizens. Lenin had compromised between socialism and capitalism: Stalin would not.[11] By his own estimate, he starved, executed or worked to death more than ten million people. The Russian empire was now the Soviet Union: despite its great industrial progress and the wound of the Revolution of 1917 and the First World War, its murder of its own citizens was sustained and brutal. Germans felt the scar of the Great War as well and many in the middle classes feared a Communist revolution like that in Russia in 1917; and in January 1933 Paul von Hindenburg, a veteran of the First World War, chose, with the backing of the conservative elites in industry, the military and the civil service, Adolf Hitler, leader of the Nazis, and not the head of the other leading party, the Communists, to be chancellor.

The old spectre of anti-Semitism haunted Europe and its long shadow would never have been so dark. The first concentration camp, Dachau, opened in March 1933. It was soon filled with Jews, socialists, homosexuals and other dissidents. This third empire or reich, after Charlemagne's and Wilhelm II's, was wrought with terror, violence and death. Any party with a component called the Order of the Death's Head was not likely to affirm life and diversity. Millions perished in the death camps: by 1942, the Holocaust or final solution was taking shape and there were nineteen principal concentration camps in Europe. International Business Machines (IBM), according to Edwin Black, became enamoured of the means of technological innovation and forgot, in the face of this technical creativity and the pursuit of profit, the ends that technology would be used for, so that it had a conscious involvement in the Holocaust and the Nazi war machine. Although computers did not exist in 1933, when Hitler came to power, the IBM punch card and card sorting system allowed for maintaining systems. Black says that IBM Germany (Dehomag), with the knowledge and cooperation of the head office in New York, made these machines available and supported them as they were established in the main concentration camps. The new form of social control and mass destruction in war needed information organized on a mass scale, and Black sets out to prove in his recent study that that is what IBM was able to help the Nazis do efficiently. Hitler needed the names of the Jews and the machines helped to deliver them.[12]

As some countries armed in the period between the two world wars, they sometimes, like Italy, France and the Soviet Union, did so too early and had a hard time retooling for what seemed to be an imminent conflict. During the 1930s, at great cost, aircraft were doubling their speed despite heavier armour and guns; tanks had bigger engines and were better armoured than their antecedents; weapons systems benefited from electrical communications, navigational devices, antisubmarine equipment and radar. Italy lacked most of this and was relatively weaker in 1940 than it was two or three years before: still Mussolini committed his country to war in hopes of creating a new Roman empire. In the spring of 1936, Addis Ababa, the capital of Ethiopia, fell to Italian forces, and Hitler entered the Rhineland in March 1936. So weak was the Italian military that whereas much of the British high command wanted Italy to remain neutral, some actually hoped that Italy would join Germany as a way to weaken it. Germany, after the rise of Hitler and his National Socialist Party in 1932–3, had a government bent on war and conquest that spent more than any other western European states on the military and soon exceeded the combined spending of France, Britain and the United States. The quest for racial purification, as Hitler had set out in Mein Kampf in the early 1920s, attended this massive and quick buildup. The speed of the rearmament also strained the German economy. Hatred, revenge, nationalism and expansion were keystones of the Nazi leader and had a wide but not universal following. Each of the powers had dissidents and those who opposed imperialism, territorial expansion and various kinds of hegemony.

The Third Reich, which is yet another allusion to the trope of the translation of empire that had persisted for so long, was like Japan in its dependence on the import of raw materials. The British empire, the United States and the Soviet Union all possessed large quantities of nickel, iron ore, copper, petroleum and other resources necessary for modern industry. Like Japan, against all odds, Germany would take on these great empires with their vast natural resources, and sooner than the military planners had generally hoped.

But the other countries were even less prepared than Germany was for war in 1939. Germany's invasion of Czechoslovakia allowed it to seize gold and money, military equipment, armament factories, ores and metals and other assets that fed a Germany economy on the brink of crisis. The plunder of labour and materials was the underpinning of this regime. They took this policy to terrible lengths probably beyond the imagination of Napoleon. Conquest had been a strategy of empire long before Cortés and Pizarro let alone Hitler. Like Japan, Germany might overtake the Dutch, the French and the British, but could it face down the Soviet Union and the United States as well? If Hitler picked up on the worst tendencies of the last kaiser and augmented, distorted and magnified them while adding many other problems to the mix, he was, as Kennedy has noted, a far cry from Frederick the Great and Bismarck, both of whom tried to protect Germany from over-exposure and situations beyond its power.[13] Neither of these earlier German leaders spoke of a thousand-year reich. The Germans helped Franco and the fascists in Spain, where the republicans had overthrown the king in 1931 and hoped to modernize Spain, which had been on a long decline. Spain had been the leading power of Europe and the world in 1600. The Spanish Civil War of 1936 to 1939 was a live testing ground for war for Germany and Italy as they supported a pro-fascist nationalist force. Britain and France, ever reluctant to go to war, failed the republicans. Both sides in this war in Spain committed atrocities.

France and the Soviet Union also maintained large military forces, so that Germany had once more to worry about powers on the western and eastern fronts. The French economy began a precipitous falling off after 1933 and with it a decline in the military. Ideological conflicts intensified in France: between 1930 and 1940, twenty-four changes in government occurred. The military ignored intelligence about Germany and France fell out with Italy over Abyssinia; it was also flanked by a fascist Spain, a neutral Belgium and a potentially hostile Germany. After the Munich agreement, the Soviet Union was less interested in cooperation with the

West. France, so heavily dependent on the importation of coal, copper, rubber, oil and other resources, came to rely on the British empire once more in its conflict with Germany. This empire had all these materials in abundance. France also relied on Britain and the United States for financial support. France expected to stop the Germans while its empire and that of Britain could then recover losses in central and eastern Europe. Britain in its turn had tried to have France be more conciliatory to Germany and less committed to its allies in central and eastern Europe. Britain itself had its own imperial preoccupations and was not prepared for the Second World War. The alliance between France and Britain started to be better coordinated in the months before the war, but that, in retrospect, came too late.

Although Britain had twice the manufacturing output of France, it was declining relative to other powers and was in a much weaker position to check Germany than it was in the First World War. After 1918, Britain had turned more in on itself, trying to forget a fruitless war and preoccupying itself with questions of greater democratization (extended the franchise), social issues and spending. Its military budget was less than a quarter of its allocations on social services. The British empire continued to change shape. Through the Balfour Declaration of 1926 and the Statute of Westminster in 1931, the self-governing dominions became independent states that could opt to follow British foreign policy or shape their own. Canada, South Africa and Eire were not that interested in any military action. Imperial unity could be achieved through consensus in war and peace. Britain, then, always had one eye overseas even as the storm gathered in Europe. Whitehall used the army, the Royal Air Force (RAF) and the Royal Navy to police territories such as India, Palestine, Egypt and Iraq and wanted to send a fleet of the navy to Singapore to protect British colonies in the east. Its industries declining steadily and then faster in the 1930s, Britain was living on its capital. Like France, Britain was cutting its military spending just as Hitler took power in Germany. By 1936, after witnessing the open military build-up in Germany and the crisis in Abyssinia, Britain began to spend much more on armaments. Before Neville Chamberlain replaced Baldwin as Prime Minister in 1937, Britain had explored the possibility with Germany of colonial and commercial concessions. This policy of appeasement might have worked if Hitler could have been appeased. That rearmament, owing to the lack of support for war among the populace and to fiscal prudence, did not begin in earnest until 1938. In this year, M. J. Bonn, of the London School of Economics, wrote *The Crumbling of Empire: The Disintegration of the World Economy*. Bonn saw that the democratic empires had greater resources than the totalitarian regimes and asserted that the clash between Fascist and Communist is a difference of aims, not methods, because while both believe in force, 'To the Communists it is a mere method, to the Fascists an end as well as a means, all of which runs contrary to developments in the democracies, whose aggressive missionary fires are dying – A strong feeling of the wickedness of domination, colonial and otherwise, is nowadays pervading the Western mind'.[14] The coming conflict, expressed in such ideas, also had a material and practical dimension, for Britain and other countries might resist the Fascist if not totalitarian movement to domination and war. Except for France, Britain did not have committed allies it could join to fight an autocrat or dictator in search of European domination. The British empire was not in a position to fight Hitler as it had Napoleon or even Kaiser Wilhelm II.

The USSR and the United States had their own brands of isolationism. In the 1930s, the Americans were not interested in British proposals to admit Japan's special place in East Asia or make special payments to Germany. The French were drawing Britain into potential conflicts in Europe that people in the constituent parts of the British empire were not enthusiastic about: the threat of Japan drew imperial resources that could have been marshalled against Germany. Britain turned to Sweden and the United States to help its arms build-up and this weakened the already delicate British economy. The British treasury warned that Britain could not sustain a long conflict as they had from 1914, but the policy of a war of attrition was the only one that the British command thought it could win. Britain left Singapore exposed to Japan and turned its focus back on Europe. Although occupying a quarter of the globe, the British empire had seen its manufacturing output dwindle to about 10 per cent of the world's production. Economics made it difficult for this overstretched empire to take a stand. It stood up to Hitler in heroic fashion and, as marvellous as that was given the nature of that regime, it was the end of the British empire, its catastrophe before its denouement.

The Rise of Japan

For many reasons, including cultural and racial prejudices, the 'white' nations continued to underestimate Japan, whose military fought with a code of courage and had developed technologically as well. Like the United States, Japan had benefited, during the First World War, from the vacuum that the western European imperial powers had left. Profiting from their demand for munitions and shipping, Japan had become a creditor while many other powers languished in debt. From 1914 to 1919, Japan's tonnage in shipbuilding rose between seven and eight times and its manufacturing increased even more than in the United States. From

1913 to 1938, its rate of manufacturing production grew over five and a half times while Britain and France had barely grown and Germany and the United States approached one and a half times. The only country whose manufacturing production grew without great fluctuations in this period was Japan. It, too, had its problems, such as an underdeveloped banking system, an agricultural sector based on intense labour and small holdings, falling demand for some of its products, such as silk, after the Great Depression and competition with more competitive western industries. In 1920, the Soviet Union was producing under 13 per cent of what Russia had in 1913, and it took until 1926 to reach that level again. From 1926 to 1938, the Soviet Union's manufacturing production augmented an astounding eight and a half times.

The years from 1913 to 1926 were much kinder to Japan, which had increased production more than two and a half times. By 1938, Japan had overtaken Italy and France in industrial production and it overtook British production by the mid-1960s. This growth in Soviet and Japanese power shifted the balance of power in the world away from the western European empires. Japan would step into the vacuum that these powers had created in eastern Asia. The continued rise of the United States would also move the world from the expansion and dominance of western Europe beginning in the fifteenth century. Japanese imperial expansion into East Asia meant that it became dependent on raw materials and spent larger amounts on the military than any of the great powers. The Japanese navy exceeded the limits placed upon it by the Washington Treaty, whereas Britain and the United States scaled back their navies. Japan had the most effective torpedoes and the third largest merchant marine in the world. Here was a modern Asian country of great economic and military power in search of an empire.

Japan's army was a dominant part of the imperial government. Its pressure to invade northern China from Manchuria in 1937 over the Marco Polo Bridge incident – the name of the event containing ironies in the history of empires and colonies – did not lead to China's surrender. Moreover, this incident bled Japan financially and had it rely on imports from disapproving western imperial powers like the Netherlands, Britain and the United States. The Japanese government also thought that Chiang Kai-shek's resistance was simultaneously being fuelled by western supplies from British and French colonies in East Asia. The leaders in Japan hoped to isolate China and take Southeast Asia, the Dutch East Indies and Borneo in order to secure petroleum and other raw materials. Japan might take the French and Dutch colonies and even those of Britain, but it would have a hard time against the United States and the Soviet Union. The Soviet tanks, aircraft and artillery had shocked the Japanese command in the battles along the border at Nomonhan during the late spring and summer of 1939.

The United States put an embargo on aeronautical materials in 1938 and abrogated the trade treaty it had with Japan while the British and Dutch banned iron-ore and oil exports after Japan overcame Indochina in the summer of 1941. These reactions isolated the Japanese. The American economy alone produced 500 per cent more steel than did its Japanese counterpart, 700 per cent more coal and 8,000 per cent more motor vehicles, providing its citizens with a national income seventeen times that in Japan. Consequently, with a spirit of realism, the Japanese command attempted to avoid or put off war with these two great military powers, but in time the conflict came to pass, no matter how difficult.

The USSR

The Soviet Union, the successor state to the Russian empire, had endured great hardship during the First World War, the revolution and civil war, its population declining from 171,000,000 in 1914 to 132,000,000 in 1921. It lost valuable farms, industry and railroads with the loss of the Baltic states, Finland and Poland. It was isolated because of strong anti-Communist attitudes in the United States, the British empire, Germany and elsewhere. Stalin's brutal smashing of the kulaks, the private owners of agricultural land in a state where over three-quarters of the population was engaged in farming, was a grab in resources and money to finance a much-needed military and industrial build-up according to the prevailing logic of security and development. No one would lend the Soviet government money on a large scale. This collectivization strategy, which the czars and Lenin did not dare to attempt, meant that agricultural production plummeted and the already low standard of living declined. Millions died in the famine of 1933.

By the late 1930s, the USSR had created a scientific and collective agriculture but at enormous human cost. Cultural and human values can never be separated from politics and economics. Private consumption in the Soviet Union was by far the lowest of the great powers (levels that would probably have caused revolution elsewhere in Europe). The state was able to skim off a huge percentage of GNP to invest in industry, education, science and the military. Education and the steep fall in the number of people working in agriculture brought about a knowledge and industrial revolution from 1928 to 1940. The number of engineers alone was reported to have risen over six times in the period. Even if one is sceptical about figures in education and production, the Soviet Union, as Kennedy has claimed, underwent a growth in national income and industrial output that was unprecedented.[15] The Soviet Union's industrial output in the late 1930s had overtaken that of Japan, Italy and France and was rivalling Britain's. Despite this success, in the USSR the agricultural sector was unproductive, transportation inadequate, and industry inflexible. Stalin's horrific purges were detrimental on an economic as well as human level: they created a shortage in skilled workers and inhibited productivity and innovation. Stalin built his organized terror on Lenin's. It was Lenin who had established Solovki, the first large Soviet concentration camp, and, as Orlando Figes has argued, military power and 'ruthless terror' were keys to the suppression of the peasant revolts in the civil war, even if famine and exhaustion dammed down the peasantry in regions like the Volga (1921–2), a crisis largely resulting from over-requisitioning by the Bolsheviks.[16] The Manchuria crisis and Hitler's accession led to great increases in the military and on defence spending. Despite great strides in technology, education, military strategy and production of tanks and aircraft, the Soviet Union still lacked in trained workers and soldiers. Stalin had purged about nine in ten generals and eight in ten colonels, so that military leadership had become a problem for the country: soon the leadership was neglecting British theory and German methods in warfare. The country grew weaker militarily between 1929 and 1939.

Like the British empire, the USSR was in a weakened position that might have affected its diplomacy in which it tried to appease and buy time. Like Germany, the Soviet Union might face war on two fronts – against the Germans in the west and the Japanese in the east. This weakness and fear of fighting on two fronts may well have helped to lead to the pact between the Soviets and Nazis in August of 1939. Germany, too, had bought some time. Eastern Europe could be carved up and then Germany could concentrate on the western front. In 1939 the Red army showed weakness and strength: it had trouble with the Finns but handled the Japanese. The pact between Molotov and Ribbentrop on 23 August 1939 made war over Poland much more actual in Britain and France. The government of the USSR played a waiting game, arming while postponing the day of war.[17]

The United States

Until the crash of 1929, the United States was becoming the pre-eminent industrial power. It was the greatest in finance and credit, held the largest stocks of gold, possessed a massive domestic market, and produced the most foodstuffs and manufactures (it had about twenty-one times more automobiles than the next country – France). The United States declined more than any other great power during the Great Depression, but it had started from a level at which its output was greater than the next six powers combined. That the United States was so self-sufficient meant that it did not have to rely on international trade for wealth.

The country was more interested in prosperity and being left alone than in building an extensive empire or in holding great sway in international politics. Only foreign raw materials to feed the great industrial machine were of concern to the United States. The American military was cut back so it was a middle power. The United States contributed greatly to the financial collapse of 1929, so that even the greatest of nations reaped what it had sown, as every other empire in history had learned and often too late. Tariff wars hurt the United States more than other nations: protectionism did not work. From 1922 to 1932, wheat exports fell forty-fold and auto exports declined over seven times from 1929 to 1932. The United States began to recover only to hit another severe slump in 1937. While from 1929 to 1938 the Soviet Union had increased its share of world manufacturing output from 5 to almost 18 per cent, the United States had slipped from just over 43 per cent to almost 29 per cent. It was still dominant in industry, but not as pre-eminent. Its middling military, caused mainly by isolationism and a desire to concentrate on domestic industry, had not built up as Germany's or even the Soviet Union's had. Britain has been called a reluctant empire in its early phases and the United States had some of these qualities as well: Americans wanted to focus on trade and prosperity and not on war and hardship. By 1937, the United States began to rearm, doubling its aircraft production in one year, and in 1938 it aimed to have a navy second to none. It would take up where the British were leaving off. The United States was, consequently, much better prepared for the Second World War than it was for the First (at least in 1914). The United States was an innovative, productive and dynamic economy that was underperforming and creating great suffering. Once the economy had to perform for war, it could do so without much trouble. The government of the United States was not as helpful as it might have been to France and Britain while they faced the build-up of fascism in Germany during the 1930s and it continued to supply Mussolini's Italy with oil even though it denounced its policies and actions. London and Washington did not cooperate well in this period, although Roosevelt himself in about 1937 started to worry more about the threats in Germany and Japan.

In 1937, the ties between Germany and Italy and Japan were in place. By 1938, secret naval talks between Britain and the United States occurred to discuss that threat. Roosevelt asked for great increases in defence spending to a budget that as a percentage of the whole was less than any of the other world powers. With the rousing of the new American giant, even if one that lacked racial purity, Hitler decided to press ahead. The more Hitler waited, the more he would face allies who would dwarf Germany's military and industrial capacity. Japan took the United States more seriously than Germany did and knew that if they waited to attack until 1944 (the mid-1940s were the apparent original targets of these two authoritarian regimes), its strength in warships would have fallen from 70 per cent to 30 per cent of the American total. Germany and Japan – looking in realistic terms – had one last chance to move before the United States and the Soviet Union came to dominate the balance of power in the world. This was soon to be an age where the capitals of western Europe would not shape world affairs. This age of western European empire was coming to an end, and three decades after the war there would be a further winding down. Western Europe would be influential but not the metropolitan centre.

The Second World War

There was no eastern front to divert the Germans as there had been in 1914. On 3 September 1939, the Germans knew that they could draw on natural resources from the Soviet Union and Sweden. Blitzkrieg warfare was successful in Poland and could be applied to the Nazi invasion of Denmark and the Netherlands. German advantages in tanks and air power allowed the Nazis to tear apart the large Allied armoured forces and infantry in the battle for France in May and June of 1940. Early victories allowed the Nazis to plunder the defeated countries. Spanish raw materials were now also easily obtained once France fell. The British and Americans agreed to the Lend-Lease programme. The Battle of Britain showed that Britain and Germany were in a stalemate in the west of Europe: Germany could not invade the British Isles and Britain did not have the army to knock Germany out of France and the Netherlands. In 1940, the British empire had mobilized under Winston Churchill and was building more tanks and aircraft than was Germany. In the North Atlantic, the Germans relied on U-boats because their surface fleet could not challenge the Royal Navy. Whereas Britain found it easy to take Italian positions in Abyssinia, Somalia and North Africa, it met its match with Rommel in Africa and with the Germans in Greece. Hitler himself, a little like Napoleon but more so as 'Russia' was not in the war, upset this balance by deciding in June 1941 to invade the Soviet Union. This allowed the British empire to preserve its territories and influence in the Middle East and undermined German shock tactics that relied on short supply lines. Germany spread itself thin at the peak of its power. Fighting in the east with poor transportation and communication was not a good choice: victory, at least enduring victory, was not a possibility. The hysteria and megalomania and propaganda of this new empire – the Third Reich – could not be sustained. If it goaded too many giants – the British empire, the United States and the Soviet Union – it might attain glory and riches for a while but the ultimate outcome would be national and imperial suicide. Japan honoured the neutrality pact it had signed with the USSR in April 1941, so, although Germany broke its own pact with the Soviet Union, Stalin did not have to worry about a Japanese attack in Siberia and could transfer his troops, used to one of the most bitter winters on earth, to stop, and then advance on, Hitler's eastern army. Owing to Tokyo's invasion of French Indochina, the West had placed an embargo on trade with Japan and frozen its assets in 1941. The Japanese, who had also signed a neutrality treaty with Italy and Germany in September 1940, chose to avoid war with the Soviet Union and the United States and, instead, to take the oil and the natural resources of Southeast Asia. The United States might intervene if the Japanese seized the Dutch East Indies, Malaya and Borneo.[18]

In search of these resources, which Japan seemed desperately to need, the generals planned new invasions and an attack on American installations in the Pacific and, above all, their fleet base at Pearl Harbor. On 7 December 1941, Japan attacked Pearl Harbor, a decision as fateful as Hitler's to invade the Soviet Union. During that month, the Soviets began counterattacks near Moscow that stymied the Blitzkrieg. Hitler also decided to declare war against the United States. Despite Japanese victories in Singapore, a British colony, and the Philippines, which had passed from the Spanish empire in 1898 into the American sphere or empire, ultimate victory would be difficult. At the time, however, the threat of Japan was palpable in the European colonial empires in East Asia and the Pacific and in China, which it had surrounded.[19] Japan also threatened Hawaii, Australia and India. In 1942, the Germans were hammering away at the Soviet army again, had pushed close to Alexandria in North Africa and had used U-boats effectively in the destruction of merchant vessels. Despite these successes and the very high level of military training and technology that Germany and Japan possessed, these two countries were stretched along vast supply lines with populations and an industrial base much smaller than their opponents. The United States was now fighting in the Pacific and the Atlantic. It would, in a matter of years, become the greatest military power in the world, whose armed forces would finally match its industrial pre-eminence.[20] Despite the growing power of the Soviet Union, the United States would become the industrial and military leader in the world that the British empire had been earlier. But the recognition of this greatness was not readily apparent, although Churchill saw it clearly.[21]

The German and Japanese empires in Europe and Asia respectively were not sustainable. Despite the German superiority in flexible military tactics to the British, Russians and Americans, they could not hold off larger armies with more tanks, aircraft, artillery, equipment and weapons. In 1942, the British Commonwealth (a new form of the empire) was producing about 25 per cent of the aircraft Britain itself was making, over 50 per cent of what Japan was producing and almost twice as many aircraft as Italy. Britain's greatest former colony, the United States, produced almost twice as many aircraft as Germany, Japan and Italy combined in both 1942 and 1943. The former British colonies in recent years, like Canada and Australia, were pulling their weight and the first group of colonies to sever the tie with Great Britain – the United States – had now overtaken the mother country and its empire as the world's foremost military and industrial power. France had disappeared under German occupation and was part of the formal and informal German empire in Europe. The East Asian colonies of the Dutch and British empires were largely under Japanese control. The British empire and Soviet Union made great contributions by raising arms production at vast rates and, combined with the huge American increases in such output, this made German or Japanese victories more unlikely even if their defeat would take a long time. For the Netherlands, its long imperial tenure was going the way of Spain and Portugal; for France, their older empire had collapsed and would be held together with desperation after the Second World War; Britain would become an island nation on its own again, so that if John Cabot's voyage to Newfoundland/Cape Breton in 1497 began this overseas empire, the handing over of Hong Kong in 1997 marked 500 years of empire. For the British, the first 150 years were tenuous and the last fifty were marked by rapid decline and decolonization.[22]

Even before Columbus sailed, there were elements in Europe that were against or wary of expansion, and these sentiments persisted to the end of the British empire.[23] The Spanish empire had endured just over 400 years, from Columbus's landfall in 1492 to the Spanish-American War in 1898. Spain had begun to decline in the seventeenth century and had lost most of its American colonies in the first decades of the nineteenth century.

Portugal had begun its expansion in 1415 and gave up Macao in 1999, so that it lasted longer than the British empire, although no modern empire was probably so strong militarily and economically for so long as that of Britain. The British generally saw their colonies leave in relative peace, whereas the French fought in Vietnam and Algeria in the 1950s and the Portuguese were at war in Angola in the 1970s. In 1963, António de Oliveira Salazar, Prime Minister of Portugal from 1933 to 1968, showed some sympathy for Africa: 'The aspirations of the African peoples do not differ from those of the majority of communities spread throughout the world, which even today yearn for liberation from the cycle of underdevelopment in which they find themselves.'[24] Salazar's position appears protean because while he seemed sympathetic, he also found fault with the idea of leaving to local inhabitants the responsibilities of government: 'This theory has been given the name of self-determination, and the movement directed to its achievement has come to be regarded as a natural force described as "the Tide of History".'[25] Using the topos of inexpressibility, Salazar said he would not criticize this position – he referred without attribution to Macmillan's 'winds of change' speech or similar ideas – but did. This fight for representative government, which was discussed in the last two chapters, persisted in the oldest of the modern western overseas European colonizers – Portugal. Salazar questioned the two main arguments for African independence – unity among the peoples of that continent and 'anti-white racism' – while advocating a new multiracial regime in Portuguese Africa: 'we hold that the economic, social, and political advancement of those territories will only be possible on a multiracial basis in which the responsibilities of leadership in all fields fall to the most qualified, irrespective of their color'.[26] This policy sounds very much like that Macmillan hoped, in 1960, would be adopted in the former British colonies and those about to achieve independence. Salazar understood the opposition to this multiracialism: 'I know we are accused of trying, by taking this stand, to ensure domination by the white race in Africa, the basis for this accusation being the fact that our multiracialism has not yet been implemented widely enough in the distribution of responsibilities throughout the Portuguese provinces in Africa' and admits that there is some truth that they were 'far from attaining satisfying results from this policy'.[27] Salazar's analysis is a mix of what would be the ANC's multiracial policy in South Africa but also the kind of paternalism that Rudyard Kipling had represented many decades before as the white man's burden. In 1961 the MPLA's (in English – the Popular Movement of the Liberation of Angola) historical perspective, which encompassed events from 1270 to the present, was quite different about the Portuguese role in Angola after it was given carte blanche in the area after the Berlin Conference of 1885 and aided by the Paris Peace Conference of 1919 (in which the imperial powers limited the acquisition of arms by 'the patriotic forces of Africa'): 'The character assumed by the Portuguese military occupation can be summed up thus: after each victory, physical liquidation of African chiefs and immediate destruction of the traditional structure (political, economic, and social) of the conquered peoples . . .'[28] The conflict over history, politics and economics ran deep between the imperial centre and the colonized people, between Portugal and Angola.

The Russian empire – the USSR after 1917 – endured from its expansion in the sixteenth century to the fall of the Berlin Wall in 1989 and subsequent events. The Soviet Union had expanded its boundaries and its informal empire and held much of that for almost fifty years. The Soviets had lost millions and millions of troops and civilians in the fight with the Nazis and that affected its demographics, industrial output, agriculture and infrastructure. Obviously, like the United States, it kept much of its territorial expansion across its landmass, but it had suffered greatly from this war as it had in the war of 1914. Even though the Red army was cut back, the USSR maintained the largest military in the world after the war, something understandable after what it had suffered in both world wars. In all this Stalin trampled the rights of his own people and crushed democracy in Poland and Czechoslovakia in the late 1940s. The strategic challenge would be for the Soviet Union to keep up or keep close enough to the United States in terms of technological and economic innovation. These two new 'imperial giants' would dominate the post-war world for almost fifty years, and the United States has become the overwhelming pre-eminent military and economic power in the past decade. In the United States, industrial expansion occurred at a rate of over 15 per cent per annum between 1940 and 1944. This one-time colony was becoming, perhaps, an imperial democracy, although a country with an anti-imperialist national mythology from revolutionary times onward and a nation with isolationist tendencies. Like Britain and the Netherlands, it was a largely Protestant power that emphasized commerce, trade and liberty. The per capita productivity and standard of living of the United States were higher than those of any state. During the Second World War, the United States produced over half the world's manufactures and about a third of all goods. The United States had military power second to none. For the first time in centuries, the Royal Navy did not rule the seas.

The Pax Britannica, with its gesture to the Pax Romana, had passed to the Pax Americana. Like the British, who enjoyed informal influence and power long before 1815, the Americans found that they filled the vacuum the British, and to a lesser extent the French, left after 1945. Adam Smith was largely the patron saint of this American order as he had often been to the British era of world affairs. The United States helped to set up the International Monetary Fund (IMF) and then the General Agreement on Tariffs and trade (GATT) and tied reconstruction and development money to agreement to abide by this framework of western capitalism that the United States was perpetuating. The Marshall Plan was instituted and was a counterbalance to open competition as the funds it made available allowed for industrial redevelopment of states devastated by the war. The United States, as Britain once had, sought out bases around the world, but they required a kind of commitment the British had tried to avoid for fear of being overstretched.

The Cold War with the Soviet Union would involve the United States in an almost imperial kind of legacy that earlier leaders, such as John Quincy Adams, had resisted earlier. On 4 July 1821 Adams had noted of the United States that 'She knows that, by once enlisting under other banners than her own, were they even the banners of foreign independence, she would involve herself, beyond the power of extrication, in all the wars of interest and intrigue, of individual avarice, envy, and ambition, which assume the color and usurp the standard of freedom'. Adams continued in a way that expressed the individual conscience and the best of the nonconformist and exceptionalist spirit of the New England colonies and later states: 'She might become the dictatress of the world; she would no longer be the ruler of her own spirit.'[29]

The old imperial order was dealt a death blow during the Second World War. In 1941, Mary Townsend of Columbia University in New York opened her study of European colonial expansion since 1871 with this declaration: 'It is universally recognized that a conflict of empires is basic to the Second World War, as it was to its predecessor of 1914–1918. Again and again Hitler has declared his determination "to break the British empire," which constitutes but a louder and less euphonious echo of William II's demand for a place in the sun.'[30] In 1944, Eric A. Walker, Vere Harmsworth Professor of Imperial and Naval History at Cambridge, spoke of fifteen colonizing powers in 1939 and 'focused on the empires and policies of the six leading Powers; that is, Great Britain, France, Belgium, the Netherlands, the United States, and the U.S.S.R., and this despite the fact that the three last-named reject the colonial idea'.[31] Walker called for honesty and courage and attention to the political dimension of empire and colonies, that ' "scheduled liberation" goes dead against the traditions and practice of the British and Americans, the only two peoples who have pursued a policy of decolonisation over a long term of years'.[32] Events also contributed to the loss of colonies or changes in them. Italy was stripped of its overseas acquisitions in 1943 and Japan suffered the same fate after the war, while Germany lost its gains in Europe and its old territories in the east such as Silesia and Prussia. Italy was on the verge of starvation and Germany, which had been devastated by heavy allied bombing, had plundered France and, this, along with fierce fighting in 1944, had left France in terrible shape.

France had suffered a kind of civil war as well as occupation and tribute to Germany. The Free French had fought fascism and had fought pro-Vichy forces in Algeria, the Levant and West Africa. Anglo-American aid had helped France re-establish itself, and British support helped to gain it an occupation zone in Germany and a seat on the Security Council of the United Nations. France, despite being extremely weak economically, attempted to hold on to the protectorates, departments and territories that made up its colonial empire – second only to the British empire. After the war the French and Portuguese would fight to try to maintain their empires, but the British would not.

The Royal Navy was still a large and effective force and the RAF was the second strategic air force in the world, but Britain could not stop the decline of its economic and political power and with it that of its empire.[33] The American development of the atomic bomb, drawing on an international team of about 100,000 scientists in the Manhattan Project, changed the technology and devastation of war beyond anything known to humankind before. And Japan, which had driven the Europeans from many of their colonies in Asia in 1940 and 1941, felt the brunt of the controversial dropping of these bombs: parts of Nagasaki and Hiroshima were incinerated on 6 August 1945. Over 140,000 people were killed instantly and many others died from the effects of fallout. Japan, whose military had sought to fight to the death and whose commitment to that tactic might have contributed to the American strategy of atomic warfare, surrendered eight days later.

War just seemed to get more and more horrific with each conflict. Between fifty and sixty million people died in the Second World War and as many were refugees. Once again the Russians (Soviets) suffered the greatest casualties, perhaps more than a third of the total in this one country. It is difficult to imagine what scars both wars left on the people of the Russian and Soviet empires. The Jewish population of Europe, so lessened through emigration before the war and through extermination during it, was drastically reduced. So many groups suffered. Death camps, massive aerial bombardments and atomic bombs made this world war perhaps even more terrible than the first in which the Germans had used chemical warfare (as Iraq was later to do on the Iranians and on its own Kurdish population many decades later).

Harry Truman, who had to make this decision, was now the head of the leading power, building on what Woodrow Wilson and Franklin Roosevelt had to do, however reluctantly, on the world stage. Even though the United States was isolationist and self-sufficient, it could not turn away from the world in quite the way it had off and on since its birth as a nation. In March 1947, Truman announced a policy – soon known as the Truman Doctrine – that spread beyond the situation in Greece, where the British could no longer sustain their interests, and that involved financial and military aid as a way of countering Communism and political crises. In June 1947 Secretary of State George C. Marshall connected dictatorships with poverty and set out his Marshall Plan, which sent billions of dollars of food, services and equipment to Europe. The United States government was trying to stop the collapse of Europe and its turning to Communism. Stalin blocked such aid to central and eastern European countries under the Soviet sphere of influence.

The United States would develop a great informal economic empire just as, to some extent, Japan would. Germany would have its own informal sphere in the European Common Market (later the European Economic Community [EEC] then the European Union [EU]), sharing some of that weight with France and later, to a degree, with Britain and Italy. Western and central Europe would contract into itself, and although it would still be a great force in the world, it would be caught between the two greatest powers, the USA and USSR. The United States economy had grown about 15 per cent a year from 1940 to 1944 and its wealth was now vast: Britain, on the other hand, divested itself of firms in its formal and informal empire in places such as Australia, India and Egypt. Amidst economic destitution in Europe at the end of the war, the Nuremburg trials were held involving twenty-four members of the Nazi leadership, half of whom were sentenced to death for crimes against humanity, a recognition of genocide as a crime in international law. And from early in the century, voices for the end of empire or decolonization grew in strength. One of the key people to resist empire was Gandhi.

Gandhi in Context: a Voice for Decolonization

A few threads among a multitude might suggest the move from the universal rights of man, as envisioned in the French Revolution, to the widespread rights of men and women of all varieties that has been the aim of the last half of the twentieth century, which, paradoxically, has had such technologies and ideologies that it may well have pursued the death wish and have been the most violent in recorded history. To echo Charles Dickens from the opening of A Tale of Two Cities, which represented London and Paris during the French Revolution – a passage I have chosen for my epigraph: 'It was the best of times, it was the worst of times'.[34] In 1849, the year after The Communist Manifesto appeared and after the collapse of the revolutionary government in France, Karl Marx moved to London, which would become his new laboratory. This was an age of revolution, this was an age of technology. Marx and Friedrich Engels, like Mary Wollestonecraft before them, were concerned with the matter of property; of Communists, they say: 'In all these movements they bring to the front, as the leading question in each, the property question, no matter what its degree of development at the time.'[35] The technological era was something that was celebrated: the Crystal Palace Great Exhibition of

1851 in Hyde Park in London; the World's Fair in Paris that highlighted the Eiffel Tower, which was built to commemorate the French Revolution and was then the tallest building in the world; and the Columbian World's Fair in Chicago in 1893 all displayed the industrial and technological progress of the leading industrial powers in the 'Victorian' age. As Dickens intimated and often represented in his novels, it was also a great age of disease, neglect and poverty. John Ruskin was another critic of the excesses of mid-Victorian England: in *Stones of Venice* (1853) he discussed technology and in *Unto this Last* (1863), laissez-faire economics. Gandhi read this last work in 1904. What was the human and what was the good and beautiful in such an age of rapid change and extremes in wealth and poverty in cities unable or unwilling to provide a healthy environment, especially for its poorest members?

The Civil Rights Act of 1866, which was a precursor to the Fourteenth Amendment of the Constitution of the United States, was a beginning in bringing equality between white and black Americans. One editorial saw the imperfections of the bill but realized that 'they could be corrected: the Senate and House of Representatives conferred freedom, and they have now defined what they mean by freedom. If a man can not own property and exercise every right that springs from its possession he is not free'.[36] Once more property and liberty were at the centre of the debate on rights. The gap between the ideals and enforcement of laws was not lost on people in their lives.

In the British empire and elsewhere as in the United States, issues of equality persisted into the twentieth century. Mahatma Gandhi became known in South Africa, where he first articulated his vision of Indian nationalism. As Anthony Parel says, Gandhi, who first learned politics in the Transvaal, was first Indian, then Gujarati then Kathiavadi and did not begin with a homeland or location from which to work outward.[37] Gandhi wrote *Hind Swaraj [Indian Home Rule]* – alternating hands when he was tired – on ship stationery on board the *Kildonian Castle*, sailing from England to South Africa from 13 to 22 November 1909.

Gandhi, who was trained as a lawyer in Britain and who translated the work himself from Gujarati into English, admired the British constitution partly for its ability to evolve and as a measure of any colonial administration and regarded Queen Victoria's Proclamation of 1858 as a charter of freedoms for Indians. These ideals were something to which the British could be held to account. *Hind Swaraj* was self-expression, a definition of home rule, a response to terrorism, a critique of modernity as being a worse threat than colonialism, an attempt to reconcile Indians and the British, a revision of dharma or practical philosophy in terms of civic humanism.[38] In this dialogue, which is reminiscent of the works of Plato, the Editor responds to the Reader:

the whole of India is not touched. Those alone who have been affected by western civilization have become enslaved. We measure the universe by our own miserable foot-rule. When we are slaves, we think that the whole universe is enslaved. Because we are in an abject condition, we think that the whole of India is in that condition. As a matter of fact, it is not so, but it is as well to impute our slavery to the whole of India. But if we bear in mind the above fact, we can see that, if we become free, India is free.[39]

Western civilization in this context is not the Christian, religious or spiritual dimension but something that undermines its own spirituality. For Indians, learning to rule themselves is the *swaraj*.

Gandhi welcomed some of the contributions of modern civilization:

civil liberty, equality, rights, prospects for improving the economic conditions of life, liberation of women from tradition, and religious toleration. At the same time, the welcome is conditional in that liberty has to harmonise with swaraj, rights with duties, empirical knowledge with moral insight, economic development with spiritual progress, religious toleration with religious belief, and women's liberation with the demands of a broader conception of humanity.[40]

Rights and duties needed to be balanced. Gandhi himself would be a martyr as would Martin Luther King, someone who also embraced, as had Millicent Fawcett and her colleagues in the moderate part of the women's movement, passive resistance in the face of discrimination and injustice. And Gandhi, who read his Thoreau on civil disobedience, was in turn someone who would influence Martin Luther King, Nelson Mandela and others in the civil rights and human rights movements. The question of gender was also slow to be resolved in the pursuit of rights and equality in a changing world.

Women as Persons, a Girl as a Target

Human rights were sometimes advanced and sometimes abused. However short this section is, it juxtaposes a brief on a case in Canada and the British empire about recognizing women as persons and a Dutch girl whom the Nazis captured and sent to a concentration camp and who came close to losing her life because she was Jewish. One is an overdue recognition of women as equal partners in humanity, another is an assault on a child, as one of many children, who suffered because of virulent racism and racial policies. Throughout this book, we have seen the neglect and abuse of women and children, especially among African slaves and indigenous

peoples, but here we see a glimmer that women might be given equal opportunities but also witness the abuse of a child, the intersection of the systematic and the personal through terror and injustice.

In Canada, the government also sets out the triumph of Emily Murphy,
who had fought so hard for women's rights. In 1916, Murphy became the
first woman magistrate in the British empire. On her first day in court, a
lawyer challenged her ruling against his client on the grounds that
Murphy was not a person and could not act as a magistrate, basing his
argument on a decision rendered in 1876 by a court in England. This decision, although obsolete, had never been overturned: it held that 'Women
are persons in matters of pains and penalties, but are not persons in
matters of rights and privileges' and added that 'Since the office of magistrate is a privilege, the current magistrate sits illegally. No decision
coming from her court may bind anyone.'[41]

On 19 October 1929, as Monique Benoit notes, the 'Famous Five'
Alberta women battled to have their gender constitutionally recognized
as 'persons' (and thus be allowed to sit in the Canadian Senate): the
Judicial Committee of the British Privy Council granted the Famous Five's
appeal to the decision of the Supreme Court of Canada in 1928 and found
in their favour. The result was 'that the word "persons" in section 24 [of
the British North America Act] includes members both of the male and
female sex . . . and that women are eligible to be summoned to and
become members of the Senate of Canada'.[42] Women could govern as well
as vote: citizens, not simply queens, could contribute to government. As
in New Zealand and elsewhere, in Canada, women came to occupy more
places in government, even if not representative of their population. This
was, and has been, a slow and ongoing process. The work of women,
as with those of Natives and minorities, in the realm of human rights
continues.

But there was also a darker side to the treatment of women in the
world. We have witnessed from the beginning of European expansion the
massacre and abuse of women and children, especially of other cultures,
but we have more testimony about recent incidents. The survivors of the
Holocaust have told some of their terrifying story. One such girl was
Rachella Velt Meekcoms, who was twelve when the Germans invaded the
Netherlands. She and her sister, Flora, were taken to Westerbork and then
Auschwitz. Looking back, Rachella makes some observations worth
remembering: 'The Dutch were very pro-Jewish and very good people as
a whole, but there were those among them also some who would give the
Jews to the Germans.'[43] After describing some of the terrible conditions
in which she found herself, Rachella observes: 'Every day was terrifying.
I lost about 20 pounds the first two weeks. We were all sick but afraid to
go to the hospital barrack because they made selections there. My number

was 81793 and my sister's was 81792. We tried always to be called up together because we held each other up.'[44] This pattern was familiar in the treatment of Natives and slaves, men, women and children, from the fifteenth century well into the nineteenth. The typology of the Black Legend of Spain warned against the Spanish bringing atrocities to the Netherlands that they had enacted in the New World. Here, the Germans were behaving barbarously with other Europeans, Germans, Dutch and others, just because they had Jewish 'blood'. And they were working them to death and disease just as Europeans had the Natives and slaves. An ideology of purity and a greed for property and booty were once more driving a government and its soldiers. And these Jewish girls thought of themselves as Dutch: 'And the Dutch girls began singing to show them. Sick and downtrodden as we were, we were singing Dutch national songs.'[45] The Dutch girls, Flora and Rachella, somehow survived and found themselves in the hands of the Danish Red Cross. The king of Denmark welcomed them and called them 'beautiful people'; and in the streets the Danish people cried to see them and shouted 'Freedom'. The girls understood why the people were crying: 'We were used to the way we looked. Such a sight we were! When we saw pictures of ourselves in the newspaper it looked like a bunch of death people walking in the street. We were so worn and filthy and bad-looking and the people kept calling out their congratulations.' And she soon adds the observation: 'We were so happy and they were so touched to see us, such a terrible sight we made.'[46] In Sweden, the Dutch consul and legation met them, and they all sang the Dutch national anthem, at which Rachella cried and cried. She soon learned she had typhus and that her sister had tuberculosis.

Later, they went back to the Netherlands. She praises the Phillips factories and says: 'so we were grateful for the years in hiding, and the Dutch people who risked their lives for us'. The first people she went to see were the family that had taken them in, and she calls them 'Marvelous people!' But she also mentions 'the other family, who betrayed us to the police' and says they were interrogated and one was put in prison'. She also observes that 'There were so many collaborators that the prisons weren't big enough after the war. Many people right after the war took the law into their own hands and there were a few killings, but there were too many to cope with'.[47] After a year, she returned to England, where she lived with her aunt and uncle, and her sister went to America. The narrative ends with her family about to go to see her sister's in America, where her sister went because she could not bear the memories of what happened in Holland. And so this is a personal testimony, so important as a countervailing story against the great movements and apparently impersonal movements of history. But if we break them down, we find individual human experiences, their voices and faces in the crowd and horizon of time.

Transitions

Even as the terrible events of the First World War, the Great Depression and the Second World War unfolded, some of the trends we have seen in earlier times occurred, with greater technology, in even more intense forms. Women, minorities, colonized peoples and indigenous peoples often continued to suffer. What came to be known as genocide, an outgrowth of pogroms and other massacres of groups, such as aboriginal peoples, was a shattering experience of the Nazi attempt at an enduring empire. Stalin's internment of opponents and groups he suspected was a kind of totalitarian solution that resembled Hitler's, but also may have sprung from the forced labour camps of the Spaniards in the New World and the concentration camps of the British in the Boer War. Over and over, in this book we have witnessed cruelty, greed and violence. This impulse to aggression, which often seems arbitrary and gratuitous, seems to have a pattern and a plan behind it. The stealing of land or property, a kind of piracy, coupled with prejudice and myths of superiority, allowed the Europeans to abuse Jews, 'heathens' and Native peoples. The technology of forced labour and enslavement led to some of the cruellest treatment of African slaves and indigenous peoples.

We saw how IBM and the Nazis were linked in the administration of genocide. The Holocaust, despite relying on IBM's punch card technology, training and service, was also personal. I have tried to bring out one voice, of a Dutch girl, stunned at the sudden barbarity of Nazi racism come into the midst of her beloved Netherlands. The administrative structures of the Spanish bureaucracy helped create its empire. All the empires we have discussed relied on bureaucracy to develop. They all had commercial companies and individuals in search of profit. At times, each empire, or one of its citizens or companies, stepped over the bounds to enter into greed and violence. Slaves and indigenous peoples suffered, and the white mythology, racism (in Japan, the West and elsewhere), economic greed, and religious or political fanaticism all contributed and continue to contribute to misery then and since and now. While empires have their benefits in technology, they have sometimes had the sorriest and most painful records of abuse of those they considered other or lesser, of those beyond the pale or who were pushed there.

Trade could have the personal aspect of pain, displacement, discrimination and even death. On a systematic level, there could be growth at the expense of targeted and marginalized groups. A transnational or global economy with new international institutions had been coming into being. Trade was global and crossed the boundaries of each state, culture or empire. The rise of the Soviet Union from the ashes of the Russian empire in 1917 and the ascent of the Nazis in Germany meant that authoritarian and totalitarian regimes with their own imperial agenda came into conflict with more traditional empires, such as those of Britain and France. The growth of Japanese imperial and colonial power in Asia was also a challenge to France, the Netherlands and Britain and their empires in Asia. Like the many shifting alliances of previous eras, the rise and fall of states and empires occurred at a remarkable pace. Even in 1945, scholars and politicians talked about the big three: Britain, the United States and the Soviet Union. But very soon it became clear that there were really only two great powers and heirs to European expansion, east and west; they were the USSR and USA. And soon they would be involved in the friction and fear of the Cold War. Meanwhile, all these societies went through rapid and uneven changes, so that in comparing powers or empires, the subjects and states are shifting.

7

Decolonization or Neo-imperialism: 1945 to the Present

෬◡ͻ

Many of the colonies in Asia and Africa that the western European empires had annexed in the last decades of the nineteenth century were in place in 1939, but by the end of the 1970s, the very empires that contained them ceased to exist. Along with the United States, Belgium, the Netherlands, Britain and France all prevailed in the Second World War, but this made no difference to the fate of their colonies. Spain and Portugal were neutral, and they did not keep their colonies. They were wealthy, but still lost their colonies, many of which had movements for independence. Nationalism had been in the colonies for some time. Many of these colonies beyond the settler colonies were culturally different from the metropole and did not have familial ties to western Europe. The United States, Canada and India had found their own nationalism and their own ways to independence and became models for others at the time of their independence. The European empires gave self-government or independence to many of their colonies before they were forced to do so. Britain allowed dependencies to develop self-government from the 1840s onwards. Still, the European gradualism gave way to sudden independence in the wake of the Second World War. Many in these European states changed their attitudes towards the holding of colonies and thought that divesting them would be for the best. And the independence of one colony led to that of another. When India became independent in 1947 and Britain evacuated the Suez Canal in 1956, British interests dissipated in east Africa and south and southeast Asia. The United States and the Soviet Union opposed colonialism and these countries became the superpowers of the period. But decolonization had its own roots.[1]

Decolonization may well have started with the revolutions in the British and Spanish American colonies from the 1770s to 1830, but the final stages of the break-up of the European empires happened in the wake of the Second World War. It was about the new dominance of American and Soviet (Russian) power in the world, in the wake of Hitler's and Hirohito's attempts at alternative empires, as the British empire declined as the dominant world power. The Russian Revolution, like the Dutch Revolt, the English Revolution, the American Revolution and the French Revolution, was against monarchy and used the rhetoric of anti-colonialism and anti-imperialism. The Cold War had global implications in the wake of the decline of western European empires. The rise of the United Nations, the debates over international human rights (which echoed Vitoria, Las Casas, Grotius and others from earlier periods), the tensions between decolonization and possible neo-imperialism or multinationalism (corporate imperialism) all contribute to the period from the Second World War to the present.

Postwar/Cold War

The ideological Cold War was beginning: Winston Churchill spoke of an iron curtain between east and west in March 1946 and the Soviets began to speak about being encircled and against Anglo-American world domination. Dwight Eisenhower, the commander of the Allied forces in Europe, later saw this struggle in the postwar era as one of freedom against slavery. Both the United States and the Soviet Union spent vast amounts on their militaries and on their build-up of nuclear arms, so that while Britain then France then a number of other countries, including Britain's former colonies, India and Pakistan, also developed nuclear bombs, their arsenal was dwarfed by the Soviet and American stockpile. This arms race in a Cold War characterized much of the period from 1945 into the early 1990s, despite various treaties to limit nuclear weapons between the USA and USSR.[2]

The Berlin Crisis of 1948–9 exemplified this antagonism among the three western occupying forces in Germany – the United States, France and Britain – and the Soviet Union. The Soviet blockade of Berlin, about 100 miles within their zone of occupation but split between the four powers, did not work because the British and Americans flew in supplies to the populace. The North Atlantic Treaty Organization (NATO), which included the United States, Canada and Britain as well as continental powers, was a military counterpart to the economics of the Marshall Plan. Here was a strategy to get Europe on its feet and to protect it from Soviet expansion and influence. The USSR countered this move with the formation of the Warsaw Pact. The Americans realized that eastern European countries would be freed of Communism by war or by the Soviet Union, which curtailed or crushed opposition in Poland, Czechoslovakia (1948, 1968), East Germany (1953) and Hungary (1956). By 1961, in order to stem the brain drain from the east, Khrushchev ordered the erection of the Berlin Wall. The Cold War spread beyond Europe. Nationalism and anti-colonialism in the rest of the world complicated the conflict between economic liberalism in the west and the socially planned economies of the Soviet Union, China and the countries under their control or influence. Nationalist movements encouraged by the Allies during the war to resist the Germans and Japanese continued their momentum against whatever western or imperial power in their territories. There were many ways to make former colonies into nations from empires.[3] The British, Americans and Russians placed Iran under military protection from 1941 to 1943, but, after the war, the Russians would not withdraw their troops until opposed by the British and Americans. In 1947, the British passed on the responsibility for safeguarding Greece and Turkey to the Americans.

The Dutch faced Sukarno's nationalist movement in Indonesia; the French, Ho Chi Minh's in Vietnam; and the British, nationalists in Malaya. The case of Indonesia shows just how confusing and volatile the situation was at the end of the Second World War. In pursuance of the Potsdam agreements, Indonesia became part of the British strategic zone, so that Lord Mountbatten, whose forces landed on 16 September 1945, had to disarm and repatriate Japanese soldiers without interfering with the friction between the Dutch and the Indonesian nationalists. The British, and even the Japanese, were called to restore order in the final months of 1945. In a strange twist, the Indonesian republican forces (Djboku) clashed with British troops while the Japanese, just months ago their enemies, reinforced them. After the Dutch returned, there were clashes and military action. The Netherlands recognized the independence of Indonesia, but tried for close relations with it until 1956. Although the Dutch tried to salvage ties between the Netherlands and Indonesia through a Dutch–Indonesian Union under the Dutch Crown, the Indonesians dissolved this on 10 August 1954.[4]

Throughout Asia, the situation was intricate and it took some time for the thinking of governments and their peoples in Europe to catch up with events. The change was monumental if not unexpected by those who knew the history of nationalist movements in Asia and Africa. Since the nineteenth century, American missionaries had put a great deal of effort into China: the Chinese revolution culminating with Mao's triumph in 1949 cut off these ties between the United States and China. The American government was caught between wanting to see the end of European colonialism and fearing that national movements would be or go Communist. The United States itself was largely consistent as it granted the Philippines independence in 1946 while encouraging the British to withdraw from India and pass on power to Nehru's parliamentary government and the Dutch to leave Indonesia by 1949.[5] The Russians developed their own A-bomb in 1949. When the North Koreans attacked across the thirty-eighth parallel in June 1950, the Cold War heated up outside Europe. After the United States and the United Nations intervened, China came to the aid of North Korea in October and November of 1950. Just as allies from the Second World War such as the United States and the Soviet Union were at Cold War in Europe, former allies, China and the United States, were involved in an actual war in Asia. About 900,000 people were killed in this conflict. The war ended in June 1953 and the United States lost over 54,000 troops, almost as many as Viet Nam, which was a more protracted conflict. Had China not come to the aid of North Korea, President Truman might well have recognized the government in Beijing (Peking) as the British had in 1950. The United States was now battling Communism, trying to contain nationalist insurgencies in Indonesia, Malaya and Viet Nam, and came to sign pacts with the Philippines, Japan, Australia and New Zealand in their war against Communism. In 1949, the Americans decided to develop a more powerful H-bomb. The Soviets responded with a similar bomb in 1953, about nine months after the American test. The Russians, who had suffered so much at the hands of the Germans in both world wars, now used German scientists and technology to build their bombs and missiles.

The contrast between the beginnings of European empire and the years during and after the Second World War was stark. In 1955, the Soviet Union was producing a large number of medium-range ballistic missiles. The Anglo-French attack on Suez in 1956 was in many ways the last independent military action by these two empires, which had been allies since 1904, and whose empires across the Atlantic were first reached in small wooden ships that, although advanced for the time, were from across such a technological divide that it was sometimes difficult, except for those involved in public policy and myth-making, to connect in the name of empire. In 1958, the Soviet Union used rocket engines to shoot Sputnik, the first satellite, into orbit and to fire an intercontinental ballistic missile 5,000 miles. This was a world in which the early explorers, Columbus, Cabot and Cartier, would think was a fantasy or dream. Even Leonardo Da Vinci might have blinked. Britain and France had their nuclear weapons, but they invested less in this balance of terror. US forces landed in Lebanon in 1958 and checked Syria, which the Soviets had backed. The Cuban missile crisis, which involved an American blockade of Cuba, showed that navies were not dead even in a world of nuclear missiles. Despite Khruschev's attempt, after Stalin's death, to reduce tensions with the West (he had among other things removed troops from Austria and handed Port Arthur back to China and Porkkala naval base to Finland), the tensions remained.[6]

With its new power, the USSR, like the USA, reached out beyond Europe. It gave so-called Third World countries an alternative to capitalism and possible neo-colonialism. The Soviet Union signed a trade pact with India in December 1953 and gave it military aid; provided aid to Egypt in 1955 for the Aswan Dam; gave loans to countries such as Iraq and Afghanistan; lent support to Guinea, Mali and Ghana; and signed a trade agreement with Cuba in 1960. Moreover, the USSR engaged in propaganda against imperialism (the western countries had their own rhetorical strategies) and offered treaties, military advisers and trade credits to states recently decolonized. During the 1960s, the Soviet Union increased aid to Iraq, Syria and Egypt, gave military and economic assistance to North Viet Nam and offered support to liberation movements in Latin America. Many countries, emerging from the influence and control of formal and informal European empires, were wary of suffering a similar fate under the sway of the Soviet Union or United States. The nationalist movements that helped to unify Italy in 1861 and Germany in 1871 and that helped to break up the Austro-Hungarian empire and to set up buffers between Russia and Germany during and after the First World War could not be controlled as much as imperial powers like Britain, France, Italy and Japan tried in the face of American opposition at the end of that war or as much as European imperialists or Western governments might later have attempted. The Second World War shattered these empires, and nationalism, which had spread from western to eastern Europe, now encompassed the globe.

The so-called white man's burden or the Social Darwinist imperialism of the late nineteenth century and early twentieth centuries was not something natural, but a passing phase. The decline of Europe and the slow and eventual rise of multicultural states like the United States, Brazil, Canada and Australia meant that empire had altered the settler colonies through slavery and immigration. These former European colonies became some of the most diverse and dynamic countries culturally and economically in the postwar era. There was a third way beyond the superpowers. At the Bandung conference of 1955, a variety of countries, some decolonized states like the Philippines and others once great imperial powers themselves such as China, Japan and Turkey, pushed for further decolonization. Originally, the General Assembly of the UN was dominated by European and Latin American countries, but after more decolonization in the late 1950s and early 1960s, it swelled with new members from recently independent countries, particularly from Africa and Asia. The Soviet Union seemed more in tune with this anti-imperialist mood, which is not surprising given the nature of the Russian Revolution and the civil wars and foreign pressures that followed, than was the United States, even though it, too, had resisted imperial Britain at its founding and had been an advocate of the decolonization of the European empires.

At the UN, politics were no longer necessarily the function of economic and military power. Men like Nehru, Tito and Nasser were influential political figures who resisted imperialism and the new superpowers. Nehru criticized British policy in Suez and the Communist party in India even as he accepted military and economic aid from the Soviet Union. Tito maintained Yugoslavian independence in the face of Russian power. In Egypt, Nasser opposed Britain, France and Israel in 1956, but while he accepted Soviet aid, he launched an anti-Soviet media campaign between 1959 and 1961. The United States suffered a great setback in Viet Nam that divided the country and left scars that are still healing ('kicking the Viet Nam syndrome' as George Bush, Sr put it). The USSR had lost influence in China and the two nations split in the late 1950s and early 1960s. Soviet strategy in the Third World was also founded on India, with whom China had a border clash in 1959 and who seemed to obtain much more aid than China ever did from Moscow. By 1964, China had exploded its own bomb (Khruschev had cancelled the nuclear agreement with China in 1959) and Sino–Soviet border clashes, which began in the wake of the Cuban missile crisis, culminated in the worst conflict in 1969. In 1963, Sukarno's government in the former Dutch colony of Indonesia, which had received a great deal of aid from Moscow, shifted its focus from the Soviet Union to China and then, in 1965, destroyed the Communist party at home. Despite long ties with the USSR, Egypt, under Anwar Sadat, expelled 21,000 Soviet advisers in 1972.

The arms race between the United States and the Soviet Union was massively expensive and expanded destructive capabilities vastly. Neither Marxism nor capitalism was accepted universally and if either was adopted to any extent, it was translated culturally. The new ideologies of these hegemonic states found resistance just as those of the old European empires had. Territories had often accepted money without the attendant ideas. The Soviets gave aid to Qaddafi, who attempted to export revolution, as Cuba did in Nicaragua and Grenada. The scramble from Africa, as Thomas Pakenham has noted, had the same hasty pace that the scramble for Africa had.[7] Much of this scramble occurred between 1957 and 1968. Marxist governments were in power in various west African states such as Guinea and the Congo, as well as in Mozambique and Ethiopia. The Belgian authorities were reluctant about the independence of the Congo and hoped to govern humanely for a long time to come in a colony that had been built on the cruel mercantilism of Leopold II. However, these authorities could not transfer power on their terms and timetable and, amid a violent and volatile climate, decided to recognize the independence of the Congo as of 30 June 1960.[8] The former Portuguese colonies of Angola and Mozambique had strong Marxist influences at the end of colonization and the beginning of independence. The Soviet Union itself invaded Afghanistan in 1979, and in 1980 Ronald Reagan denounced it as the 'evil empire'.

The rise of China was another complicating factor in the decolonization of the western European empires.[9] This was and is another giant on the world scene. China and the USSR competed for power as the voice of Communism across the world. The empire of ideas, although not something pursued in detail in this book, had and has its own dominion. China actually siphoned great Soviet military concentrations away from eastern Europe. Whereas the Soviet Union emphasized the industrial worker, China often celebrated the peasant. China criticized the Russian invasions of Czechoslovakia in 1968 and Afghanistan in 1979. While the USSR supported India, China lent aid to Pakistan. In Albania, the Chinese were a thorn in the Soviets' backyard, whereas in North Vietnam the Soviets returned the favour. Mao's denunciation of the Soviets for backing down over Cuba, its border war with India in 1962 and the Cultural Revolution (1965–8) did not win him friends in Washington.

It is sometimes easy to think about decolonization as something that is the formal business of states alone. State power was significant in the British empire and played a key role in decolonization. In the White Paper of 1948, British policy was clearly expressed: 'The central purpose of British colonial policy is simple. It is to guide the colonial territories to responsible government within the Commonwealth in conditions that ensure to the people concerned both a fair standard of living and freedom from oppression from any quarter.'[10] This is the responsible government that Americans had insisted on, that Canadians had also demanded and that Lord Durham, as we saw in chapter 5, had recognized in 1838–9. Rights and prosperity were not then, or in 1948, matters that were divorced in the British framework. Putting these ideals into practice was not always easy. Business, as well as government, played a key role in colonization and decolonization. The decolonizing effort affected people, businesses and other parts of society. While this comes as no surprise, this dimension is too often overlooked. One example is the British winding down of empire on the Gold Coast of Africa. Whether or not the independence of Ghana and the consequences of the birth of that nation in 1957 weakened British business there, companies from Britain still play a key role there today. This persistence of British business in Ghana, according to Sarah Stockwell, was not due to a concerted effort by the governments and business sector in Britain in order to manipulate the process of independence to favour British capital. Rather, British firms were unable to influence imperial policy. Instead, British businesses had to develop

political and business strategies that were not part of official decolonization and this relation needs to be explored in colonies throughout
the British empire at the time of independence from the United States
onwards.[11] Similar intensive and systematic studies could be undertaken
in regard to the colonies of the various European empires during and after
they achieved independence. The retreat from empire has a rich historiography: the British case is well documented.[12] Others consider decolonization another form of imperialism or a neo-imperialism.[13] It is a kind
of cautionary tale that it is easy to settle into new manifestations of imperialism by declaring it over and done with.[14] Still others see a friction
among colony, nation and empire. In 1960, amid the final stages of decolonization, Stewart C. Easton, for example, viewed nationalism as a
European phenomenon that was used by its colonies for two distinct main
purposes – to curb local powers and to drive out the colonial or imperial
power itself.[15]

In the West old allies were sometimes divided. The colonial wars in
Indochina (1950–4) and Algeria (1956–62) as well as the Suez crisis of
1956 kept France off balance after the Second World War even though
American aid and Europe's economic recovery from the late 1940s had
benefited France.[16] Despite Anglo-American support during and after the
war, Charles De Gaulle blocked British entry into the European Common
Market (EEC, later called the European Union or EU) in 1957 and was
critical of Washington. De Gaulle celebrated the first French nuclear test
in 1960, sought reconciliation with West Germany in 1963, began taking
France out of the NATO military structure, expelled NATO from its headquarters in Paris in 1966, shut down American bases in France and sought
better relations with Moscow. All the while, De Gaulle wanted Europe to
be independent of the two superpowers. De Gaulle's own career was on
the rocks in 1968, the year of student and work revolts and the invasion
of Czechoslovakia. Another leader saw the importance of Europe taking
back some control of its destiny. Willy Brandt led West Germany into economic ties with East Germany, Poland and the Soviet Union between
1969 and 1973, so that financial, technology and cultural exchanges
could be made between east and west. Arms reduction and the Helsinki
Accords of 1975 on human rights moved Europe in that direction.

The United States was more able to abide by this change than the USSR
because these countries were on its doorstep and had been for some time.
There was a history there of military and economic competition. There
were many protests within the United States over the Vietnam War:
domestic and world opinion in this war, which was more open to the
media than any conflict before, as well as the desire not to bring China
and the USSR into the war kept the American government from throwing all it had into southeast Asia. The US economy was overheated by

money spent on Lyndon Johnson's Great Society and on Vietnam while the USSR was spending its revenues on achieving nuclear parity with the United States. Popular support for the United States waned in allied states and countries in the Third World because of the American support for a questionable regime in South Vietnam. The fall of Saigon in April 1975 was critical to the American psyche and to its place in the world because defeat and isolation, not of its choosing, were not usual for the United States. Despite domestic turmoil and division (and the part that the Watergate scandal would play), Richard Nixon and Henry Kissinger devised a flexible and imaginative foreign policy in a changing world, establishing regular relations with China. After Nixon's departure in August 1974, Kissinger stayed on in Gerald Ford's administration, but he did not have as much scope as he had had. Congress had increasing powers, which meant that aid to Laos, Cambodia, South Viet Nam and Angola dried up.

The oil crisis of 1973 sent shocks through the world economic system. Despite these changes in global politics and economics, the United States still wielded great influence in the world. From 1976, Jimmy Carter sought fairness in global relations and helped to bring about the Camp David agreement between Israel and Egypt. Washington did not, perhaps could not, shape a consistent foreign policy based on human rights. National self-interest and democratic ideals created friction as much as John Quincy Adams said they would. Having imperial influence even without being a formal political empire meant that the United States, as Jimmy Carter would realize more than most, was in danger of losing its soul. The crisis in Afghanistan and in Iran made the last phase of Carter's presidency especially difficult.

Ronald Reagan decided to change course in 1980 and to check Soviet expansion through a rhetoric of good and evil and a renewed arms race that might well crush the USSR economically. As the United States was stretched, it continued to embody contradictions, refusing to see that the world was more than a drama of conflict between the USA and USSR. By 1984, the United States had taken itself out of UNESCO, one of the symbols of a multitudinous and multilateral world that the government of the United States, consciously or not, had helped to form. Western Europe, Japan and China were all key players in the world. The Soviet economy, which had slowed considerably, could not keep up with American spending: it had had its own Viet Nam in Afghanistan. Muslim fundamentalism, if no friend to capitalism, was not a support to Communism. The Chinese and Soviets were perhaps even more suspicious of each other than of the Americans.

The economic transformation of Japan and Germany after the Second World War is a reminder that the power of trade is as significant as military power and that they are not always related. Japan was a technological powerhouse given to innovation and quality of goods. Although there have been fluctuations, China, from the early 1950s, has experienced steady economic growth and may well be the engine-house of the world in the twenty-first century. Western Europe itself, despite its economic and military decline, recovered magnificently from the ruins of two world wars. The victory of the British empire might well have kept it from making the reforms that Germany and Japan had made. The Germans talked about the English disease, a mixture of poor management, the stifling of innovation, poor productivity and a defiant labour movement. Neither the joining of the EEC nor North Sea oil could keep Britain's industrial base from eroding. A country with the third highest GNP in the world in 1945 was slipping fast. In 1917–18, Lenin saw that Germany had raised itself to a level with England and Japan with Russia, so that the relative strength of imperial powers changes rapidly.[17]

The rebuilding of Europe after the Second World War helped to create a much stronger international economy than the steps taken after the First World War. After some years of hardship, the world manufacturing output expanded about threefold from 1950 to 1970. This period was also one of decolonization. This process of emancipation was part of modernization and, after the First World War, Europe had to begin to accept the move to self-governance among the colonies. After the Second World War, all that the denial of such a sea-change would do or staying too long in a territory would accomplish, as Rudolf von Albertini noted, was to increase tensions further.[18] Stewart C. Easton toured the colonies, proclaimed in 1964 that the creation of new independent states in Asia and Africa was a 'revolutionary' change that had caught people 'almost unawares' and declared: 'The postwar retreat from colonialism and the appearance of the new nations at the United Nations raises many profound questions.'[19] Independence did not come easily for colonies. Africa had about 5,000 languages and had been divided geometrically rather than by boundaries that made sense to the people who lived there. In 1963, the Organization of African Unity was founded and their first decisions promoted peace because they decided to forego unity and to respect the divisive boundaries that the Scramble had created. This decision protected the smaller states.[20] In India, Hindus and Muslims fought each other. In North Africa and the Middle East many Muslims were not Arab and vice versa. Despite these and other problems, the peoples of the so-called Third World managed to throw off the empires of Britain, France, Belgium and the Netherlands. In Britain, while Churchill thought it important to hold on to colonies, Clement Attlee and the Labour Party thought that this went against social justice.

Just when Britain had promised India independence in the 1930s, the war began and 2,000,000 Indian soldiers fought for the empire. In 1947

India and Pakistan were new states created from the colony of India but not without the massacre of hundreds of thousands of people in clashes between Hindus and Muslims. A radical Hindu assassinated Gandhi, a Hindu himself, in 1948. From 1945 to 1965, Britain shrank from the world's most extensive empire to an island with few dependencies and in that period half a billion Asians gained their independence from the British empire.

After the revolution of 1949, China, under its Communist leader, Mao Zedong (1893–1976), would not tolerate western colonial hegemony within its borders or if it affected its interests. Another Communist leader, Ho Chi Minh (1890–1969), drove out the French in 1954 and the Geneva Convention of that year created, as states independent from France, North and South Vietnam and Laos. This decolonization threw this region into the Cold War between the apparent heir if not heir apparent to western European imperialism, the United States, and the Soviet Union, the state that claimed to have overthrown the czarist regime of the Russian Empire. In 1955, Achmed Sukarno, who led Indonesia to independence from a reluctant Netherlands, sponsored the Bandung Convention. This was a meeting of non-aligned states attempting to modernize and to stand up to the superpowers.

In the Middle East, Britain gave up Palestine to the United Nations, but the friction between Arabs and Jews persisted. In this region the United States played the anti-imperialist in the Suez Crisis of 1956, when Gamel Nasser – who had seized power from the king of Egypt, whose country had won its independence from Britain after the war – had nationalized the Suez Canal which allowed Britain to dominate Asian trade and to control oil. When the USSR had threatened these western imperial powers who were on the wane and the new Jewish state, the USA did not back Britain, France and Israel in their opposition to Nasser's nationalization of the canal, which he said was dug by force by 120,000 Egyptians who had lost their lives.

The sixth Pan-African Congress met in 1945 and considered force as a possibility against European colonialism. In Africa, many British colonies, beginning with Ghana in 1957, earned their independence peacefully, although the Sudan and Kenya involved conflict. The French colonies of Morocco and Algeria won their independence from France through conflict in 1956 and 1962 respectively. The fight for Algeria was long and savage on both sides. At home, there were protests over the French army's harsh practices at home and in Algeria and this violence helped the collapse of the Fourth Republic. Charles de Gaulle negotiated the independence of this most prized of French colonies and had to remake France in a new image. By the time Algeria had attained independence, the French empire in Africa was nought. In 1960, Ivory Coast,

Dahomey, Senegal, Upper Volta, Niger, Mauritania, Gabon, Mali, Chad and the Central African Republic all became sovereign states. That year, Nigeria gained independence from Britain, and Kenya and Zanzibar followed suit in 1963. The Congo (Zaire) became independent from Belgium in 1960 and Rwanda and Burundi in 1962. In 1951 Libya and in 1960 Somalia cut their ties with Italy. A conflict occurred in the Spanish colony of the Western Sahara, which achieved independence in 1975. Another ancient imperial power, Portugal, experienced rebellions in Guinea Bissau, Angola and Mozambique, the first becoming a state in 1974 and the second and third gaining independence in 1975. The imperial wheel had come full circle.[21]

Political changes at home had contributed to decolonization. Salazar was unlikely to give up Angola when there was a large settler population and because the indigenous forces of nationalism there were divided. A revolution in Portugal changed everything. On 25 April 1974, a leftist military junta staged a coup and accepted the view that there could be no last military victory in Angola. This change of government, like the Labour victory in Britain in 1945 and de Gaulle's in France in 1958, affected decolonization.[22] We saw that military political changes and alliances at home had affected how Spain and France had behaved in continental America after the American and French Revolutions. Internal and external factors played a part in the break-up of empires and the change from colonies to nations.

During the 1960s and 1970s, various factors complicated decolonization and the Cold War between the USA and USSR. Multinational corporations from the United States, Europe and Japan employed Europeans for their skills after the Second World War and then branched out into other areas of the globe. Was this a new imperialism or a breaking down of national boundaries and an imperial past? By the 1970s, companies in Japan and western Europe, often with the support of their governments, were now strong rivals to multinationals and tried to match them in research and development.[23] Healthcare and education began to be centres of the economy rather than heavy industry and manufacturing. The student body of universities grew sixfold from 1950 to 1969 in the United States, and many western European countries experienced a great expansion in post-secondary education. By 1960, the six European Common Market countries had a larger percentage of gross world product than the United States did. By the 1970s – Britain joined in 1973 and other countries followed – western Europe outstripped the United States in overseas trade by about a three-to-one ratio. Although it was the leading single producer in so many areas, the United States was falling into debt at the beginning of the 1970s. For the oil-producing countries of the Middle East, it was another measure against colonialism when the Organization of

Petroleum Exporting Countries (OPEC) set the conditions for trade in oil and their restriction of the flow of oil raised prices, cost industry, produced inflation and unemployment and drove up interest rates in Europe and North America. Limits to growth and stagflation were upon the West. Before the Second World War, the British had tried to control the petroleum industry.

Communications played a role in crucial changes. As radio had done, so too did television and the computer alter communication and the world of economics, politics and culture. In 1943, the British had used Colossus, the first electronic computer, to decode German diplomatic and military messages. Computers would shrink from the size of an enormous room in the 1940s to a desktop in the 1980s and would become vastly more powerful. The space race from the 1950s between the Soviets and Americans was another technological dimension with political, military and economic implications.

Civil rights movements, often based on the peaceful tactics of the suffragettes and Gandhi, were used in the United States from the 1950s to decolonize the state from within, that is, to seek equal treatment for Africans and Latin-Americans in the great republic. Women continued to pursue equal opportunities and treatment in Europe and the United States. Violent protests could also erupt, as in the wake of the assassination of Martin Luther King on 4 April 1968. In that year students and workers took to the streets in France and troops from the Soviet Union and its eastern European allies in the Warsaw Pact put down the democratic movement of the Prague Spring. During the 1970s, tensions between the Soviet Union and the United States lessened as they sought arms control.

Old grievances remained against one-time imperial powers as the Basques and Irish Republican Army sought independence from Spain and Britain respectively. The United States pulled out of Viet Nam and lost the war. In some key countries in the world of Islam, such as Iran, the majority Shi'ites were challenging the ruling minority Sunnis. The Iranian Shi'ites, led by Ayatollah Khomeni, who had been in exile in Paris, overthrew the Shah in 1979 and refused to release hostages taken from the United States embassy. In September 1980, Iraq's president, Saddam Hussein, attacked Iran, perhaps hoping that the Shi'ites in his country would focus on fighting the Iranians (Persians) who were not Arabs. Ethnicity might trump religiosity. Oil also complicated this, as well as other wars, in the region. In 1979, the Soviet Union supported a coup led by some Communists in Afghanistan against the government and all the Soviet technology and forces could not defeat the Islamic forces. By the end of the 1990s, when the Russian empire in its Soviet phase was unravelling, the Taliban took control. The invasion by American and allied forces in the wake of 11 September 2001, when the two towers of the World Trade Center were destroyed and the Pentagon was badly damaged in Washington in a guerrilla or terrorist attack on civilians, drove this Islamic party from power for what was alleged to be support of the Al-Qaeda, a militant group that was blamed for the attack on the United States. Hussein in Iraq also took advantage of the vacuum that the crumbling or reshaping (depending on the viewpoint) of the Soviet Union left. After the end of the Iran–Iraq war in 1988, Iraq was in debt and had lost hundreds of thousands of troops and civilians. Hussein saw one part of the solution to these problems in the invasion and annexation of Kuwait, the country with the world's highest per capita income, in August 1990.[24] The USSR supported the United Nations' condemnation of Iraq. The coalition led by the USA defeated Iraq readily.

During the 1980s, Japan was rising fast as an economic power and relations between countries in the northern and southern hemisphere (except New Zealand and Australia) became strained because of economic disparities. Economic power was shifting from the Atlantic to the Pacific. Besides Japan, Hong Kong, China, Singapore, Taiwan and South Korea were investing in high-tech industries. Japan's massive investment made it a leader in electronics and consumer products: the quality of its goods and its modernization made it the world's second largest economy. Japan and Asia helped to finance the growing American debt that helped, through bonds, to drive the growth in military spending because low taxes were politically popular in the United States. During the 1990s, many of these Asian tigers, except for China, stumbled and succumbed to troubles in their financial institutions.

Leaders in the West, like Margaret Thatcher, worried about the decline of the West and turned on the economic democracy that had been erected to fight totalitarianism earlier in the century and favoured, instead, competitiveness, privilege and individualism as nineteenth-century liberals had. Britain, a pioneer of the welfare state, was also a pioneer in its dismantling. Mrs Thatcher was able to achieve victory when she was not popular with wide segments of the populace because of the patriotism of the Falklands (Malvinas) War with Argentina, a conflict between the shadow of what was once the greatest empire in world history and a country that was once part of its informal empire that had declined from wealth into desperation. This war was about losses before it had begun. It was not Churchill facing down the Nazis, but a prime minister trying to salvage past glory and some bright future in a struggle with a military junta that had turned on its opponents and some of its own people. Ronald Reagan came to power in 1980 amid the crisis with Iran and he took up a programme similar to Mrs Thatcher's, which came to be known as Reaganomics. Reagan returned to the rhetoric of the Cold War and called the USSR the evil empire. The huge military build-up to counter that in the Soviet Union during the 1970s continued, although some of Reagan's predecessors in the USA spent more as a percentage of GNP than he did. John Major and Tony Blair in Britain and Bill Clinton in the United States followed many of their predecessors' policies. The problems of disparity in incomes and of urban decay were often overlooked in practice – that is, in the structures of economics – no matter how much verbal recognition of these challenges was expressed. Imperial powers often experience the friction of defence and domestic spending and can overstretch their resources. Germany and France faced similar problems like stagflation and high unemployment, but neither the governments of Helmut Kohl, who assumed power in 1982, or that of François Mitterand chose the same divisive strategy as their Anglo-American counterparts. Germany and France had developed powerful economies that were still among the few leading ones in the world.

The Soviet empire broke up in 1989 and the USSR came apart in the 1990s. The Solidarity movement in Poland – with the blessing of the Pole John II, who had become pope in 1978 – sought economic reform and was outlawed in 1981. In the Soviet bloc, the standard of living had been decaying for some time. In the USSR, a quarter of the grain rotted, the birth-rate fell and pollution was high. In 1985, Mikhail Gorbachev, the new Soviet leader, proposed a restructuring of the economy (*perestroika*) and thereby hoped to improve innovation and productivity, and openness (*glasnost*). Ronald Reagan was impressed by these policies, including Gorbachev's unilateral arms cuts, which he enacted to try to inject money into the domestic economy to enhance the standard of living and quality of life for the people. In 1985, the two leaders met and began to thaw out the Cold War. Gorbachev pulled out Soviet troops from Afghanistan in 1989. But not everyone thought his reform was far-reaching. In the spirit of freedom of information and debate, Boris Yeltsin denounced *perestroika* as not going far enough and quit the Politburo in 1989. In that year, Chinese students, inspired by Soviet reforms, demonstrated, using technology, such as fax machines and electronic mail, to get their story out to the world. Workers joined them. On 4 June 1989, the government crushed the protest and later executed about a thousand leaders. In Europe, Communism lost the power of government in just over a year. In June 1989 Solidarity defeated the Communists in Poland; in August Czechoslovakia opened its borders to the west; in October the Communist party was no longer the official party in Hungary; in November, the East German Politburo resigned and the Berlin Wall was opened, and Alexander Dubcek, the Czech leader during the Prague Spring of 1968, called for the end of Stalinist government and the reformers assumed power; in December Romanian leader Nicolae Ceausescu lost power and was executed; during the spring of 1990, Lithuania seceded from the USSR and Estonia and Latvia followed suit; in October 1990 Germany was united again after more than forty years while Gorbachev set the course for a transition to a market economy; Yeltsin became President of the Russian Republic after defeating a Communist candidate; in August 1990, while Gorbachev was on vacation, there was an attempted coup in Moscow, which Yeltsin faced down and found hundreds of thousands of supporters in the streets of Leningrad and Moscow.

The last great formal empire with its capital in Europe fell after more than four centuries of expansion. The United States is the heir to the western European empires, through tradition and settlement, but not through geography. On 3 October 1990, Germany was fully integrated as a polity. While this unity salved scars, it also led to new strains. The Soviet empire contained more than 100 ethnic groups and in Soviet central Asia alone there were about 50,000,000 Muslims. Yugoslavia and the USSR fractured. Almost a decade of civil war and ethnic cleansing (genocide) attended the break-up of Yugoslavia into Slovenia, Croatia, Bosnia-Herzegovina, the Federal Republic of Yugoslavia (which included Montenegro and Kosovo) and the Republic of Macedonia. NATO and the UN intervened, but might have done so earlier. This was a conflict in a complex region not well understood, whose divisions had some of their origins in the Ottoman and Habsburg empires. At the end of August 1991, the Soviet Parliament suspended the operations of the Communist Party; from September 1991, when the Baltic states declared their independence, other republics in the USSR followed suit. On 1 January 1992, the USSR dissolved and twelve of the fifteen former Soviet republics formed the Commonwealth of Independent States (CIS). Gorbachev ceded power to Yeltsin. Organized crime and corruption in Yeltsin's government created an undertow for the movement to reform, openness and democracy. The war in Chechnya also involved a clash with Muslim forces. The people of the new Russia and what was its empire suffered under these changes. People were free to travel and the educated could go out into the world and prosper. Russia is still in flux and Vladimir Putin's government is a test of whether the country, with the vastest resources in the world, can unlock the potential of its people and live in a prosperous democracy. Instability was not just a matter of the fall of, or challenge to, Communism in Europe and China. In India, Tamil nationalists assassinated a reforming leader, Rajiv Gandhi, grandson of Jawaharlal Nehru, and some unrest remains.

Matters of modernization and globalization, which had long been present even before the expansion of the European empires, continued to intensify. The debate over globalization has many sides: it builds opportunity; it destroys communities and the land and devours resources; it allows people to move to find opportunity; it exports terror; it creates a

McWorld of logos; it is a force that breaks down hierarchies and privilege; it is a new imperialism that guards the perks of rich individuals and nations. The protests against the World Trade Organization (WTO) in Seattle and elsewhere suggest that there are keen differences on the consequences of globalization.[25]

Sometimes quantification can hide the human in the movement of history. Poverty, violence and prejudice can drive people from the land, village and city of their birth. The migration of peoples has long been a part of human culture, society and history. Britain and Ireland produced almost half the European emigration between 1870 and 1890 and the United States received almost two-thirds of these people. Immigration mainly from Europe transformed Australia, New Zealand, Canada, the United States and South America during the nineteenth and twentieth centuries, supplementing the earlier British migrations to those areas. Countries like Canada and Australia developed official policies of multiculturalism during the 1960s and 1970s. In the 1990s, multiculturalism was at the centre of a debate in the United States, which had taken as its credo 'out of many, one' and had become a 'melting pot'. Besides the massive movements of immigrants, there was also since 1945 a vast scale of global migration. Refugees have been moving decade after decade. Perhaps 100,000,000 people have been victims of war, political persecution and uneven economic development while tens of millions have fled in search of economic opportunity and safety. Some of the destinations have been the United States, Canada, Australia, France, Britain, Sweden, Germany, Saudi Arabia, Nigeria, Singapore, Iran and South Africa. Illegal immigration from places like Mexico and China became a matter of debate in the United States. Sweatshops in Western capitals and modern slavery in the charcoal industry in Brazil and in the carpet business in India – no matter how prohibited by law – continued. Women and children suffered much in these upheavals. Suffragettes and feminists in the nineteenth and twentieth centuries in the British empire, the United States and elsewhere may have won the vote and have gained equality before the law, but, in many cultures, the lot of women and the children they brought into the world, although improved, was still precarious.

Disease and ecological problems continue to affect the nations of the world. The spread of diseases like AIDS (acquired immune deficiency syndrome) affected the poorest in Africa more than anywhere else, although from the 1970s the disease spread globally. The inability or lack of will of the wealthy countries of the world to help the poor, sick and dying is one of the most baffling and callous aspects of life. Ecological disasters, which resulted from the industrial and nuclear world, affected many countries, for instance the sinking of the *Exxon Valdez* in Alaska, the chemical leak at Bhopal in India and the nuclear meltdown at Chernobyl in the Soviet Union.

Communications and transportation have developed greatly in the past century or so and have influenced the configuration of communities and states. The influence of American popular culture, through film from Hollywood, advertising generated by Madison Avenue and television and spread through multinational companies, reached all corners of the globe. Literature, as the awarding of the Nobel Prize to many beyond the West shows, became more global, even though many of the writers sought the large and rich markets in the English or French languages. The nation came under stress between continuity and change: migration was altering the nation. Trading blocs, technology like the internet and organizations such as the European Union all intensified that challenge to the traditional nation state as developed in Europe from the Middle Ages. Home and exile, metropolitan centre and periphery, were intertwined. The world was global, but was somewhere that had moved beyond the colonial, or was it a new kind of colonialism, more informal but still strong?[26]

In cultural and literary theory a debate arose over what is now called postcolonialism. After whose empires and colonies is a key question, but the process of decolonization has occurred rapidly since the Second World War. Is the United States an example of a great series of colonies coming together to lead an anti-colonial movement from the 1770s onwards, or has it emerged as an economic power so great that it has reinvented colonialism in an informal phase based on financial leverage? In 1989 Andrei Sakharov called the USSR 'the last empire on the planet'.[27] With the Soviet Union and the United States after the First and Second World Wars, do we have new imperial powers, new forms of empire, or forces for decolonization (a way Lenin and some presidents of the United States thought of their respective nations)? Do we have a neocolonialism or new imperialism? Studies of imperialism and colonialism covered much of the ground that postcolonial critique later did. The ambivalence of empire was there from the start, but anti-colonial attitudes have picked up ground with formal decolonization, particularly in the last six decades of the twentieth century. There remain at the beginning of the twenty-first century some surviving outposts not only of the British empire (Bermuda voted against independence) but also of other nations: New Zealand, Australia, the United States, France, the Netherlands, Denmark, Spain and Portugal. Still, a United Nations Special Committee on Decolonization can attest to the diversity of territories. The special status of Nunavut in Canada also suggests that there is decolonization occurring within some nation states.[28]

The very language of English was something in which, as Salman Rushdie suggested, the empire wrote back to the metropolitan centre. The politics of language and the language of politics merged. Postcolonialism owes much to Edward Said, whose work *Orientalism* (1978) was in part a critique of French and British imperialism from the Enlightenment onwards and the ways it made the East something other to colonize. He was preoccupied with imperialism, and, later in his career, with the translation of empire to the American forms of imperialism, as seen by Noam Chomsky. Said turned his criticism to the American media in *Covering Islam*. Gayatri Chakravorty Spivak set out a critique of imperialism past and present by using theoretical positions such as deconstruction (a showing and displacing of the workings and assumptions of texts) and feminism (seeing the world or reading texts in terms of women and from their point of view). Homi Bhabha has brought to bear on the experience of colonization the idea of mimicry, a parodic repetition that destabilizes identity, and examined the hybridity of colonial authority, which, as I have argued, often requires a myth of origins, whether that is the translation of empire from ancient Greece and Rome or in the legal foundation of Columbus's discovery of the New World. Bhabha has explored the ambiguities and continuities between colonizer and colonized while exposing and questioning the stereotypes imperialists use to justify the colonization of subject peoples. The danger in the displacement and critique of empire and colony, which is an opposition that is intricate and overlapping, is a re-inscription of the categories of imperialism and colonialism, empire and colony. The translation of study can reinforce the translation of empire.[29]

The First and Second Gulf Wars under Presidents Bush, father and son, and the civil war and conflict in Yugoslavia under Bill Clinton raise the same issues about decolonization, neocolonialism and postcolonialism. In an interview with the *Washington Post*, reported by the Associated Press, José Maria Aznar, the Prime Minister of Spain, said that many Europeans see George W. Bush as an emperor and find that difficult to accept. Aznar himself offered the view that negative reactions to the empire come with power in the translation of empire: 'Spain was a superpower "and some still harbour resentment," he said. "Britain was a superpower. France was a superpower. It's your turn now. It's been your turn for a long time." '[30] With the passing of Britain, the United States was the new imperial power or is often perceived as such. The return of Hong Kong and Macao to China was probably more symbolic than effective means for China to increase its political and economic influence. This was another end to European imperialism.

The attacks on Washington and New York on 11 September 2001, after a decade of prosperity and a new technological economy in the United States and thus in the world because of its general leadership in trade, brought together again what the British and Soviets experienced in Afghanistan and the British were caught in Palestine. This was not a new Crimean War and the World Trade Towers were not the King David Hotel. As this is being written, the United States is spending massive amounts of money after invading Afghanistan with support from the Security Council and Iraq without it. It is divided from its allies. A million marched against the war in London, but Tony Blair took Britain into the war none the less. For some, this was leadership, for others betrayal. Even after the allied victory, which depended so much on the technical superiority of the United States, George W. Bush has an approval rating that splits his nation between admiration and denunciation – much like Blair, his chief ally. The war persists.

A critic of the war, Naomi Klein, contended early on in the war: 'Iraq is being transformed into the world's largest shopping mall. It's the sale of the century – bomb it, then buy it.'[31] Others, like Harry G. Gelber, see a more multiracial world inside Europe and elsewhere that is interdependent and cannot simply be characterized in terms of colonialism, even though that is often how the debate will continue to describe it.[32] The controversy over war and empire continues. There have long been voices of dissent and affirmation of expansion and 'empire'.

Voices for the Liberation of Africans and Their Descendants in America: King and Mandela in Context

The figures of Martin Luther King and Nelson Mandela, like that of Gandhi, as well as the League of Nations and the United Nations, represent an international movement towards rights, one that slowly moved towards a practice of the ideals of equality set out in the American and French Revolutions. In the shadow of the assassination of Lincoln and the end of the American Civil War, this legal and political change came, sometimes all too slowly, but was coming none the less. Paradoxically, out of the empires – for example, the Dutch, British and French – and their ruins developed an ideology of rights and freedoms and new groups and nations that would demand the very rights the ranks of European and settler societies would claim for themselves. Amid the rubble of Europe, which had experienced self-immolation, and the remnants of empire that were no longer sustainable first in Asia and then in Africa, decolonization accelerated after the Second World War.

Martin Luther King had one eye on the lack of adequate human rights for African Americans in the United States and similar situations beyond its borders. On 16 April 1963, King had written his 'Letter from Birmingham Jail', which he had addressed to eight members of the clergy from Alabama, and had connected civil rights in the United States with independence from colonialism overseas: 'The nations of Asia and Africa are moving with jet-like speed toward gaining political independence, but we stiff creep at horse-and-buggy pace toward gaining a cup of coffee at a lunch counter.'[33] King gained attention across the country when he was arrested and jailed in Birmingham. On 28 August 1963, King organized a march on Washington, where, on the steps of the Lincoln Memorial, he began with a celebration of freedom and then appealed to the figure of Lincoln in his 'I Have a Dream' speech. King added: 'But one hundred years later, the Negro still is not free.'[34] King echoed Lincoln and appealed to his memory. In appealing to American political, legal and constitutional history, King spoke directly about the problems for African Americans and for the country as a whole: 'When the architects of our republic wrote the magnificent words of the Constitution and the Declaration of Independence, they were signing a promissory note to which every American was to fall heir. This note was a promise that all men, yes, black men as well as white men, would be guaranteed the unalienable rights of life, liberty, and the pursuit of happiness.' With the pacing and pauses of a great orator, King declares what has happened to that promise: 'It is obvious today that America has defaulted on this promissory note insofar as her citizens of color are concerned.' That dream King had was of healing and community, not of violence and separation: 'I have a dream that one day on the red hills of Georgia the sons of former slaves and the sons of former slave owners will be able to sit down together at the table of brotherhood.' The speech culminates in a cry for liberty that culminates with a line from Negro spirituals – 'Free at last! free at last! thank God Almighty, we are free at last!' This inclusive vision was a practical utopia, an actual activism built on a dream. This speech and the event it marked in Washington helped strengthen the movement to desegregation and contributed to the passing of the Civil Rights Act in 1964.

Something else bolstered King and the movement the next year. King won the Nobel Prize and began his speech on 10 December 1964 in Oslo in Norway with 'I accept the Nobel Prize for Peace at a moment when twenty-two million Negroes of the United States of America are engaged in a creative battle to end the long night of racial injustice'.[35] A nation of Americans slightly bigger than the population of Canada was waiting for justice to result from King's peaceful tactics. Like Gandhi, King appealed in this speech to a spirituality, the way nations and people ought to be, not as they are. Christianity was not about bullets or nuclear annihilation. In this address, King brought up India and Africa, quietly but indirectly alluding to the non-violent work of Gandhi and those who marched for Indian independence, but making a specific reference to the urgency in South Africa. Although King was infused with the Bible, he ended by alluding to the English Romantic poets, William Wordsworth on 'man's inhumanity to man' and John Keats' 'beauty is truth and truth beauty' as an answer to cruelty and greed. There is room for the ideal in a movement that suffers violence and discrimination: this peaceful march needs to transform not only those who walk with it but those who surround it regardless of their colour. The day before he was assassinated, King gave a speech in Memphis, Tennessee ('I've Been to the Mountaintop'), enumerating different places in the stations of history where he would not stop: 'I would go on, even to the great heyday of the Roman Empire. And I would see developments around there, through various emperors and leaders.' King called his own nation sick and said it was in trouble. He saw a movement towards freedom in many parts of the world where black people wanted liberty. Beyond the denial of free speech in his country which prides itself in freedom, he wanted to stress the strength and wealth of black Americans. King could then keep going towards the mountain-top. He could take the entire nation back to the well the founding fathers dug so deep in the Declaration of Independence and the Constitution. At the end, with the Bible and Negro spirituals in mind, King's last words in his last public speech would be prophetic, his vision, like that of Gandhi, too great for his assassin: 'And I've seen the promised land. I may not get there with you. But I want you to know tonight, that we, as a people, will get to the promised land. And I'm happy, tonight. I'm not worried about anything. I'm not fearing any man. Mine eyes have seen the glory of the coming of the Lord.'[36] He was shot on the balcony the next day by a white man, who could not let his people go there. On 24 January 1998, a statue of Mahatma Gandhi was unveiled in Atlanta at the Martin Luther King Jr Historical Site as a way of marking the fiftieth anniversary of the independence of India and just a week shy of the fiftieth anniversary of his assassination. Henry David Thoreau's 'On the Duty of Civil Disobedience' influenced Gandhi and King both, and, in *Stride Toward Freedom* (1958), King had also paid tribute to his debt to Gandhi, especially in articulating the power of love.[37]

King would inspire others, such as Nelson Mandela, but there were white men, like Harold Macmillan, prime minister of Britain, who advocated rights for Africans in South Africa. Later, Presidents John Kennedy and Lyndon Johnson would seek to protect and extend civil rights for black Americans. Macmillan – who, like Winston Churchill, had an American mother – became prime minister on 10 January 1957 and continued to preside over the decolonization of the British empire. He met President Dwight Eisenhower on 20 March 1957 in Bermuda and consulted with Eisenhower over winding down the empire. The body of one top-secret telegram in the late 1950s ended with 'all this "liquidation of colonialism" is going so well that I would be sorry if there was any hitch, especially one in the Caribbean'.[38] Africa, as well as the Caribbean, concerned the prime minister at this time.

Macmillan was the first British prime minister to speak before the Houses of Parliament in Cape Town, South Africa. His 'winds of change' speech there on 3 February 1960 set out, diplomatically but directly, a vision of a world of equal nations where people of different backgrounds could come together in their countries and in the world as a community. He thought that South Africa could be a leader in Africa owing to its wealth and knowledge as an industrialized country, but that it needed to embrace 'the new Africa of to-day'; 'I understand and sympathize with your interest in these events and your anxiety about them', yet the silent qualification created a transition to the world of Macmillan and the government he led: 'Ever since the break-up of the Roman Empire one of the constant facts of the political life in Europe has been the emergence of independent nations. They have come into existence over the centuries in different forms with different kinds of government. But all have been inspired by a deep, keen feeling of nationalism, which has grown as the nations have grown.' Macmillan's typology between past and present, Roman empire and contemporary empires (including the British empire), set out a sympathetic movement from empire to nation. He then moved into the present: 'In the twentieth century, and especially since the end of the war, the processes which gave birth to the nation states of Europe have been repeated all over the world. We have seen the awakening of national consciousness in peoples who have for centuries lived in dependence on some other power.' Macmillan came to focus on the most recent events that had caused anxiety for the white government of South Africa: 'Fifteen years ago this movement spread through Asia. Many countries there, of different races and civilizations, pressed their claim to an independent national life. To-day the same thing is happening in Africa.'[39] Although Macmillan tried to soften the point, he asserted that national policies must accept 'this growth of national consciousness' as a fact and take it into account, so that South Africa, which 'sprung from Europe, the home of nationalism' and which created 'the first of the national Africanisms' must face this actuality. This national consciousness was worldwide, but was here in Africa: 'The wind of change is blowing through this Continent.' Paradoxically, 'this tide of national consciousness which is now rising in Africa is a fact for which you and we and the other nations of the Western world are ultimately responsible': nationalism is part of the great advancements that 'Western civilisation' has made in science, agriculture, communication and, above all, education.[40] Not embracing this fact of the growth of national consciousness would imperil the precarious balance between East and West, between 'the free world' and the Communists: Macmillan asks whether non-aligned countries will become Communist or 'will the great experiments in self-government that are being made in Asia and Africa, especially within the Commonwealth, prove so successful, and by their example so compelling, that the balance will come down in favour of freedom and justice?'[41] In this struggle for the minds of peoples between Communism and freedom, each nation must make its own choice. The implication is that the imperial centre in its last acts of devolution would not dictate to its last or former colonies.

Britain was concerned about and responsible for this winding down of empire and this birth of nations. In these countries Britain had the aim 'to raise the material standards of life' in 'a society that respects the rights of individuals' and in which people share in political responsibility and power and in which merit alone was the criterion for economic and political advancement.[42] Moreover, minorities of all kinds in the various new and emerging nations needed 'to live together in harmony'. Macmillan quoted a speech of his foreign Minister, Selwyn Lloyd, to the General Assembly of the United Nations on 17 September 1959, in which he advocated that all people of different backgrounds in territories had the right to security, freedom and well-being:

> we (that is the British) reject the idea of any inherent superiority of one race over another. Our policy, therefore, is non-racial; it offers a future in which Africans, Europeans, Asians, the Peoples of the Pacific and others with whom we are concerned, will all play their full part as citizens in the countries where they live, and in which feelings of race will be submerged in loyalty to new nations.

As politely as the Prime Minister of South Africa and the parliamentarians listened to Macmillan, they advocated apartheid or the segregation of white and black South Africans and later imprisoned black leaders like Nelson Mandela. South Africa withdrew from the Commonwealth in 1961.

Nelson Mandela resisted this regime: like Gandhi, he was engaged in politics in the Transvaal. On 21 September 1953, Mandela wrote his presidential address, 'No Easy Walk to Freedom', to the African National Congress (ANC) in that area, but because he was subject to a banning order, someone else had to read it. Mandela was confident that with more than forty times the number of blacks than whites in Africa the day of reckoning was at hand. There were already examples of resistance: 'The entire continent is seething with discontent and already there are powerful revolutionary eruptions in the Gold Coast, Nigeria, Tunisia, Kenya, the Rhodesias and South Africa.' The oppressed would achieve justice. Mandela also speculated on what criticism of imperialists had effected against him and his fellow ANC leaders: 'We have been gagged because we have emphatically and openly condemned the criminal attacks by the imperialists against the people of Malaya, Vietnam, Indonesia, Tunisia and Tanganyika and called upon our people to identify themselves unreservedly with the cause of world peace and to fight against the war policies of America and her satellites.' For Mandela, the United States was not a former colony who was leading the way in decolonization. With images similar to those King would later use, Mandela spoke of the struggle for freedom of black Africans in their own country: 'there is no easy walk to freedom anywhere, and many of us will have to pass through the valley of the shadow (of death) again and again before we reach the mountain tops of our desires'. The long march to the mountain-top was not on an easy road but through death and violence.

The translation of empire was a theme Mandela expatiated on without calling it that. He saw the waning of the old empires – especially of Britain – and the rise of the new empire: the United States. This new power concerned Mandela because in it he saw a new imperialism that was more dangerous still than the earlier European form:

> Whilst the influence of the old European powers has sharply declined and whilst the anti-imperialist forces are winning striking victories all over the world, a new danger has arisen and threatens to destroy the newly won independence of the people of Asia and Africa. It is American imperialism, which must be fought and decisively beaten down if the people of Asia and Africa are to preserve the vital gains they have won in their struggle against subjugation. The First and Second World Wars brought untold economic havoc especially in Europe, where both wars were mainly fought. Millions of people perished whilst their countries were ravaged and ruined by the war. The two conflicts resulted, on the one hand, in the decline of the old imperial powers.
>
> On the other hand, the U.S.A. emerged from them as the richest and most powerful state in the West, firstly, because both wars were fought thousands of miles away from her mainland and she had fewer casualties. Whereas the British Empire lost 1,089,900 men, only 115,660 American soldiers died during the First World War. No damage whatsoever was suffered by her cities and industries. Secondly, she made fabulous profits from her allies out of war contracts. Due to these factors the U.S.A. grew to become the most powerful country in the West.[43]

Mandela tried to expose the good intentions of the United States, which profited from the European wars. This was a country that took advantage of the weakness of its allies and not simply of its enemies. Just when the blacks of South Africa had shuffled off one imperial power, they had to put up with a totalitarian government and a new empire. This feigning new imperialism that disavowed imperial motives was the pressing danger Africans faced:

> American imperialism is all the more dangerous because, having witnessed the resurgence of the people of Asia and Africa against imperialism and having seen the decline and fall of once powerful empires, it comes to Africa elaborately disguised. It has discarded most of the conventional weapons of

the old type of imperialism. It does not openly advocate armed invasion and conquest. It purports to repudiate force and violence. It masquerades as the leader of the so-called free world in the campaign against communism. It claims that the cornerstone of its foreign policy is to assist other countries in resisting domination by others. It maintains that the huge sums of dollars invested in Africa are not for the exploitation of the people of Africa but for the purpose of developing their countries and in order to raise their living standards.

This imperial force was much less bald in its new form. The translation of empire does not mean stasis but an imitation with difference or a variation on a theme. Mandela intimated that exploitation was the chief aim of American political and economic interests in Africa and elsewhere. He did not see the same danger from Communist powers like the Soviet Union and China who did not maintain bases in Africa but asserted that the United States used Communism as a distraction from its own imperialism. The end of this article was even more explicit in exposing the American threat that Mandela maintained was the chief danger for Africa:

> The people of Africa are astir. In conjunction with the people of Asia, and with freedom-loving people all over the world, they have declared a full-scale war against all forms of imperialism. The future of this continent lies not in the hands of the discredited regimes that have allied themselves with American imperialism. It is in the hands of the common people of Africa functioning in their mass movements.

For Mandela, the people were the source for resistance to imperialism. This sounds a little like the patriots in the American Revolution.

In the early 1990s, at the time South Africa was beginning to change its politics, Mandela, perhaps in response to a world that had altered so much since the 1950s, was more conciliatory to Europe and the United States. That did not mean that he still was not direct about history, politics and discriminatory legal and economic legacies. In addressing the European Parliament on 13 June1990, Mandela was direct in his assessment of the positive and negative legacies of Europe in the history of tyranny and racism (racialism): 'Your actions in pursuit of the cause of the release of all South African political prisoners and the emancipation of our people from racial bondage, have served as a vindication of the nobility of the human spirit. They have demonstrated the undiminished strength of the universal human conscience which guarantees the transience of all tyrannies.'[44] This nobility had overcome some less positive aspects of European history, which was ambivalent on the question of race. Mandela stressed the dilemma of inflicting and suffering racism. He pursued one of the great themes of colonialism from the early Spanish chroniclers of empire onwards – genocide – and a practice that became more systematic in the twentieth century.

The course of events in Mandela's life and in the world may well have transformed his views, at least in public, of imperialism from those he held in the 1950s. Although Mandela never shrank from exposing injustice at home and abroad when he saw it, he came to drop or place in a more minor key the theme of imperialism in the speeches he made in the 1990s. For instance, in relations with the United States, Mandela took, in June 1990, a very different tack than he had done during the 1950s. Speaking to representatives of American business on 16 June, Mandela said: 'It is that we look forward to the time when you will join hands with our people to form a partnership of freedom and prosperity for the peoples of South Africa and the United States of America.'[45] After Mandela's address to business leaders, he spoke to a joint session of Congress and the Senate on 26 June 1990. He set out the aspirations he saw for South Africa:

> We fight for and visualize a future in which all shall, without regard to race, colour, creed or sex, have the right to vote and to be voted into all effective organs of state. We are engaged in a struggle to ensure that the rights of every individual are guaranteed and protected, through a democratic constitution, the rule of law, an entrenched bill of rights which should be enforced by an independent judiciary, as well as a multi-party political system.[46]

Rights and rule of law without discrimination were the chief goals of his movement. Part of that forthright address was to link economics, laws and human rights. The system of discriminatory laws had made life hard for black South Africans in terms of their dignity and livelihood. The heart of the battle was the fight for humanity and the recognition of what is human in all people. Mandela reminded the Houses of Congress that in this struggle it would be a mistake for those fighting oppression to sacrifice their own humanity.

Investment was now an important part of Mandela's new South Africa. Speaking to leaders in British business, he encouraged a partnership in this renewed nation in a way not too different from that Harold Macmillan had offered to South Africa in 1960: 'Your economic interest in South Africa is substantial, both in terms of trade as well as direct and indirect investment. This very fact imposes on all of us an obligation to keep up our dialogue and provides us with the basis for a shared hope for, and a deep interest in the smooth transition of our country to a full democracy with a thriving and advancing economy.'[47] Mandela then proposed a specific bond between British business and an inclusive South Africa: 'The message we bring to you today is a simple one. It is that we look forward to the time when you will join hands with our people to form a partnership of freedom and prosperity for the peoples of South Africa and the kingdom.' This would be a new phase in a long partnership between British investors and South Africa: it would now help to underwrite a multiracial democracy. The one-time imperial centre had tried to break apartheid in Macmillan's time and would now be called on to help end it now.

Mandela also spoke to members of the Commonwealth and former parts of the British empire. On 15 October 1990, he addressed a banquet in India hosted by President Venkataraman and sought to forge a bond between the countries, reminding them that some Indian labours were indentured against their will and taken to South Africa in the nineteenth century.[48] Mandela emphasized the emergence of a nation that is multicultural in its identity. Appealing to a common historical situation, Mandela reminded his hosts of more specific connections:

> It is that history which makes it possible for each one of us to claim the immortal Mahatma Gandhi as our national hero. It is that history which drove us and drives us still to look to the examples he set to decide what we should make of our own destiny. It is that history which brought Jawarlal Nehru's daughter the late Indira Gandhi to our country, which she visited as a young woman. It is that history which brings us here today and brings us to a country with an unequalled record of struggle against the criminal system of apartheid.

Gandhi began his political life in South Africa. Just as Martin Luther King mentioned Gandhi in his Nobel speech, so too did Mandela refer to King in his.[49] This web of allusion, among others, connected Gandhi, King and Mandela and also linked them to those in Britain and North America who advocated liberty, fought slavery and favoured civil disobedience. There were others, among the black population, such as Bishop Tutu, and the white population, such as F. W. de Klerk, who also fought apartheid. De Klerk, the co-winner of the Nobel Peace Prize for 1994 who dedicated his prize to UNICEF and thereby the education of children as the hope for peace, emphasized the connection between economic development and democracy: 'And hand in hand with economic development goes democracy. Wherever economic growth occurs it promotes the establishment of representative and democratic institutions – institutions which invariably develop a framework for peace. It is highly significant that there has never been a war between genuine and universal democracies. There have been countless wars between totalitarian and authoritarian states.'[50] White views of apartheid were always split in South Africa.

Canada also had some influence in South Africa before and after the new constitution in the mid-1990s. In 1961, the prime minister of Canada, John Diefenbaker, had spoken against apartheid; in 1998, Mandela addressed Parliament there. He honoured one Canadian and spoke about Canada's help in creating peacekeeping at the United Nations: 'On my way here today, I had the honour of unveiling, at your Human Rights Monument, a plaque dedicated to John Humphrey, author of the first draft of the Universal Declaration of Human Rights. I would like, if I may, to pay tribute to his contribution to the central philosophy of your country and his dedication to the cause of human rights worldwide.'[51] Mandela also honoured another Canadian, Lester Pearson, who was committed to the United Nations and who won the Nobel Prize for his role in one of the episodes of the end of the French and British empires: the Suez Crisis of 1956. Human rights was something that could bind together all peoples, including those who live in nations born of empire, in this case the British empire, as was and is the case of India, Canada and South Africa. Many of Mandela's black compatriots did not see the day of independence for a multiracial South Africa – nor did Indira Gandhi, Pearson and Macmillan – but the ideal and practice of multicultural democracy are going on in India, Canada, South Africa and in the imperial heartland – Britain. Freedom and not bondage was what every human deserved.

Slavery: Persistence

But slavery and servitude endure with their inhumane living and working conditions. In 1980 Arab masters in Mauritania, where the Portuguese first carried away slaves in 1441, were said to have 90,000 black African slaves. Slavery persists into the twenty-first century throughout the world, whether among children working on rugs in India or charcoal operations in Brazil or among diplomats living with immunity in world capitals. The exploitation of labour – which so many saw in the nineteenth and early twentieth centuries from Adam Smith through Karl Marx to V. I. Lenin – contains a shadowland between those who live on starvation wages in poor conditions and those who are kidnapped, coerced and terrorized as slaves for sex or cheap labour. Wordsworth's 'man's inhumanity to man' is a disease of the spirit as much as a matter of law and economics. What black Africans suffered and what adverse effects Africa and other places now experience in another new era of globalization is a matter of lived experience – of suffering and death and not simply a katascopic vantage from afar (a bird's eye view), a statistic seen on high or a stereoscopic view in search of a topography, a grounding.

All this was an aspect of trade and technology sometimes occluded or elided in a standard view of economic growth. Britain helped to put an end to the slave trade even as it benefited from it. Slavery ended at the apogee of British power and left scars in the United States, which would remain with it as a legacy even in its rise to the status of world power. This inheritance of slavery has been a part of world trade, so that it affected many people and their businesses and governments even in places that did not have slaves, or at least slaves from Africa.[52]

Transitions and Coming to Conclusions

Empires in the west probably began in Mesopotamia: the looting of the museum in Baghdad that contained many of these antiquities is itself a parable of empire. The story of empires and colonies is also one of culture, identity and law. As I was finishing the first writing of this book, I saw an image on the television screen of someone flashing a light into the mouth of a bedraggled Saddam Hussein, who, I assumed, had recently been caught. He had no privacy. He was there to be displayed and interpreted. But this was a man cast out into the light, not an actor playing a character, no matter how much political theatre is a part of human culture. Was he a prisoner of war? Did the Geneva Convention apply? If so, should he be shown to the world in this way, whatever his alleged crimes? What did international law say about this head of state whose country was invaded? Should he stand trial? If so, where and in what jurisdiction? Whatever anyone thinks of this man, whether a leader or a tyrant, his capture took place in a dugout near the Tigris river, which we were taught as school-children was the cradle of civilization.

This might have been a Western interpretation of the origins of the West, but this river, along with the Euphrates, was where the myth and history began, whether in religious writings or in archaeology. And many had dreamt of empire there by the banks of this river, and the translation of empire, with so many changes in religion, politics, and technology, continues even as it is thrown into question. There were other rivers of origin for other cultures, but for the coalition forces, they were facing their own past knowingly or not.

Looking at a human, surprised and disoriented, is there something universal there beyond the specific politics? What is a person and how should he or she live? What are persons and how can they live together? What legacy is there in the ambivalence of empire and colonies? Is it possible to be postcolonial people living between utopia and dystopia? Joyce's Stephen Daedalus spoke about the nightmare of history, or was it one damn thing after another?

In the wake of these western empires, is it possible to have a United Nations beyond the imperial? Albert Einstein and Bertrand Russell argued for new ways of thinking in the nuclear age: I wonder what they would have thought about Saddam Hussein by the Tigris. But that is more a supposition, a road not taken, the what-if of fiction or the story in history, the rhetorical assumption that Thucydides made because he wasn't there to hear Pericles' oration.

Empires and colonies are a longstanding theme in and of history. With the meetings of cultures and the estrangement of time, there might be some possibility of getting past the ironic blindness of ethnocentrism. Peoples need identities, but those self-definitions can become tyrannical in any place or state. The intricacies of imperialism and colonization do not make for easily discernible patterns of rise and fall, growth and decay. Empire is protean but cannot really be personified. The shape of its time is the retrospection of interpretation.

8
Conclusion

☙

As this book has taken some time to write, during the course of its writing and rewriting, the United States and Britain invaded Iraq, Saddam Hussein was caught, tried and hanged, and literally all hell has broken loose on the streets of Iraq after what, for the American and British troops, was a swift victory. The situations of Afghanistan and Iraq become more complex, as though civil wars have erupted and civilians – men, women and children – die. Only today Iran released the fifteen British personnel captured in the gulf that Iraq and Iran share on their southern coasts. One of the questions is whether there exists an Anglo-American imperial order that Kaiser Willem II railed against and Goldwin Smith said would upset the international order and would be resisted by force. Another is whether the United States is being drawn into a more formal empire as Britain was in the last decades of the nineteenth century.

There is some controversy whether the United States is an imperial democracy or not even an empire. It has displayed the reluctance of a former colony that fought to be free of an empire and the desire to be an even greater empire that some of its early presidents and citizens articulated. It does govern and has governed some territories that were not states in the union or were never intended as such. That means that the United States seems to have had imperial aspects to its polity. Whatever side one comes down on in this controversy, it is important to recognize that the theme of empire and colony is as important today as ever. Are nations who depend on others for support and military protection colonies? Is an informal empire an empire none the less? For instance, is the United States operating today in parts of the world the way Britain did in Latin America – as an economic hegemon? Like earlier empires, and most recently, the British empire, does the United States use military power to assure resources and trade that favours it?

The events since 1989 and, more recently, from 11 September 2001, make such questions urgent. Each of us lives in a world of patterns and systems, but we all have a personal stake in what is happening. The history of the United States, and the other empires in Europe and elsewhere that we have discussed, might well provide us with some themes within themes to consider when thinking about empires and colonies. Here are some of the key points that arise from the expansion of western European empires from about 1415 to the Second World War and their contraction, decolonization and disappearance after 1945.

In the Introduction, I argued that it was important not to attribute everything to 'empire' because it was a changing term and because some of the negative events in these empires also happened outside them. Feudalism, capitalism and Communism were all capable of cruelty, war, pollution and environmental degradation. Not all empires were the same over thousands of years or in different parts of the world. Even within an empire, a 'colony' might be self-governing and have a majority of European settlers, or it could be a protectorate or have some other form. The Russian and Austrian empires contained different kinds of constituent parts, as did the British empire. The power and shapes of empires change over time. That is why I structured the book in terms of European events, as, while examining the world, the book has had at its core the expansion of Europe, especially of the seaborne empires of western Europe and the United States, whose early settlers came from Britain and the Continent.

Another key aspect of the book is an emphasis on the role of culture and of the personal or individual. Although I set out the economic, political and military elements of the expansion of empire in a framework – including of other empires like Russia (Soviet Union), Japan and China – I also balanced this macro-narrative with the micro-history of individuals, their voices in counterpoint to the grand structure of historical forces. This strategy was chosen because although empires and colonies over many centuries is a vast subject that no one book can set out exhaustively, it is important to provide some specifics and to make human the impersonal statistics and movements in history. While I argued that the story of empire is not a simple moral tale, I did not want the ethical dimension to get lost in the dates, statistics and other stuff of history. In order to decentre this myth of progress, of Europe bringing civilization to the world, I selected the voices of Natives, slaves, Africans, women, children and critics of empire. They were meant to unsettle the largely European male world of government and policy in the making of empire. These voices, from the fifteenth century to the present, provide a counterbalance, as part of what I have argued is the contradiction and ambivalence found in empires and colonies. Even within each person, then and now, there are divisions in the mind.

It is easier to condemn the past than to see the faults that matter most in the present. There is, then, a certain irony for those who went before in empires and colonies and those of us who come after. I, too, am full of contradictions and ambivalence. That is not to say that I should give to the Portuguese and Spanish who set sail for Africa and Asia, and to Columbus who came across the New World en route to Asia, a teleological or proleptic sense. They did not know what they would find. They could not foresee the extent of the empires they represented. The first expansion was halting and tentative.

Navigational, military and administrative technologies were important to the Europeans. It is good to remember that they were not as powerful economically as India and China until the late eighteenth or early nineteenth century. Moreover, power is not everything, and one reason I have emphasized culture and alternative voices as well is that there can be a tendency in books about empire to concentrate on the powerful and measures of power. This story is not simply that of the powerful or the victors. In creating a teleology, it is easy to read history backwards and then forwards again. Nor would the Europeans have gained territories had not, in many places, the indigenous peoples suffered diseases that weakened and killed them. With increasing power, the Europeans sometimes developed racist ideologies to go along with beliefs of religious superiority. The industrial and technological revolutions fed what might now be called a rationalization, delusion or fantasy.

In the English-speaking world in which there is still a memory of the British empire and in which the United States is the world's leading power, it is doubly important to remember that the Portuguese and Spanish set out the framework for early modern empires well before England did. They moved maritime Europe closer to Africa and Asia and brought the Americas into a global economy. The Spaniards debated the pros and cons of expansion and the status of Natives long before the English and French did. The ecological imperialism of the Spaniards in the Canary Islands and the fate of the Guanches set the scene for how they, the Portuguese and other Europeans settled the New World and then other colonies in Asia, Oceania, and elsewhere. The figures of the Native serve as a reminder that the plundering of people and lands occurred no matter what rationalizations the Europeans found. In the New World, the Spaniards, for instance, worked the Natives to death and then needed African labour to increase their profits. Slavery played a role early in this expansion, something that Portugal got involved with in Africa in the 1440s. The church promoted empire and opposed some of its excesses. Gold and God were connected.

Even before the Reformation, the French challenged the papal donations dividing the unknown world between Portugal and Spain. Throughout this period, France played a major role in Europe and overseas. They struggled with Portugal for Brazil. Louis XIV, the French navy and Napoleon played central parts in the story of empire in Europe and overseas. For instance, Louis XIV put pressure on the Dutch in Europe and made it harder for them to manage their empire. The French navy helped the Americans defeat the British in the War of Independence. Napoleon sold Louisiana to the United States and invaded Spain, which helped the Spanish colonies in continental America go their own way and become independent.

The Dutch Revolt weakened the Spanish empire, which was the strongest of the European empires, and the Netherlands became the great commercial and naval power of Europe. The Dutch empire became a model for, and rival to, England, which had helped it overcome Spain but which now envied the rise of the Netherlands. A haven for artists and intellectuals, a great tolerant nation, the Netherlands really helped change the nature of empire and set the stage for Britain and the United States to build commercial empires built on sea power. Hugo Grotius' contribution to the law of the seas and international law is a case in point. There were limits to Dutch tolerance, as Grotius had later to leave for Sweden. Like Portugal, the Netherlands is a small nation, so it easy to forget how great a power it was in Europe and the world. But Enlightenment thinkers, such as Abbé Raynal, made a distinction between the feudal empire of Portugal and the new empires like Holland. Yet, even the new empires used old institutions such as slavery. At first the Dutch resisted the slave trade, but they, too, got drawn in.

Another aspect of empire I stressed was the internal division within European states. 'Spain', for instance, was really a collection of states within what we now call Spain. Overseas, early on, as with the Pizarros, there was civil and internal strife. When Portugal and Spain were joined under the same king, Philip, in 1580, it wasn't inevitable that by 1640, Catalonia and Portugal would revolt. France suffered a long civil war between Protestants and Catholics in the sixteenth century that weakened its colonial effort. The first British empire collapsed in a civil war between the British and British Americans. This was the first great instance of decolonization in this era of seaborne empires and the Spanish and Portuguese colonies in continental America soon followed suit. That led all the European states, as they lost their interests in America from 1775 to 1821, to look elsewhere for imperial expansion. Africa and Asia, Oceania and Australasia were some of those places.

During the nineteenth century, we saw that the mistreatment of Native peoples and their lands continued. Despite a movement to abolish slavery and to more humanitarianism from the late eighteenth century, the misuse of Natives in Australia, New Zealand and North America occurred. The Portuguese enslavement of Africans from the 1440s and the Spanish abuse of Natives in the New World were preludes to later wars and ecological destruction. Disease, abuse and neglect were part of the experience of Natives in New Zealand and the United States, the two examples I concentrated on. Technologies and trade brought new animals and plants to a habitat that changed it for its inhabitants. The spectres of slavery and enforced labour and their legacies, as well as ideologies of racial superiority, made it doubly hard for Africans and for aboriginal peoples. The voices and writings of indigenous peoples and former slaves in this period, like those of Phillis Wheatley, Equiano and Red Cloud, qualify this narrative of manifest destiny or the advancement of European civilization.

The British empire introduced the Industrial Revolution and helped to transform itself, Europe and the world. Part of the ambivalence of empire is that although there were horrors like the treatment of Native peoples and slavery, there was also the creation of the industrial and technological world in which we now live and continue to modify. This world has degraded the environment massively and has many flaws and problems, including alienation and a disregard for nature. None the less, most people would not go back to pre-industrial life. Whether British innovations were based on good fortune, innovation, capitalism or empire or some combination, they did usher in a world that differs from what went before more perhaps than any period of human history. This was a revolutionary break from an order based on nature and biology and not on coal and fossil fuels. So just as triumphalism is uncritical, so is the denunciation of the modern seaborne empires and especially the British which innovated the most radically. The United States became a great innovator as well.

Despite this contribution, there were also continued abuses, which the voices continue to bring out, and Leopold II of Belgium is such an example. His agents' treatment of the local peoples to make great profit in rubber was gruesome. The use of contracts by the Dutch in Indonesia, which was a system of enforced labour, was something Leopold took as his model. Every empire made positive contributions, but every empire had its share of abuses, many of them barely imaginable to the humanitarian soul.

The Black Legend of Spain warned of a typology between Old World and New World. The argument went that the Spaniards, if not resisted, would do in the Netherlands what they had to the Natives in the New World. William Wordsworth wrote about man's inhumanity to man, and this inhumanity among people had always occurred in Europe as overseas. Michel de Montaigne and Jean de Léry reminded people of this French typology, for in the civil wars Protestants and Catholics committed atrocities against each other that were every bit as horrible as those perpetrated in the New World. The Europeans continued to massacre indigenous peoples into the twentieth century. Despite the franchise for women, soldiers massacred or abused men, women and children. Beginning in 1933, as Edwin Black has argued, IBM, which was founded in 1896 as a census tabulating company by Herman Hollerith, a German inventor, helped the Nazis, from the time Hitler came to power until well into the Second World War, to identify and catalogue German and then European Jewry, a step necessary in the plans for conquest and genocide. According to Black, Thomas Watson, the chairman of IBM, was able to use his subsidiary, IBM Germany (or Dehomag), many of whose managers were devoted Nazis, and, when it became illegal in the United States to trade with the Nazis, IBM sought a series of cover-ups through undated letters, oral agreements and intermediaries in Geneva to help the Nazis. IBM updated its Hollerith punch card technology and leased the machines, supplied the punch cards, trained Nazis, and serviced the machines that Hitler required to carry out his ghastly task. Nor did the Allies ever ask too many questions about the Holleriths inspected at Auschwitz, the Warsaw Ghetto and elsewhere, but gave the inventory back to IBM. The Allies, under Roosevelt and Eisenhower, were doing statistical work of their own concerning the bombing of Germany, and they needed IBM. They turned to it when they were taking a census of the country. The Nazis would have killed Jews, but their efficiency was based on IBM's technology. The Solution Company was a part of the Final Solution.

In serving an ideology of hatred, purity and dominance, who knows what might have been done earlier with the technology that IBM developed? To make this personal, I appealed to the voice, and one voice on purpose, of one of the survivors of the Holocaust. This was a girl, Rachella Velt Meekcoms, who was twelve when the Germans invaded the Netherlands. She and her sister, Flora, survived Westerbork and then Auschwitz. In her narrative, she looks back and tells a poignant and beautiful story of the ugliness and terror. Her story of forced labour and disease might have been told by a Taino after Columbus's landfall or a member of Sitting Bull's tribe, but it was the story of someone who had survived the most organized genocide in history. I do not know whether Rachella is alive. She would be about seventy-seven now.

The privacy and dignity and human rights of an individual are fragile beside the centralizing and controlling power of the state and military and of multinational corporations, the heirs to the earlier companies the English, Dutch and others set up for exploration, trade and empire. The clash of controlling totalitarian states was a key development in the twentieth century. Were there grace and place enough, we would hear the individual stories and voices of many Jews and others – men, women, and children – killed and tortured because of race hatred or some other kind of myth or intolerance. We have heard some of the voices of Natives and slaves from earlier periods who were caught up in land-hunger and sometimes in the intolerant ideology of European settlers. There are degrees, and it is the very systematic nature of some of the examples we have discussed in this book – not isolated and random acts – that is the hardest. In the pattern there are eyes, faces and voices, all individual. This is the culture of the human in the machinery of economics, politics and, most specifically, ideology. This book, in general, is an attempt to show the tension between the group and the individual, the general and the particular. Both are important, but in the path of greed and ideological purity and righteousness, human rights can be moved aside or trampled.

Las Casas, the abolitionists, Mary Prince, Thoreau, Lincoln, Sitting Bull, Gandhi, Martin Luther King, Mandela and others all spoke up against injustice and discrimination. Even in the nuclear age, where destruction is always near, different peoples found themselves in new nations, now almost 200, and the United Nations has a mandate to promote international cooperation and peace no matter how hard that is. The technological and medical breakthroughs are marvels, but the world is divided into the rich and poor nations and there may well be more neglect of, and less investment in, these states now than there was under colonialism. In informal empires, the strong states do not raise taxes and provide services as they would if that nation were a constituent colony. Sometimes citizens, foundations, non-governmental organizations (NGOs) and governments have come together to help and to support people in the 'Third World'. Often these problems are forgotten or remembered all too briefly. In such a time and place, some wonder whether decolonization is really a re-colonization under a new phase of informal empire. Is this an age of neocolonialism and not postcolonialism? Is the United States the leader of this movement that hides its imperialism and self-interest as Mandela suggested in the 1950s or is the USA a reluctant power that gets involved and recoils from formal empire as it seems to have done in the past? Will it, like Britain in the late nineteenth century, have to formalize empire in order to protect its interests economically and in continuing the legacy of an empire of liberty? Will this great flexible republic harden into a hard and inflexible empire? These are open questions that arise from this book. These implications rest with the reader. In the question of empires and colonies, we inhabit paradox, contradiction and ambivalence. The world has never been richer, the world has never been poorer. These are the best of times and the worst of times.

Notes and References

∽◔◡◔∽

Introduction

1 Alexis de Toqueville, *Democracy in America*, trans. J. P. Mayer, ed. George Lawrence (1966; Garden City, NY: Doubleday, 1969), 412–13.

2 *The Oxford English Dictionary*, 2nd edn (Oxford: Oxford University Press, 1989). This is the source for the discussion of all the definitions in this paragraph.

3 Although I am still drawing on this edition of the *Oxford English Dictionary*, I also consulted – for the cognates of the Greek words that also designate settler, colonist or people sent away from home and to send away from home, to transplant and to emigrate – my copy of *A Lexicon Abridged from Liddell & Scott's Greek–English Lexicon*, 22nd edn (New York: Harper & Brothers, 1888), 84. Like 'empire', 'emperor' is a word that derives from Latin through the French: it appeared in English to designate the sovereign of the Roman empire about the first quarter of the thirteenth century. 'Imperator', which in Latin first meant a military commander, became in the Roman republic a title indicating honour that was 'bestowed on a victorious general by the acclamation of the army on the field of battle' and was later 'conferred by the senate on Julius Caesar and on Augustus, with reference to the military powers with which the chief of state was invested', a precedent adopted by subsequent rulers of the Roman empire except Tiberius and Claudius. The emperor of this empire had dominion or lordship over the dependencies or colonies.

4 Here, I continue to draw on the OED, but see also Peter Martyr (Petrus Martyr Anglerius), *De orbe nouo decades* (Alcalá de Henares, 1516); Richard Eden, *The Decades of the newe worlde of west India, . . .* (London, 1555, rpt. no place, [New York?], 1966); Samuel Purchas, *Purchas His Pilgrims* (London, 1613), VIII.ii.612; Thomas Hobbes, *Leviathan* (London, 1651), II.xxii.118; Edmund Burke, *Sp. Conc. America, Works*, III.73; J. R. Seeley, *The Expansion of England* (London, 1883), 38; see also Adam Smith, *The Wealth of Nations* (London, 1776), II.IV.vii.177. For an account of definitions of 'colonies' that relates to

colonies that remained during the 1990s, see Robert Aldrich and John Connell, *The Last Colonies* (Cambridge: Cambridge University Press, 1998), 2–9.

5 Aldrich and Connell, *The Last Colonies* (Cambridge: Cambridge University Press, 1998), 3.

6 Hans Kohn argued during the 1950s that 'Not every "imperial" relationship is "colonial"'; see his 'Reflections on Colonialism' in *The Idea of Colonialism*, ed. Robert Stausz-Hupé and Harry W. Hazard (New York: Frederick A. Praeger, 1958), 3.

7 For all discussions of empire and colonization, the key matter of focus is particularly significant owing to the sheer range of material: as late as 1944, E. A. Walker could write: 'Since there were fifteen colonising Powers in 1939, it has plainly been impossible to deal here with the empires of all of them in detail'; see Walker, *Colonies* (1944; Cambridge University Press, 1945), vii.

8 Preface and Acknowledgments, in Norman Etherington, *Theories of Imperialism: War, Conquest and Capital* (London: Croom Helm, 1984), n.p. [1–5]; see Eric Stokes, 'Late Nineteenth Century Colonial Expansion and the Attack on the Theory of Economic Imperialism: A Case of Mistaken Identity?' *Historical Journal* 12 (1969): 285–301.

9 See Etherington, *Theories of Imperialism*, 280–3, for this discussion.

10 Seymour Phillips, 'The outer world of the European Middle Ages' in Stuart B. Schwartz, ed. *Implicit Understandings* (Cambridge: Cambridge University Press, 1994), 44–5. See J. K. Wright, *The Geographical Love of the Time of the Crusades: A Study in the History of Medieval Science and Tradition in Western Europe* (New York: Dover Publications, 1965 reprint of 1925 edn), 233–5; Ernst Breisach, *Historiography: Ancient, Medieval & Modern* (Chicago: University of Chicago Press, 1983), esp. 13, 23, 29–30, 46–51, 172–9.

11 Phillips, 'The outer world', 53; see also Phillips, *The Medieval Expansion of Europe*, 2nd ed. (Oxford: Oxford University Press, 1998), ch. 9.

12 See William McNeill, *Plagues and Peoples* (New York: Anchor Books, 1976); Michael Dols, *The Black Death in the Middle East* (Princeton: Princeton University Press, 1977); Amaryta Sen, *Poverty and Famines: An Essay on Entitlement and Deprivation* (Oxford: Clarendon Press, 1981); Janet Abu–Lughod, *Before European Hegemony: The World System A.D. 1250–1350* (New York: Oxford University Press, 1989); Clive Ponting, *A Green History of the World: The Environment and the Collapse of Great Civilizations* (New York: Penguin Books, 1991); Alfred W. Crosby, *Ecological Imperialism: The Biological Expansion of Europe, 900–1900* (New York and Cambridge: Cambridge University Press, 1986, rpt. 1991); Jared Diamond, *Guns, Germs, and Steel: The Fates of Human Societies* (1997; New York: Norton, 1999); Kenneth Pomerantz, *The Great Divergence: China, Europe, and the Making of the Modern World Economy* (Princeton: Princeton University Press, 2000); Robert B. Marks, *The Origins of the Modern World: A Global and Ecological Narrative from the Fifteenth to the Twenty-first Century*, 2nd edn (Lanham: Rowman & Littlefield, 2007).

13 See Jonathan Hart, 'A Comparative Pluralism: the Heterogeneity of Methods and the Case of Possible Worlds', *Canadian Review of Comparative Literature* [*CRCL/RCLC*] 15 (1988): 320–45.

14 Aristotle, *Poetics*. Alternative history and counterfactual history blur the line between history and fiction. See, for instance, Geoffrey Hawthorn, *Plausible Worlds: Possibility and Understanding in History and the Social Sciences* (Cambridge: University of Cambridge Press, 1991); *Virtual History: Alternatives and Counterfactuals*, ed. Niall Ferguson (London: Papermac, 1998); *What if?: The World's Foremost Military Historians Imagine What Might Have Been*, ed. Robert Cowley (New York: Berkeley Books, 1999); Karen Hellekson, *The Alternate History: Refiguring Historical Time* (Kent, OH: Kent State University Press, 2001).

15 Clifford Geertz, *Available Light: Anthropological Reflections on Philosophical Topics* (Princeton and Oxford: Princeton University Press, 2000, rpt. 2001), 16.

16 See, for instance, D. Hay, *Europe: the Emergence of an Idea* (Edinburgh: Edinburgh University Press, 1957), esp. ch. 1.

17 Hans Kohn, 'Reflections on Colonialism', *The Idea of Colonialism*, ed. Robert Strausz-Hupé and Harry W. Hazard (New York: Frederick A. Praeger, 1958), 11, see 3; in this collection, there are some other wide-ranging essays on colonialism and anti-colonialism across the world.

18 Kohn, 2, see 3.

19 Jean-Marie André, 'Avant–Propos', *L'Idéologie de 'impérialisme romain* (Paris: Société les Belles Lettres, 1974), 7.

20 Michael Twaddle, 'Imperialism and the State in the Third World', *Imperialism and the State in the Third World*, ed. Michael Twaddle (London: British Academic Press, 1992), 1.

21 Twaddle, 1; see Wolfgang J. Mommsen, *Theories of Imperialism* (New York: Random House, 1980) and Anthony Brewer, *Marxist Theories of Imperialism: a Critical Survey*, 2nd edn (London: Routledge, 1990).

Chapter 1

1 See H. Inalcik and D. Quataert, *An Economic and Social History of the Ottoman Empire 1300–1914* (Cambridge: Cambridge University Press, 1995) and S. Deringil, *The Well-Protected Domains. Ideology and the Legitimization of Power in the Ottoman Empire* (London: I. B. Taurus, 1998).

2 J. H. Parry makes this point clearly. See his *The Establishment of European Hegemony: 1415–1715: Trade and Exploration in the Age of the Renaissance* (New York: Harper, 1961, rpt. 1965), 15. Despite changes to the discipline since I read Parry as an undergraduate, his work is valuable and qualifies Eurocentrism, especially early in the story of European expansion.

3 See Parry, esp. 36–43.

4 Alvise Cadamosto, *The Voyages of Cadamosto and Other Documents on Western Africa in the Second Half of the Fifteenth Century* (London: The Hakluyt Society, 1937), 54, see 55. See also Carter G. Woodson, 'Attitudes of the Iberian Peninsula', *Journal of Negro History* 20 (1935): 202; Margaret T. Hogden, *Early Anthropology in the Sixteenth and Seventeenth Centuries* (Philadelphia: University of Pennsylvania Press, 1964); Winthrop D. Jordan, *White Over Black: American Attitudes toward the Negro, 1550–1812* (Chapel

Hill, NC: University of North Carolina Press, 1968); Lyle N. McAlister, *Spain and Portugal in the New World 1492–1700* (Minneapolis: University of Minnesota Press, 1984), 54–5. On Spain, see also Henry Kamen, *Empire: How Spain Became a World Power 1492–1763* (2002; New York: HarperCollins, 2003). One of the classic studies on European expansion is J. H. Parry, *The Establishment of the European Hegemony 1415–1715: Trade and Exploration in the Age of the Renaissance*, 3rd edn (New York: Harper, 1966). For a more detailed discussion, see my *Representing the New World; English and French Uses of the Example of Spain* (New York and London: Palgrave, 2001), 15–48. Pope Alexander VI, *Copia dela bula dela concession* (Logroño [1511]). See also Edgar Prestage, *The Portuguese Pioneers* (London: Adam & Charles Black, 1933, rpt. 1966), 3; Charles Verlinden, *The Beginnings of Modern Colonization*, trans. Yvonne Freccero (Ithaca, NY: Cornell University Press, 1970), 33, see esp. 34–76. This essay was published in French as 'Esclavage médiévales dans la colonisation de l'Amérique', *Cahiers de l'Institut des Hautes Etudes de l'Amérique Latine* 6 (1961): 29–45. See McAlister, 42–5. See Thomas T. Allen, *Commodity and Exchange in the Mongol Empire: A Cultural History of Islamic Textiles* (Cambridge: Cambridge University Press, 1997), esp. 5, 103–5. Lynn Hunt et al., *The Making of the West: Peoples and Cultures* (Boston and New York: Bedford/St. Martin's, 2001), 482–95; on Mehmed II and Pasti, see 489. See also Philip Ziegler, *The Black Death* (Harmondsworth: Penguin, 1970); Harry A. Miskimin, *The Economy of Early Renaissance Europe, 1300–1460* (Cambridge: Cambridge University Press, 1975); David Nirenberg, *Communities of Violence: Persecution of Minorities in the Middle Ages* (Princeton: Princeton University Press, 1996). Hunt et al. eds., 496–515.

5 Carter G. Woodson, 'Attitudes of the Iberian Peninsula', *Journal of Negro History* 20 (1935): 202; Margaret T. Hogden, *Early Anthropology in the Sixteenth and Seventeenth Centuries* (Philadelphia: University of Pennsylvania Press, 1964); Winthrop D. Jordan, *White Over Black: American Attitudes toward the Negro, 1550–1812* (Chapel Hill, NC: University of North Carolina Press, 1968); McAlister, 54–5. On Spain, see also Henry Kamen, *Empire: How Spain Became a World Power 1492–1763* (2002; New York: HarperCollins, 2003). On European expansion, see J. H. Parry, *The Establishment of the European Hegemony 1415–1715: Trade and Exploration in the Age of the Renaissance*, 3rd edn (New York: Harper, 1966).

6 The English challenged the pope's authority but had in 1155 appealed to the pope to lend authority to Henry II's conquest of Ireland. *The Avalon Project: The Bull of Pope Adrian IV Empowering Henry II to Conquer Ireland. A.D. 1155.* The document is located at this URL: <http://www.yale.edu/lawweb/avalon/medieval/bullad.htm>. See Lyttleton's 'Life of Henry II.', vol. v, 371. Although such a bull was issued for the purpose of this conquest, whether the extant document is authentic is still a matter of debate among scholars.

7 See Frances Gardiner Davenport, *European Treaties bearing on the History of the United States and its Dependencies to 1648* (4 vols., Washington, DC, 1917), I, 1, 9–10.

8 Davenport, *European Treaties*, 1, 10–12, 34. For the treaty of 1479 and its ratification, see ibid., 36–41 (trans. 42–8).

9 All the bulls and treaties mentioned here, as well as other documents, can be found in ibid. Ibid., 77–8.

10 This is Green's legal view in L. C. Green and Olive P. Dickason, *The Law of Nations and the New World* (Edmonton: University of Alberta Press, 1989), 7. This book provides a good discussion of the bulls and of the legal aspects of the colonization of the Americas; see esp. 4–6.

11 McAlister, 51–2.

12 Cadamosto, 54, see 55.

13 For a more detailed discussion, see my *Representing the New World*, 15–48.

14 Pope Alexander VI, *Copia dela bula dela concession* (Logroño [1511]).

15 Kamen, xxv, 6–7. On Spain, see Henry Kamen, *Spain 1469–1714: A Society of Conflict* (London: Longmans, 1991); John Edwards, *The Spain of the Catholic Monarchs 1474–1520* (Oxford: Blackwell, 2000).

16 Christopher Columbus, *The Four Voyages of Christopher Columbus*, Cecil Jane ed. (1929 and 1932; New York: Dover, 1988), vol. 1, 2.

17 Columbus 8.

18 Mark A. Burkholder and D. S. Chandler, *From Importance to Authority: The Spanish Crown and the American Audiencias, 1687–1808* (Columbia, MO: University of Missouri Press, 1977), 1 and J. M. Ots y Capdequí, *El estado español en las Indias*, 4th edn (Buenos Aires: Fondo de Cultura Económica, 1965), 45.

19 Kamen, 28–33, 49–50.

20 Carter G. Woodson, 'Attitudes of the Iberian Peninsula', 202; Margaret T. Hogden, *Early Anthropology in the Sixteenth and Seventeenth Centuries* (Philadelphia: University of Pennsylvania Press, 1964); Winthrop D. Jordan, *White Over Black: American Attitudes toward the Negro, 1550–1812* (Chapel Hill, NC: University of North Carolina Press, 1968); McAlister, 54–5.

21 The bull *Romanus pontifex*, 8 January 1455, in Davenport, *European Treaties*, 21.

22 Hugh Thomas, *The Slave Trade* (New York: Simon & Schuster, 1997), 46–7, 86, 89. See also Carl Sauer, *The Early Spanish Main* (Berkeley: University of California Press, 1966) for more on Queen Isabella and Columbus.

23 Charles Henry Cunningham, *The Audiencia in the Spanish Colonies: As illustrated by the Audiencia of Manilia (15–83–1800)* (Berkeley: University of California Press, 1919), 3, see 1.

24 The First Letters Patent Granted to John Cabot and his Sons, London, 5 March 1496 in H. P. Biggar, *The Precursors of Jacques Cartier 1497–1534* (Ottawa, 1911), 7 (translation 9).

25 For a helpful discussion of the geographical and cultural contexts that shaped Spain before the emigration to the western Atlantic, see Ida Altman, 'Spain in the Era of Exploration', *1492: An Ongoing Voyage*, ed. John R. Hébert (Washington: Library of Congress, 1992), 64–77.

26 The Petition of John Cabot and his Sons, 5 March 1496 in Biggar, *Precursors*, 6. On Cabot and his successors, see, for example, Lucien Campeau, 'Les Cabot et l'Amérique', *Revue d'Histoire de l'Amérique Française* 14 (1960): 317–52 and John L. Allen, 'From Cabot to Cartier: The Early Exploration of

Eastern North America, 1497–1543', *Annals of the Association of American Geographers* 82 (1992): 500–21.

27 The First Letters Patent Granted to John Cabot and his Sons, London, 5 March 1496 in Biggar, *Precursors*, 7 (translation 9).

28 Dispatch of Ferdinand and Isabella to Gonzales de Puebla, their ambassador to England, 28 March 1496 in ibid., 10–11 (translation, 11).

29 Ayala in Biggar, *Precursors*, 27 (translation, 28).

30 Ibid.

31 For a detailed discussion of the Cabots and the Portuguese, see H. P. Biggar, *Voyages of the Cabots and of the Corte-Reals* (Paris, 1903) and also James. A. Williamson, *The Voyages of the Cabots and the English Discovery of North America under Henry VII and Henry VIII* (London, The Argonaut Press, 1929), 119f, 200–3. For treatments of the Cabots, see Henry Harrisse, *Jean et Sébastien Cabot* (Paris, 1882) and John T. Juricek, 'John Cabot's First Voyage, 1497', *Smithsonian Journal of History* 2 (1967), 1–22. See also Allen, 'From Cabot', 500–21.

32 Williamson, *Voyages*, 204. For a study of the Corte Reals, including documents, see Henry Harrisse, *Les Cort-Real et leurs voyages au nouveau-monde* . . . (Paris, 1883).

33 On the English, French, and Portuguese fisheries in Newfoundland, see K. G. Davies, *The North Atlantic World in the Seventeenth Century* (Minneapolis: University of Minnesota Press, 1974), 12–17.

34 The tax regards 'das pescarias da Terra Nova' (96) (the fisheries of Newfoundland). Letter from the king of Portugal in regard to the tithe on Newfoundland codfish in Biggar, *The Precursors*, 96–7 (translation 97–8).

35 See Selma Barkham, 'The Basques: Filling a Gap in Our History between Jacques Cartier and Champlain', *Canadian Geographical Journal* 96 (1978): 8–19.

36 Ramusio, *Navigationi et Viaggi* (Venetia, 1550), III, 423 verso, cited in Biggar, Introduction, *The Precursors*, xxii. See also Charles-André Julien, *Histoire de l'expansion et de la colonisation françaises* (Paris, 1948), I, 336; Carl Ortwin Sauer, *Sixteenth-Century North America: The Land and the People as Seen by Europeans* (Berkeley: University of California Press, 1971), 51–2; Eugène Guénin, *Ango et ses pilotes, d'après des documents inédits, tirés de archives de France, Portugal et d'Espagne* (Paris, 1901). See also Raymonde Litalien, *Les explorateurs de l'Amérique du Nord, 1492–1795* (Sillery, Québec: Septentrion, 1993), 53. For another account of Essomericq, see Frank Lestringant, *Le Huguenot et le sauvage: L'Amérique et la controverse coloniale, en France, au temps des Guerres de Réligion (1555–1589)* (Paris: Klincksieck, 1990), 29.

37 Warrant of Queen Joanna to John de Agramonte Covering an Agreement with King Ferdinand for a Voyage to Newfoundland, 8, 29 October 1511 in Biggar, *The Precursors*, 102–7; translation 107–11. See also Letters Patent from Queen Joanna confirming the appointment of Agramonte as captain of the expedition, 29 (?) October, 1511 in ibid., 111–12.

38 Warrant, in ibid., 102–3; the translation reads 'the secret of Newfoundland', '(except that two of the pilots may be Bretons or belong to some other

nation which has been there)', 'our son', 'the Most Serene King of Portugal' in ibid., 107.

39 Warrant in ibid., 103–5.

40 See Luca Codignola, 'The Holy See and the Conversion of the Indians', *America in European Consciousness, 1493–1750*, ed. Karen Ordahl Kupperman (Chapel Hill, NC: University of North Carolina Press, 1995), 199.

41 King Ferdinand's letter to Sebastian Cabot, September 13, 1512 in ibid., 115 (translation 116).

42 Biggar includes a number of French documents pertaining to the Newfoundland fishery – a pardon to the mate of a Newfoundland fishing vessel, January 1513 in ibid., 116–18; an agreement between the monks of the Abbey of Beauport and the inhabitants of the Island of Bréhat, which mentions Newfoundland cod, 14–17 December 1514 in ibid., 118–23; documents concerning vessels going from Bayonne to Newfoundland, vessel of 18 February 1520 in ibid., 124, and a vessel for 6 March 1521 in the same volume in ibid., 125–6. For discussions of the fisheries, see Charles de la Morandière, *Histoire de la pêche française de la morue* (Paris: G.P. Maisonneuve et Larose, 1962) and Harold Innis, *The Cod Fisheries: The History of an international Economy*, rev. edn (Toronto: University of Toronto Press, 1954, rpt. 1978).

43 Letter from Vice-Admiral Fitzwilliam to Cardinal Wolsey, 21 August 1522, and another from Fitzwillam to Henry VIII in Biggar, *The Precursors*, 142–3.

44 *Fontes rerum canariarum*, ix, 15, 33, cited in Felipe Fernández-Armesto, *Before Columbus: Exploration and Colonization from the Mediterranean to the Atlantic 1229–1402* (Philadelphia: University of Pennsylvania Press, 1987), 180–1. See also Fernández-Armesto's discussion on these pages. See Fernández-Armesto, 248, 250–1. Columbus's desire for gold in the service of God was textual and practical, for such dreams were also fed in his reading of Polo. *The Four Voyages of Columbus*, trans. and ed. Cecil Jane (2 vols., London, 1930, 1933; rpt New York, 1988), 2 vols. in 1 vol., I, 11 n.3; II, 3 n. 4, 5. See also Jane's Introduction, II, lvii. Marcel Trudel, 'New France, 1524–1713', *Dictionary of Canadian Biography*, gen. ed. George W. Brown, vol. 1, 1000–1700 (Toronto: University of Toronto Press, 1966), I, 26; see also 27–37. Fernández-Armesto, *Before Columbus*, 5–6, 218. His book concentrates mainly on the expansion of Portugal, Genoa and Castile.

45 See Jacques Cartier, *Voyages au Canada avec les relations des voyages en Amérique de Gonneville, Verranzano et Roberval*, ed. Charles-André Julien, R. Herval, Th. Beauchesne (Paris: F. Maspero, 1981), 40. This includes a modern-spelling version of Gonneville. See Charles-André Julien's Introduction to this volume, which is reprinted from his *Les Français en Amérique dans la première moitié du XVIe siècle* (Paris: Presses universitaires de France, 1946), 10. The original source of knowledge about the New World here was Portugal, and, in this account at least, the French voyage does not seem to have much official backing.

46 Philip P. Boucher, *Les Nouvelles Frances: France in America, 1500–1815: An Imperial Perspective* (Providence, RI: John Carter Brown Library, 1989).

47 Binot Paulmier de Gonneville, *Relations authentique . . .* in *Les Français* (1946), ed. Julien et al., 37. See note 7 on that page.

48 Ibid., 37. The editors gloss this Latin inscription at ibid., 37–8; my translation.

49 On Díaz and the role of writing for Cortés and his associates, see J. H. Elliott, 'Cortés, Veláquez and Charles V', Hernán Cortés, *Letters from Mexico*, trans. Anthony Pagden (1971; New Haven: Yale University Press, 1986), xvi.

50 Ibid., 38.

51 Gonneville is not alone in misreading the signs. For a discussion of how Verrazzano and Cartier misread the Natives' religious beliefs, see Stephen Greenblatt, *Marvelous Possessions: The Wonder of the New World* (Chicago: University of Chicago Press, 1991), 102–4.

52 Gonneville, *Relation*, 39.

53 Gonneville, *Relation*, 44, see 40–3. The editors have calculated the number of men lost; ibid., 44.

54 Ibid., 44–5. See Julien, 'Introduction', *Les Français* (1946), 5.

55 See Gonneville, *Relation*, 25.

56 Max Savelle with the assistance of Margaret Anne Fisher, *The Origins of American Diplomacy: The International History of Angloamerica, 1492–1763* (New York: Macmillan, 1967), 17.

57 E. L. Jones, *The European Miracle: Environments, Economies and Geopolitics in the History of Europe and Asia* (Cambridge: Cambridge University Press, 1981). See also Diamond, *Guns, Germs, and Steel*, esp. 409–19.

58 Paul Kennedy, *The Rise and Fall of the Great Powers: Economic Change and Military Conflict From 1500 to 2000* (1987; New York: Vintage, 1989), 4–30. Below, I will be distilling Kennedy and supplementing his analysis in this section.

59 Zhang Ting-yu, *History of the Ming*, trans. Dun J. Li in *The Bedford Anthology of World Literature: The Early Modern World, 1450–1650*, Book 3 (Boston and New York: Bedford/St.Martin's, 2004), 256, see 252; also in *The Civilization of China* (Upper Saddle River, NJ: Pearson Education, 1975).

60 Kennedy, 9–13.

61 Urs Bitterli, *Cultures in Conflict: Encounters Between European and Non-European Cultures, 1492–1800*, trans. Ritchie Robertson (1986; Cambridge: Polity, 1989), 133–4.

62 Kennedy, 17; see 17–30 as a basis for my discussion below. See also J. U. Nef, *War and Human Progress* (Cambridge, MA: Harvard University Press, 1950); W. H. McNeill, *The Pursuit of Power: Technology, Armed Forces and Society Since 1000 A.D.* (Chicago: University of Chicago Press, 1983).

63 See Ross Chambers, *Room for Maneuver: Reading (the) Oppositional (in) Narrative* (Chicago: University of Chicago Press, 1991); Ross Chambers, 'No Montagues Without Capulets: Some Thoughts on "Cultural Identity"', in Jonathan Hart and Richard Bauman ed., *Explorations in Difference: Law, Culture and Politics* (Toronto: University of Toronto Press, 1995); see Michel Serres, *Hermes III: La Traduction* (Paris: Minuit, 1974) and *The Parasite*, trans. Lawrence R. Schehr (Baltimore: Johns Hopkins University Press, 1982); René Girard, *Le Bouc emissaire* (Paris: Grasset, 1982); Jean-Luc Nancy, *The Inoperative Community*, trans. Peter Connor (Minneapolis: University of Minnesota Press, 1991); Michel de Certeau, *Heterologies: Discourse on the Other*, trans. Brian Massumi (Minneapolis: University of Minnesota Press,

1986), ch. 5. See also Tzvetan Todorov, *La Conquête de l'Amérique* (Paris: Editions du Seuil, 1982) and *The Conquest of America: The Question of the Other*, trans. Richard Howard (New York: Harper & Row, 1984); Deborah Root, 'The Imperial Signifier: Todorov and the Conquest of Mexico', *Cultural Critique* 9 (1988): 197–219.

64 Cadamosto, 55.

65 Cadamosto, 68.

66 Cadamosto, 69.

67 William D. Phillips, Jr., and Carla Rahn Phillips, *The Worlds of Christopher Columbus* (Cambridge: Cambridge University Press, 1992), 110–24. At his death Cecil Jane left an unfinished introduction, which he worked on until two days before he died and in which he covered seven of twenty-one topics for the proposed Introduction and printed in that form because the Hakluyt Society thought 'no other person could complete it in a manner which would do justice to its author', as Edward Lynum describes in his brief 'Prefatory Note' to the second volume of Jane's edition of Columbus's *Voyages*. Nonetheless, Jane left a detailed, balanced and useful examination of contemporary Spanish representations of these negotiations, including a discussion of the views of Peter Martyr and Bartolomé de Las Casas; see Cecil Jane, 'Introduction: The Negotiations of Columbus with Ferdinand and Isabella', *The Four Voyages of Columbus*, Cecil Jane, ed. (1929 and 1932; New York: Dover, 1988), vol. 2, xiii–lxxv. This second volume was originally part of four volumes and was later bound into one volume to include all four volumes. Jane wrote an Introduction, and there are two indices, to both original volumes that came to be combined (which leaves the separate pagination of the original volumes from the Hakluyt Society). For another helpful account, see John Cummins, 'Planning and Persuasion', *The Voyage of Christopher Columbus: Columbus' Own Journal of Discovery Newly Restored and Translated by John Cummins* (London: Weidenfeld and Nicolson, 1992), 31–45 and see also 'Appendix I', the procurator's questions to Columbus, 195–203, in the same volume, for subsequent questioning.

68 This is a vast field of postmodern, postcolonial and other recent theories, so that I have refrained from creating a vast list. There is, for instance, a debate over the status of narrative in fictions and history, something I have discussed in relation to the dramatic in a number of places, including *Theater and World* (Boston: Northeastern University Press, 1992) and in relation to theory in *Northrop Frye: The Theoretical Imagination* (London and New York: Routledge, 1994), so that I have avoided repeating myself here. For a recent discussion of narrative and history in the possession of the New World, see Howard Marchitello, *Narrative and Meaning in Early Modern England: Browne's Skull and Other Histories* (Cambridge: Cambridge University Press, 1997), 92–123. For a view of contemporary Latin America in terms of the relation between fiction and history, see Lois Parkinson Zamora, *The Usable Past: The Imagination of History in Recent Fiction of the Americas* (Cambridge: Cambridge University Press, 1997), esp. 1–39, 196–210. On the relation between truth and lying, Montaigne had much to say, particularly in 'Du démentir'. In a chapter appropriately called 'The Storyteller', Natalie Zemon

Davis raises an interesting relation between the culture of truth and fiction as opposed to ideas of their relation: 'Where does self-fashioning stop and lying begin? Long before Montaigne posed that question to his readers in a self-accusatory essay, Pansette's inventiveness posed it to his judges'; see *The Return of Martin Guerre* (Cambridge, MA: Harvard University Press, 1983), 103.

69 Marvin Lunenfeld, ed., *1492 Discovery, Invasion, Encounter Sources and Interpretations* (Lexington, MA: DC Heath, 1991), 201.

70 Bartolomé de Las Casas, *History of the Indies*, trans. and ed. André Collard (New York: Harper & Row, 1971), Book III, 181–7.

71 Ibid.

72 Ibid.

73 Jr. Vine Deloria, 'Afterword'. *America in 1492: The World of the Indian Peoples Before the Arrival of Columbus*, ed. Alvin M. Josephy, Jr (1991. New York: Random House, 1993), 429–43, 429–30.

74 Gordon Brotherston, *Image of the New World: The American Continent Portrayed in Native Texts*. (London: Thames and Hudson, 1979), 15. See also Fernando Alvarado Tezozomoc, *Crónica Mexicáyotl*, trans. Adrián León (México D.F.: UNAM, 1975) and *Crónica Mexicana*. (México D.F.: Porrúa, 1975); *Les Figures de l'indien*, ed. Gilles Therien (Montréal: Université du Québec à Montréal, 1988); Ronald Wright, *Stolen Continents: The 'New World' Through Indian Eyes* (Boston and New York: Houghton Mifflin, 1992.)

75 Brotherston, 21.

76 Deloria, 432–35.

77 Alfred W. Crosby, *Ecological Imperialism; The Biological Expansion of Europe, 900–1900* (New York and Cambridge: Cambridge University Press, 1986, rpt. 1991), 70–103.

78 David E. Stannard, *American Holocaust: The Conquest of the New World* (New York and Oxford: Oxford University Press, 1992, rpt. 1993), 57–74. I am indebted to Stannard here and below. See also *Lewis Hanke, Aristotle and the American Indians: A Study in Race Prejudice in the Modern World* (Bloomington: Indiana University Press, 1959); Kirkpatrick Sale, *The Conquest of Paradise: Christopher Columbus and the Columbian Legacy* (New York: Alfred A. Knopf, 1990). On pacification, see also Sauer, *The Early Spanish Main* (Berkeley: University of California Press, 1966), 89.

79 Eric R. Wolf, *Europe and the People Without History* (Berkeley: University of California Press, 1982, rpt. 1990), 133–4.

Chapter 2

1 For example, see C. A. Bayly, *Imperial Meridian: The British Empire and the World, 1780–1830* (London: Longman, 1989).

2 Jonathan Hart, *Representing the New World* (New York: Palgrave, 2001).

3 Sanjay Subrahmanyam, *The Portuguese Empire in Asia 1500–1700: A Political and Economic History* (London and New York: Longman, 1993), 2–8.

4 See, for instance, James Westfall Thompson, *The Wars of Religion in France, 1559–1576* (New York: Ungar, 1957).

5 Schiller wrote a history of the revolt: see his *Geschichte des Abfalls der vere-inigten Niederlande von der spanischen Regierung* (1788) or *The Revolt of the Netherlands*. For a key modern study, see Pietr Geyl, *The Revolt of the Netherlands, 1555–1609* (New York: Barnes & Noble), 1966. The original volume was part of *De geschiedenis van de Nederlandsche Stam*, 3 vols., 1930–59 – translated into English as *The Revolt of the Netherlands, 1555–1609* and *The Netherlands in the Seventeenth Century*.

6 Subrahmanyam, 9–10, 28–29, 55–67. See Judith Banister, *China's Changing Population* (Stanford: Stanford University Press, 1987); A. J. R. Russell-Wood, *The Portuguese Empire, 1415–1808: A World on the Move* (1992; Baltimore: The Johns Hopkins University Press, 1998).

7 This narrative owes a debt to Subrahmanyam's discussion, 30–54. See also Charles R. Boxer, *The Portuguese Seaborne Empire, 1415–1825* (London: Hutchinson & Co., 1969); A. C. Saunders, *A Social History of Black Slaves and Freedmen in Portugal, 1441–1555* (Cambridge: Cambridge University Press, 1982).

8 Subrahmanyam, 78–100. The quotation below occurs in Subrahmanyam, and my discussion here and above are indebted to him. See A. R. Disney, 'The Portuguese Empire in India, c. 1550–1650', in *Indo-Portuguese History: Sources and Problems*, ed. John Correia-Afonso, S.J. (Bombay: Oxford University Press, 1981), 148–73.

9 K. C. Fok, 'Early Ming Images of the Portuguese', *Portuguese Asia: Aspects in History and Economic History* (Stuttgart: Franz Steiner Verlag, 1987), 145, quoted in Subrahmanyam, 101. The discussion that follows is indebted to Subrahmanyam, 102–6.

10 Henry Kamen, *Empire: How Spain Became a World Power 1492–1763* (2002; New York: HarperCollins, 2003), esp. 49–51.

11 Vitorino Magalhães Godinho, *Ensaios*, vol. 2, (Lisbon: Sá da Costa, 1968) and A. H. Oliveira Marques, *History of Portugal, Volume 1: From Lusitania to Empire* (New York: Columbia University Press, 1972), 306–22.

12 Subrahmanyam, 107–43. See also Tikiri Abeyasinghe, *Portuguese Rule in Ceylon, 1594–1612* (Colombo: Lake House, 1966); Charles R. Boxer, *The Portuguese Seaborne Empire, 1415–1825* (London: Weidenfeld and Nicholson, 1969); Peter John Bury, 'The Indian Contribution to Portuguese Rule in the East, 1500–1580' (PhD thesis, University of Cambridge, 1975); Henry Kamen, *Inquisition and Society in Spain in the Sixteenth and Seventeenth Centuries* (London: Weidenfeld and Nicholson, 1985); *The Rise of Merchant Empires: Long-distance Trade in the Early Modern World 1350–1750*, ed. James D. Tracy (Cambridge: Cambridge University Press, 1990).

13 See Subrahmanyam, 107–43.

14 H. V. Livermore, 'Portuguese History', *Portugal and Brazil: An Introduction*, ed. H. V. Livermore (Oxford: The Clarendon Press, 1953), 62–4.

15 This brief discussion is indebted to J. H. Parry, *The Establishment of the European Hegemony: 1415–1715* (New York: Harper, 1961, rpt. 1965), 60–75.

16 Om Prakash, *The Dutch East India Company and the Economy of Bengal,*
    1630–1720 (Princeton: Princeton University Press, 1985), 3, 7.
17 Livermore, 62–4.
18 Felipe Fernández-Armesto, *The Spanish Armada: The Experience of War in*
    1588 (Oxford: Oxford University Press, 1988), vi, 273–6.
19 'An answer made to serten of the kinges counsell as consernyng the kinges
    shippes to be occupyed', *Records of the Drapers' Company of London*, vol.
    VII (1514–50), 167–70, 175–6 in ibid., 134–42; see 136–7.
20 Confirmation of the letters patent to Fagundes, 13 March and 22 May 1521,
    in ibid., 127–9; translation 129–31.
21 Agreement with Gomez for the discovery of a northwest passage, in ibid.,
    145–7 (translation 147–50).
22 Rastell's son sailed to America in 1536; on the use of allegory by father
    and son, see Jeffrey Knapp, *An Empire Nowhere: England, America,*
    and Literature from Utopia *to* The Tempest (Berkeley: University of
    California Press, 1992), 45. On the failures of the voyages of John Rastell
    and later of Humphrey Gilbert, see Mary C. Fuller, *Voyages in Print:*
    English Travel to America, 1576–1624 (Cambridge: Cambridge University
    Press, 1995), 32.
23 John Parker, *Books to Build an Empire: A Bibliographical History of English*
    Overseas Interests to 1620 (Amsterdam: N. Israel, 1965), 27.
24 Elaine Sanceau, *The Land of Prester John: A Chronicle of Portuguese*
    Exploration (New York: Alfred A. Knopf, 1944), 229.
25 Parker, 28–30.
26 Ibid.
27 Ibid. Lestringant notes that Thorne is one of a number of English and French
    explorers of North America to appear in a list in Hakluyt's *Divers Voyages*
    (1582); see Frank Lestringant, *Le Huguenot et le sauvage* (Paris: Klincksieck,
    1990), 214.
28 More generally, James Axtell has chronicled the phenomenon of the 'White
    Indian'; see Axtell, 'The White Indian', *The Invasion Within: the Contest of*
    Cultures in Colonial North America (New York: Oxford University Press,
    1985), 302–28. Nicholas Canny and Peter Hulme have noted that some
    English abandoned their colonies for assimilation amongst the Natives, espe-
    cially before 1622; see Canny, 'The Permissive Frontier: the Problem of
    Social Control in English Settlements in Ireland and Virginia 1550–1650' in
    The Westward Enterprise, ed. K. R. Andrews, N. P. Canny and P. E. H. Hair
    (Liverpool: Liverpool University Press, 1978), 17–44; Hulme, *Colonial*
    Encounters: Europe and the Native Caribbean, 1492–1697 (1986; London:
    Routledge, 1992), 143. Jeffrey Knapp picks up on that theme of fragility and
    failure and includes a reminder that is easily forgotten: the most famous
    English voyagers (Drake, Cavendish, Frobisher, Hawkins) had all perished
    at sea; see Knapp, *Empire*, 63. Henry Hudson, Humphrey Gilbert and others
    also died during their voyages, something apparently much less common
    among the Spanish and the French.
29 Parker, *Books*, 28–30.
30 Ibid.

31 H. P. Biggar, *A Collection of Documents Relating to Jacques Cartier and The Sieur de Roberval* (Ottawa: Public Archives of Canada, 1930), xviii.

32 Theodore K. Rabb, *Enterprise & Empire: Merchant and Gentry Investment in the Expansion of England, 1575–1630* (Cambridge MA: Harvard University Press, 1967), 1.

33 'Paget to King Henry VIII' in H. P. Biggar, *Collection*, 444.

34 Biggar, 'Introduction', *Collection*, xxxv.

35 Parker, *Books*, 65–6. See Nicholas Canny's work on the English in Ireland; Canny, *The Elizabethan Conquest of Ireland: A Pattern Established 1565–76* (Hassocks, Sussex: Harvester Press, 1976); 'The Permissive Frontier', 17–44; 'Identity Formation in Ireland: The Emergence of the Anglo-Irish' in *Colonial Identity in the Atlantic World, 1500–1800*, ed. Nicholas Canny and Anthony Pagden (Princeton: Princeton University Press, 1987), 159–212; *Kingdom and Colony: Ireland in the Atlantic World 1560–1800* (Baltimore: Johns Hopkins University Press, 1988).

36 See ibid. and also Canny, *Elizabethan Conquest*, 54, 133–4. For another discussion of the connection between Ireland and the New World, see David B. Quinn, *Ireland and America: Their Early Associations, 1500–1640* (Liverpool: Liverpool University Press, 1991). Quinn discusses the Irish and Spanish America; ibid., 11–16.

37 Humphrey Gilbert, *Discourse of a Discoverie for a New Passage to Cataia* (London, 1576), j ii recto – j ii verso.

38 T. O. Lloyd, *The British Empire 1558–1995*, 2nd edn (Oxford: Oxford University Press, 1996; rpt 2000), 15.

39 Canny, *Kingdom*, 1–6.

40 Ibid., 85, 133–4.

41 Ibid., 566.

42 'June 11, 1578. Patent granted to Sir Humphrey Gilbert by Elizabeth I' in *New American World: A Documentary History of North America to 1612*, ed. David B. Quinn (5 vols. New York: Arno Press, 1979), III, 186.

43 Ibid., 188–9.

44 J. Parker, *Books*, 70, see 69.

45 Abraham Fleming, '. . . Capteine Forbisher' in Dionyse Settle, *True Reporte of the Laste Voyage into the West and Northwest Regions* (London, 1577), A i verso.

46 Settle, *True Reporte*, Ci verso–Cii recto; see Biiii verso.

47 George Beste, 'The Epistle Dedicatory' to 'A True Discourse of the Late Voyages of Discoverie for Finding of a Passage to Cathaya, by the North-weast, under the Conduct of *Martin Frobisher* General . . .' in *The Three Voyages of Martin Frobisher*, ed. Richard Collinson (London, 1867), 17–18.

48 J. Parker, *Books*, 72, 104–8. John Parker observes that it is curious that no book is extant describing Drake's pre-eminent Elizabethan voyage (107). See Augustín de Zárate, *Discovery and Conquest of the Provinces of Peru* (London, 1581), j 4 verso. In an account printed almost fifty years later, Drake's chaplain, Francis Fletcher, described the Spanish as thinking they do favours in whipping and torturing the Natives. See Francis Fletcher, *The World Encompassed by Sir Francis Drake* (London, 1628), 104.

49 Ibid., 13.

50 J. Parker, *Books*, 102–3, 105. For good accounts of the war in the Low Countries, see Pieter Geyl, *The Revolt of the Netherlands*; Charles Wilson, *Queen Elizabeth and the Revolt of the Netherlands* (London: Macmillan, 1970); Geoffrey Parker, *The Dutch Revolt* (Harmondsworth: Penguin, 1979); Jonathan I. Israel, *The Dutch Republic and the Hispanic World 1606–1661* (Oxford: Clarendon Press, 1982); Hugh Dunthorne, 'The Dutch Revolt in English Political Culture 1585–1660' in *From Revolt to Riches: Culture and History of the Low Countries 1500–1700*, ed. Theo Hermans and Reiner Salverda (London: Centre for Low Country Studies, 1993), 235–47.

51 Jacques Cartier, *A Shorte and Briefe narration of the Two Navigations and Discoveries to the Northwest Partes called New France* (London, 1580), B ii recto.

52 Samuel Eliot Morison, *The European Discovery of America: The Northern Voyages A.D. 500–1600* (New York: Oxford University Press, 1971), 574–5.

53 See 'A Report of the Voyage and Successe Thereof, Attempted in the Yeere of Our Lord, 1583. by Sir Humphrey Gilbert . . .', in Richard Hakluyt, *The Principall Navigations Voiages and Discoveries of the English Nation . . .* (London, 1589), facsimile, ed. David Beers Quinn and Raleigh Ashlin Skelton (Cambridge: Cambridge University Press, 1965), 680–1.

54 The phrase is Jack Beeching's; see his 'Introduction' in Richard Hakluyt, *Voyages and Discoverie: The Principal Navigations Voyages, Traffiques and Discoveries of the English Nation*, ed. Jack Beeching (1972; Harmondsworth: Penguin, 1985), 18. For Beeching's comments on 'Discourse', see ibid., 16–18. Lestringant leaves out a discussion of 'Discourse' in his section on Hakluyt in Paris, which might be because Hakluyt's role in the disappearance of French manuscripts could be of more interest to the French reader than a secret document to the English Crown; see Lestringant, *Le Huguenot*, 213–18. Both aspects of Hakluyt's work in Paris were, however, complementary and should be seen together. David Armitage discusses Hakluyt in terms of the relation between his humanism and ideology; see Armitage, 'The New World and British Historical Thought From Richard Hakluyt to William Robertson' in *America in European Consciousness, 1493–1750*, ed. Karen Ordahl Kupperman (Chapel Hill, NC: University of North Carolina Press, 1995), 52–9.

55 'Discourse' was a state paper that remained in manuscript and was not published until 1877, when it appeared in Boston. For an informative examination of the context of this state paper (one that informs my account), see David B. Quinn and Alison M. Quinn, 'Introduction', Richard Hakluyt, *Discourse of Western Planting* (London: Hakluyt Society, 1993), xv–xxxi, esp. xv.

56 For a reconstruction of Hakluyt's reading, particularly of works pertaining to Spanish colonies in the New World, see ibid., xviii–xx.

57 Hakluyt, 'Discourse', 12. For a text about the persecution of Protestants in Spain, see Reginalus Gonsalvius Montanus, *A discovery and playne declaration of sundry subtill proactises of the Holy Inquisition of Spayne* (n.p.

[London?], 1569). David Quinn thinks that Hakluyt was probably aware of this work, which also includes a description of the taking of an English ship. See Quinn's Commentary to the 'Discourse', 135.

58 Ibid., 28. For a brief discussion of piracy, see the Quinns' 'Commentary', 143.

59 Hakluyt, *Discourse*, 28.

60 Hakluyt, *Discourse*, 28–9. On the penal laws and French fur trade, see the Quinns' 'Commentary', 144, especially notes to lines 636 and 665–78.

61 Ibid.

62 Ibid., 52.

63 T. O. Lloyd, *The British Empire 1558–1995*, 2nd edn, 2, 9.

64 Paul Fauchille, *Traité de Droit International Public* (Paris, 1925), I, part 2, 687, cited in L. C. Green and Olive P. Dickason, *The Law of Nations and the New World* (Edmonton: University of Alberta Press, 1989). 7. For similar references to François Ier on Adam's will, see Lyle N. McAlister, *Spain and Portugal in the New World 1492–1700* (Minneapolis: University of Minnesota Press, 1984), 199 and Anthony Pagden, *Lords of all the World: Ideologies of Empire in Spain, Britain and France c. 1500–c. 1800* (New Haven: Yale University Press, 1995), 47.

65 Raymonde Litalien, *Les explorateurs de l'Amérique du Nord, 1492–1795* (Sillery, Québec: Septentrion, 1993), 53.

66 Max Savelle, *The Origins of American Diplomacy: The International History of Angloamerica, 1492–1763*. With the assistance of Margaret Anne Fisher (New York: Macmillan, 1967), 19–21.

67 Charles-André Julien, *Les Voyages de découvertes et les premiers établissements* (Paris: Presses Universitaires de France, 1948), 115–17, 135–8; David. B. Quinn and Alison M. Quinn, 'Commentary' in Richard Hakluyt, *Discourse*, 187. In *Les Français* Charles-André Julien outlines Le Veneur's principal part in the Cartier expedition and the family connections and friendships behind this; see Julien, 'Introduction', *Les Francais en Amérique pendant la première moitié du XVIe siècle. Introduction par Ch. A. Julien. Textes des voyages de Gonneville, Verrazano, J Cartier et Roberval. Avec deux cartes hors-texte, Edités par Ch.-A. Julien, Herval, Th. Beauchesne* (1. éd., Paris: Presses universitaires de France, 1946), I, 11. Some of this material he says he owes to the groundbreaking work in Baron de La Chapelle, 'Jean Le Veneur et le Canada', *Nova Francia* 6 (1931), 341–3.

68 On Cartier, see François-Marc Gagnon, *Jacques Cartier et la découverte du Nouveau Monde* (Québec: Musée du Québec, 1984). Patricia Seed asserts that the French had ceremonies of possession that involved a 'conquest by love'. René Laudonnière thought that the Spanish had recognized one territory in the New World as being French because they saw signs and the French coat of arms that Verrazzano had supposedly left; see Laudonnière, *Histoire notable de la Floride . . .* (Paris, 1586), 38 and Patricia Seed, *Ceremonies of Possession in Europe's Conquest of the New World, 1492–1640* (Cambridge: Cambridge University Press, 1995), 56. Seed also mentions that Gonneville and Cartier had used tricks to take possession from the Natives because they could not gain consent for their actions. See ibid., 57.

69 See René Laudonnière, *Histoire notable de la Floride située es Indes Occidentales* (Paris, 1586) in *Les Français en Amérique pendant la deuxième moitié su XVIᵉ siècle* (Paris: PUF, 1958), 38, cited in Patricia Seed, *Ceremonies*, 56. Seed discusses Gonneville and this French ploy of a conquest by love in such ceremonies of planting a cross, pillar or royal standard; ibid., 56–63.

70 Julien, *Les Français* (1946), I, 13.

71 'To this great enterprise the King officially assigned the elevated purpose of propagating Christianity; for, ever since the Pope's division of new lands between Portugal and Spain, the role of missionary was the only justification France could use for her actions without affronting the Holy See. This was an obvious diplomatic façade, since the first baptism by the French in North America did not take place until 1610'. M. Trudel, 'Section One: Introduction to the New World' in *Canada: Unity in Diversity*, ed. Paul G. Cornell et al. (Toronto: Holt, Rinehart and Winston of Canada, 1967), 9.

72 Julien, *Les Français* (1946), I, 14.

73 See Keller et al., *Creation of Rights of Sovereignty*, 23–5, cited in Olive Dickason, 'Concepts of Sovereignty at the Time of First Contacts' in Green and Dickason, *The Law*, 221, 287.

74 As late as 1971, Justice Richard Blackburn had confirmed *terra nullius* in Australia, and it took until 1992 for the High Court of Australia to reject it. See Tim Rowse, *After Mabo: Interpreting Indigenous Traditions* (Melbourne: Melbourne University Press, 1993), 8, 21.

75 'Copia de lo que el embaxador de França scrivé á Su Magestad á los XXVII de diziembre 1540' in H. P. Biggar, *A Collection of Documents Relating to Jacques Cartier and The Sieur de Roberval* (Ottawa: Public Archives of Canada, 1930), 169–71.

76 '[El Emperador] al Cardenal de Toledo' in Biggar, *Collection*, 283–4 (translation, ibid).

77 Savelle, 21.

78 André Thevet, *La Cosmographie vniverselle*, vol. 2, livre 1, cap. 11, f. 498 verso; see A. C. de C.M. Saunders, *A Social History of Black Slaves and Freedmen in Portugal 1441–1555* (Cambridge: Cambridge University Press, 1982), 11–12, 33.

79 Jean de Léry, *History of a Voyage to the Land of Brazil*, trans. and introduction by Janet Whatley (Berkeley: University of California Press, 1990), 9, see 4.

80 Morison, *The European Discovery of America*, ix.

81 As Arthur Ray says, 'In the 1560s and 1570s more than a thousand whaling men were summering – and sometimes wintering – there [on the strait of Belle Isle in eastern Canada] every year'; see Ray, 'When Two Worlds Met', *The Illustrated History of Canada*, ed. Craig Brown (1987; Toronto: Lester Publishing, 1991), 21.

82 See Frank Lestringant, 'The Philsopher's Breviary: Jean de Léry in the Enlightenment' in *New World Encounters*, ed. Stephen Greenblatt (Berkeley: University of California Press, 1993), 127.

83 Another aspect of the French response to the New World is the work of André Thevet, who claimed to be Cartier's friend and whose self-promotion

and his advocacy for French expansion is something I have discussed elsewhere and so have relegated my analysis to the notes in this chapter. See Jonathan Hart, 'Strategies of Promotion: Some Prefatory Matter of Oviedo, Thevet and Hakluyt', *Imagining Culture: Essays in Early Modern History and Literature*, ed. J. Hart (New York: Garland, 1996), 73–94.

84 See Cornelius Jaenen's series of important articles on the French view of America and, especially, Amerindians; see his 'Conceptual Frameworks for French Views of America and Amerindians', *French Colonial Studies* 2 (1978), 1–22; 'French Attitudes Towards Native Society', in *Old Trails and New Directions*, ed. Carol Judd and Arthur Ray (Toronto, 1980), 59–72; 'France's America and Amerindians: Image and Reality', *History of European Ideas* 6 (1985), 405–20.

85 Julien, 'Introduction', *Les Français* (1958), II, v, see vi–viii. On Spain and France in Florida, see Sauer, *Sixteenth*, 189–227.

86 On Gouges, see Lestringant, *Le Huguenot*, 156–64, 174–5.

87 On Le Challeux, see Lestringant, *Le Huguenot*, 113–15, 152–5.

88 See Steele, *Warpaths*, 7–20. On the French failure in Florida, including dissension amongst the French, and their piracy, as well as a balanced account of the conflict between Spain and France in this region, see ibid., 25–8. Apparently, the Spanish expedition to Florida, 1565–8, cost the king one-fifth of the military budget for his empire ; ibid., 27. For other discussions of this conflict, which, along with the war in the Netherlands, fed the Black Legend, see Eugene Lyon, *The Enterprise of Florida: Pedro Menéndez de Avilés and the Spanish Conquest of 1565–1568* (Gainsville, FL, 1976) and Paul E. Hoffman, *The Spanish Crown and the Defense of the Caribbean, 1565–1585: Precedent, Patrimonialism, and Royal Parsimony* (Baton Rouge, 1980), 218–28.

89 *Histoire Novvelle dv Novveav Monde, Contenant en somme ce que les Hespagnols ont fait iusqu'à present aux Indes Occidentales, & le rude traitement qu'ils ont fait à ces poures peuples-la. Extraite de l'italien de M. Hierosme Benzoni Milanois, qui ha voyagé XIIII ans en ce pays-la: & enrichie de plusieurs Discours & choses dignes de memoire. Par M. Vrbain Chavveton. Ensemble, Vne petite Histoire d'vn Massacre commis par les Hespagnols sur quelques François en la Floride. Auec un Indice des choses plus remarkable* (Geneva, 1579); my translation here and below.

90 Biggar, *Collection*, xviii.

91 Pagden, *Lords*, 67, 93. See also Marcel Trudel, *The Beginnings of New France*, trans. Patricia Claxton (Toronto: McClelland and Stewart, 1973), 48–50 and W. J. Eccles, 'Sovereignty Association, 1500–1783', *Essays on New France* (Toronto: Oxford University Press, 1987), 159.

92 Of these three expeditions, Boucher says: 'The intention of these expeditions was to imitate the Spanish pattern of exploration, conquest, and exploitation of land and aborigines. The search for golden cities and dense populations of aboriginal serfs galvanized the energies of these would-be conquistadors'. Philip P. Boucher, *Les Nouvelles Frances: France in America, 1500–1815: An Imperial Perspective* (Providence: John Carter Brown Library, 1989), 5, see 12.

93 Philippe Du Plessis-Mornay, 'Discours au roy Henri III sur les moyens de diminuer l'Espagnol' (1584) in *Mémoire et correspondence* (12 vols. Paris, 1824–5), II, 590. He advocated an attack on Spain and a settling of the isthmus of Darien. For a discussion of Du Plessis-Mornay in the context of 'Protestant geopolitics', see Frank Lestringant, *Le Huguenot*, 123–4, see 119–26; for his relation to the ill-fated Scottish 'Darien Venture' of 1698–9, which had some of the same goals, see David Armitage, 'The British Empire and the Civic Tradition 1656–1742' (unpublished PhD dissertation, Cambridge University, 1992), 132, see 124–59. Armitage also discusses works that further prove my point about the persistence of earlier ways of representing Spain; see William Paterson, 'Proposal for Settling on the Isthmus of Darien, Releasing the nations from the Tyranny of Spain . . .' (B.L. Add. MS 12437), 1 January 1701/2, [appears under the title, 'Memoir Upon Expeditions against Spanish America'] in Paterson, *The Life and Writings of William Paterson, Founder of the Bank of England*, ed. Saxe Bannister (3 vols. London, 1859), I, 140–1, cited in Armitage, 'The British', 133; Charles Davenant, *An Essay upon Universal Monarchy* (1701) in *Essays upon I. The Balance of Power. II. The Right of Making War, Peace, and Alliances. III. Universal Monarchy* (London, 1701), cited in ibid., 142. Armitage and Pagden also speak about Andrew Fletcher's and David Hume's view of Spain and universal monarchy; see ibid., 141–6; Pagden, *Lords*, 63, 70, 118–20. As Louis XIV sought to assert the right of his grandson, Philip of Anjou, over the claim of the Austrian Habsburgs to the Spanish throne (the Parlement registered Philip as successor to the French throne in February 1701), the threat of universal monarchy, which helped to set off the War of Spanish Succession, returned, a fear that Spain under Emperor Charles V and even Philip II had engendered in France and England.
94 Paul Kennedy, *The Rise and Fall of the Great Powers: Economic Change and Military Conflict From 1500 to 2000* (1987; New York: Vintage, 1989), 56–5; see Robin Briggs, *Early Modern France, 1560–1715* (Oxford: Oxford University Press, 1977).
95 Kennedy, 52–55; see also David Maland, *Europe in the Seventeenth Century* (London: Macmillan, 1966), Jonathan Israel, 'A Conflict of Empires: Spain and the Netherlands, 1618–1648', *Past and Present* 76 (1977), 34–74 and his *The Dutch Republic and the Hispanic World* (1982) cited before. On the growth of Dutch sea power, see George Raudens, *Empires: Europe and Globalization 1492–1788* (Phoenix Mill: Sutton Publishing, 1999), 75–91.
96 The outline of the Dutch in Brazil, although not many of the points of interpretation, at the beginning of this section derive from one of the standard works in English in the field, C. R. Boxer's *The Dutch in Brazil 1624–1654* (1957; Hamden, CT: Archon Books, 1973), esp. 1–3. See also J. Franklin Jameson, *Willem Usselincx, Founder of the Dutch and Swedish West India Companies* (New York: London, G. P. Putnam's Sons, 1887) and Catharina Ligtenberg, *Willem Usselincx* (Utrecht: A. Oosthoek, 1914).
97 Pedro de Magalhães Gandavo, *Historia da provincia sācta Cruz a que vulgarmente chamamos Brasil* (Lisboa, 1576).
98 Simão de Vasconcellos, *Chronica da Companhia de Jesu do estado do Brasil: e do que obrarão seus filhos nesta parte do Nouo Mundo* (Lisboa, 1663).

99 Lloyd, 13. The British launched the East India Company with 68,000 pounds; in 1602 the Dutch East India began with 500,000 pounds capital.

100 Anthony Farrington, *Trading Places: The East India Company and Asia 1600–1834* (London: The British Library, 2002), 41–47, and Lloyd, 14.

101 Farrington, 48.

102 Kennedy, *The Great Powers*, 66–70; see Charles Wilson, *The Dutch Republic and the Civilization of the Seventeenth Century* (London: Weidenfeld & Nicolson, 1968); Geoffrey Parker, *The Dutch Revolt* (London: Penguin:, 1977); Jonathan Israel, *The Dutch Republic*.

103 Ecology makes a brief but important appearance in a recent history of the Spanish empire; see Kamen, *Empire*, 270–2, 282. For a recent discussion of disease in the New and Old Worlds and among slaves in the African slave trade, see Mark Harrison, *Disease and the Modern World: 1500 to the Present Day* (Cambridge: Polity, 2004), esp. 72–90. On disease and European expansion in this period and related matters, see Paul Slack, *The Impact of Plague in Tudor and Stuart England* (Oxford: Clarendon Press, 1985); Mary Dobson, *Contours of Death and Disease in Early Modern England* (Cambridge: Cambridge University Press, 1997); David Herlihy, *The Black Death and the Transformation of the West* (Cambridge, MA: Harvard University Press, 1997); Noble David Cook, *Born to Die: Disease and the New World Conquest, 1492–1650* (New York: Cambridge University Press, 1998); J. N. Hays, *The Burdens of Disease: Epidemics and Human Response in Western History* (New Brunswick, NJ: Rutgers University Press, 2000).

104 David Stannard, *American Holocaust: The Conquest of the New World* (New York and Oxford: Oxford University Press, 1992, rpt. 1993), 75–95. See Ross Hassig, *Aztec Warfare: Imperial Expansion and Political Control* (Norman: University of Oklahoma Press, 1988). Pedro de Cieza de León, *The Incas*, trans. Harriet de Onis (Norman: University of Oklahoma Press, 1959), quoted in Stannard, 80.

105 Chilam Balam, quoted in Stannard, 86. See also Nathan Wachtel, *The Vision of the Vanquished: The Spanish Conquest of Peru Through Indian Eyes, 1530–1570*, trans. Ben and Sian Reynolds (Sussex: The Harvester Press, 1977), 31.

106 Jared Diamond, *Guns, Germs, and Steel: The Fates of Human Societies* (New York and London: W. W. Norton, 1997, rpt. 1999), 67, see 68–81 for the following discussion.

107 Almagro quoted in Stannard, 88; see 89–92. See also John Hemming, *The Conquest of the Incas* (New York: Harcourt Brace Jovanovich, 1970), esp. 363–4.

108 Eric R. Wolf, *Europe and the People Without History* (Berkeley: University of California Press, 1982, rpt. 1990), 135. See Stannard, 88–92.

109 Stannard, 92–5. See Wolf, 149–51. See also Carlo M. Cipolla, *Cristofano and the Plague: A Study in the History of Public Health in the Age of Galileo* (London: William Collins Sons, 1973); John Hemming, *Red Gold: The Conquest of the Brazilian Indians, 1500–1760* (Cambridge, MA: Harvard University Press, 1978); Paul Slack, *The Impact of the Plague in Tudor and*

Stuart England (London: Routledge & Kegan Paul, 1985); Russell Thornton, *American Indian Holocaust and Survival: A Population History Since 1492* (Norman: University of Oklahoma Press, 1987).

110 For a detailed contextual and thematic discussion of the miscegenation policy in Australia, the United States and Brazil that is important for understanding each group, including the Aborigines, see Patrick Wolfe, 'Land, Labor, and Difference: Elementary Structures of Race', *The American Historical Review* 106 (3) June 2001, 866–905.

111 Diamond, *Guns*, 78.

112 James Lockhart, *The Nahuas After the Conquest: A Social and Cultural History of the Indians of Central Mexico, Sixteenth Through Eighteenth Centuries* (Stanford: Stanford University Press, 1992), 330. See also Hernán Cortés, *Letters from Mexico*, trans. and ed. Anthony Pagden (New Haven: Yale University Press, 1986) and David J. Weber, *The Spanish Frontier in North America* (New Haven: Yale University Press, 1992).

113 Anthony Pagden, *The Fall of Natural Man: The American Indian and the Origins of Comparative Ethnology* (1982; Cambridge: Cambridge University Press, 1986), 119.

114 See R.A. Gutiérrez, *When Jesus Came, the Corn Mothers Went Away: Marriage, Sexuality, and Power in New Mexico, 1500–1846* (Stanford: Stanford University Press, 1991), 48. Octavio Paz considers La Malinche to be a figure that plays out the conflict and contradictions in the Mexican past: she is to be embraced and scorned at the same time. See his *El labertino de la soledad* (Mexico: Fondo de Cultura Economica, 1959), esp. 78–9.

115 Miguel Leon-Portilla, ed. *The Broken Spears: The Aztec Account of the Conquest of Mexico* (1959; Boston: Beacon Press, 1992), 3, Bernal Díaz, *The Conquest of New Spain*, trans. J. M. Cohen (Harmondsworth: Penguin, 1963, rpt. 1983), 86–7, see below. For a suggestive and influential discussion of go-betweens in the context of Herodotus, Díaz and Montaigne, see Stephen Greenblatt, *Marvelous Possessions: The Wonder of the New World* (Chicago: University of Chicago Press, 1991), 119–51.

116 Leon-Portilla 125. See Bernardino de Sahagún, *Florentine Codex: General History of the Things of New Spain Book 12*, trans. Arthur J. O. Anderson and Charles E. Dibble (Santa Fe, NM: The School of American Research and University of Utah, 1975).

117 Díaz, *The Conquest of New Spain*, 65.

118 Ibid., 73.

119 Ibid., 81.

120 Inga Clendinnen, *Ambivalent Conquests: Maya and Spaniard in Yucatan, 1517–1570* (New York: Cambridge University Press, 1987), 18. See Gonzalo Fernández de Oviedo y Valdés, *Historia general y natural de las Indias (1535–1547)* (Madrid: Ediciones Atlas, 1959), 32:3, 6; Bernal Díaz del Castillo, *La Conquista de La Nueva España* (4 vols. Paris and Buenos Aires: Sociedad de Ediciones Louis-Michaud, n.d.), ch. 29; Diego de Landa, *Landa's Relación de las cosas de Yucatán*, trans. and ed. Alfred M. Tozzer (Cambridge, MA: Peabody Museum, Harvard University, 1941), 8 n. 38. For another discussion of White Indians, see Cornelius Jaenen, *Friend and Foe:*

Aspects of French-Amerindian Contact in the Sixteenth and Seventeenth Centuries (Toronto: McClelland and Stewart, 1976).

121 Donald Chipman, 'Isabel Moctezuma: Pioneer of *Mestizaje*', in *Struggle and Survival in Colonial America*, ed. D. Sweet and G. Nash (Berkeley: University of California Press, 1981), 214–27, 216.

122 Whatley, "Introduction", Léry, *History*, xix.

123 Editions in 1578, 1580, 1585, 1594, 1599–1600, 1611.

124 Michel de Montaigne, *Essais* (Paris: Garnier Freres, 1962). *The Essays of Montaigne*, trans. E. J. Treichmann (London: Oxford University Press, 1953), 180.

125 Ibid. [1st page verso-2nd page recto]. This should refer to Chauveton's *Histoire Novvelle dv Novveav Monde . . . Extraite de l'italien de M. Hierosme Benzoni Milanois . . .* (Geneva. 1579);

126 Ibid. [2nd page recto].

127 Gordon Brotherston, *Image of the New World: The American Continent Portrayed in Native Texts* (London: Thames & Hudson, 1979), 28–32, 48–53; see Jonathan Hart, 'Images of the Native in Renaissance Encounter Narratives', *ARIEL* 25 (1994), 55–76.

128 See Hart, 'Images' (1994).

129 See J. Jorge Klor de Alva, Foreword, in Miguel Leon-Portilla, ed. *The Broken Spears: The Aztec Account of the Conquest of Mexico* (1959; Boston: Beacon Press, 1992), xii–xxi.

130 Portilla, ed. *The Broken Spears*, 56–7.

131 Lynn Hunt et al., eds., *The Making of the West: Peoples and Cultures* (Boston and New York: Bedford/St. Martin's, 2001), 496–515.

132 Kennedy, 17; see 17–30 as a basis for my discussion below. See also J. U. Nef, *War and Human Progress* (Cambridge, MA: Harvard University Press, 1950); W. H. McNeill, *The Pursuit of Power: Technology, Armed Forces and Society Since 1000 A.D.* (Chicago: University of Chicago Press, 1983).

133 Maria Augusta Lima Cruz, 'Exiles and Renegades in Early Sixteenth Century Portuguese Asia', *Historiography of Europeans in Africa and Asia, 1450–1800*, ed. Anthony Disney (Aldershot: Variorum, 1995), 235, 248, see 236–47. The original version, also translated by Sanjay Subrahmanyam, appeared in the *Indian Economic and Social History Review* 23 (1986), 249–62.

134 Peter Burke, *The European Renaissance: Centres and Peripheries* (Oxford: Blackwell, 1998), 157, 196, 210–11. See also Charles R. Boxer, *Three Historians of Portuguese Asia* (Barros, Couto, Bocarro) (Macão: Imprensa Nacional, 1948) and his *João de Barros. Portuguese Humanist and Historian of Asia* (New Delhi: Concept Publishing Company, 1981); Donald Lach, *Asia in the Making of Europe: The Century of Discovery* (Chicago: University of Chicago Press, 1965).

135 K. C. Fok, 'Early Ming Images of the Portuguese', in *Historiography*, ed. A. Disney, 113–14, 125, see 115–24.

136 Fok 114; see Yen Ts'ung-chien, *Shu-yü chou-tzu-lu* (Ku-kung po-wu-kuan edition, 1930), ch. 9, esp. 17.

137 Michael Murrin, *History and Warfare in Renaissance Epic* (Chicago: University of Chicago Press, 1994), 182–6. See also Geoffrey Parker, *The Military Revolution: Military Innovation and the Rise of the West, 1500–1800* (Cambridge: Cambridge University Press, 1988) and his *Empire, War, and Faith* (London: Allen Lane, 2002).

138 See Kennedy, 14–15, to which my discussion is indebted; on the Portuguese expulsion from Japan, see G. B. Sansom, *The Western World and Japan* (London: Cresset Press, 1950); Charles R. Boxer, *Fildagos in the Far East, 105–7; his *A Portuguese Embassy (1644–1647)* (London: Kegan Paul, Trench, Trübner & Co., Ltd., 1928); and his *The Christian Century in Japan, 1549–1650* (Berkeley: University of California Press, 1951), 383–9 and, more recently, A. J. R. Russell-Wood, *The Portuguese Empire*, 24, 81.

139 On the role of gunpowder in imperial expansion, see W. H. McNeill, *The Age of Gunpowder Empires 1450–1800* (Washington, DC: American Historical Association, 1989).

Chapter 3

1 Sanjay Subrahmanyam, *The Portuguese Empire in Asia 1500–1700: A Political and Economic History* (London and New York: Longman, 1993), 144–80 here and above. See also H. V. Livermore, *Portugal: A Short History* (Edinburgh: Edinburgh University Press, 1973); Geoffrey Parker, *The Military Revolution: Military Innovation and the Rise of the West, 1500–1800* (Cambridge: Cambridge University Press, 1988) and his *Empire, War, and Faith* (London: Allen Lane, 2002); R. A. Stradling, *Philip IV and the Government of Spain, 1621–1665* (Cambridge: Cambridge University Press, 1988); Geoffrey V. Scammell, *The First Imperial Age: European Overseas Expansion, c. 1400–1715* (London: Unwin Hyman, 1989).

2 Subrahmanyam, 181–215. See John E. Will, Jr., *Embassies and Illusions: Dutch and Portuguese Envoys to K'ang-his, 1666–1687* (Cambridge, MA: Harvard University Press, 1984). On Portugal and China, see A. J. R. Russell-Wood, *The Portuguese Empire, 1415–1808: A World on the Move* (1992; Baltimore: The Johns Hopkins University Press, 1998), esp. 79–80, 96–7, 199–200, 215–16.

3 For the statistics of Spain's decline, see Paul Kennedy, *The Rise and Fall of the Great Powers* (New York: Random House, 1987), 41–55. On the business of empire in this period, see Henry Kamen, *Empire: How Spain Became a World Power 1492–1763* (2002; New York: HarperCollins, 2003), 314–29.

4 Geoffrey Parker, *Spain and the Netherlands, 1559–1659* (London: Fontana/Collins, 1979), esp. 17–42, 86–105, 122–34, and his *The Army of Flanders and the Spanish Road 1567–1659: The Logistics of Spanish Victory and the Defeat in the Low Countries War* (Cambridge: Cambridge University Press, 1972); John Lynch, *Spain under the Habsburgs* (1964; Oxford: Oxford University Press, 1969), esp. I: 53–58, 77, 347–8, II:70; Carlo Cipolla, *Guns and Sails in the Early Phase of European Expansion*

1400–1700 (London: Collins, 1965) and his *The Economic Decline of Empires* (London: Methuen, 1970); Fernand Braudel, *The Mediterranean and the Mediterranean World in the Age of Philip II*, trans. Siân Reynolds (London: Collins, 1972), 2 vols., esp. II: 700–05, 840–42; I. A. A. Thompson, *War and Government in Habsburg Spain 1560–1620* (London: Athlone Press, 1976); R. A. Stradling, *Europe and the Decline of Spain: A Study in the Spanish System, 1580–1720* (London: Allen & Unwin, 1981); J. H. Elliott, *Imperial Spain, 1469–1716* (Harmondsworth: Penguin, 1970); see Kennedy, 43–55. On the economic strength of the Netherlands, see Jonathan I. Israel, *Dutch Primacy in World Trade, 1585–1740* (Oxford: Clarendon, 1989).

5 J. H. Elliott, *Spain and Its World 1500–1700* (New Haven and London: Yale University Press, 1989), 217.

6 Elliott, *Spain and Its World*, 221–2.

7 Gaspar de Guzmán Olivares, BL Add. Ms. 25, 689 f. 237, consulta del Conde duque a SM, quoted in Elliott, *Spain and Its World*, 234.

8 André de Barros, *Vida do apostolico padre Antonio Vieyra da Companhia de Jesus, chamado por antonomasia o Grande* (Lisboa, 1746).

9 Kennedy, *Great Powers*, 55.

10 Kennedy, 32–41.

11 C. R. Boxer, *The Dutch in Brazil 1624–1654* (1957; Hamden, CT: Archon Books, 1973), 10–28.

12 Boxer, 31, 43–48.

13 Boxer, 73–74, 82–83, 108–20, 251–58.

14 The discussion above and below is indebted to Charles Wilson, *The Dutch Republic and the Civilization of the Seventeenth Century* (London: Weidenfeld and Nicolson, 1968), esp. 1–41, which remains a clear and balanced account. See Pieter Geyl, *History of the Low Countries: Episodes and Problems. The Trevelyan Lectures 1963 with Four Additional Essays* (London: Macmillan, 1964).

15 For a discussion on Grotius and indeed the Dutch contribution to intellectual currents of the period, see Jonathan I. Israel, *Radical Enlightenment: Philosophy and the Making of Modernity 1650–1750* (Oxford: Oxford University Press, 2001), esp. 447–54.

16 Wilson, *The Dutch Republic*, 42–73, 206–29 for the discussion above.

17 Anthony Farrington, *Trading Places: The East India Company and Asia 1600–1834* (London: The British Library, 2002), 48.

18 Farrington, 41–7, and T. O. Lloyd, *The British Empire 1558–1995*, 2nd edn (Oxford: Oxford University Press, rpt. 2000), 14.

19 Kennedy, 59–63; see also on the economy Ralph Davis, *English Overseas Trade 1500–1700* (London: Macmillan, 1973); Brian Murphy, *A History of the British Economy, 1086–1970* (London: Longman, 1973); D. C. Coleman, *The Economy of England 1450–1750* (Oxford: Oxford University Press, 1973); see on the military, C. Barnett, *Britain and Her Army 1509–1970: A Military, Political and Social Survey* (London: Allen Lane, 1970); Kenneth R. Andrews, *Trade, Plunder and Settlement* (Cambridge: Cambridge University Press, 1983); Paul M. Kennedy, *The Rise and Fall of*

British Naval Mastery (London: Allen Lane, 1976). On the sea power of the Netherlands, see Jaap R. Bruijn, *The Dutch Navy at the Seventeenth and Eighteenth Centuries* (Columbia: University of South Carolina Press, 1993).

20 Max Savelle, *The Origins of American Diplomacy: The International History of Angloamerica, 1492–1763*, with the assistance of Margaret Anne Fisher (New York: Macmillan [1967]), 21–2. See Frances Gardiner Davenport, *European Treaties bearing on the History of the United States and its Dependencies to 1648* (Washington, DC: Carnegie Institution of Washington, 1917): I: 213.

21 Kennedy, 56–5; see Robin Briggs, *Early Modern France, 1560–1715* (Oxford: Oxford University Press, 1977).

22 Boxer, 4–9.

23 François Valentijn, *François Valentijn's Description of Ceylon*, trans. and ed. Sinnappah Arasaratnam (London: Hakluyt Society, 1978), 226, 231, 258–60. Two helpful books on the Dutch colonies are W. Ph. Coolhaus, *A Critical Survey of Studies on Dutch Colonial History* (S-Gravenhage: Martinus Nijhoff, 1960) and Om Prakash, *The Dutch East India Company and the Economy of Bengal, 1630–1720* (Princeton: Princeton University Press, 1985). On the Portuguese, for instance, see Sanjay Subrahmanyam, *The Portuguese Empire in Asia, 1500–1700: A Political and Economic History* (London: Longman, 1993). A useful general work is *Historiography of Europeans in Africa and Asia, 1450–1800*, ed. Anthony Disney (Aldershot: Variorum, 1995).

24 Willem Piso, *De Indiae utriusque re naturali et medica libri quatuordecim* (Amsterdam, 1658).

25 Michael Hemmersam, *West-Indianische Reissbeschreibung* (Nuremburg, 1663). For a helpful catalogue of this and other related books once exhibited at the John Carter Brown Library in 1988, see Dagmar Schäffer, *Portuguese Exploration to the West and the Formation of Brazil 1450–1800* (Providence, RI: The John Carter Brown Library, 1988), esp. 65–6. A key study remains important; see Charles R. Boxer, *The Dutch in Brazil*.

26 Om Prakash, *The Dutch East India Company and the Economy of Bengal, 1630–1720* (Princeton: Princeton University Press, 1985), 3, 7.

27 Prakash, 261.

28 Farrington, 48–53.

29 R. B. [Nathaniel Crouch], *The English Empire* (London 1685), 6–7. This is a very rare book. The third edition (1698) was issued by the same printer; the only ostensible difference at the beginning between the 1685 and 1698 editions, first and third, is that the 1698 edition drops the very brief first paragraph in chapter 1. I am using the British Library copy.

30 R.B., 29.

31 R.B., 44.

32 R.B., 44–6.

33 R.B., 60–1 here and below.

34 T. O. Lloyd,, 3.

35 See R.B., 213–14.

36 Farrington, 64, 80–86.
37 See Robert Johnson, *Nova Britannia, Offring Most Excellent Fruites by Planting in Virginia* (London, 1609), A 3 recto.
38 Ibid.
39 Robert Johnson, *The New Life of Virginea: Declaring the Former Successe and Present Estate of that Plantation, Being the Second Part of* Noua Britannia (London, 1612) in *Tracts*, ed. Force, I, 19. I have also consulted the copy in Houghton Library, Harvard, and, where indicated, will refer to this edition in the discussion that follows in the main text. Once again, Johnson dedicated his work to Thomas Smith. For brief discussions of Johnson, both of which relate to Providence, work and resources, see Jeffrey Knapp, *An Empire Nowhere: England, America, and Literature from* Utopia *to* The Tempest (Berkeley: University of California, 1992), 231 and Mary C. Fuller, *Voyages in Print: English Travel to America, 1576–1624* (Cambridge: Cambridge University Press, 1995), 86–7.
40 Johnson, 7.
41 Ibid., 7–8.
42 Ibid., 15–16.
43 T. A., 'To the Hand' in John Smith, *A Map of Virginia with a Description of the Covntrey, the Commodities, People, Government and Religion . . .* (Oxford, 1612), * 2.
44 William Symonds, 'The Proceedings of the English Colonie in Virginia . . .' in John Smith, *A Map of Virginia with a Description of the Covntrey, the Commodities, People, Government and Religion . . .* (Oxford, 1612), 63–81. Symonds's tract comprised part two of the book. On a later crisis in the relation with the Natives, see Alden T. Vaughan, ' "Expulsion of the Savages": English policy and the Virginia Massacre of 1622', *William and Mary Quarterly* 35 (1978), 57–84.
45 See John Smith, *A Description of New England* (London, 1616), 20.
46 Samuel Purchas, *Hakluytus Posthumous or Purchas His Pilgrimes Contayning a History of the World in Sea Voyages and Lande Travells by Englishmen and others* (20 vols. Glasgow, 1906), XIV, 427–8. This edition, which consists of twenty volumes, is a reprint of the 1625 edition. I have also consulted the 1613, 1614, 1617 and 1626 editions. See also Purchas, *Hakluytus*, I, xxiv–xxvii for discussion of the editions. The 'Publisher's Note' asserts the last edition (1626) to be a distinct work and not volume five of the 'Pilgrimes' as it is often considered.
47 Purchas, I, xlix.
48 For a useful study, including translation and background such as Cromwell's 'Western Design', especially in Hakluyt, Purchas, Gage, Stevens and others, see Colin Steele, *English Interpreters of the Iberian New World From Purchas to Stevens: A Bibliographical Study. 1603–1726* (Oxford: Dolphin Book Co., 1975); and for a helpful annotated bibliography, including a good account of the versions of Las Casas, see A. F. Allison, *English Translations from the Spanish and Portuguese to the Year 1700: An Annotated Catalogue of the Extant Printed Versions (excluding Dramatic Adaptations)* (London: Dawson of Pall Mall, 1974).

49 Thomas Gage, *The English-American his Travail by Sea and Land: Or a New Survey of the West Indias* . . . (London, 1648), A 3 verso, see A 3 recto.

50 See Thomas Gage, *Nouvelle Relation des Indes Occidentales, contenant les voyages de Thomas Gage* . . . (Paris, 1676), ã iij recto; my translation here and below; see ã iij verso.

51 Philip Boucher, *Les Nouvelles Frances: France in America, 1500–1815: An Imperial Perspective* (Providence, RI: John Carter Brown Library, 1989), 54.

52 See ibid., 31.

53 On Virginia's problems, temporal and spiritual (and of its neighbour Maryland), see Anon., *Virginia and Maryland. – Or, the Lord Baltamore's Prited Case, Uncased and Answered. – Shewing, the Illegality of his Patent* . . . (London, 1655); Hammond, *Leah and Rachel* (London, 1656); R.G., *Virginia's Cure: or an Advisive Narrative concerning Virginia. Discovering the True Ground of the Churches Unhappiness, and the only true Remedy* . . . (London, 1662), 'A List of Those That Have Been Executed for the Late Rebellion in Virginia, by Sir William Berkeley, Governor of the Colony . . .' in *Tracts*, ed. Force, II, 1–48; III, 1–32 and 1–20; I, 1–4.

54 David Armitage, 'The British Empire and the Civic Tradition 1656–1742' (unpublished PhD dissertation, Cambridge University, 1992), 61–2; see Karen Ordahl Kupperman, 'Errand to the Indies: Puritan Colonization from Providence Island through the Western Design', *William and Mary Quarterly* 44 (1988), 70–99.

55 Roger Williams to John Winthrop 15 February 1654/5 in *The Correspondence of Roger Williams*, ed. Glenn W. LaFantasie (2 vols. Providence, RI: Published for The Rhode Island Historical Society by Brown University Press/University Press of New England, 1988), II, 248, quoted in Armitage, 'The British Empire', 63. In Gage's terms the true Rome was attacking the Romish Babylon. Apparently, Cromwell found it hard to assimilate the defeat of the English in a providential framework just as Philip II had with the defeat of the armada. Roger Williams reported this retrospectively; see Williams to John Leverett, 11 October 1675 in *The Correspondence of Roger Williams*, quoted in ibid., 66–7.

56 Bartolomé de Las Casas, *The Tears of the INDIANS: BEING An Historical and True Account of the Cruel Massacres and Slaughters of above Twenty Millions of innocent People; Committed by the Spaniards in the Islands of Hispaniola, Cuba, Jamaica, & c. As also, in the Continent of Mexico, Peru, and Other Places of the West-Indies, to the Total Destruction of those Countries. Written in Spanish by Casaus, and Eye-witness of those Things; and Made English by J. P.* (London, 1656), A 3 recto–A 3 verso. Some of the pages of the prefatory matter are numbered and some are not and their numbers are extrapolated from the numbered pages. Another translation came out after the Glorious Revolution: *POPERY Truly Display'd in Bloody Colours: Or, a Faithful NARRATIVE of the Horrid and Unexampled Massacres, Butcheries, and all manner of Cruelties, that Hell and Malice could invent, committed by the Popish Spanish Party on the Inhabitants of West-India* . . . (London, 1689).

57 Las Casas, *The Tears*, A 3 verso–A 4 verso.

58 Ibid., A 4 verso–A 6 recto.

59 For a fine discussion of Harrington that argues that *Oceana* was not a utopia and was 'a blue-print, not a fantasy', see Armitage, 'The British Empire', 17, 80–91.

60 See Anonymous, 'Preface' in Bartolomé de Las Casas, *An Account of the First Voyages and Discoveries Made by the Spaniards in America* (London, 1699), no pagination.

61 See André Saint-Lu, *Las Casas Indigéniste: études sur la vie et l'œuvre du défenseur des Indiens* (Paris: L'Harmattan, 1982), 168–9. Allison speculates that the reason for this English version of Las Casas (1699) might 'have had some connection with the Spanish opposition to the Darien Expedition of 1698–1700'; Allison, *English Translations*, 42. On the 1699 English version and general information on the French and English translations of Las Casas, see Steele, *English Interpreters*, 107–8, 175–6.

62 John Harris, *Navigantium atque Itinerantium Bibliotheca: or, a Compleat Collection of Voyages and Travels: Consisting of above Four Hundred of the most Authentick Writers; Beginning with Hackluit, Purchass, & c. in English; Ramusio in Italian; Thevenot, &c in French; De Bry, and Grynæi Novus Orbis in Latin; the Dutch East-India Company in Dutch: And Continued, with Others of Note, that have Publish'd Histories, Voyages, Travels, or Discoveries, in the English, Latin, French, Italian, Spanish, Portuguese, German, or Dutch Tongues. . . .* (London, 1705).

63 Harris devoted several chapters in the second volume to Thévenot's travels in the Middle East; see ibid., Book II, chapters, ix–xi.

64 Harris, 'The Epistle Dedicatory', ibid., 1; neither the 'Epistle' nor the Address 'To the Reader' is paginated; each is two pages. There will, therefore, be no additional notes to page numbers in these two brief prefatory pieces. Unlike Gage, Harris was presenting a collection and obviously did not see the need of criticism.

65 John Oldmixon *The British Empire in America . . .* (London, 1708), xxxv.

66 Marcel Trudel, *Histoire de la Nouvelle-France*, vol. 2, *Le Comptoir, 1604–1627* (Montreal: Fides, 1966), 9–15. See W. J. Eccles, *France in America* (1972; Vancouver: Fitzhenry and Whiteside, 1973), 14–15.

67 All of the editions of Lescarbot's *Histoire de la Nouvelle France* (1609, 1611–12, 1617–18) included an appendix consisting of a short collection of poems, *Les Muses de la Nouvelle France*. The last two editions involved a reshaping and a completion of the account of New France until the date of composition. See Anthony Pagden, *Spanish Imperialism and the Political Imagination, Studies in European and Spanish-American Social and Political Theory 1513–1830* (New Haven: Yale University Press, 1990), 4.

68 Marc Lescarbot, *Histoire de la Nouvelle-France . . .* (Paris, 1609), ã ij recto, ã iij recto and verso, ã iiij recto; my translations here and below.

69 Lescarbot, *Histoire* (1609), b ij verso.

70 Ibid., b iij recto–b iij verso.

71 Ibid., b iiij recto.

72 Ibid.

73 See Frank Lestringant, *Le Huguenot et le Sauvage* (Paris: Klincksieck, 1990), 267.

74 Ibid., 266–70.

75 Lescarbot, *Histoire* (1609), b iv verso. In his address to Pierre Jeannin in the 1612 edition, Lescarbot used this language of republicanism; see Marc Lescarbot, *Histoire de la Nouvelle-France* . . . (Paris, 1612), jx.

76 Pierre d'Avity, sieur de Montmartin, described America in his *Les Estats, empires et principavtez dv monde* . . . (Paris, 1613), 133–4.

77 In 1615 Edward Grimeston translated D'Avity (he used 'Avity' whereas modern historians seem to use 'd'Avity') and dedicated it to the Earl of Suffolk, who has provided the translator protection in France, the Netherlands and Spain. Pierre d'Avity, 'The Epistle Dedicatorie' in *The Estates, Empires, & Principallities of the World* . . ., trans. Edward Grimeston (London, 1615), n.p. [2pp.]. As a result of these differences, I include my own translations and, in key places, compare d'Avity's original with Grimeston's translation.

78 D'Avity, *Les Estats*. British Isles (1–42), France (131), Spain and its possessions (132–333), of which the New World (257–333). I am using d'Avity's headings, which included Ireland under the rubric of 'Grande-Bretagne'. Portugal is placed under the Spanish possessions.

79 Ibid., 263–4; d'Avity, *Les Estats*, 263.

80 D'Avity, *The Estates*, 222, see 221.

81 Ibid., 265.

82 D'Avity, *Les Estats*, 322. As d'Avity's syntax and diction here is difficult if not awkward, I have taken some liberties in the translation to render the two sentences in a clear and coordinated sentence. Grimeston left out this passage, so that he kept his promise, in the prefatory matter, to make changes in d'Avity's text.

83 Sagard, quoted in W. J. Eccles, *The Ordeal of New France* (Toronto: Canadian Broadcasting Corporation, 1967), 21–2.

84 Philip Boucher, *Les Nouvelles Frances*, 24–7.

85 For background on these companies and Richelieu's colonial policy, which has informed my discussion here and below, see Mathé Allain, 'French Colonial Policy in America and the Establishment of the Louisiana Colony' (unpublished PhD dissertation, The University of Southwestern Louisiana, 1984), 17–31. On the number of companies with royal charters, see Emile Salone, *La Colonisation de la Nouvelle-France: Étude sur les origines de la nation canadienne française* (Paris, n.d.), 18. See also Marcel Trudel, *The Beginnings of New France, 1524–1622* (Toronto: McClelland and Stewart, 1973), 171.

86 On religious policy in New France and on the status of French Protestants, see J. Saintoyant, 'Des Politiques religieuses et indigènes des diverses colonizations européenes avant le XIXe siècle', *Revue d'Histoire des Colonies Françaises* 23 (1935), 235–304 and Cornelius Jaenen, 'The Persistence of Protestant Presence in New France', *Proceedings of the Second Meeting of the Western Society for French History* (1974), 29–40, cited in Allain, 'French Colonial', 27.

87 Gabriel Sagard, 'Av Lecteur', *Histoire dv Canada et voyages qve les freres mineurs Recollets y ont faicts pour la conuersion des Infidelles* . . . (Paris, 1636).

88 Ibid., 787.
89 Gabriel Sagard, *Le Grand Voyage du Pays des Hurons*, ed. Réal Ouellet and Jack Warwick (Montréal: Presses de l'Université de Montréal, 1990), quoted and translated in Luca Codignola, 'The Holy See and the Conversion of the Indians in French and British North America, 1486–1760' in *America in European Consciousness, 1493–1750*, ed. Karen Ordahl Kupperman (Chapel Hill: University of North Carolina Press, 1993), 215. On Sagard's view of the Natives, see Dickason, *Myth*, 78–9.
90 Boucher, *Les Nouvelles*, 28. On Le Jeune, see Peter A. Goddard, 'Christianization and Civilization in Seventeenth-Century French Colonial Thought' (unpublished D.Phil. dissertation, University of Oxford, 1990), 57–119; Rémi Ferland, 'Procédés de rhétorique et fonction conative dans les Relations du Père Paul LeJeune' (unpublished PhD dissertation, Université Laval, 1991); Yvon Le Bras, *L'Amérindien dans les* Relations *du Père Paul Le Jeune* and Pierre Dostie, *Le Lecteur suborné dans cinq textes missionaires de la Nouvelle-France*, 2 vols. in 1 vol. (Sainte-Foy: Éditions de la Huit, 1994); Dostie begins at 159. Ferland, who is interested in rhetoric and discourse analysis, examines Le Jeune's work in terms of one of Roman Jakobson's six inalienable factors of communication – 'la fonction "conative" ' – or the orientation towards the addressee to modify his comportment or opinion, the purest form of which occurs in the imperative or vocative; ibid., 4. Le Bras and Dostie are both interested in exploring the Amerindian as other in Le Jeune and various French missionaries like Gabriel Sagard and Louis Hennepin. Neither of these authors touches on the example of Spain or any other topics concerning Spain.
91 Francisco Bressani, *Breve Relatione d'alcvne missioni de' PP. della Compagnia di Giesù nella Nuova Francia* (Macerata, 1653) in *The Jesuit Relations and Allied Documents*, ed. Reuban Gold Thwaites (73 vols., Cleveland: Burrows Bros. Co., 1896–1901), XXXVIII, 227–8. Bressani was also a mapmaker; see Olive Dickason, *The Myth of the Savage and the Beginnings of the French Colonialism in the Americas* (Edmonton: University of Alberta Press, 1984), 110.
92 Goddard, 'Christianization', viii, 183–212.
93 Jean Baptiste Du Tertre, *Histoire générale des isles de S. Christophe . . .* (Paris, 1654), 396–8.
94 Ibid., 24.
95 Philip Boucher, *Les Nouvelles*, 49–51.
96 Blaise François de Pagan, Comte de Merveilles, *Relation historique et géographique* (Paris, 1655); see also Philip Boucher, *Les Nouvelles*, 37.
97 Blaise François de Pagan, *An Historical & Geographical Description of the Great Country & River of the Amazones in America . . .* trans. William Hamilton (London, 1661), A 3 recto.
98 Ibid., A 3 verso.
99 Louis Hennepin, *Description de la Louisiane, nouvellement decouverte au Sud'Oüest de la Nouvelle France, par ordre du roy. Auec la carte du pays: les mœurs & la maniere de vivre des sauvages. Dedie'e a sa Majeste. . .* (Paris, 1683); my translation here and below. Besides mentioning that

Hennepin was a Recollet missionary, the title page listed him as a 'Notaire Apostolique'. I am using the 1688 edition at Houghton Library, Harvard, which is a reprint, page for page, of the edition of 1683. Philip Boucher calls much of Hennepin's work 'unreliable because he did not accompany La Salle to the mouth of the Mississippi'; Boucher, *Les Nouvelles*, 59, 64–6.

100 Hennepin, 'Epistre', ã ii verso, see ã ii recto.

101 On Hennepin, in a study that concentrates on the representations made to the reader and on the way the Native is represented, see Dostie, *Le Lecteur*, 183–94, 213, 219. Dostie discusses Sagard, Le Jeune and other French missionaries in New France; ibid., 161–70.

102 Kennedy, *Great Powers*, 100–1.

103 Kennedy, 101–5.

104 Kennedy, 105–6.

105 For a detailed discussion of the role of the Netherlands in slavery, see Johannes Menne Postma, *The Dutch in the Atlantic Slave Trade, 1600–1815* (Cambridge: Cambridge University Press, 1990).

106 Boxer, 31, 43–48.

107 'Code Noir . . . Mars 1685' *Receuils de Réglemens, Édits, Déclarations et Arrêts, Concernant le Commerce, l'Administration de la Justice, & la Police des Colonies Françaises de l'Amerique, & les Engagés. Avec Le Code Noir, Et l'Addition audit Code. Nouvelle Édition* (Paris: Libraires Associés, M.DCC.LXV.), 67; see 67–83 [supplements of the changes to the Code Noir appear on 84–174]; Baldwin Room copy, Toronto Reference Library. The phrase is 'les peuples que la Divine Providence a mis sous notre obéissance'. In consulting the *Dictionnaire de L'Académie française*, 1st Edition (1694) the word in this context is glossed as being put under a king's domination: 'On dit, *Vivre sous l'obeïssance d'un Prince*, pour dire, Estre sous sa domination: & on dit dans le mesme sens. *Les Peuples qui sont sous l'obeïssance, dans l'obeïssance du Roy. il a reduit, rangé cette Province sous son obeïssance. dans tous les pays, dans toutes les terres de l'obeïssance du Roy. se soustraire de l'obeïssance d'un Prince. rentrer dans l'obeïssance de son Prince' (135)*. This dictionary is now online: see *Dictionnaire de l'Académie Française Database Project* directed by R. Wooldridge & I. Leroy-Turcan, the ARTFL Project and The University of Chicago at <http://www.lib.uchicago. edu/efts/ARTFL/projects/dicos/ACADEMIE/PREMIERE/>. I chose 'obeisance' in the sense of definitions 2 and 2 b in the OED, which, when taken together, combines authority and dominion, both senses of the word having long histories in the English language and being related to 'obedience'. See *Oxford English Dictionary Online* (Second Edition, 1989). Using the same dictionaries with their access to etymologies and historical contexts, I have chosen 'memorandum' for the original term: 'Memoire. s. m. Escrit pour instruire, pour faire ressouvenir de quelque chose. *J'oublieray vostre affaire, si vous ne m'en donnez un memoire. memoire instructif' (38)*.

108 'Code Noir . . . Mars 1685', 67–77. S'attrouper. v. n. p. S'assembler en troupe. Il est deffendu par les Ordonnances de s'attrouper. il s'attroupa une quantité de gens. au son du tocsin les paysans des environs s'attrouperent; see *Dictionnaire de L'Académie française*, 1st Edition (1694), 602; for 'fouet', see

the same source: Foüet, se dit aussi Des coups de verges dont on chastie les enfants. Donner le foüet. meriter le foüet. avoir le foüet. sujet au foüet. craindre le foüet. menacer du foüet. Il se dit aussi Des coups de verges dont la Justice fait chastier quelques criminels; & dans ce sens on dit, Condamné au foüet. avoir le foüet par les carrefours. avoir le foüet sous la custode (481); children and criminals receive this corporal punishment. Whip or whisk are usual translations for foüet. The Code referred to 'le jarret', which also could have been translated as hock or ham. The fleur-de-lys was a royal emblem of France, which still appears on the flag of Quebec. For more on the Code Noir, see 6531. – Documents Historiques: Le Code Noir at <http://www.haiti-reference.com/>; Louis Sala-Molins, *Le Code noir, ou Le calvaire de Canaan*, 4eme. Edition (Paris: Presses universitaires de France, 1987); *Le code noir / introduction et notes de Robert Chesnais* (Paris: L'esprit frappeur, 1998).

109 Leonard Guelke, 'Freehold Farmers and Frontier Settlers, 1657–1780', *Historiography of Europeans in Africa and Asia, 1450–1800*, ed. Anthony Disney (Aldershot: Variorum, 1995), 174–7, see 175–216; for an earlier version, see *The Shaping of South African Society, 1652–1840* (Middletown CT: Wesleyan University Press, 1989), 66–108.

110 Neil Salisbury, 'Squanto: Last of the Patuxets', in D. Sweet and G. Nash, ed. *Struggle and Survival in Colonial America* (Berkeley: University of California Press, 1981), 228–46, 241–2.

111 William Bradford, *Of Plymouth Plantation 1620–1647*, ed. Samuel Eliot Morison (New York: Alfred A. Knopf, 1952, rpt. 1991), 81.

112 Ibid., 81n.3, 83 n.8–9.

113 Ibid., 83, see *Purchas His Pilgrimes* IV.1778.

114 Bradford, 83.

115 Ibid., 84, see 83.

116 Ibid., 85.

117 Ibid., 87.

118 Ibid., 114.

119 See Kennedy, 14–15, to which my discussion is indebted; on the Portuguese expulsion from Japan, see G. B. Sasom, *The Western World and Japan* (London: Cresset Press, 1950); Charles R. Boxer, *Fidalgos in the Far East, 1550–1770: Fact and Fancy in the History of Macao* (The Hague: M. Nijhoff, 1948) 105–7; his *A Portuguese Embassy (1644–1647)* (London: Kegan Paul, Trench, Trübner & co., ltd., 1928); and his *The Christian Century in Japan, 1549–1650* (Berkeley: University of California Press, 1951), 383–9 and, more recently, A. J. R. Russell-Wood, *The Portuguese Empire*, 24, 81. his *A Portuguese Embassy (1644–1647)* (London: Kegan Paul, Trench, Trübner & Co., Ltd., 1928); and his *The Christian Century in Japan, 1549–1650* (Berkeley: University of California Press, 1951), 383–9 and, more recently, A. J. R. Russell-Wood, *The Portuguese Empire*, 24, 81.

120 Sanjay Subrahmanyam, *The Portuguese Empire in Asia, 1500–1700: A Political and Economic History* (London: Longman, 1993), 277.

121 On the role of gunpowder in imperial expansion, see W. H. McNeill, *The Age of Gunpowder Empires 1450–1800* (Washington, DC: American Historical Association, 1989).

122 Lynn Hunt et al., *The Making of the West: Peoples and Cultures* (Boston and New York: Bedford St. Martin's, 2001), 667–70. See G. Vernadsky, *The Tsardom of Muscovy 1547–1682* (New Haven: Yale University Press, 1969); Marc Raeff, *Understanding Imperial Russia: State and Society in the Old Regime*, trans. Arthur Goldhammer (New York: Columbia University Press, 1984) and Lindsey Hughes, *Russia in the Age of Peter the Great* (New Haven: Yale University Press, 1998).

123 For discussion on nature and children, see Peter Coates, *Nature: Western Attitudes Since Ancient Times* (Cambridge: Polity, 1998); Colin Heywood, *A History of Childhood: Children and Childhood in the West from Medieval to Modern Times* (Cambridge: Polity, 2001). Interestingly enough, in regard to the execution of witches, which often meant the killing of women, the Spanish Inquisition very much limited any trials against witches in the colonies (although Mexico was somewhat of an exception), and there was one such execution in New France and none in the Dutch colonies. The English colonies, perhaps because they were subject to less metropolitan control, were more prone to witch trials in which, like that at Salem, children often accursed women of being possessed by the devil. See Wolfgang Behringer, *Witches and Witch-Hunts: A Global History* (Cambridge: Polity, 2004), 143–7.

Chapter 4

1 W. D. Hussey, *The British Empire and Commonwealth 1500 to 1961* (Cambridge: Cambridge University Press, 1963), 102–3, see 104–18. On the Mughal empire, see also Niall Ferguson, *Empire: The Rise and Demise of the British World Order and the Lessons for Global Power* (New York: Basic Books, 2002), 29–31. On the Mughals, the British and India, see Linda Colley, *Captives: Britain, Empire and the World* (2002; London: Pimlico, 2003), esp. 241–65. On related topics concerning the British empire in context, see C. A. Bayley, *Indian Society and the Making of the British Empire* (Cambridge: Cambridge University Press, 1988) *and Imperial Meridian: The British Empire and the World, 1780–1830* (London: Longman, 1989); T. A. Heathcote, *The Military in British India: The Development of the British Land Forces in South Asia, 1600–1947* (Manchester: Manchester University Press, 1995); Nancy F. Koehn, *The Power of Commerce, Economy and Governance in the First British Empire* (Ithaca, NY: Cornell University Press, 1995); Anthony Pagden, *Lords of All the World: Ideologies of Empire in Spain, Britain and France c. 1500–c.1800* (New Haven and London: Yale University Press, 1995); Matthew H. Edney, *Mapping an Empire: The Geographical Construction of British India, 1765–1843* (Chicago: University of Chicago Press, 1997); David Armitage, *The Ideological Origins of the British Empire* (Cambridge: Cambridge University Press, 2000); Susan Brigden, *New Worlds, Lost Worlds: The Rule of the Tudors, 1485–1603* (London: Allen Lane, 2000); David B. Abernethy, *The Dynamics of Global Dominance: European Overseas Empires 1415–1980* (New Haven: Yale University Press, 2001).

2 Richard Koebner, *Empire* (Cambridge: Cambridge University Press, 1961), 297.

3 See, for instance, Bernard Bailyn, *The Ideological Origins of the American Revolution* (Cambridge, MA: Harvard University Press, 1967); Piers Mackesy, *The War for America 1775–1783* (Lincoln: University of Nebraska Press, 1993), Tom Pocock, *Battle for Empire: The Very First World War* (London: Michael O'Mara, 1998), and Fred Anderson, *Crucible of War: The Seven Years' War and the Fate of Empire in British North America, 1754–1766* (London: Faber, 2000).

4 Paul Kennedy, *The Rise and Fall of the Great Powers* (New York: Random House, 1987), 84–6. On free trade, see Bernard Semmel, *The Rise of Free Trade Imperialism* (Cambridge: Cambridge University Press, 1970).

5 Kennedy, 87–8; see Alice Clare Carter, *The Dutch Republic in Europe in the Seven Years War* (London: Macmillan, 1971) and Carter's *Neutrality or Commitment: the Evolution of Dutch Foreign Policy, 1667–1795* (London: Edward Arnold, 1975).

6 Léon Pètre et Joseph Trillat, *La France Outre-Mer* (Paris: Les Editions Jos. Vermaut, [.n.d.]), 17; even though the book is undated, in their preliminary note, the authors cite an event in 1931, so I am assuming the work is after that.

7 See Geoffrey Brunn, *Europe and the French Imperium, 1799–1815* (New York: Harper & Brothers, 1938); Edward Vose Gulick, *Europe's Classical Balance of Power* (New York: W. W. Norton, 1967); Derek Mackay and H. M. Scott, *The Rise of the Great Powers 1648–1815* (London: Longman, 1983), and Kennedy, esp. 84–9.

8 Adam Smith, quoted in Goldwin Smith, *Commonwealth or Empire: A Bystander's View of the Question* (New York and London: Macmillan, 1902), 62 here and below. Alberta copy inscribed by Smith to H. N. Barry.

9 Jonathan Mayhew, *Two Discourses* . . . (London, 1760), 56–57 (see 8, 33, 38, 54), quoted in Richard Koebner, *Empire*, 118, 332.

10 Achille Viallate, *Essais d'Histoire Diplomatique Américaine* (Paris: Librairie Orientale et Américaine, n.d.) et 7. The Introduction is signed June 1905. Viallete says that the study of American diplomacy (which had to do in part with boundaries) was especially appropriate because of the Spanish-American war, as 'the foundations of a "much-greater America"' ('d'une "Plus-grande Amérique"') (iii, see I-ii); my translation.

11 Alexis de Tocqueville, *Democracy in America*, ed. J.P. Mayer and trans. George Lawrence (1966; Garden City, NY: Doubleday & Company, 1969), 412, see 413.

12 See Richard Pares, *War and Trade in the West Indies 1739–63* (Oxford: Clarendon Press, 1936); Walter Louis Dorn, *Competition for Empire 1740–1763* (New York: Harper & Brothers, 1940); A. T. Mahan, *The Influence of Sea Power upon History 1660–1783* (London: Methuen, 1965); Max Savelle, *Empires to Nations: Expansion in America, 1713–1824* (Minneapolis: University of Minnesota Press, 1974); Kennedy, 92–115, esp. 93.

13 Kennedy, 97, see 94–115. I am once more indebted to Kennedy. See also Paul Kennedy, *The Rise and Fall of British Naval Mastery* (London: Allen Lane,

1976). For a more recent study, see Angus Maddison, *The World Economy: A Millennial Perspective* (Paris: Development Centre of the Organisation for Economic Co-operation and Development, 2001).

14 Pierre François-Xavier Charlevoix, *Histoire et description générale de la Nouvelle-France avec le journal historique d'un voyage fait par ordre du Roi dans L'Amérique Septentrionale* (3 vols. Paris, 1744), I, 2, quoted in Philip Boucher, *Les Nouvelles Frances: France in America, 1500–1815: An Imperial Perspective* (Providence, RI: John Carter Borwn Library, 1989), 86.

15 Charlevoix, I, iii–iv. On Charlevoix, see Bruce Trigger, 'The Historian's Indian: Native-Americans in Canadian Historical Writing from Charlevoix to the Present', *Canadian Historical Review* 67 (1986), 315–42.

16 For a recent key study of the Enlightenment, see Jonathan I. Israel, *Radical Enlightenment: Philosophy and the Making of Modernity 1650–1750* (Oxford: Oxford University Press, 2001).

17 Guillaume-Thomas Raynal, *Histoire philosophique et politique des établissemens et du commerce des Européens dans les deux Indes* (La Haye: Gosse fils, 1776), 1:119, see 1:113–14, 118. My translation.

18 Raynal, 1: 119.

19 Raynal, 1:119.

20 Raynal, 1:119–20.

21 Raynal, 1:120.

22 Raynal 1:120.

23 Raynal, 1:120.

24 Raynal, 1:139.

25 Raynal, 1: 139.

26 Kennedy, *Great Powers*, 79–84; see P. G. M. Dickson, *The Financial Revolution in England: A Study in the Development of Public Credit 1688–1756* (London: Macmillan, 1967); Charles Wilson, *Anglo-Dutch Commerce and Finance in the Eighteenth Century* (Cambridge: Cambridge University Press, 1966); James C. Riley, *International Government Finance and the Amsterdam Capital Market 1740–1815* (Cambridge: Cambridge University Press, 1980); and J. F. Bosher, *French Finances, 1770–1795: From Business to Bureaucracy* (Cambridge: Cambridge University Press, 1970); Ralph Davis, *The Rise of the Atlantic Economies* (London: Weidenfeld and Nicolson, 1973); John Garretson Clark, *La Rochelle and the Atlantic Economy During the Eighteenth Century* (Baltimore: Johns Hopkins University Press, 1981); Angus Calder, *Revolutionary Empire: The Rise of the English-Speaking Empires from the Fifteenth Century to the 1780s* (1981; rev. ed. London: Pimlico, 1998); Carolyn Webber and Aaron Wildavsky, *A History of Taxation and Expenditure in the Western World* (New York: Simon and Schuster, 1986); Maddison (2001). On the economics of Spain to the end of the Seven Years War, for instance financiers, see Henry Kamen, *Empire: How Spain Became a World Power 1492–1763* (2002; New York: HarperCollins, 2003), esp. 40–1, 84–9, 292–6, 403–05.

27 Anthony Farrington, *Trading Places: The East India Company and Asia 1600–1834* (London: The British Library, 2002), 48–53.

28 Farrington, 98–106.

29 Philip Schofield, 'Editorial Introduction', Jeremy Bentham, *Colonies, Commerce, and Constitutional Law: Rid Yourselves of Ultramaria and Other Writings on Spain and Spanish America*, ed. Philip Schofield (Oxford: Clarendon Press, 1995), xv–xvi.

30 Bentham, Letter 15, Part 1, *Colonies*, 126–27.

31 Bentham, Letter 16, Part 1, 130.

32 See Bailyn (1967); Ian R. Christie and Benjamin W. Larabee, *Empire and Independence, 1760–1776* (New York: Norton, 1976); Calder, *Revolutionary Empire* 1981; rev. 1998); Theodore Draper, *A Struggle for Power: The American Revolution* (New York: Times Books, 1996).

33 On the Dutch and revolution more generally, see Simon Schama, *Patriots and Liberators: Revolution in the Netherlands, 1780–1813* (New York: Alfred Knopf, 1977).

34 See also Carter, *The Dutch Republic* (1971); Douglass C. North and Robert Paul Thomas, *The Rise of the Western World: A New Economic History* (Cambridge: Cambridge University Press, 1973); J. H. Parry, *Trade and Dominion: The European Overseas Empire in the Eighteenth Century* (London: Weidenfeld and Nicolson, 1971); Peter Padfield, *Tides of Empires: Decisive Naval Campaigns and the Rise of the West*, 2 vols, (London: Routledge & Kegan Paul, 1979, 1982) and his *Maritime Supremacy & the Opening of the Western Mind: Naval Campaigns that Shaped the Modern World, 1588–1782* (London: John Murray, 1999).

35 D. K. Fieldhouse, *The Colonial Empires: A Comparative Survey from the Eighteenth Century* (1965; London: Weidenfeld and Nicolson, 1966), 50–4.

36 See, for instance, Beverly Lemire, *Fashion's Favourite: The Cotton Trade and the Consumer in Britain, 1660–1800* (Oxford: Oxford University Press, 1991).

37 Kennedy, Great Powers, 121, 132–3, especially, but I am indebted to 115–39 here and below. See John Edward Douglas Binney, *British Public Finance and Administration 1774–1792* (Oxford: Clarendon Press, 1958); Glen St. John Barclay, *The Empire Is Marching: A Study of the Military Effort of the British Empire* (London: Weidenfeld & Nicolson, 1976); Winfried Baumgart, *Imperialism: The Idea and Reality of British and French Colonial Expansion* (rev. ed. Oxford: Oxford University Press, 1982); Geoffrey Best, *War and Society in Revolutionary Europe, 1770–1870* (London: Fontana, 1982); Frank Tallett, *War and Society in Early-modern Europe, 1495–1715* (London: Routledge, 1992); M. S. Anderson, *War and Society in Europe of the Old Regime, 1618–1789* (Montreal: McGill-Queen's University Press, 1998). Napoleon's invasion of Russia led to a backlash against the cultural and intellectual influence of Paris on the life of the Russian aristocracy. Leo Tolstoy represents this, among much else, in his *War and Peace*, trans. Louise and Aylmer Maude (Oxford: Oxford University Press, 1991, rpt.1998). For a discussion of Tolstoy and this aspect of the history of Russian culture, see Orlando Figes, *Natasha's Dance: A Cultural History of Russia* (2002; London, 2003), 101–18. On Napoleon's influence in Europe and beyond, see Geoffrey Brunn, *Napoleon and His Empire* (1972); Martyn Lyon, *Napoleon Bonaparte and the Legacy of the French Revolution* (Basingstoke: Macmillan, 1994) and

Lynn Hunt et al., *The Making of the West: Peoples and Cultures* (Boston/New York: Bedford/St. Martin's, 2001), esp. 798.

38 See Lester D. Langley, *The Americas in the Age of Revolution, 1750–1850* (New Haven: Yale University Press, 1997).

39 D. K. Fieldhouse, *The Colonial Empires: A Comparative Survey from the Eighteenth Century*, 2nd edn (Houndsmills and London: Macmillan Education, 1982, rpt. 1987), 104; my discussion above and below is indebted to 100–25.

40 Fieldhouse, 112–20.

41 Fieldhouse, 120–2. See Abernethy (2001) and Maddison (2001).

42 Fieldhouse, 122–5.

43 Dominic Lieven, *Empire: The Russian Empire and Its Rivals* (2000; New Haven and London: Yale University Press, 2001), 206–9, 272.

44 John P. LeDonne, *The Russian Empire and the World, 1700–1917: The Geopolitics of Expansion and Containment* (New York and Oxford: Oxford University Press, 1997), esp. 23–30, 39–41 and Peter Englund, *The Battle That Shook Europe: Poltava and the Birth of the Russian Empire* (1992; London and New York: I. B. Taurus, 2003).

45 Lieven, 158–9.

46 See, for instance, Frederick Jackson Turner, *The Frontier in American History* (New York: H. Holt and Co., 1920). On the World Columbian exposition, see Jonathan Hart, *Columbus, Shakespeare, and the Interpretation of the New World* (New York and Houndmills: Palgrave Macmillan, 2003), esp. 48–74.

47 David J. Weber, *The Spanish Frontier in North America* (New Haven and London: Yale University Press, 1992), 147–8, 179–83, 236–7, 269–70.

48 Ray Allen Billington with James Blaine Hedges, *Westward Expansion: A History of the American Frontier*, 4th edn (New York: Macmillan, 1974), 9. For a most recent version, see Ray Allen Billington and Martin Ridge, *Westward Expansion: A History of the American Frontier, Sixth Edition, An Abridgement* (Albuquerque: University of New Mexico Press, 2001), 10.

49 Billington, *Westward Expansion, 4th edn*, 16.

50 Billington, *Westward Expansion, 4th edn*, 17.

51 For a recent discussion, see Mark Harrison, *Disease and the Modern World: 1500 to the Present Day* (Cambridge: Polity, 2004), esp. 72–90. See Alfred W. Crosby, *The Columbian Exchange: Biological and Cultural Consequences of 1492* (Westport, CT: Greenwood, 1972); Francis Jennings, *The Invasion of America: Indians, Colonialism, and the Cant of Conquest* (Chapel Hill, NC: University of North Carolina Press, 1975); William Cronon, *Changes in the Land: Indians, Colonists, and the Ecology of New England* (New York: Hill & Wang, 1983); Terry G. Jordan and Matti Kaups, *The American Backwoods Frontier: An Ethnic and Ecological Interpretation* (Baltimore, MD: Johns Hopkins University Press, 1989); Ian Steele, *Warpaths: Invasions of North America* (New York: Oxford University Press, 1994); *In the Wake of Contact: Biological Responses to Contact*, eds. Clark Spencer Larsen and George R. Milner (New York: Wiley-Liss, 1994); Colin G. Calloway, *The American Revolution in Indian Country: Crisis and Diversity in Native*

American Communities (New York and Cambridge: Cambridge University Press, 1995) and his *New Worlds for All: Indians, Europeans, and the remaking of Early America* (Baltimore, MD: Johns Hopkins University Press, 1997); Andrew Cayton, *Frontier Indiana* (Bloomington: Indiana University Press, 1996); Eric Hinderaker, *Elusive Empire: Constructing Colonialism in the Ohio Valley, 1673–1800* (New York and Cambridge: Cambridge University Press, 1997); Noble David Cook, *Born to Die: Disease and the New World Conquest, 1492–1650* (New York and Cambridge: Cambridge University Press, 1998); Gary Clayton Anderson, *The Indians of the Southwest, 1580–1830* (Norman: University of Oklahoma Press, 1999). See also Billington, *Westward Expansion,4th edn*, 121–9.

52 Weber, 282–5.

53 Weber, 271–82. See also *The Louisiana Purchase and American Expansion, 1803–1898*, eds. Sanford Levinson and Bartholomew H. Sparrow (Lanham: Rowan & Littlefield, 2005). In this volume, for the first incorporation debate, see Gary Lawson and Guy Seidman, 19–40; on Jefferson and expansion, see Peter S. Onuf, 41–68; on the Louisiana Purchase and the American Civil War, 69–82; on Texas, see David P. Currie, 111–28.

54 Weber, 283–301.

55 Thomas Jefferson to the President of the United States (James Madison), April 27, 1809, in *12 The Writings of Thomas Jefferson*, ed. Albert Ellery Bergh (1905), 275, 277, quoted in Gary Lawson and Guy Seidman, *The Constitution of Empire: Territorial Expansion and American Legal History* (New Haven and London: Yale University Press, 2004), 1,

56 Lawson and Seidman, 4–7. For other views on legal aspects of U.S. expansion, see *The Louisiana Purchase and American Expansion, 1803–1898*; for instance, Lawson and Seidman, 19–140; Christina Duffy Burnett on the constitution, 181–208; and Bartholomew Sparrow on internal and external empires, 231–50.

57 Bartholomew H. Sparrow, 'Empires External and Internal: Territories, Government Lands, and Federalism in the United States', in *The Louisiana Purchase and American Expansion, 1803–1898*, ed. Sanford Levinson and Bartholomew H. Sparrow (Lanham: Rowan & Littlefield, 2005). 231.

58 Lawson and Seidman, 202–05.

59 Charles Darwin, *The Voyage of the Beagle* (Garden City, NY: Doubleday, 1962), 434, quoted in Alfred W. Crosby, *Ecological Imperialism: The Biological Expansion of Europe, 900–1900* (New York and Cambridge: Cambridge University Press, 1986, rpt. 1992), 217. Crosby cites this passage again at 244.

60 Charles Darwin, *The Voyage of the Beagle* (1839), ch. 18, Dec. 30.

61 See K. R. Howe, *Where the Waves Fall: A New South Sea Islands History from First Settlement to Colonial Rule* (Sydney: George Allen & Unwin, 1984); James Belich, *Making Peoples: A History of the New Zealanders: From Polynesian Settlement to the End of the Nineteenth Century* (Auckland: Allen Lane, 1996).

62 Raewyn Dalziel, 'Southern Islands: New Zealand and Polynesia', *The Nineteenth Century*, ed. Andrew Porter with Alaine Low, Volume III of the

Oxford History of the British Empire, gen. ed. Wm. Roger Louis (Oxford and New York: Oxford University Press, 1999), 573; see 574–96.

63 Dalziel, 573.

64 Dalziel, 576–7. See also Belich, *Making Peoples* (1997).

65 Dalziel, 573–5.

66 Crosby, 223, see 218–37, to which my discussion is indebted.

67 Dalziel, 575–6.

68 Dalziel, 575.

69 Crosby, 218–37. See Harrison M. Wright, *New Zealand, 1769–1840. Early Years of Western Contact* (Cambridge, MA: Harvard University Press, 1959); D. Ian Pool, *The Maori Population of New Zealand, 1769–1971* (Auckland: University of Auckland Press, 1977). For a discussion of the Maori and the Polynesian migration, see Jared Diamond, *Guns, Germs, and Steel: The Fates of Human Societies* (New York and London: W. W. Norton, 1997, rpt. 1999), 53–66.

70 For more studies of slavery, see Philip Curtain, *The Atlantic Slave Trade: A Census* (Madison: University of Wisconsin Press, 1969); Roger Anstey, *The Atlantic Slave Trade and British Abolition, 1760–1810* (London: Macmillan, 1975); James Walvin, *England, Slaves and Freedom, 1776–1838* (Basingstoke: Macmillan, 1986); Ira Berlin, *Many Thousands Gone: The First Two Centuries of Slavery in North America* (Cambridge, MA: Harvard University Press, 1998); Richard Drayton, 'The Collaboration of Labour: Slaves, Empires and Globalizations in the Atlantic World, c.1650–1950', in *Globalization in World History*, ed. A. G. Hopkins (London: Pimlico, 2002), 98–114; Jonathan Hart, *Contesting Empires: Opposition, Promotion, and Slavery* (New York: Palgrave Macmillan, 2005), esp. 91–159.

71 Montesquieu, *Spirit of Laws*, bk. 15, CH. 1, *The Founders' Constitution*, Volume 1, Chapter 15, Document 4, The University of Chicago Press at <http://presspubs.uchicago.edu/founders/documents/v1ch15s4.html>.

72 Montesquieu, *Spirit of Laws*, bk. 15, CH. 5.

73 Montesquieu, bk. 15, CH. 7.

74 Thomas Jefferson to Antoine Louis Claude Destutt de Tracy, January 26, 1811 – *Thomas Jefferson Papers Series 1. General Correspondence. 1651–1827* (American Memory, Library of Congress). Rather than insert 'sic' after 'it's', I think it is fair to say that this was a literate equivalent as a possessive as the form we use today: 'its'. See Simone Goyard Fabre, 'Avant Propos', Antoine-Louis-Claude Destutt de Tracy, *Commentaire sur "L'esprit des lois" de Montesquieu* (Caen: Centre de philosophie politique et juridique, 1992), [1–3], Bibliothèque Nationale de France [BNF]. For Jefferson's English translation, see Destutt de Tracy, *A commentary and review of Montesquieu's Spirit of laws* (Philadelphia, Printed by William Duane, 1811).

75 See M. de Bovis, *Essais sur l'esprit des lois colonials* (Paris: impr. de Everat, 1820), 6; BNF; my translation. This book discusses other aspects of slavery in the colonies; see esp. 5–7, 35–6.

76 'Code Noir . . . Mars 1685' *Receuils de Réglemens, Édits, Déclarations et Arrêts, Concernant le Commerce, l'Administration de la Justice, & la Police*

des Colonies Françaises de l'Amerique, & les Engagés. Avec Le Code Noir, Et l'Addition audit Code. Nouvelle Édition (Paris: Libraires Associés, M.DCC.LXV.), 67; see 67–83 [supplements of the changes to the Code Noir appear on 84–174]; Baldwin Room copy, Toronto Reference Library. See also n. 107 on p. 322 of this volume.

77 'Code Noir . . . Mars 1685', 67–77. S'attrouper. v. n. p. S'assembler en troupe. Il est deffendu par les Ordonnances de s'attrouper. il s'attroupa une quantité de gens. au son du tocsin les paysans des environs s'attrouperent; see *Dictionnaire de L'Académie française*, 1st Edition (1694), 602; see also n. 108 on p. 322 of this volume.

78 Paul Kennedy, *Great Powers*, 79–84; see Dickson, *The Financial Revolution in England* (1967); Wilson, *Anglo-Dutch* (1966); Riley, *International Government Finance* (1980); and Bosher, *French Finances*, (1970); Davis, *Rise* (1975); Clark, *La Rochelle* (1981); Calder, *Revolutionary Empire* (1981); C. Webber and A. Wildavsky, *History of Taxation* (1986); Abernethy (2001).

79 Kennedy, 97, see 94–115. I am once more indebted to Kennedy. See also Paul Kennedy, *The Rise and Fall of British Naval Mastery* (London: Allen Lane, 1976).

80 Henry Folmer, *Franco-Spanish Rivalry in North America 1524–1763* (Glendale, CA: Arthur H Clark Company, 1953), 309–10.

81 Martin Kitchen, *The British Empire and Commonwealth: A Short History* (1994; London: Macmillan, 196), 16.

82 Thomas, 153–61, 170–82, 197–203, 231, 247–61, 270–8; see Elizabeth Donnan, *Documents Illustrative of the History of the Slave Trade to America*, 4 vols. (Washington, DC: Carnegie Institution of Washington, 1930–35); see I: 97; UNESCO, *The Atlantic Slave Trade from the Fifteenth to Nineteenth Century* (Paris: UNESCO, 1979); Moses Finlay, *Ancient Slavery and Modern Ideology* (London: Chatto & Windus, 1980); Robin Blackburn, *The Making of New World Slavery: From the Baroque to the Modern 1492–1800* (London: Verso, 1997); Quenum Alphonse 'Some Remarks on the Christian Churches and the Atlantic Slave Trade from the Fifteenth to the Nineteenth Century', *From Chains to Bonds: The Slave Trade Revisited* (Paris: UNESCO; New York, Berghahn Books, 2001), 267–73.

83 H. M. Feinburg, 'New Data on European Mortality in West Africa: The Dutch on the Gold Coast, 1719–1760', *Historiography*, ed. Anthony Disney, 70, 7283, see 69–82; see the earlier version in *Journal of African History* 15 (1974), 357–71. For a more recent assessment of disease and death among slaves and Europeans, see Harrison, 78–90.

84 Robin Hallett, 'The European Approach to the Interior of Africa in the Eighteenth Century', *Historiography*, ed. A. Disney, 68, see 53–67; for the first appearance of this article, see *Journal of African History* 4 (1963), 191–206.

85 See, for instance, Alfred W. Crosby, *Ecological Imperialism: The Biological Expansion of Europe, 900–1900* (Cambridge: Cambridge University Press, 1986, rpt. 2000) and David E. Stannard, *American Holocaust: The Conquest of the New World* (Oxford: Oxford University Press, 1992, rpt. 1993).

86 For extensive statistics, which I draw on, see Hugh Thomas, *The Slave Trade: The Story of the Atlantic Slave Trade* (New York: Simon & Schuster, 1997).

87 Hugh Thomas, *The Slave Trade*, 481–2, 523, 577, 611–13.

88 An address to the public, from the Pennsylvania Society for promoting the abolition of slavery, and the relief of free negroes, unlawfully held in bondage . . . Signed by order of the Society, B. Franklin, President. Philadelphia, 9th of November, 1789. Pennsylvania Society for promoting the abolition of slavery. Philadelphia, 1789. Library of Congress. American Memory. An American Time Capsule: Three Centuries of Broadsides and Other Printed Ephemera. Library of Congress, Rare Book and Special Collections Division. Printed Ephemera Collection; Portfolio 147, Folder 10.

89 Jeremy Belknap, *A Discourse, Intended to Commemorate the Discovery of America by Christopher Columbus; Delivered at the Request of the Historical Society in Massachusetts, on the 23rd Day of October 1792, Being the Completion of the Third Century Since that Memorable Event* (Boston: Belknap and Hall, 1792), 19.

90 Ibid., 46–7.

91 For this painting, see Hugh Honour, *The New Golden Land* (New York: Pantheon Books, 1975), plate 150.

92 C. R. Boxer, *The Golden Age of Brazil 1695–1750: Growing Pains of a Colonial Society* (Berkeley: University of California Press, 1962, rpt. 1964), 1.

93 Jefferson, who had written about 'life, liberty and the pursuit of happiness', lived in a colony –Virginia, whose population at the time was nearly half African slaves. See Ferguson, *Empire*, 101.

94 *General Treaty signed in Congress at Vienna* (London, 1816), 132, quoted in Thomas, 585. See Thomas, 291–302, 315, 370–71, 414, 423–24, 449–63, 482–84, 499–510, 526–85.

95 Olive Patricia Dickason, *Canada's First Nations: A History of the Founding Peoples from Earliest Times*, 3rd edn (Toronto: Oxford University Press, 2002), 155–6. Richard White says his study 'tells how Europeans and Indians met and regarded each other as alien, as other, as virtually nonhuman'. See R. White, *The Middle Ground: Indians, Empires, and the Republics in the Great Lakes Region, 1650–1815* (New York: Cambridge University Press, 1991, rpt. 1993), ix.

96 Dickason, 160–2, 198. Her clear and extensive account from the Native point of view makes an important contribution to the historiography. For an account of the conflict with the Métis, see Dickason, 240–51.

97 Treaty With the Six Nations: 1789, Avalon Project, Yale Law School at <http://www.yale.edu/lawweb/avalon/ntreaty/six1789.htm>.

98 Unnamed Women and Red Jacket (Seneca), 1791, *Great Speeches*, 35.

99 Red Jacket, 'You Say That You Are Right', in Susan Hazen-Hammond, *Timelines of Native American History: Through the Centuries with Mother Earth and Father Sky* (New York: Perigree Book, 1997), 91.

100 These comments are derived from a paper I wrote in Roman Law for E. J. Weinrib in 1975–6; see R. H. Barrow, *The Romans* (Harmondsworth: Penguin, rpt. 1990).

101 Queen Elizabeth to the Troops at Tilbury, 9 August 1588, British Library MS Harley 6798, art. 18, fol. 87; see *Elizabeth I: Collected Works*, pp. 325–6; on-line, see 'Transcription of Tilbury speech' at <http://www3.newberry.org/elizabeth/exhibit/europeamerica/5.xx.html>. Michael Wood, in Episode 2, 'The Lost Years', of his series 'In Search of Shakespeare' (PBS television; <www.pbs.org>; the series was broadcast 4–25 February 2004) asserted that the Tilbury speech was written down after Elizabeth's death. On women in the early modern period (and especially on Elizabeth I and on witchcraft in the colonies), see Merry E. Weisner, *Women and Gender in Early Modern Europe* (New York: Cambridge University Press, 1993, rpt. 1999), esp. 229–30, 242, 251–2.

102 *The Glory of Women: or, A Looking-Glasse for Ladies*, trans. H.C. Gent. (London: T.H. for Frances Coles, 1652); British Library.

103 Abigail Adams, Letter to John Adams, September 22, 1774. Massachusetts Historical Society. Africans in America. Revolution at <http://www.pbs.org/wgbh/aia/part2/2h23.html>.

104 Aristotle, *Politics*, VII.14.21–22 (1333b–1334a, p. 290).

105 Maria De Fleury, *British Liberty Established, and Gallic Liberty Restored; or, the Triumph of Freedom. A Poem* (London: Peterborough-House Press, 1790), A4r, B1v. British Library.

106 Mary Wollestonecraft, *A Vindication of the Rights of Woman* (Boston: Peter Edes for Thomas and Andrews, 1792), chapter ix; online see <http://www.bartleby.com/144/9.html>. See Mary Wollestonecraft, *Vindication of the Rights of Woman and A Vindication of the Rights of Men*, ed. Janet Todd (Oxford: Oxford University Press, World's Classics, 1999 (Reprint of *Political Writings*, 1994)), pp. 63–283.

107 Olaudah Equiano, *The Life of Olaudah Equiano, or Gustavus Vassa, the African* (London, 1789; rpt. Leeds, 1814; New York: Dover, 1999). The American edition appeared in 1791, the German edition in 1790, and the Dutch edition in 1791. By 1837, there were nine more editions; see Note (1999), iv. The Dover edition uses the Leeds edition of 1814, which is corrected, as does Henry Louis Gates, Jr. in *The Classic Slave Narratives*, ed. H. L. Gates, Jr. (1987; New York: Signet, 2002). 26.

108 Ibid., 2.

109 Ibid.

110 Ibid., 3.

111 Ibid., 23.

112 Ibid., 32.

113 Ibid., 74–5.

114 Ibid., 76.

115 Ibid., 81.

116 Ibid., 180. A number of helpful studies of specific slave societies exist. See, for instance, Robert C.-H. Shell, *Children of Bondage: A Social History of the Slave Society at the Cape of Good Hope, 1652–1838* (Hanover: Wesleyan/New England, 1994).

117 Phillis Wheatley, *Poems on Various Subjects, Religious and Moral* (London: Archibald Bell, 1773).

118 See J. R. Beard, *Toussaint L'Ouverture: A Biography and Autobiography* (Boston: James Redpath, 1863); C. L. R. James, *The Black Jacobins: Toussaint L'Ouverture and the San Domingo Revolution* (New York: Vintage, 1989).

Chapter 5

1 William H. McNeill, 'European Expansion, Power and Warfare Since 1500', *Imperialism and War: Essays on Colonial Wars in Asia and Africa*, eds. J. A. de Moor and H. L. Wesselionhg (Leiden: E. J. Brill/Universitaire pers Leiden, 1989), 12–21 for which I am indebted for the discussion in this paragraph. On the military, health and the tropics, see Philip D. Curtain, *Disease and Empire: The Health of European Troops in the Conquest of Africa* (New York: Cambridge University Press, 1998). On race, see Michael L. Krenn, *The Color of Empire: Race and American Foreign Relations* (Washington, DC: Potomac Books, 2006), which is divided into chapters on white, brown, yellow and black and which has a useful appendix of documents from 1751 to 1967.

2 A contrary view was taken about 120 years after the British government took control over India; see R. C. Dutt, *England and India 1785–1885: A Record of Progress During a Hundred Years* (London: Chatto & Windus, 1897). For reference information about the British empire, see Chris Cook, *Britain in the Nineteenth Century 1815–1914* (London and New York: Longman, 1999), 236–47.

3 Paul Kennedy, *The Rise and Fall of the Great Powers* (New York: Random House, 1987), 148–50 for here and below. The original calculations on industrialization are from P. Bairoch, 'International Industrialization Levels from 1750 to 1980', *Journal of Economic History* 11 (1982), 290ff. and David Kenneth Fieldhouse, *The Colonial Empires: A Comparative Study from the Eighteenth Century* (London: Weidenfeld & Nicolson, 1966), 178. See also P. Deane, 'The Cotton Industry' and E. J. Hobsbawm, 'The British Standard of Living, 1790–1850', and R. M. Hartwell, ' The Rising Standard of Living in England, 1800–1850' in Sima Lieberman, ed. *Europe and the Industrial Revolution* (Cambridge, MA: Schenkman Publishing Co., 1972), 85–98, 163–91, 209–35, and Keith Robbins, *The Eclipse of a Great Power: Modern Britain* (London and New York: Longman, 1983), esp. 49–56. For another view of European economics, see C. P. Kindleberger, *A Financial History of Western Europe* (London: Allen and Unwin, 1984) and of global economies, see David Landes, *The Wealth and Poverty of Nations* (London: Little, Brown, 1998).

4 See Daniel Headrick, *The Tools of Empire: Technology and European Imperialism in the Nineteenth Century* (New York: Oxford University Press, 1981). On technology and power, especially as pertaining to military, administration and medicine, see Philip Curtain, *The World and the West: The European Challenge and the Overseas Response in the Age of Empire* (New York: Cambridge University Press, 2000), 19–37.

5 See John Gallagher, 'Foxwell Buxton and the New African Policy, 1838–1842', *Cambridge Historical Journal* 1 (1950), 58 and John Gallagher and Ronald Robinson, 'The Imperialism of Free Trade', 53–55; see 56–72.

6 See Gallagher and Robinson and also *The Robinson and Gallagher Controversy*, ed. Wm. Roger Louis (New York: New Viewpoints, 1976), esp. Louis' note on 53–4.

7 V. I. Lenin, *Imperialism, the Highest Stage of Capitalism, Selected Works*, [n.d.], v:71, quoted in Gallagher and Robinson, 55.

8 In January 1840, Macaulay published an essay on Lord Clive, who was a hero of the Seven Years War, in India as James Wolfe was at Quebec. See Lord Macaulay [Thomas Babington], *Historical Essays*, ed. Alan Westcott (New York: Macmillan, 1926), 160–251.

9 E. H. Nolan, *The Illustrated History of the British Empire in India and the East From the Earliest Times to the suppression of the Sepoy Mutiny in 1859 with a Continuation to the end of 1878.* 3 vols. London: Virtue & Co, n.d), I:v. This edition is an update of the one of 1859.

10 *The Making of the West: Peoples and Cultures*, eds. Lynn Hunt et al. (Boston/New York: Bedford/St. Martin's, 2001), 873–75. See also Winifred Baumgart, *Imperialism: The Idea and Reality of British and French Colonial Expansion* (Oxford: Oxford University Press, 1982), Fernand Braudel, *A History of Civilizations* (New York: Penguin Books, 1993) and Marc Ferro, *Colonization: A Global History* (London: Routledge 1997).

11 See Kennedy, *The Rise and Fall* , esp. 151–8, for detailed economic figures for Britain.

12 Catherine Hall, *Civilising Subjects: Metropole and Colony in the English Imagination, 1830–1867* (Cambridge: Polity, 2002), 84–5, 98, 105; see 86–139.

13 Andrew Porter, 'An Overiew, 1700–1914', *Missions and Empires*, ed. Norman Etherington (Oxford: Oxford University Press, 2005), 40, 47. I also owe a debt to Porter's discussion, 40–63.

14 John Rosselli, *Lord William Bentinck* (London: Chatto & Windus for Sussex University Press, 1974), 213, quoted in Porter, 'An Overview', 49.

15 Aylward Shorter, *Cross and Flag in Africa: The 'White Fathers' during the Colonial Scramble (1892–1914)* (Marynoll, NY: Orbis Books, 2006), esp. xxi

16 Alan Lester, 'Humanitarians and White Settlers in the Nineteenth Century', *Missions and Empires*, ed. Norman Etherington (Oxford: Oxford University Press, 2005), 81; see 80–85. See J. Guy, 'Class, Imperialism and Literary Criticism', *Journal of Southern African Studies* 23 (1997), 219–41.

17 Lester, 'Humanitarians', 80–4.

18 For documents relating to the debate for and against the Louisiana Purchase and to Jefferson's instructions to Lewis in 1803, see Michael Roth, *Issues of Western Expansion* (Westport, CT: Greenwood Press, 2002), 25–34.

19 For the early history of New Mexico and for Native–European relations, see Ramón Gutiérrez, *When Jesus Came, the Corn Mothers Went Away: Marriage, Sexuality, and Power in New Mexico, 1500–1846* (Stanford, CA: Stanford University Press, 1991).

20 James Kirby Martin et al., *American and Its People, Second Edition* (New York: HarperCollins, 1993), 403–9, 432–5. For commentary and documents on discrimination, for instance of the Chinese in California, see Roth,

213–36. On the role of women, see Judy Yung, *Unbound Voices: A Documentary History of Chinese Women in San Francisco* (Berkeley: University of California Press, 1999). There were shocks to all Native cultures, no matter how long established, when they came into contact with European cultures. See, for example, Ronald Spores, *The Mixtecs in Ancient and Colonial Times* (Norman: University of Oklahoma Press, 1984).

21 By the time of these encounters between Natives and newcomers/invaders/settlers, there was a long history. For background on Native interactions with Iberian, Dutch, British and French interactions, see John E. Kicza, *Resilient Cultures: America's Native Peoples confront European Colonization* (Upper Saddle River, NJ: Prentice Hall, 2003).

22 The Indian Removal Act (U.S. Statutes at Large 4 (1830): 411–12) and Frelinghuysen's speech (Register of Debates in Congress, Washington DC, Vol. 6, 311–16), in Roth, 44–6.

23 See the intricate decision in The Cherokee Nation v. The State of Georgia, 30 U.S. 1 (1831) and Worcester v. The State of Georgia, 315 U.S. 515 (1832), in Roth, 48–51, 56–8. See also Anthony F. C. Wallace, *The Long, Bitter Trail: Andrew Jackson and the Indians* (New York: Hill & Wang, 1993).

24 Martin et al., 306–12. There were massacres and violence that occurred on both sides, although the settlers had numbers and the US army on their side. See, for instance, documents related to the Sand Creek Massacre, in which a militia in the Colorado territory in November 1864 attacked an unguarded encampment while the Natives slept and killed, scalped and mutilated men, women and children they were supposed to protect (using cannon as well, Roth, 141–7). On massacres, see David Stannard, *American Holocaust: The Conquest of the New World* (New York: Oxford University Press, 1992) and Elliott West, *The Contested Plains: Indians, Goldseekers, and the Rush to Colorado* (Lawrence: University of Kansas Press, 1998).

25 Sitting Bull, in 48th Congress, 1st session, 1883, Senate Report No. 283, Serial 2164, 80–1, in Roth, 188. This speech also occurs in *Great Speeches by Native Americans*, ed. Bob Blaisdell (New York: Dover, 2000), 169–70. For commentary on and documents about the battle between Custer and the Natives, see Roth, 167–89. For the Native perspective, see Geogory F. Michno, *Lakota Noon: The Indian Narrative of Custer's Defeat* (Missoula: Mountain Press, 1997). See also Robert M. Utley, *The Lance and the Shield: The Life and Times of Sitting Bull* (New York: Henry Holt, 1993). For commentary on and documents about Wounded Knee in 1890, see Roth, 239–66. See also Robert V. Hine and John Mack Faragher, *The American West: A New Interpretative History* (New Haven: Yale University Press, 2000).

26 Martin et al., 412–19. For documents related to Manifest Destiny, the annexation of Mexico and the war with Mexico, see Roth, 66–76.

27 Martin et al., 419–21.

28 For the discussion above, see Martin et al., 421–34. For documents related to the Mormons and to the Mexican War, see Roth, 71–6, 87–98. See also Leonard J. Arrington, *Great Basin Knowledge: An Economic History of the Latter-Day Saints, 1830–1900* (Cambridge, MA: Harvard University Press, 1958); Leonard J. Arrington and David Bitton, *The Mormon Experience: A*

History of the Latter-Day Saints (New York: Alfred A. Knopf, 1979); John D. Eisenhower, *So Far from God: The U. S. War with Mexico* (New York: Random House, 1989).

29 Arrell Morgan Gibson with John S. Whitehead, *Yankees in Paradise: The Pacific Basin Frontier* (Albuquerque: University of New Mexico Press, 1993), esp. 93–101.

30 On imperialism, I am indebted to Martin et al., 654–86. For the quotation from Sherman, see Jan P. Nederveen Pieterse, *Empire & Emancipation: Power and Liberation on a World Scale* (1989; London: Pluto Press, 1990), 271; see 261–98.

31 See, for instance, David Healy, *US Expansionism: the Imperialist Urge in the 1890s* (Madison, WI: University of Wisconsin Press, 1970) and Thomas Schoonover, *Uncle Sam's War of 1898 and the Origins of Globalization* (Lexington: University of Kentucky Press, 2003).

32 George F. Parker, *Recollections of Grover Cleveland* (New York: Century Co., 1909), 249–50, quoted in Lewis L. Gould, *The Spanish-American War and President McKinley* (1980; Lawrence: University of Kansas Press, 1982), 1. See Charles G. Dawes, *A Journal of the McKinley Years*, ed. Bascom N. Timmons (Chicago: Lakeside Press, 1950), 115.

33 Felix C. Tejera, 'An American Dilemma: The Cuban Question, 1895–1897' (Florida State University, Department of History, PhD dissertation, 1975), vii.

34 For a brief account of some of these views, see Louis A. Pérez, *The War of 1898: The United States and Cuba in History and Historiography* (Chapel Hill: University of North Carolina Press, 1998), 116–19. Earlier assessments on the historiography of 1898, see Ernest May, 'American imperialism: A Reinterpretation', *Perspectives in American History* (1967): 121–283; Edward Crapol, 'Coming to Terms with Empire: The Historiography of Late-Nineteenth-Century American Foreign Relations', *Diplomatic History* 16 (1992): 573–97; Joseph Fry, 'Imperialism, American Style, 1890–1916)', *American Foreign Relations Reconsidered, 1890–1993*, ed. Gordon Martel (London: Routledge, 1994), 52–70. For examples of this historiography, see David Starr Jordan, Imperial Democracy (Boston: s.n., 1898); John R. Musick, *Cuba Libre: A Story of the Hispano-American War* (New York: Funk & Wagnalls Company, 1900); Carl Russell Fish, *The Path of Empire* (New Haven: Yale University Press, 1920); Foster Rhea Dulles, *Prelude to World Power, – 1860–1900* (New York: Macmillan, 1965); Ernest May, *Imperial Democracy: The Emergence of America as a Great Power* (New York: Harcourt, Brace & World, 1961); H. Wayne Morgan, *America's Road to Empire: The War with Spain and Overseas Expansion* (New York: Wiley, 1965); Irving Werstein, *1898: The Spanish-American War* (New York: Cooper Square Publishers, 1966); James A. Field Jr., 'American Imperialism: The "Worst Chapter"', *Quarterly* 96 (1997).

35 William McKinley, *Speeches and Addresses of William McKinley from March 1, 1897 to May 30, 1900* (New York: Doubleday & McClure Co., 1900), 188–9.

36 Jean Badreux, *La Guerre: L'Espagne ey les Etats-Unis* (Montreal: Leprohon & Leprohon, 1898), 4. Severo Gómez Núñez, *La Guerra Hispano-*

Americana: La Habana Influencia de las Plazas de Guerra (Madrid: Imprenta del Cuerpo de Artillería, 1900), esp. 153–5.

37 Thomas Hart Baker, Jr., 'Imperial Finale: Crisis, Decolonization, and War in Spain, 1890–1898' (Princeton University, PhD dissertation, 1976), esp. iii–v, 1–2, 401.

38 D. J. Connor, *Representations of the Cuban and Philippine Insurrections on the Spanish Stage 1887–1898* (Tempe, AZ: Bilingual Press/ Editorial Bilingüe, 2001), esp. 155–60.

39 The issues concerning the press were larger than that one business. On the political and economic importance to Spain of the loss of Cuba, see Rosario Sevilla Soler, *La Guerra de Cuba y la Memoria Collectiva: La Crisis del 98 en la Prensa Sevillana* (Sevilla: C.S.I.C., 1996), esp. 15–17, 25–6; on the sinking of the Maine and other events, see Félix Santos, *1898 La Prensa y la Guerra de Cuba* (Bilbao: Asociació Julián Zugazagoitia, 1998), esp. 11–21.

40 Gonzalo de Quesada, and Henry Davenport Northrop, *Cuba's Great Struggle for Freedom*, entered according to Act of Congress, in the year 1898, by J. R. Jones, In the Office of the Librarian of Congress, at Washington, DC: All Rights Reserved, iii.

41 See Jonathan Hart, *Representing the New World* (New York and London: Palgrave Macmillan, 2001).

42 White, Constitutional Record, 55th Cong., 3rd Sess., 265, excerpt in Traverso, 124.

43 Theodore Roosevelt, 'Appendix B', *The Rough Riders* (1899; New York: Signet Classics, 1961), 192.

44 Goldwin Smith, *Commonwealth or Empire: A Bystander's View of the Question* (New York and London: Macmillan, 1902), 1–2.

45 G. Smith, 2.

46 G. Smith, 49–50.

47 G. Smith, 50.

48 Quoted in H. J. Mackinder, 'The Geographical Pivot of History', *Geographical Journal* 23.6 (1904), 441 and Kennedy, 196, see also Kennedy, 194–256, which has influenced my discussion. See also E. A. Benians et al., eds., *The Cambridge History of the British Empire* [vol. 3, *The Empire-Commonwealth 1870–1919*] (Cambridge: Cambridge University Press, 1959); Walter LaFeber, *The New Empire: An Interpretation of American Expansion 1860–1898* (Ithaca, NY: Cornell University Press, 1963); Hugh Seton-Watson, *The Russian Empire 1801–1917* (Oxford: Clarendon Press, 1967); William Appleman Williams, *The Roots of the Modern American Empire: A Study of the Growth and Shaping of Social Consciousness in a Marketplace Society* (New York: Random House, 1969); Sybil Eyre Crowe, *The Berlin West African Conference 1884–85* (Westport, CT: Negro Universities Press, 1970); C. J. Bartlett, *The Global Conflict, 1880–1970: The International Rivalry of the Great Powers* (London: Longman, 1984); Charles Townshend, ed., *The Oxford Illustrated History of Modern War* (Oxford: Oxford University Press, 1997); Douglas Porch, *Wars of Empire* (London: Cassell, 2000), esp. 99–155.

49 See David Good, *The Economic Rise of the Habsburg Empire* (1984) and Kennedy, 158–82 here and below.

50 On Africa and other regions, see Henri Brunschwig, *Mythes et réalités de l'Imperialisme colonnial français 1871–1914* (Paris: A. Colin, 1960); Paul T. Kennedy, *African Capitalism: The Struggle for Ascendancy* (Cambridge: Cambridge University Press, 1988); Franz Ansprenger, *The Dissolution of the Colonial Empires* (London: Routledge, 1989); Crawford Young, *The African Colonial State in Comparative Perspective* (New Haven: Yale University Press, 1994). On the expansion of France, see Robert Aldrich, *Greater France: A History of French Overseas Expansion* (Basingstoke: Macmillan, 1996).

51 For documents concerning the building of a transcontinental railway in the United States, see Roth, 130–41. See also David Haward Bain, *Empire Express: Building the First Transcontinental Railroad* (New York: Viking, 1999); Stephen E. Ambrose, *Nothing Like It in the World: The Men Who Built the Transcontinental Railroad, 1863–1869* (New York: Simon and Schuster, 2000).

52 Hunt et al., 875–76. See also Mikiso Hane, *Modern Japan: A Historical Survey* (Boulder: Westview Press, 1992).

53 Orlando Figes, *Natasha's Dance: A Cultural History of Russia* (2002; London: Penguin, 2003), 145, see 143–6; on Turgenev, see 107–8.

54 Hunt et al., 849–56 for above. See also Barbara Alpern Engel, *Between the Fields and the City: Women, Work, and Family in Russia, 1861–1914* (Cambridge: Cambridge University Press, 1994); Philip Nord, *The Republican Moment: Struggles for Democracy in Nineteenth-Century France* (Cambridge, MA: Harvard University Press 1995); Sudhir Hazareesingh, *From Subject to Citizen: The Second Empire and the Emergence of Modern French Democracy* (Princeton: Princeton University Press, 1998); Robert B. Edgerton, *Death and Glory: The Legacy of the Crimean War* (Boulder, CO: Westview Press, 1999).

55 Mary Evelyn Townsend, *The Rise and Fall of Germany's Colonial Empire 1884–1918* (New York: Macmillan, 1930), 1.

56 Kennedy, 182–93. See Hunt et al. 858–62. See A. J. P. Taylor, *The Struggle for Mastery in Europe, 1848–1918* (Oxford: Clarendon Press, 1954); Rondo E. Cameron, *France and the Economic Development of Europe 1800–1914: Conquests of Peace and Seeds of War* (Princeton: Princeton University Press, 1961); Trevor Nevitt Dupuy, *A Genius for War: The German Army and the General Staff, 1807–1945* (Englewood Cliffs, NJ: Prentice-Hall, 1977); François Caron, *An Economic History of Modern France* (New York: Columbia University Press, 1979); Paul M. Kennedy, *The Rise of the Anglo-German Antagonism, 1860–1914* (London: Allen & Unwin, 1980); Michael Eliot Howard, *The Franco-Prussian War: The German Invasion of France, 1870–1871* (1961; London: Methuen, 1981); Roger Price, *An Economic History of Modern France, 1730–1914*, rev. ed. (London: Macmillan, 1981). For background on war, technology and economics, see Michael Howard, *War in European History* (Oxford: Oxford University Press, 1976); Jeremy Black, *War in European History, 1494–1660* (Washington, DC: Potomac

Books, 2006); *An Economic History of Europe: From Expansion to Development*, ed. Antonio Di Vittorio (London Routledge, 2006).

57 E. J. Hobsbawm, *The Age of Empire 1875–1914* (London: Weidenfeld and Nicholson, 1987), 56, 60, see esp. 57–83; see also, J. A. Hobson, *Imperialism* (London, 1902) and Wolfgang J. Mommsen, *Max Webber and German Politics 1890–1920* (Chicago: University of Chicago Press, 1984), esp. 77. A more recent view is A. N. Porter, *European Imperialism, 1860–1914* (Basingstoke: Macmillan, 1994).

58 See George Grant, *Technology and Empire*: Perspectives on North America (Toronto: House of Anansi, 1969). See also Daniel R. Headrick, *The Tools of Empire: Technology and European Imperialism in the Nineteenth Century* (New York: Oxford University Press, 1981) and Alfred W. Crosby, *Ecological Imperialism: The Biological Expansions of Europe, 900–1900* (1986; Cambridge: Cambridge University Press, 1993); *Nature and Empire: Science and the Colonial Enterprise*, ed. Roy MacLeod (Chicago: University of Chicago Press, 2000); *War at Sea in the Middle Ages and the Renaissance*, eds. John B. Hattendorf and Richard W. Unger (Woodbridge, Suffolk: Boydell Press, 2003; Pamela Kyle Crossley, Lynn Hollen Lees, John W. Servos, *Global Society: The World Since 1900* (Boston: Houghton Mifflin, 2004); *Maritime Empires: British Imperial Maritime Trade in the Nineteenth Century*, eds. David Killingray, Margarette Lincoln and Nigel Rigby (Woodbridge, Suffolk: Boydell Press in association with the National Maritime Museum, 2004); *City, Country, Empire: Landscapes in Environmental History*, ed. by Jeffry M. Diefendorf and Kurk Dorsey (Pittsburgh: University of Pittsburgh Press, 2005). On imperialism and Africa, see Halford Lancaster Hoskins, *European Imperialism in Africa* (1930; New York, Russell & Russell, 1967); *European Imperialism and the Partition of Africa*, ed. E. F. Penrose (London: F. Cass, 1975); Woodruff D. Smith, *European Imperialism in the Nineteenth and Twentieth Centuries* (Chicago: Nelson-Hall, 1982); Ambe J. Njoh, *Planning Power: Town Planning and Social Control in Colonial Africa* (London: UCL Press, 2007).

59 R. Owen, *The Middle East and the World Economy 1800–1914* (London: I. B. Taurus, 1993). See also Ekmeleddin Ihsanoglu, *Science, Technology, and Learning in the Ottoman Empire: Western Influence, Local Institutions, and the Transfer of Knowledge* (Aldershot, Hampshire: Ashgate/Variorum 2004).

60 Hunt et al., 900–4, to which this discussion of Africa here and below is indebted. See Jean Comaroff and John Comaroff, *Of Revelation and Revolution: Christianity, Colonialism, and Consciousness in South Africa* (Chicago: University of Chicago Press, 1991), Robert T. Harrison, *Gladstone's Imperialism in Egypt: Techniques of Domination* (Westport, CT: Greenwood Press, 1995) and H. L. Wesseling, *Divide and Rule: The Partition of Africa, 1880–1914*, trans. Arnold J. Pomerans (Westport, CT: Praeger, 1996); *Missions, States, and European Expansion in Africa*, ed. Chima J. Korieh, Raphael Chijioke Njoku (New York: Routledge, 2007).

61 See, for example, *From Slave Trade to Legitimate Commerce: The Commercial Transition in Nineteenth-Century West Africa*, ed. Robin Law

(Cambridge: Cambridge University Press, 1995) and *From Slave Trade to Empire: Europe and the Colonisation of Black Africa, 1780s-1880s*, ed. Olivier Pétré-Grenouilleau (London: Routledge, 2004).

62 For an interesting discussion of race and empire, see Allison Blakely, *Blacks in the Dutch World: The Evolution of Racial Imagery in Modern Society* (Bloomington: Indiana University Press, 1993). See Hunt et al., 904–9, 922.

63 Colin Newbury, 'The Partition of Africa', *The Oxford History of the British Empire*, ed. Wm. Roger Louis, Volume III, *The Nineteenth Century*, ed. Andrew Porter (Oxford: Oxford University Press, 1999), 624–35 for the discussion above and 636–50 below. See also Eric Axelson, *Portugal and the Scramble for Africa* (Johannesburg: Witwatersrand University Press, 1967).

64 Sir Reginald Coupland, *The Exploitation of East Africa 1856–1890: The Slave Trade and the Scramble* (1939; Evanston, IL: Northwestern University Press, 1967), 484–5.

65 R. J. Hammond and quoted in his *Portugal and Africa 1815–1910: A Study in Uneconomic Imperialism* (Stanford, CA: Stanford University Press, 1966), 108–32, see ix. For the plates of Pinheiro, see the ones on the page between pages 144 and 145 in Hammond's book for the events of 1889–90 and the ultimatum and for the ones concerning the Camões centenary and the Congo Treaty, see the plates on the page between 112 and 113. On Camões, see James Nicolopulos, *The Poetics of Empire in the Indies: Prophecy and Imitation in La Araucana and Os Lusíadas* (University Park: Penn State University Press, 2000), esp. 221–69.

66 Robbins, 18; see 19–24.

67 The above discussion draws on Newbury, 636–49. See also *France and Britain in Africa: Imperial Policy and Colonial Rule*, eds. Prosser Gifford and Wm. Roger Louis (New Haven: Yale University Press, 1971); D. M. Schreuder, *The Scramble for Southern Africa, 1877–1895: The Politics of Partition Reappraised* (Cambridge: Cambridge University Press, 1980); Antoine Jean Bullier, *Partition et repartition: Afrique du Sud, histoire d'une stratégie ethnique (1880–1980)* (Paris: Diffusion, Didier érudition, 1988); *Postmodernism, Postcoloniality and African Studies*, ed. Zine Magubane (Trenton, NJ: Africa World Press, 2003); Rachael Gilmour, *Grammars of Colonialism: Representing Languages in Colonial South Africa* (Houndmills, Basingstoke: Palgrave Macmillan, 2006); *Rethinking Settler Colonialism: History and Memory in Australia, Canada, Aotearoa New Zealand and South Africa*, ed. Annie Coombes. (Manchester: Manchester University Press, 2006).

68 Thomas Pakenham, *The Scramble for Africa 1876–1912* (New York: Random House, 1991), xxiii, 586–7, 600–01, 606–9, 615–28 for the discussion above. See H. Drechsler, *Let us Die Fighting: The Struggle of the Herero and Nama against German Imperialism, 1884– 1915* (London: Zed Press, 1980); Gilbert Gwassa, *The Outbreak and Development of the Maji Maji War 1905–1907*, ed. Wolfgang Apelt (Köln: Köppe, 2005).

69 Pakenham, 577–79. See Hansard, 1 Mar 1901, XC, quoted in Pakenham, 578.

70 Hansard, 17 Jun 1901, XCV, 573–83, quoted in Pakenham, 579. See Pakenham, 641.

71 Packenham, 665–8.

72 Woodruff D. Smith, *The German Colonial Empire* (Chapel Hill: University of North Carolina Press, 1978), 20–1. See also Richard A. Voeltz, *German Colonialism and the South West Africa Company, 1884–1914* (Athens, OH: Ohio University, Center for International Studies, 1988); W.O. Henderson, *The German Colonial Empire, 1884–1919* (London: F. Cass, 1993); Juhani Koponen, *Development for Exploitation: German Colonial Policies in Mainland Tanzania, 1884–1914* (Helsinki: Tiedekirja; Hamburg: Lit Verlag (Münster), 1994). For German points of view, see Hans-Ulrich Wehler, *Bismarck und der Imperialismus* (Cologne: Kiepenheuer u. Witsch, 1969); *Deutsche Kolonialzeitung*, 17 October 1891, 142–5; C. A. Lüderitz, ed., *Die Erschliessung von Deutsch-Südwest-Afrika* (Oldenburg: G. Stalling, 1945).

73 This became apparent in Tagore's presidential address to the Congress in 1908 when he called for Indian strength in the face of British rule. See Radindranath Tagore, *Towards Universal Man* (London: Asia Publishing House, 1961), 116–24.

74 J. Forsyth, *A History of the Peoples of Siberia. Russia's North Asian Colony 1581–1990* (Cambridge: Cambridge University Press, 1992). For some earlier background on the fur trade, see J. Martin, *Treasure of the Land of Darkness. The Fur Trade and its Significance for Medieval Russia* (Cambridge: Cambridge University Press, 1986).

75 Hunt et al., 904–9, 922, to which I am indebted for this discussion of colonialism in Asia.

76 E. J. Hobsbawm, *The Age of Empire, 1875–1914* (London: Weidenfeld & Nicolson, 1987), 57, see 65–6 specifically but 58–71 generally for the discussion below.

77 D. K. Fieldhouse, *The Colonial Empires: A Comparative Survey from the Eighteenth Century*, 2nd edn (Houndsmills and London: Macmillan Education, 1982, rpt. 1987), 349–52.

78 Fieldhouse, 325–34 for which my discussion is indebted. For a different approach, see Robert B. Marks, *The Origins of the Modern World*, 2nd edn (Lanham: Rowman & Littlefield, 2007).

79 Fieldhouse, 257–360. See Curtain, *The World and the West*, 3–17.

80 Fieldhouse, 367, see 364–71, to which my discussion is indebted. See Curtain, *World*, 38–52.

81 Hobsbawm, 67, see 70 for the comment on cement.

82 Hobsbawm, 62–8. On the affects of imperialism on the land and on biology, see John M. MacKenzie, *The Empire of Nature: Hunting, Conservation, and British Imperialism* (Manchester: Manchester University Press, 1988) and Crosby, *Ecological Imperialism*. See also Philip Curtain, *Death by Migration* (New York: Cambridge University Press, 1989) and his *Disease and Empire* (New York and Cambridge: Cambridge University Press, 1998).

83 Kennedy, *Great Powers*, 214, see 209–13 for here and below; see also Paul M. Kennedy's Introduction to the volume he edited, *The War Plans of the Great Powers 1880–1914* (London: Allen & Unwin, 1979).

84 Lieven, *Empire*, 160–1.
85 A. Sked, *The Decline and Fall of the Habsburg Empire 1815–1918* (London: Longman, 1989). See also R. J. W. Evans, *The Making of the Habsburg Monarchy 1551–1700* (Oxford: Oxford University Press, 1979); J. P. Bled, *Franz Joseph* (Oxford: Blackwell, 1994); C. Ingrao, *The Habsburg Monarchy 1618–1815* (Cambridge: Cambridge University Press, 1994).
86 On Austria-Hungary and France, see Kennedy, *Great Powers*, 215–24; on the Habsburg empire and its successor in a German and a wider context, see Robert A. Kann, *A History of the Habsburg Empire 1526–1918* (Berkeley: University of California Press, 1974); L. L. Farrar, *Arrogance and Anxiety: The Ambivalence of German Power 1849–1914* (Iowa City, IA: University of Iowa Press, 1981); David F. Good, *The Economic Rise of the Habsburg Empire, 1750–1914* (Berkeley: University of California Press, 1984); on France, see Henri Brunschwig, *French Colonialism, 1871–1916: Myths and Realities, trans.* William Granville (London: Pall Mall Press, 1966); Jean Ganiage, *L'expansion coloniale de la France sous la Troisième Republique 1871–1914: Avec la collaboration de Daniel Hémery* (Paris: Payot, 1968); A.S. Kanya-Forstner, *The Conquest of the Western Sudan: A Study in French Military Imperialism* (Cambridge: Cambridge University Press, 1969); Raoul Girardet, *L'idée coloniale en France de 1871 à 1962* (Paris: La Table Ronde, 1972); John F. V. Keiger, *France and the Origins of the First World War* (London: Macmillan, 1983).
87 Hunt et al. ed, 905–7.
88 Norman Stone, *Europe Transformed 1878–1919* (Glasgow: Fontana, 1983), 212–13, quoted in Kennedy, *Great Powers*, 237. My discussion of the economy of the Russian empire is indebted to Kennedy, 232–42.
89 Besides Kennedy for a discussion of the economics of the Russian empire, see the following more specialized discussions: Steven G. Marks, *Road to Power: The Trans-Siberian Railroad and the Colonization of Asian Russia, 1850–1917* (Ithaca, NY: Cornell University Press, 1991) and Christine D. Worobec, *Peasant Russia: Family and Community in the Post-Emancipation Period* (Princeton: Princeton University Press, 1991); John P. LeDonne, *The Russian Empire and the World, 1700–1917: The Geopolitics of Expansion and Containment* (New York: Oxford University Press, 1997). The Russian empire was also of interest to the government of the United States and other groups in the U. S.; see Carey, Mathew, *The Russian Empire in Europe and Asia* (Philadelphia: M. Carey, 1814); United States. Department of the Treasury, Bureau of Statistics, *The Russian Empire and the Trans-Siberian Railway* (Washington, Government Print Office, 1899); Victor A. Yakhontoff, *The Russian Empire and the Soviet Union in the Far East*, (New York, American Russian Institute for Cultural Relations with the Soviet Union, 1936). In Britain, there was similar interest; see Baron von Haxthausen, *The Russian Empire, Its People, Institutions and Resources*, trans. Robert Farie (London: Chapman and Hall, 1856); S. B. Boulton, *The Russian Empire: Its Origin and Development* (London: Cassell, Petter, Galpin, 1882).
90 For the case of New Zealand, see, for instance, Jean E. Rosenfeld, *The Island Broken in Two Halves: Land and Renewal Movements Among the Maori of*

New Zealand (University Park: Penn State University Press, 1999), 125, see esp. 1–22, 292–3. See also Keith Sinclair, *The Origins of the Maori Wars* (Wellington: New Zealand University Press, 1957) and *A History of New Zealand* (Auckland: Penguin Books, 1988); John Williams, *Politics of the New Zealand Maori: Protest and Cooperation, 1891–1909* (Auckland: Oxford University Press, 1969). On a famous challenge to *terra nullius* in Australia as regards to its indigenous peoples, see Tim Rowse, *After Mabo: Interpreting Indigenous Traditions* (Melbourne: Melbourne University Press, 1993). See also The Law Reform Commission, *Aboriginal Customary Law-Recognition?* (Sydney: ARLC, 1980); Peter Poynton, *Aboriginal Australia: Land, Law and Culture* (London: Institute of Race Relations, 1994). More recently, see *Pacific Answers to Western Hegemony: Cultural Practices of Identity Construction*, ed. Jürg Wassmann (Oxford: Berg, 1998); John Toohey, *Background Paper on Aboriginal Customary Laws: Reference, an Overview* (Perth, W.A.: Law Reform Commission of Western Australia, 2004); Chris Cunneen and Melanie Schwartz, *Customary Law, Human Rights and International Law: Some Conceptual Issues* (Perth, W.A.: Law Reform Commission of Western Australia, 2005); Greg McIntyre, Aboriginal Customary Law: Can It Be Recognised? (Perth, W.A.: Law Reform Commission of Western Australia, 2005); Law Reform Commission of Western Australia, *Aboriginal Customary Laws: The Interaction of Western Australian Law with Aboriginal Law and Culture: Final Report* (Perth, W.A.: Law Reform Commission of Western Australia, 2006).

91 Hunt et al., 891–908 has informed my discussion here and below.
92 Olive Patricia Dickason, *Canada's First Nations: A History of Founding Peoples from Earliest Times*, 3rd edn (Toronto: Oxford University Press, 2002), 203.
93 See Olive P. Dickason, *The Myth of the Savage And the Beginnings of French Colonialism in the Americas* (1984; Edmonton: University of Alberta Press, 1997).
94 Dwight D. Eisenhower; this section on the United States is indebted to Kennedy, *Great Powers*, 242–9; see also John J. Valentine, *"Imperial democracy": Dutch Colonizers in Malaysia, Annexation of the Philippines* (San Francisco, CA, [no pub.] 1899). Ernest R. May, *Imperial Democracy: The Emergence of America as a Great Power* (New York: Harcourt, Brace & World, 1961) and May's *American Imperialism: A Speculative Essay* (New York: Atheneum, 1968); Dana Gardner Munro, *Intervention and Dollar Diplomacy in the Caribbean 1900–1921* (Princeton: Princeton University Press, 1964); Thomas J. McCormick, *China Market: America's Quest for Informal Empire* (Chicago: Quadrangle Books, 1967); Bradford Perkins, *The Great Rapprochement: England and the United States, 1895–1914* (New York: Atheneum, 1969); Graham A. Cosmas, *An Army for Empire: The United States Army in the Spanish-American War* (Columbia, MO: University of Missouri Press, 1971); Richard D. Challener, *Admirals, Generals and American Policy 1898–1914* (Princeton: Princeton University Press, 1973); William Woodruff, *America's Impact on the World: A Study of the Role of the United States in the World Economy 1750–1970* (New York:

Wiley, 1973); Thomas Andrew Bailey, *A Diplomatic History of the American People*, 9th edn (Englewood Cliffs, NJ: Prentice-Hall, 1974); Charles S. Campbell, *From Revolution to Rapproachement: The United States and Britain, 1783–1900* (New York: Wiley, 1974); Marcello de Cecco, *Money and Empire: The International Gold Standard 1890–1914* (Oxford: Blackwell, 1974); Gerald F. Linderman, *The Mirror of War: American Society and the Spanish-American War* (Ann Arbor, MI: University of Michigan Press, 1974); Harold G. Vatter, *The Drive to Industrial Maturity: The U. S. Economy, 1860–1914* (Westport, CT: Greenwood Press, 1975); David F. Trask, *The War with Spain in 1898* (New York: Macmillan, 1981); Robert Dallek, *The American Style of Foreign Policy* (New York: Knopf, 1983); Porch, *Wars of Empire* (2000).

95 D. K. Fieldhouse: *The Colonial Empires: A Comparative Survey from the Eighteenth Century*, Second Edition (London: Macmillan, 1982, rpt. 1987), 280.

96 Fieldhouse, 202–3. See also W. P. Morrell, *Britain in the Pacific Islands* (Oxford: Clarendon Press, 1960); A Ross, *New Zealand Aspirations in the Pacific in the Nineteenth Century* (Oxford: Clarendon Press, 1964); *Tides of History: The Pacific Islands in the Twentieth Century*, eds. K.R. Howe, Robert C. Kiste, Brij V. Lal (Honolulu: University of Hawaii Press, 1994)

97 Alfred W. Crosby, *Ecological Imperialism: The Biological Expansion of Europe, 900–1900* (New York and Cambridge: Cambridge University Press, 1986, rpt. 1991), 237–52 to which I am indebted for the discussion above.

98 BPPCNZ, VI, 167, quoted in Crosby, 261.

99 Daizel, 587–91. See Claudia Orange, *The Treaty of Waitangi* (Wellington: Allen & Unwin, 1987) and her *An Illustrated History of the Treaty of Waitangi* (Wellington: Bridget Williams Books, 2004); Ian Pool, *Te Iwi Maori: A New Zealand Population Past, Present and Projected* (Auckland: Auckland University Press, 1991); *Sovereignty and Indigenous Rights: The Treaty of Waitangi in International Contexts*, ed. William Renwick (Wellington: Victoria University Press, 1991). For other general views, see Paul G. McHugh, *Maori Land Laws of New Zealand: Two Essays* (Saskatoon: University of Saskatchewan, Native Law Centre, 1983); *Pacific Answers to Western Hegemony: Cultural Practices of Identity Construction*, ed. Jürg Wassmann (Oxford: Berg, 1998); *Voyages and Beaches: Pacific Encounters, 1769–1840*, eds. Alex Calder, Jonathan Lamb, Bridget Orr (Honolulu: University of Hawaii Press, 1999); Bryan Gilling and Vincent O'Malley, *The Treaty of Waitangi in New Zealand History* (Wellington: Treaty of Waitangi Research Unit, Stout Research Centre, Victoria University of Wellington, 2000); *Telling Stories: Indigenous History and Memory in Australia and New Zealand*, eds. Bain Attwood and Fiona Magowan (Crows Nest, N.S.W.: Allen & Unwin, 2001).

100 Dalziel, 573. See W. H. Oliver and B. R. Williams, *The Oxford History of New Zealand* (Oxford and Wellington: Oxford University Press, 1981) and the Second Edition, edited by Geoffrey W. Rice (Auckland: Oxford University Press, 1992).

101 See Crosby, 252–68. See also Harold Miller, *Race Conflict in New Zealand, 1814–1865* (Auckland: Blackwood & Janet Paul, 1966); Peter Adams, *Fatal Necessity. British Intervention in New Zealand, 1830–1847* (Auckland: Auckland University Press, 1977).

102 Jared Diamond, *Guns, Germs, and Steel: The Fates of Human Societies* (New York and London: W. W. Norton, 1997, rpt. 1999), 350–2.

103 Hugh Thomas, *The Slave Trade: The Story of the Atlantic Slave Trade* (New York: Simon & Shuster 1997), 804–5. I am using Thomas's estimated statistics as the basis of my analysis here. For some other studies of slavery, see the following: Gilberto Freyre, *The Masters and the Slaves: A Study in the Development of Brazilian Civilization* (Berkeley: University of California Press, 1986), which examines hybridity and slavery in Portuguese colonial society in Brazil and the sexuality and family life of the African slave in Brazil; Michael Graton, *Empire, Enslavement and Freedom in the Caribbean* (Princeton: Marcus Weiner Publishers, 1997), which begins with the historical roots, discusses British imperial policy and free wage labour from 1780 to 1890; and Robert William Fogel, *The Slavery Debates: A Retrospective, 1952–1990* (Baton Rouge: Louisiana State University Press, 2003), a book by a Nobel Prize winner on the controversy over the economics of slavery.

104 For a black and white reproduction of this painting, see Hugh Honour, *The European Vision of America* (Cleveland: The Cleveland Museum of Art, 1975), Plate 316.

105 See, for instance, Valerie Smith, *Self-Discovery and Authority in Afro-American Narrative* (Cambridge, MA: Harvard University Press, 1987) and her *Not Just Race, Not Just Gender: Black Feminist Readings* (New York: Routledge, 1998).

106 Gates, Introduction, *Classic Slave Narratives*, 9; see William Andrews, 'Six Women's Slave Narratives, 1831–1909', in *Black Women's Slave Narratives*, ed. W. L. Andrews (New York: Oxford University Press, 1987).

107 Mary Prince, 'The History of Mary Prince, A West Indian Slave. (Related by Herself)', in *The Classic Slave Narratives*, ed. Henry Louis Gates, Jr. (1987; New York: New American Library, 2002), 255, see 253–4.

108 Ibid., 288.

109 Douglass, quoted in James M'Cune Smith, 'Introduction', Frederick Douglass, *My Bondage and My Freedom* (New York, Miller, Orton & Mulligan, 1855), 8–9. For an on-line version of this text, see Avalon Project: My Bondage and Freedom by Frederick Douglass; 1855 at <http://www.yale.edu/lawweb/avalon/treatise/douglas/douglas01.htm>.

110 *First Inaugural Address of Abraham Lincoln, Monday, Monday, March 4, 1861,* Avalon Project, Yale Law School, here and below at <http://www.yale.edu/lawweb/avalon/presiden/inaug/lincoln1.htm>.

111 Abraham Lincoln, *Emancipation Proclamation*; September 22, 1862, the Avalon Project, at <http://www.yale.edu/lawweb/avalon/emancipa.htm>.

112 Abraham Lincoln, January 4, 1855 (Notes on the history of the African slave trade), *The Abraham Lincoln Papers at the Library of Congress, Series 1. General Correspondence. 1833–1916*, ms. 2pp. [431 marked on first page], here and below.

113   From Abraham Lincoln to James N. Brown [Fragment of a Draft or Copy], October 18, 1858; the complete text of Lincoln's letter to Brown is in *Collected Works*, III, 327–28.

114   Olive Patricia Dickason, *Canada's First Nations: A History of the Founding Peoples from Earliest Times*, 3rd edn (Toronto: Oxford University Press, 2002), 155–6.

115   Dickason, *Canada's First Nations*, 253. The Order-in-Council is quoted from George Brown and Ron Macguire, eds., *Indian Treaties in Historical Perspective* (Ottawa: Canada, Indian and Northern Affairs Canada, Corporate Policy, Research Branch, 1979), 32. On difference generally and in Canada, see *Explorations in Difference: Law, Culture, and Politics*, ed. Jonathan Hart and Richard W. Bauman (Toronto: University of Toronto Press, 1996). On aboriginal rights and law in Canada, see also *The Quest for Justice: Aboriginal Peoples and Aboriginal Rights*, eds. Menno Boldt and J. Anthony Long in association with Leroy Little Bear (Toronto: University of Toronto Press, 1985); *Speaking Truth to Power: A Treaty Forum* (Ottawa: Law Commission of Canada; (Vancouver: British Columbia Treaty Commission, 2001); Michael J. Bryant & Lorne Sossin, *Public Law: An Overview of Aboriginal, Administrative, Constitutional, and International Law in Canada* (Toronto: Carswell, 2002); Paul G. McHugh, *Aboriginal Societies and the Common Law: A History of Sovereignty, Status, and Self-determination* (Oxford: Oxford University Press, 2004); David W. Elliott, *Law and Aboriginal Peoples in Canada*, 5th ed. (Concord, ON: Captus Press, 2005); Joseph Eliot Magnet, *Litigating Aboriginal Culture* (Edmonton, AB: Juriliber, 2005); Thomas Isaac, *Aboriginal Title* (Saskatoon: Native Law Centre, University of Saskatchewan, 2006).

116   *Great Speeches*, 132; from *New York Times*, 17 June 1870; short excerpt in *Timelines*, 155.

117   *Great Speeches*, 169; see James Creelman, *On the Great Highway: The Wanderings and Adventures of a Special Correspondent* (Boston: Lothrop Publishing, 1901), 299–302. Textual production and delays affected many works, such as those by Columbus, Jean de Léry, Shakespeare, James Joyce and others, so that this transmission and delay are reminiscent of Marco Polo dictating his story to Rusticello, a French writer of romance, while he was in prison. I have discussed some aspects of textual transmission and authorship in earlier works such as *Columbus, Shakespeare and the Interpretation of the New World* (New York and London: Palgrave Macmillan, 2003).

118   Benjamin Franklin to Peter Collinson, 9 May 1753, in Leonard W. Labaree, ed., *Papers of Benjamin Franklin* (New Haven: Yale University Press, 1959), 36 vols, vol. 4:481–2. See also J. Norman Heard, *White into Red: A Study of the Assimilation of White Persons Captured by Indians* (Methuchen, NJ: Scarecrow Press, 1973) and James Axtell, 'The White Indians', *The Invasion Within: The Contest of Cultures in Colonial North America* (New York: Oxford University Press, 1985), 302–27.

119   Harriet Taylor Mill, excerpt from 'Enfranchisement of Women', *Westminster Review* (July 1851): 295–6; reprinted in Ann P. Robson and John M. Robson, eds., *Sexual Equality: Writings by John Stuart Mill,*

Harriet Taylor Mill, and Helen Taylor (Toronto: University of Toronto Press, 1994), 178–203.

120 To help celebrate Women's Equality Day, the National Women's History Project developed a quiz; this is my source for the list of countries that got the vote before the United States, although Britain is listed as doing so in 1919 and not 1918 as in many other sources; see <http://www.nwhp.org/events/equality-day/equality-day-quiz.html>.

121 See this connection on the website of the United States National Park Service at <http://www.nps.gov/wori/ugrrexhibit.htm> and <http://www.nps.gov/wori/ugrrpanel per cent205.htm>.

122 Declaration of Sentiments at <www.nps.gov/wori/declaration.htm>.

123 Mary Ann Müller, 'An Appeal to the Men of New Zealand' (1869), *The New Zealand Mail*, 1 June 1878, 7; online at <http://www.nzhistory.net.nz/Gallery/Suffragists/appeal.html>.

124 For the website, see <http://www.nwhp.org/events/equality-day/equality-day-quiz.html>.

125 '110 Years of Women's Suffrage', New Zealand Women and the Vote: Suffrage and Beyond, <http://www.nzhistory.net.nz/Gallery/Suffragists/index.html>.

126 For a brief discussion of decolonization and neocolonialism, see Raymond F. Betts, *France and Decolonisation* (London: Macmillan, 1991), 128–9.

Chapter 6

1 E. J. Hobsbawm, *The Age of Empire: 1875–1914* (London: Guild Publishing, 1987), 75.

2 M. J. Bonn, *The Crumbling of Empire: The Disintegration of the World Economy* (London: George Allen & Unwin, 1938), 7, see 8–10, 415–17. On economics and related military and ideological matters, see Wolfe W. Schmokel, *Dream of Empire: German Colonization, 1919–1945* (New Haven: Yale University Press, 1964); Wm. Roger Louis, *Imperialism at Bay: The United States and the Decolonization of the British Empire 1941–1945* (New York: Oxford University Press, 1978); B. R. Tomlinson, *The Political Economy of the Raj, 1914–1947: The Economics of Decolonization* (London: Macmillan Press, 1979); John Gallagher, *The Decline, Revival and Fall of the British Empire*, ed. Anil Seal. (Cambridge: Cambridge University Press, 1982); W. O. Henderson, *The German Colonial Empire 1884–1919* (London: F. Cass, 1993); Adam Hochschild, *King Leopold's Ghost: A Story of Greed, Terror, and Heroism in Colonial Africa* (Boston: Houghton Mifflin, 1998); David S. Landes, *The Wealth and Poverty of Nations* (London and New York: Norton, 1998); Niall Ferguson, *The Cash Nexus: Money and Power in the Modern World, 1700–2000* (London: Allen Lane, 2001) and his *Empire: The Rise and Demise of the British World Order and the Lessons of Global Power* (New York: Basic Books, 2002).

3 On Egypt, see Robert Tignor, 'Decolonization and Business: The Case of Egypt', *Journal of Modern History*, 59 (1987), 479–505 and *Capitalism and Nationalism at the End of Empire: State and Business in Decolonizing Egypt, Nigeria and Kenya, 1945–1963* (Princeton: Princeton University Press, 1998).

See also Elizabeth Monroe, *Britain's Moment in the Middle East, 1914 to 1956, 2nd ed.* (Baltimore: Johns Hopkins University Press, 1981).

4 See Kennedy, *Great Powers,* 249–56; Oron J. Hale, *Germany and the Diplomatic Revolution 1904–1906* (Philadelphia: University of Pennsylvania Press, 1931); Luigi Albertini, *The Origin of the War of 1914,* trans. and ed. Isabella M. Massey, 3 vols. (London: New York, Oxford University Press, 1952–57); George W. . Monger, *The End of Isolation: British Foreign Policy 1900–07* (London: T. Nelson, 1963); C. J. Lowe, *The Reluctant Imperialists: British Foreign Policy 1878–1902,* 2 vols. (London: Routledge & Kegan Paul, 1967); Zara S. Steiner, *Britain and the Origins of the First World War* (London: Macmillan, 1977); D. C. B. Lieven, *Russia and the Origins of the First World War* (London: Macmillan, 1983); Felix Gilbert, *The End of the European Era, 1890 to the Present,* 3rd edn (New York: W.W. Norton, 1984); *The Cambridge History of Warfare,* ed. Geoffrey Parker (New York: Cambridge University Press, 2005); T. Iván Berend, *An Economic History of Twentieth-century Europe: Economic Regimes from Laissez-faire to Globalization* (Cambridge: Cambridge University Press, 2006). For more specific studies in economic history, see Jeremy Adelman, *Frontier Development: Land, Labour, and Capital on the Wheatlands of Argentina and Canada, 1890–1914* (Oxford: Clarendon Press, 1994) and his *Republic of Capital: Buenos Aires and the Legal Transformation of the Atlantic World* (Stanford, CA: Stanford University Press, 1999); Volker Rolf Berghahn, *Imperial Germany, 1871–1918: Economy, Society, Culture, and Politics,* rev. edn (New York: Berghahn Books, 2005). A recent work on the imperial is Michael Hardt and Antonio Negri, *Empire* (Cambridge, MA: Harvard University Press, 2000).

5 Lewis H. Gann, 'Western and Japanese Colonialism: Some Preliminary Comparisons', *The Japanese Colonial Empire, 1895–1914,* eds. Ramon H. Myers and Mark R. Peattie (Princeton: Princeton University Press, 1984), 497, see 498–525, which is a suggestive and helpful survey; the other essays in this collection are also germane. See also Masahiro Yamamoto, *Nanking: Anatomy of an Atrocity* (Westport, CT: Praeger, 2000).

6 Kennedy, *Great Powers,* 276, see 256–75. See also William L. Langer, *The Diplomacy of Imperialism 1890–1902,* 2nd edn (New York: Knopf, 1951); Ian Hill Nish, *The Anglo-Japanese Alliance: The Diplomacy of Two Island Empires, 1894–1907* (London: University of London, 1966); Arthur J. May, *The Passing of the Habsburg Monarchy, 1914–1918,* 2 vols. (Philadelphia: University of Pennsylvania Press, 1966); Ernest R. May, *The World War and American Isolation* (Cambridge, Harvard University Press, 1966); F. S. Northedge, *The Troubled Giant: Britain Among the Great Powers, 1916–39* (London: London School of Economics and Political Science; Bell, 1966); C. J. Lowe, *The Reluctant Imperialists: British Foreign Policy 1878–1902,* 2 vols. (London: Routledge & Kegan Paul, 1967); A. J. Ryder, *The German Revolution of 1918* (Cambridge: Cambridge University Press, 1967); Max Beloff, *Imperial Sunset,* 2 vols. (London: Methuen, 1969); Bernadotte E. Schmitt and Harold C. Vedeler, *The World in the Crucible 1914–1919* (New York: Harper & Row, 1984); Lewis H. Siegelbaum, *The Politics of Industrial Mobilization in Russia, 1914–1917: A Study of the War-industries*

Committees (London: Macmillan in association with St Antony's College, Oxford, 1983); Richard Pipes, *A Concise History of the Russian Revolution* (New York: Knopf, 1995); Arno J. Mayer, *The Furies: Violence and Terror in the French and Russian Revolutions* (Princeton: Princeton University Press, 2000); *The Anglo-Japanese Alliance, 1902–1922*, ed. Phillips Payson O'Brien (London: RoutledgeCurzon, 2004).

7 On Indian nationalism, see D. A. Low, *Britain and Indian Nationalism* (Cambridge: Cambridge University Press, 1997). For the fading of empire in Asia and Africa during the twentieth century, see D. A. Low, *Eclipse of Empire* (Cambridge: Cambridge University Press, 1991, rpt., 1993). On India, 1917 to 1947, see 58–100.

8 See Kennedy, 275–85; for the peace at the end of the First World War, see Margaret Macmillan, *Paris 1919: Six Months that Changed the World* (2002; New York: Random House, 2003).

9 Kennedy, 285–91.

10 On economic relations between Britain and India, see B. R. Tomlinson, *The Political Economy of the Raj 1914–1947: The Economics of Decolonization in India* (London: Macmillan, 1979); R.P.T. Davenport-Hines and Geoffrey Jones, eds., *British Business in Asia since 1860* (Cambridge: Cambridge University Press, 1989); Maria Misra, *Business, Race, and Politics in British India, c.1850–1960* (Oxford: Clarendon Press, 1999).

11 Stalin's position was embodied through writing as well as through action. See Joseph Stalin, *Marxism and the National and Colonial Question*, trans. A. Feinberg (London: Martin Lawrence, 1936).

12 *The Making of the West: Peoples and Cultures*, ed. Lynn Hunt et al. (Boston/New York: Bedford/St. Martin's, 2001), 1006–8, 1026–8, 1034–7, 1052–4. See Edwin Black, *IBM and the Holocaust: The Strategic Alliance Between Nazi Germany and America's Most Powerful Corporation* (New York: Crown Publishers, 2001), esp. 5–9. On totalitarianism, see Hannah Arendt, *The Origins of Totalitarianism* (New York: Harcourt, 1951); James Young, *The Texture of Memory: Holocaust Memorials and Meaning* (New Haven: Yale University Press 1993); Abbott Gleason, *Totalitarianism: The Inner History of the Cold War* (New York: Oxford University Press, 1995); Simon Tormey, *Making Sense of Tyranny: Interpretations of Totalitarianism* (Manchester, UK: Manchester University Press, 1995); Peter Fritzsche, *Germans into Nazis* (Cambridge, MA: Harvard University Press, 1998).

13 Kennedy, 309, see 291–310, which has influenced my discussion. See Hunt et al, 1046–7, 1053–4.

14 M. J. Bonn, *The Crumbling of Empire: The Disintegration of the World Economy* (London: George Allen & Unwin, 1938), 415, 417.

15 Kennedy, 323, see 311–27 for numbers and analysis to which I am indebted here and below.

16 Orlando Figes, *A People's Tragedy: The Russian Revolution 1891–1924* (London: Pimlico, 1996), 767–68, fig. 98 and caption following 768.

17 On the Great Depression and related matters, see Paul Kennedy 311–27; see also Ian Brown, *The Economies of Africa and Asia in the Interwar Depression* (London: Routledge, 1989); Dietmar Rothermund, *The Global Impact of the*

Great Depression, 1929–1939 (London: Routledge, 1996); David M. Kennedy, *Freedom from Fear: The American people in Depression and War, 1929–1945* (New York: Oxford University Press, 1999).

18 On the British in Malaya from this time to the end of empire, see Nicholas J. White, *Business, Government, and the End of Empire: Malaya, 1942–1957* (Oxford: Oxford University Press, 1996). On cultural change in Asia and elsewhere, see Philip Curtin, *The World and the West* (New York: Cambridge University Press, 2000), esp. 53–108.

19 On the French in the region, see Robert Aldrich, *The French Presence in the South Pacific, 1842–1940* (London: Macmillan, 1990).

20 For a study of this shift in the world, which in my view represented a translation of empire at least informally, see William Roger Louis, *Imperialism at Bay, 1941–1945: The United States and the Decolonization of the British Empire* (Oxford: Clarendon Press, 1977).

21 Kennedy, 333–43; on this pronouncement by Churchill, see Ronald H. Spector, *Eagle Against the Sun: The American War with Japan* (New York: Viking, 1985), 123 and Kennedy, 347. The rapid growth of Allied production of aircraft and tanks (especially on the part of the USA and USSR) and major vessels (USA) in relation to the output in these categories by Japan and Germany can be seen in Hunt et al., 1054–55 and *The Hammond Atlas of the Twentieth Century* (London: Times Books, 1996), 103.

22 On decolonization in the wake of the First World War, see, for instance, R. F. Holland, *European Decolonization, 1918: An Introductory Survey* (London: Macmillan, 1985).

23 See Stephen Howe, *AntiColonialism in British Politics: The Left and the End of Empire, 1918–1964* (Oxford: Clarendon Press, 1993). See also Partha Sarathi Gupta, *Imperialism and the British Labour Movement, 1914–1964* (New York: Holmes & Meier, 1975).

24 António de Oliveira Salazar, 'The Civilized Man's Burden', in Ronald H. Chilcote, *Emerging Nationalism in Portuguese Africa: Documents (*Stanford, CA: Hoover Institution Press, Stanford University, 1972), 2; see Salazar's *The Road for the Future* (Lisbon: Secretariado Nacional de Informação, 1963), 16–20.

25 Salazar, 3.

26 Salazar, 3–4.

27 Salazar, 4.

28 'The MPLA's Historical Perspective', in Chilcote, *Emerging*, 184, see 181–83; see Movimento Popular de Libertação de Angola, Angola. *Exploitation esclavagiste. Resistance Nationale* ([Léopoldville (?)], 1961), pp. 5–42.

29 John Quincy Adams, quoted in Robert L. Beisner, *Twelve Against Empire: The Anti-Imperialists 1898–1900* (New York: McGraw-Hill, 1968), iii. See Kennedy, 348–65.

30 Mary Evelyn Townsend with Cyrus Henderson Peake, *European Colonial Expansion Since 1871* (Chicago: J. B. Lippincott, 1941), v.

31 Eric A. Walker, *Colonies* (Cambridge: Cambridge University Press, 1944, rpt. 1945), vii.

32 Walker, 139, see 136–8, 160–2.

33 On the decline and fall of the British Empire, see, for instance, Colin Cross, *The Fall of the British Empire, 1918–1968* (London: Hodder & Stoughton, 1968); John Darwin, *Britain and Decolonization: The Retreat from Empire in the Post-War World* (London: Macmillan, 1987) and, in a comparative context, in M. E. Chamberlain, *Decolonization: The Fall of European Empires*, 2nd edn (Oxford: Blackwell, 1999), esp. 15–69.

34 Charles Dickens, *A Tale of Two Cities* (London: Chapman and Hall, 1859); see *A Tale of Two Cities*, ed. Andrew Sanders, World's Classics (Oxford: Oxford University Press, 1990).

35 MANIFESTO OF THE COMMUNIST PARTY: IV, The Avalon Project, at <http://www.yale.edu/lawweb/avalon/treatise/communist_manifesto/manfour.htm>.

36 'The Civil Rights Bill', Editorial, *Harper's Weekly*, April 1966, 243; see 'The Impeachment of Andrew Johnson' at <http://www.impeach-andrewjohnson.com/05AJFirstVetoes/iiia-11.htm>.

37 Anthony Parel, Introduction, in M. K. Gandhi, *Hind Swaraj and Other Writings* (Cambridge: Cambridge University Press, 1997), xx–xxi; see this Introduction, xiii–lxii, to which I am indebted here and below.

38 Parel, xiv–xvii.

39 Gandhi, *Hind Swaraj*, 72–3.

40 Parel, xvii–xviii.

41 Quoted in Nellie McClung, *The Stream Runs Fast: My Own Story* (Toronto: Thomas Allen Limited, 1945), 186; my account is indebted to Monique Benoit, 'Are Women Persons? The "Persons" Case', *The Archivist*, No 119, Government Archives and Records Disposition, National Archives of Canada at <http://www.archives.ca/04/042412_e.html>.

42 Benoit and the decision quoted by her at <http://www.archives.ca/04/042412_e.html>

43 Rachella Meekcoms, in *Voices From the Holocaust*, ed. Sylvia Rothchild (New York: New American Library, 1981), 174.

44 Meekcoms, 179–80.

45 Meekcoms, 181.

46 Meekcoms, 183.

47 Meekcoms, 185.

Chapter 7

1 On decolonization, see, for instance, Janet Elizabeth Hannan Hyman, 'Political Decolonization: the Philippines, Ceylon, Syria and the Lebanon, and Iraq', thesis (PhD), Radcliffe College, 1940; Arend Lijphart, *The Trauma of Decolonization; the Dutch and West New Guinea* (New Haven, Yale University Press, 1966); John Sturgus Bastin and Henry J. Benda, *A History of Modern Southeast Asia: Colonialism, Nationalism, and Decolonization* (Englewood Cliffs, NJ: Prentice-Hall, 1968); Kwame Nkrumah, *Consciencism: Philosophy and Ideology for De-colonization* (New York: Modern Reader Paperbacks, 1970); Adrian Pelt, *Libyan Independence and the United Nations; A Case of Planned Decolonization Foreword by U. Thant* (New Haven, Published for the

Carnegie Endowment for International Peace [by] Yale University Press, 1970);
Rudolf von Albertini, *Decolonization; the Administration and Future of the
Colonies, 1919–1960*, trans. Francisca Garvie (Garden City, NY, Doubleday,
1971); Yassin El-Ayouty, *The United Nations and Decolonization: the Role of
Afro-Asia* (The Hague, Martinus Nijhoff, 1971); Selwyn D. Ryan, *Race and
Nationalism in Trinidad and Tobago: A Study of Decolonization in a
Multiracial Society* (Toronto: University of Toronto Press, 1972); Robert
Stephen Wood, *France in the World Community. Decolonization, Peacekeeping
and the United Nations* (Leiden, Sijthoff, 1973); Henri Grimal, *Decolonization:
the British, French, Dutch, and Belgian Empires, 1919–1963*, trans. Stephan
De Vos (Boulder, CO: Westview Press, 1978); Guy Viêt Levilain, *Cultural
Identity, Négritude, and Decolonization: The Haitian Situation in the Light of
the Socialist Humanism of Jacques Ro[u]main and René Dépestre* ([New York:
American Institute for Marxist Studies], 1978); Franz-Wilhelm Heimer, *The
Decolonization Conflict in Angola, 1974–76: An Essay in Political Sociology*
(Genève: Institut universitaire de hautes études internationales, 1979); *A
Memorandum Concerning the Decolonization of the Union of Soviet Socialist
Republics/Submitted to the Members of the 35th U.N. General Assembly by the
Ad Hoc Committee Consisting of the World Councils of Byelorussians,
Estonians, Latvians, Lithuanians, Turkestanians, and Ukrainians* (New York:
[s.n.], 1980); *The Decolonization of Africa: Southern Africa and the Horn of
Africa: Working Documents and Report of the Meeting of Experts Held in
Warsaw, Poland, from 9 to 13 October 1978* (Paris: Unesco Press, 1981); D. K.
Fieldhouse, *The Colonial Empires: A Comparative Survey from the Eighteenth
Century*, 2nd edn (Houndsmills and London: Macmillan Education, 1982, rpt.
1987), 395–428; Bassey E. Ate, *Decolonization and Dependence: The
Development of Nigerian-U.S. Relations, 1960–1984* (Boulder, CO: Westview
Press, 1987); *Decolonization and African Independence: The Transfers of
Power, 1960–1980*, eds. Prosser Gifford and Wm. Roger Louis (New Haven:
Yale University Press, 1988); Raymond F. Betts, *France and Decolonisation
1900–1960* (London: Macmillan, 1991), 49–124 and his *Decolonization*, 2nd
edn., (New York: Routledge, 2004); David Birmingham, *The Decolonization
of Africa* (Athens, OH: Ohio University Press, 1995); Clive J. Christie, *A
Modern History of Southeast Asia: Decolonization, Nationalism and
Separatism* (London: Tauris Academic Studies, 1996); Toyin Falola,
Development Planning and Decolonization in Nigeria (Gainesville: University
Press of Florida, 1996); John D. Hargreaves, *Decolonization in Africa, 2nd edn.*
(London: Longman, 1996); Norrie Macqueen, *The Decolonization of
Portuguese Africa: Metropolitan Revolution and the Dissolution of Empire*
(London: Longman, 1997); Muriel Evelyn Chamberlain, *Decolonization: The
Fall of the European Empires*, 2nd edn. (Oxford: Blackwell, 1999);
*Imperialism, Decolonization, and Africa: Studies Presented to John
Hargreaves: With an Academic Memoir and Bibliography*, ed. Roy Bridges,
(Basingstoke: Macmillan, 2000); Phillip Chiviges Naylor, *France and Algeria:
A History of Decolonization and Transformation* (Gainesville: University Press
of Florida, 2000); *The United States and Decolonization: Power and Freedom*,
eds. David Ryan and Victor Pungong (Basingstoke: Macmillan, 2000); James

D. Le Sueur. *Uncivil War: Intellectuals and Identity Politics during the Decolonization of Algeria*; foreword by Pierre Bourdieu (Philadelphia: University of Pennsylvania Press, 2001); John Dunham Kelly and Martha Kaplan, *Represented Communities: Fiji and World Decolonization*. (Chicago: University of Chicago Press, 2001); David D. Newsom, *The Imperial Mantle: The United States, Decolonization, and the Third World* (Bloomington: Indiana University Press, 2001); Ebere Nwaubani, *The United States and Decolonization in West Africa, 1950–1960* (Rochester, NY: University of Rochester Press, 2001); John Springhall, *Decolonization since 1945: The Collapse of European Overseas Empires* (Houndmills, Basingstoke: Palgrave, 2001); *The Last Empire: Thirty Years of Portuguese Decolonization*, eds. Stewart Lloyd-Jones and António Costa Pinto (Bristol: Intellect, 2003); Mark T. Berger, *The Battle for Asia: From Decolonization to Globalization* (London: RoutledgeCurzon, 2004); Messay Kebede, *Africa's Quest for a Philosophy of Decolonization* (Amsterdam: Rodopi, 2004). On the British empire, Niall Ferguson has a chapter on the denouement, called 'Empire for Sale'; see his – *Empire: The Rise and Demise of the British World Order and the Lessons for Global Power* (2002; New York: Basic Books, 2003), 291–356. See also Robin W. Winks, *Failed Federations: Decolonization and the British Empire* ([Nottingham:] University of Nottingham [1970?]); John Darwin, *Britain and Decolonisation: The Retreat from Empire in the Post-war World* (New York: St. Martin's Press, 1988); Allister Hinds, *Britain's Sterling Colonial Policy and Decolonization, 1939–1958* (Westport, CT: Greenwood Press, 2001); William Roger Louis, *Ends of British Imperialism: The Scramble for Empire, Suez and Decolonization: Collected Essays* (London: I.B. Tauris, 2006).

2   On British economic decline, see E. J. Hobsbawm, *Industry and Empire; From 1750 to the Present Day* (Harmondsworth: Penguin, 1969); Correlli Barnett, *The Audit of War: The Illusion & Reality of Britain as a Great Nation* (London: Macmillan, 1986); and *The Making of the West: Peoples and Cultures*, ed. Lynn Hunt et al. (Boston/New York: Bedford/St. Martin's, 2001), 1073. On decolonization, see, for instance, L. von Albertini, *Decolonization* (1971); Correlli Barnett, *The Collapse of British Power* (London: Eyre Methuen, 1972); Grimal, *Decolonization* (1978); T. Smith, *The Pattern of Imperialism: The United States, Great Britain and the Late-Industrializing World Since 1915* (Cambridge, 1981); R. F. Holland, European Decolonization, 1918–1981: An Introductory Survey (New York: St Martin's Press, 1985); D. A. Low, *Eclipse of Empire* (1991; Cambridge: Cambridge University Press, 1993); Frances Gouda, *Dutch Culture Overseas: Colonial Practice in the Netherlands Indies, 1900–1942* (Amsterdam: Amsterdam University Press, 1995). On Churchill, Eisenhower and general ideas about the beginnings of the Cold War, see Robert Dallek, *The American Style of Foreign Policy* (New York: Knopf, 1983), 170; Michael Balfour, *The Adversaries: America, Russia and the Open World, 1941–1962* (London: Routledge & Kegan Paul, 1981), 71; Paul Kennedy, *The Rise and Fall of the Great Powers* (New York: Random House, 1987), 366–72; on the nuclear issue, see Frederick S. Dunn, B. Brody et al., *The Absolute Weapon: Atomic Power and World Order*, ed. Bernard Brodie (New York: Harcourt, Brace,

1946); Wilfrid L. Kohl, *French Nuclear Diplomacy* (Princeton: Princeton University Press, 1971); Lawrence Freeman, *Britain and Nuclear Weapons* (London: Macmillan; published for the Royal Institute of International Affairs, 1980); J. Baylis, *Anglo-American Defense Relations, 1939–80: The Special Relationship* (London: Macmillan, 1981); John Prados, *The Soviet Estimate: U. S. Intelligence Analysis and Russian Military Strength* (New York: Dial Press, 1982); David Holloway, *The Soviet Union and the Arms Race* (New Haven: Yale University Press, 1983); Robert Aldrich, *Greater France: A History of French Overseas Expansion* (Basingstoke: Macmillan, 1996); Niall Ferguson, *The Pity of War* (London: Allen Lane, 1998); Philip Curtain, *The World and the West* (New York: Cambridge University Press, 2000); *Marks of Distinction: American Exceptionalism Revisited*, ed. Dale Carter (Aarhus: Aarhus University Press, 2001); Ferguson, *Empire* (2003), 291–356.

3 On nationalism, see for instance, Frank Füredi, *Colonial Wars and the Politics of Third World Nationalism* (London: I.B. Tauris, 1994) and Harry G. Gelber, *Nations Out of Empires: European Nationalism and the Transformation of Asia* (London: Palgrave, 2001). Gelber gives a sweeping view over centuries of the European empires in Asia and the exchange between Asian and European cultures (including their ironies) and points out the variety of meanings in the words such as 'colony', 'colonization', and 'decolonization' (esp. 212–24). Philip Curtain discusses resistance to European rule and the independence of Indonesia and Ghana. See his *The World and the West* (New York: Cambridge University Press, 2000), 193–274. On the connection between Britain and Australia, see David Day, *The Great Betrayal: Great Britain, Australia and the Onset of the Pacific War, 1939–42* (London: Angus & Robertson, 1988). On the background to relations between Britain and Japan, see Douglas Ford, *Britain's Secret War against Japan, 1937–1945* (London; New York: Routledge, 2006). For a more general history of the times, see *The Oxford History of the Twentieth Century*, eds. Michael Howard and Wm. Roger Louis (Oxford; New York: Oxford University Press, 1998).

4 Grimal, *Decolonization* (1965; London: Routledge & Kegan Paul, 1978), 185–213.

5 For more on the economics and politics of India and the East Indies, see B.H.M. Vlekke, *The Story of the Dutch East Indies* (Cambridge, MA: Harvard University Press, 1946); Jacob Cornelius Van Leur, *Indonesian Trade and Society*, trans. James C. Holmes and A. van Marle (The Hague: Van Hoeve, 1955); Brian Roger Tomlinson, *The Political Economy of the Raj 1914–47: The Economics of Decolonisation in India* (London: Macmillan, 1979) and *The Economy of Modern India 1860–1970* (Cambridge: Cambridge University Press, 1993).

6 For a wide-ranging analysis based on the thesis that great powers seek alliances to achieve a balance of power, see Paul Kennedy, *Rise and Fall*, 366–438. On the Cold War, see James Cronin, *The World the Cold War Made: Order, Chaos, and the Return of History* (New York: Routledge, 1996); John Gaddis, *We Now Know: Rethinking Cold War History* (Oxford: Clarendon Press, 1997); Vladislav Zubok and Constantine Pleshakov, *Inside the*

Kremlin's Cold War: From Stalin to Khrushchev (Cambridge, MA: Harvard University Press, 1996); Elena Zubkova, *Russia after the War: Hopes, Illusions, and Disappointments, 1945–1957* (Armonk, NY: M.E. Sharpe, 1998); Henry Heller, *The Cold War and the New Imperialism: A Global History, 1945–2005* (New York: Monthly Review Press, 2006). On Russian imperialism, see *Russian Empire: Some Aspects of the Tsarist and Soviet Colonial Practices*, ed. Michael S. Pap (Cleveland, OH: John Carroll University and the Ukrainian Historical Association, 1985).

7 Thomas Pakenham, *The Scramble for Africa 1876–1912* (New York: Random House, 1991), 671; see 669–80.

8 Grimal, *Decolonization*, 322–39.

9 See, for example, Aron Shai, *The Fate of British and French Firms in China, 1949–54: Imperialism Imprisoned* (Basingstoke: Macmillan in association with St Antony's College, Oxford, 1994); D. Clayton, *Imperialism Revisited: Political and Economic Relations between Britain and China, 1950–54* (Basingstoke: Macmillan, 1997).

10 Quoted in W. D. Hussey, *The British Empire and Commonwealth 1500 to 1961* (Cambridge: Cambridge University Press, 1963), 347.

11 Sarah Stockwell, *The Business of Decolonization: British Business Strategies in the Gold Coast* (Oxford: Clarendon Press, 2000), 236–37. For other related works, see Kathleen Mary Stahl, *The Metropolitan Organization of British Colonial Trade: Four Studies* (London: Faber, 1951); Thomas Lionel Hodgkin, *Nationalism in Colonial Africa* (London: Muller, 1956); *Colonialism in Africa, 1870–1960*, ed. Lewis H. Gann and Peter Duignan 5 vols. (Cambridge: Cambridge University Press, 1969–75), iv, *The Economics of Colonialism*; Frederick Pedler, *The Lion and the Unicorn in Africa: A History of the Origins of the United Africa Company, 1787–1931* (London: Heinemann Educational, 1974) and *Business and Decolonization in West Africa: c.1940–1960: A Personal Memoir* (Oxford; [s.n.], 1989); Yusuf Bangura, *Britain and Commonwealth Africa: The Politics of Economic Relations, 1951–75* (Manchester: Manchester University Press, 1983); Stephen Constantine, *The Making of British Colonial Development Policy 1914–60* (London: Cass, 1984); Anne Phillips, *The Enigma of Colonialism: British Policy in West Africa* (London: Currey, 1989); John D. Hargreaves, *Decolonization in Africa* (Harlow: Longman, 1988); Douglas Rimmer, *Staying Poor: Ghana's Political Economy 1950–1990* (Oxford: Pergamon Press for the World Bank, 1992); D. K. Fieldhouse, *Merchant Capital and Economic Decolonization: The United Africa Company, 1929–87* (Oxford: Oxford University Press, 1994); L. J. Butler, *Industrialisation and the British Colonial State: West Africa 1939–1951* (London: Cass, 1997).

12 See, for instance, J. M. Lee, *Colonial Development and Good Government: A Study of the Ideas Expressed by the British Official Classes in Planning Decolonization, 1939–1964* (Oxford: Clarendon Press, 1967); John G. Darwin, *Britain and Decolonization: The Retreat from Empire in the Post-War World* (Basingstoke: Macmillan Education, 1988) and *The End of the British Empire: The Historical Debate* (Oxford: Basil Blackwell, 1991); P. J. Cain and A.G. Hopkins, *British Imperialism*, 2 vols. (Harlow: Longman,

1993); Philip Murphy, *Party Politics and Decolonization: The Conservative Party and British Colonial Policy in Tropical Africa, 1951–64* (Oxford: Clarendon Press, 1995); Curtain, *World and West* (2000), 193–274; Robert Johnson, *British Imperialism* (Basingstoke: Palgrave Macmillan, 2003); Ferguson, *Empire* (2003), 291–356.

13 For instance, imperialism and neocolonialism were linked in Kwame Nkrumah's *Neo-Colonialism, The Last Stage of Imperialism* (London: Thomas Nelson & Sons, 1965).

14 See Kwame Nkrumah, *Neo-Colonialism: The Last Stage of Imperialism* (London: Nelson, 1965); J. Lonsdale and R. Robinson, 'The Imperialism of Decolonization', *Journal of Imperial and Commonwealth History* 22 (1994), 462–511. On neo-colonialism, see Kiernan, *America* (2005), 283–94.

15 Stewart C. Easton, *The Twilight of European Colonialism: A Political Analysis* (New York: Holt, Rinehart and Winston, 1960), 3–5.

16 There are some comparative studies of decolonization in empires: see, for example, *Decolonisation and After: the British and French Experience, eds.* W. H. Morris-Jones and Georges Fischer (London: Cass, 1980), 86–104; Miles Kahler, *Decolonization in Britain and France: The Domestic Consequences of International Relations* (Princeton: Princeton University Press, 1984); Jacques Marseille, *Empire colonial et capitalisme français: Histoire d'un divorce* (1984; Paris: Seuil, 1989); Frederick. Cooper, *Decolonization and African Society: The Labour Question in French and British Africa* (Cambridge: Cambridge University Press, 1996).

17 See Robert Gilpin, *War and Change in World Politics* (Cambridge: Cambridge University Press, 1981) and Kennedy, *Rise and Fall*, 437, see 373–438 for my discussion above. On aspects of economics and politics, see Rupert Emerson, *From Empire to Nation: The Rise of Self-Assertion of Asian and African Peoples* (Cambridge MA: Harvard University Press, 1960); Edward. Taborsky, *Communist Penetration of the Third World* (New York: R. Speller, 1973); Maurice Parodi, *L'économie et la société française de 1945 à 1970* (Paris: A. Colin, 1971); Robert D. Keohane, *After Hegemony: Cooperation and Discord in the World Political Economy* (Princeton: Princeton University Press, 1974); Raymond Aron, *The Imperial Republic: The United States and the World, 1945–1973*, trans. Frank Jellinek (London: Weidenfeld & Nicolson, 1975); Paul Bairoch, *The Economic Development of the Third World Since 1900* (Berkeley: University of California Press, 1975); Ronald Steel, *Pax Americana*, rev. ed. (New York: Penguin, 1977); A. W. DePorte, *Europe Between the Superpowers: The Enduring Balance* (New Haven: Yale University Press, 1979); George C. Herring, *America's Longest War: The United States and Vietnam, 1950–1975* (New York: Knopf, 1979); Michael Mandelbaum, *The Nuclear Revolution: International Politics Before and After Hiroshima* (Cambridge and New York: Cambridge University Press, 1981); L. S. Stavrianos, *Global Rift: The Third World Comes of Age* (New York: Morrow, 1981); Henry S. Bradsher, *Afghanistan and the Soviet Union* (Durham, NC: Duke University Press, 1983); Adam B. Ulam, *Dangerous Relations: The Soviet Union in World Politics 1970–1982* (New York: Oxford University Press, 1983); Norman A. Graebner, *America as a World Power: A Realist Appraisal from Wilson to Reagan: Essays*

(Wilmington, DE: Scholarly Resources, 1984); Alan S. Milward, *The Reconstruction of Western Europe, 1945–1951* (London: Routledge, 1984); Glenn Blackburn, *The West and the World Since 1945* (New York: St. Martin's Press, 1985); Akira Iriye, *The Origins of the Second World War in Asia and the Pacific* (London, New York: St Martin's Press, 1987); Stanley Karnow, *Vietnam: A History*, rev. ed. (1983; New York: Penguin, 1991); Henry Kissinger is a controversial figure, to some a flexible visionary who understood Realpolitik and to others a violator of human rights and a perpetrator of war crimes. Beyond these black and white views, for many, there is probably more of an ambivalence towards Kissinger. He obviously understood the traditions of European diplomacy; see Henry Kissinger, *A World Restored: Metternich, Castlereagh and the Problems of Peace 1812–1822* (Boston: Houghton Mifflin, 1957). On the rise of the west and on the benefit of world history, see William H. McNeill, *Mythistory and Other Essays* (Chicago: University of Chicago Press, 1986), esp. 43–106. On the atomic bomb, American aid to Europe and the Nuremburg trials, see Hunt et al. (2001), 1061–3, 1075–81. Richard Rhodes, *The Making of the Atomic Bomb* (New York: Simon and Schuster, 1986). On the numbers of dead in Europe, see Hunt et al, 1064–5 and *The Hammond Atlas of the Twentieth Century* (London, 1996), 102. On controversies over the United States as an empire or as an embodiment of imperialism, see *Cultures of United States Imperialism*, eds. Amy Kaplan and Donald E. Pease (Durham, NC: Duke University Press, 1993); V. G. Kiernan, *America: The New Imperialism: From White Settlement to World Hegemony* (London and New York: Verso, 2005); *Lessons of Empire: Imperial Histories and American Power*, ed. Craig Calhoun et al. (New York and London: The New Press, 2006); Christopher Layne and Bradley A. Thayer, *American Empire: A Debate* (New York and London: Routledge, 2007).

18 Rudolf von Albertini, *Decolonization: The Administration and Future of the Colonies, 1919–1960*, trans. Francisca Garvie (1966; Garden City NY: Doubleday, 1971), 525.

19 Stewart C. Easton, *The Rise and fall of Western Colonialism: A Historical Survey from the Early Nineteenth Century to the Present* (London and Dunmow; Pall Mall Press, 1964), v–vi.

20 Pakenham, *Scramble*, 680.

21 Hunt et al., 1084, 1090–97. See also J. P. D. Dunbabin, *The Post-Imperial Age: The Great Powers and the Wider World* (London; New York: Longman, 1994); John D. Hargreaves, *Decolonization in Africa* 2nd edn. (London: Longman, 1996, rpt. 1999); W. David McIntyre, *British Decolonization, 1946–1997: When, Why, and How Did the British Empire Fall?* (Basingstoke: Macmillan, 1999). On early maritime power, see *War at Sea in the Middle Ages and the Renaissance*, eds. John B. Hattendorf and Richard W. Unger (Woodbridge: Boydell Press, 2003); on cotton, see *The Fibre that Changed the World: The Cotton Industry in International Perspective, 1600–1990s*, ed. Douglas A. Farnie and David J. Jeremy (Oxford: Oxford University Press, 2004); and on human rights, see *Human Rights and Revolutions*, eds. Jeffrey N. Wasserstrom et al., 2nd edn (Lanham, MD: Rowman & Littlefield Publishers, 2007).

22 Fieldhouse, *The Colonial Empires*, 408.

23 On the advancement of Asian economies, see *World Bank, East Asian Miracle: Economic Growth and Public Policy* (New York: Oxford University Press, 1993). On trade, science, research and development, see Zaheer Baber, *The Science of Empire: Scientific Knowledge, Civilization, and Colonial Rule in India* (Albany: State University of New York Press, 1996); 'The Technology of Japanese Imperialism: Telecommunications and Empire-building, 1895–1945', thesis (Ph. D.)—Harvard University, 1996 and (by the same author) *Technology of Empire: Telecommunications and Japanese Imperialism, 1930–1945* (Cambridge, MA: Harvard University Press, 2003); *Universities and Empire: Money and Politics in the Social Sciences during the Cold War*, ed. Christopher Simpson (New York: New Press; distributed by Norton 1998); *China and Historical Capitalism: Genealogies of Sinological Knowledge*, eds. Timothy Brook and Gregory Blue (Cambridge and New York: Cambridge University Press, 1999); *The Silk Roads: Highways of Culture and Commerce*, ed. Vadime Elisseeff (New York: Berghahn Books; Paris UNESCO Pub., 2000); *China: Empire and Civilization*, gen. ed. Edward L. Shaughnessy (Oxford and New York: Oxford University Press, 2000); *Gender, Colonialism and Education: The Politics of Experience*, eds. Joyce Goodman and Jane Martin (London: Woburn Press, 2002); Jeffry A. Frieden, *Global Capitalism: Its Fall and Rise in the Twentieth Century* (New York: Norton, 2006).

24 Some of the background to these conflicts was a history of empire and colony. For the case of Iran, see Geoffrey Jones, *Banking and Empire in Iran* (Cambridge: Cambridge University Press, 1986). On Islam, see *The Oxford History of Islam*, ed. John L. Esposito (Oxford and New York: Oxford University Press, 1999).

25 Hunt et al., 1113–77 to which my narrative is indebted; see Walter Laqueur, *The Age of Terrorism* (London: Weidenfeld & Nicolson, 1987); David Caute, *Sixty-Eight: The Year of the Barricades* (London: Paladin, 1988); Adrian Guelke, *The Age of Terrorism and the International Political System* (London: Tauris, 1995); Dennis B. Smith, *Japan since 1945: The Rise of an Economic Superpower* (Basingstoke: Macmillan1995); Edward Singer, *Twentieth Century Revolutions in Technology* (Commack, NY: Nova Science Pub., 1998); on globalization, see, for instance, Naomi Klein, *No Logo* (New York: Picador, 1999). For other recent works on technology and globalization, see *Does Technology Drive History? The Dilemma of Technological Determinism*, eds. Merritt Roe Smith and Leo Marx (1994; Cambridge, MA: MIT Press, 1996); Pamela Kyle Crossley, Lynn Hollen Lees, John W. Servos, *Global Society: The World Since 1900* (Boston: Houghton Mifflin, 2004); *Globalization with a Human Face*, eds. Jung Min Choi, John W. Murphy, and Manuel J. Caro (Westport, CT: Praeger Publishers, 2004).

26 Hunt et al., 912–15, 1177–89. See *The Hammond Atlas of the Twentieth Century* (London: Times Books, 1996), 183

27 Andrei Sakharov, Royal Institute of International Affairs, 20 June 1989, quoted in J. E. Chamberlain, 93

28 Robert Aldrich and John Connell, *The Last Colonies* (Cambridge: Cambridge University Press, 1998), 1, 156–68, 235. On indigenous issues, see *Native*

America: Problems and Prospects, ed. Russell Thornton (Madison: University of Wisconsin Press, 1998).

29 Salman Rushdie, 'The Empire Writes Back with a Vengeance', *The Times*, 3 July 1982, 8, rpt. in his *Imaginary Homelands* (Harmondsworth: Granta/ Penguin, 1990). Edward Said, *Orientalism* (London: Routledge & Kegan Paul, 1978) and *Covering Islam* (New York: Vintage, 1997); see his *Culture and Imperialism* (London: Chatto & Windus, 1993). For works considering his idea of Orientalism, see Robert Young, 'Discovering Orientialism', *White Mythologies: Writing History and the West* (London: Routledge, 1990) and John M. MacKenzie, *Orientalism: History, Theory and the Arts* (Manchester: Manchester University Press, 1995). When I was a participant in Said's seminar at the School of Criticism and Theory at Dartmouth College in 1988, he said how much he did not like the word the 'West' because there was no such thing. It was a manufactured idea. At Harvard, when I was a visiting scholar, I heard Gayatri Spivak speak at the Center for Literary Theory and hosted Homi Bhabha at University of Alberta, where I had invited him as a Distinguished Visitor, so that I have had the pleasure of hearing Said, Spivak and Bhabha at some length. Gayatri Chakravorty Spivak, 'Imperialism and Sexual Difference', *Oxford Literary Review* 8 (1986), esp. 234–37 and *In Other Worlds: Essays in Cultural Politics* (London: Routledge, 1988). For related work on subalterns, see Antonio Gramsci, 'History of the Subaltern Classes: Some Methodological Criteria', in Q. Hoare and G. Nowell Smith, eds., *Selections from the Prison Notebooks* (London: Lawrence and Wishart, 1971) and Ranajit Guha and Gayatri Chakravorty Spivak, eds. *Selected Subaltern Studies* (Oxford: Oxford University Press, 1988). Homi K. Bhabha, 'Of Mimicry and Man: The Ambivalence of Colonial Discourse', *October* 28 (1984), 125–33, and *The Location of Culture* (London: Routledge, 1993) as well as the volume he edited, *Nation and Narration* (London: Routledge, 1990). For related works, see Peter Hulme, *Colonial Encounters: Europe and the Native Caribbean, 1492–1797* (London: Methuen, 1986), Nicholas Thomas, *Colonialism's Culture* (London: Polity, 1994), Anne McClintock, *Imperial Leather: Race, Gender, and Sexuality in the Colonial Contest* (London: Routledge, 1995), Robert Young, *Colonial Desire: Hybridity in Theory, Culture and Race* (London: Routledge, 1995). For a clear overview, see Peter Childs and R. J. Patrick Williams, *An Introduction to Post-Colonial Theory* (London: Longman, 1997). For some of my work on the colonial and postcolonial, see Jonathan Hart and Terry Goldie, 'Postcolonial Theory', *Encyclopedia of Contemporary Literary Theory* (Toronto: University of Toronto Press, 1993), 155–8 and Jonathan Hart, 'Cultural Appropriation: Colonialism and Postcolonialism', in *Columbus, Shakespeare and the Interpretation of the New World* (New York and London: Palgrave Macmillan, 2003), 149–73, 213–19.

30 The Associated Press, Washington, 'Bush acts like emperor, Spanish leader says', *The Edmonton Journal*, Thursday, 15 January 2004, A 10.

31 Klein, quoted in Geoff McMaster, 'Klein Decries Economic Pillage of Iraq', *University of Alberta Express News*, 17 November, 2003, 1. McMaster is interviewing Klein, whose talk concluded the Parkland Institute's conference,

'Challenging Empire'. Klein's *No Logo: Taking Aim at the Brand Bullies* has been translated into 27 languages. I had the pleasure of meeting Klein when I was at Princeton University and I wish to thank her for her generous suggestions. If memory serves, the first full draft of my book was completed at the end of 2003 and the last in March 2007. The Conclusion, as it stands, was completed on 4 April 2007, and that explains the layering of the references in my book.

32 Gelber, 223–4. For another point of view, see Paul Bairoch, *Economics and World History: Myths and Paradoxes* (Chicago: University of Chicago Press, 1993).

33 'Martin Luther King's Letter from Birmingham Jail', April 16, 1963, at <http://almaz.com/nobel/peace/MLK-jail.html>. This version keeps all original typographical errors.

34 'The I Have a Dream Speech', The United States Constitution Online, at <http://www.usconstitution.net/dream.html>.

35 'Martin Luther King's Nobel Prize Acceptance Speech', December 10, 1964, Oslo, Norway at <http://www.nobelprizes.com/nobel/peace/MLK-nobel.html> for quotations from this speech here and below.

36 Martin Luther King, 'I've Been to the Mountaintop', at <http://www.afscme.org/about/kingspch.htm>, © American Federation of State, County and Municipal Employees, 2002.

37 Martin Luther King, *Stride, Toward Freedom: The Montgomery Story* (New York: Harper & Brothers, 1958).

38 Top Secret, Foreign Office telegram No. 2938 to Washington, 2; see page 76 of Public Record Office Reference, PREM 11/2880.

39 *Souvenir of the Visit of the RT. Hon Harold Macmillan Prime Minister of the United Kingdom to the Houses of Parliament, Cape Town, Wednesday, 3rd February, 1960*, Printed on the authority of Mr Speaker (Parow: Cape Times Limited [n.d. 1960??]), 7 [ms. 12], Public Record Office Reference, PREM 11/4937.

40 Macmillan, 8 [ms. 13].

41 Macmillan, 8 [ms. 13].

42 Macmillan, 9 [ms. 14].

43 Mandela, 'A New Menace in Africa', No.30, March 1958, here and below at <http://www.anc.org.za/ancdocs/history/mandela/1950s/nm55-56.html#Education>.

44 ADDRESS OF THE DEPUTY PRESIDENT OF THE AFRICAN NATIONAL CONGRESS NELSON MANDELA, AT THE EUROPEAN PARLIAMENT, Strasbourg, 13 June 1990 at <http://www.anc.org.za/ancdocs/history/mandela/1950s/sp530921.html> here and below.

45 MANDELA MESSAGE TO USA BIG BUSINESS, 19 June 1990 at <www.anc.org.za/ancdocs>.

46 ADDRESS TO THE JOINT SESSION OF THE HOUSES OF CONGRESS OF THE U.S.A., Washington, DC, June 26, 1990, here and below, at <www.anc.org.za/ancdocs>.

47 STATEMENT OF THE DEPUTY PRESIDENT OF THE AFRICAN NATIONAL CONGRESS, NELSON MANDELA, TO THE CONFEDERATION OF BRITISH INDUSTRY, London, 4 July 1990, at <www.anc.org.za/ancdocs>.

48 SPEECH BY THE DEPUTY PRESIDENT OF THE AFRICAN NATIONAL CONGRESS, NELSON MANDELA, AT THE BANQUET HOSTED BY THE PRESIDENT OF THE REPUBLIC OF INDIA, New Delhi, 15 October 1990, here and below at <www.anc.org.za/ancdocs>.

49 Nelson Mandela – *Nobel Lecture, Acceptance and Nobel Lecture, Norway, 1994* at <*http://www.nobel.se/peace/laureates/1993/mandela-lecture.html*>.

50 F. W. de Klerk, Acceptance and Nobel Lecture, Norway, 1994, at <http://www.nobel.se/peace/laureates/1993/mandela-lecture.html>.

51 Speech by President Mandela to the Joint Sitting of the Canadian Parliament, Ottawa, 24 September 1998, here and below, at <www.anc.org.za/ancdocs>.

52 Thomas, 593–623, 629, 656–5, 672–3, 712, 726–45, 774–85, 790–3, 861–2. On China, the Exhibition of 1851, and economic and political imperialism, see Hunt et al, 823–25, 841. See also Jonathan Sperber, *The European Revolutions, 1848–1851*, 2nd edn (Cambridge and New York: Cambridge University Press, 2005). On slavery and economic contexts, see also William Law Mathieson, *Great Britain and the Slave Trade* (London: Longmans, Green and Co., 1929); Hugh G. Soulsby, *The Right of Search and the Slave Trade in Anglo-American Relations, 1814-* (Baltimore: Johns Hopkins University Press, 1933); Christopher Lloyd, *The Navy and the Slave Trade: The Suppression of the African Slave Trade in the Nineteenth Century* (London: Longmans, Green, 1949); Arthur F. Corwin, *Spain and the Abolition of Slavery in Cuba* (Austin: Published for the Institute of Latin American Studies by the University of Texas Press, 1967); C. L. R. Boxer, *The Portuguese Seaborne Empire, 1415–1825* (London: Hutchinson, 1969) Philip D. Curtain, *The Atlantic Slave Trade, A Census* (Madison: University of Wisconsin Press, 1969); W. E. F. Ward, *The Royal Navy and the Slavers: The Suppression of the Atlantic Slave Trade* (London: Allen & Unwin, 1969); Leslie Bethell, *The Abolition of the Brazilian Slave Trade: Britain, Brazil and the Slave Trade Question, 1807–1869* (Cambridge: Cambridge University Press, 1970); Seymour Dreschler, *Econocide: British Slavery in the Era of Abolition* (Pittsburgh: University of Pittsburgh Press, 1977); Enriqueta Vila Vilar, *Hispanoamérica y el comercio de esclavos* (Seville: Escuela de Estudios Hispano-Americanos, 1977); *Forced Migration: The Impact of the Export Slave Trade on African Societies*, ed. Joseph E. Inikori (London: Hutchinson, 1982); Maldwyn A. Jones, *The Limits of Liberty: American History, 1607–1980* (Oxford: Oxford University Press, 1983); David Brion Davis, *Slavery and Human Progress* (New York: Oxford University Press, 1984); Stuart Schwartz, *Sugar Plantations in the Formation of Brazilian Society: Bahia, 1550–1835* (Cambridge: Cambridge University Press, 1985); John Lynch, *The Spanish American Revolutions, 1808–1826*, 2nd edn (London: Norton, 1986); David Eltis, *Economic Growth and the Ending of the Atlantic Slave Trade* (New York: Oxford University Press, 1987); Robin Blackburn, *The Overthrow of Colonial Slavery 1776–1848* (London: Verso, 1988); *The Atlantic Slave Trade: Effects on Economies, Societies, and Peoples in Africa, the Americas, and Europe*, eds. Joseph E. Inikori and Stanley L. Engerman (Durham: Duke University Press, 1992); Jean-Michel Déveau, *France au temps des négriers* (Paris: France-Empire, 1994) and his *L'or et les esclaves:*

histoire des forts du Ghana du XVIe au XVIIIe siècle (Paris: UNESCO: Karthala, 2005); David Turley, *Slavery* (Oxford: Blackwell, 2000); Jonathan Hart, *Contesting Empires: Opposition, Promotion, and Slavery* (New York: Palgrave Macmillan, 2005).

Index